Grammar for CAE and Proficiency

with answers

**Self-study grammar
reference and practice**

MARTIN HEWINGS

CAMBRIDGE
UNIVERSITY PRESS

CAMBRIDGE UNIVERSITY PRESS
Cambridge, New York, Melbourne, Madrid, Cape Town,
Singapore, São Paulo, Delhi, Mexico City

Cambridge University Press
The Edinburgh Building, Cambridge CB2 8RU, UK

www.cambridge.org
Information on this title: www.cambridge.org/9780521713757

First published 2009
7th printing 2013

Printed in Italy by L.E.G.O. S.p.A.

A catalogue record for this publication is available from the British Library

ISBN 987-0-521-71375-7 Paperback

Acknowledgements

My thanks go firstly to Fiona Davis for her encouragement, constructive suggestions, and eye for detail. Fiona's considerable editorial expertise has helped me enormously in writing the book. Thanks, too, to Lynn Townsend for guiding the project so professionally, and to Lynn, Nora McDonald and Linda Matthews for their work in the final stages.

Nick Witherick and Peter Sunderland gave extensive feedback on drafts of the book. Their experience was invaluable in helping me revise the grammar reference and exam practice material in particular. Thanks are also due to Sam Brown, Claire Fooks, Nathalie Key, Suzanne Hewings and Hannah Templeton for their assistance in drafting sample answers.

At home, thanks to Ann and Suzanne for being always willing to listen, help and support.

The author and publishers acknowledge the following sources of copyright material and are grateful for the permissions granted. While every effort has been made, it has not always been possible to identify the sources of all the material used, or to trace all copyright holders. If any omissions are brought to our notice, we will be happy to include the appropriate acknowledgements on reprinting.

HarperCollins Publishers Ltd for the text on p. 9 from *Bel Canto*. Copyright © Ann Patchett 2001. Reprinted by permission of HarperCollins Publishers Ltd; The Economist for the adapted text on p. 10 *The Economist*. Copyright © The Economist Newspaper Limited, London, 19 December 2006; Alite Ltd for the adapted text on p. 11 from Alite Ltd Newsletter, www.alite.co.uk; Tom Kirkwood for the text on p. 21 from BBC Reith Lecture, Radio 4, 2001; BBC News Online for the text on p. 22. Copyright © bbc.co.uk; Sir David Attenborough for the text on p. 78 'Why do birds eat seeds?' from *The Life of Birds* by Sir David Attenborough; International Masters Publishers for the adapted text on p. 79 from *Reflexology* Leaflet. Reproduced with the permission of International Masters Publishers AB. Copyright © 1999 International Masters Publishers AB. All rights reserved; Text on p. 97 'My life as a human speed bump' by George Monbiot, The Green Living Guide, *The Guardian* 23 October 2006; Telegraph Media Group Ltd for the adapted text on p. 116 from 'Gadgets to make your home energy efficient' *Daily Telegraph* 14 April 2007, for the text on p. 168 'Terrible Orchestra' by Alexander McCall Smith, *Daily Telegraph* 1 November 2007. Copyright © Telegraph Media Group Limited; Hodder & Stoughton Limited and MBA Literary Agents for the text on p.117 from *Natural Flights of the Human Mind*. Copyright © 2006 by Clare Morrall, published by Sceptre. Reproduced by permission of Hodder & Stoughton Limited and MBA Literary Agents on behalf of the author; Penguin Books Ltd for the text on p. 127 from *Eyewitness Travel Guides: Spain* (Dorling Kindersley 1996, 1997). Copyright © 1996, 1997 Dorling Kindersley Limited, London. Reproduced by permission of Dorling Kindersley Ltd; BBC.co.uk for the text on p. 143 from www.bbc.co.uk /nature/animals/mammals/explore/instincts.shtml, and for the text on p. 159 from www.bbc.co.uk/science/humanbody/mind/articles /psychology/what_is_psychology.shtml. Reproduced by permission of BBC.co.uk; Nick Rennison for the extracts on pp. 206-207, from the *Waterstone's Guide to Popular Science*. Reproduced with permission of the editor, Nick Rennison

Alamy/Adrian Sherratt p129(r), Alamy/Aflo Co Ltd p90, Alamy/Andrew Paterson p179, Alamy/Arco Images GmbH p95(t), Alamy/Chad Ehlers p62(t), Alamy/Clare Burdier p81, Alamy/Classic Stock 101(c), Alamy/David Frazier Photolibrary Inc p33, Alamy/David Noble Photography p225 (l), Alamy/DBImages p24 (tr), Alamy/Dennis MacDonald p43, Alamy/Direct Photo.org pp1(tr), 149, Alamy/Helene Rogers p108, Alamy/Image Source Pink p190, Alamy/JBP p129(l), Alamy/Jennifer Sena p53 (r), Alamy/John van Decker p78, Alamy/Jon Arnold Images Ltd p141, Alamy/Keith Morris p153, Alamy/Ken Weingart p53 (l), Alamy/Miguel Angel Munoz p95(b), Alamy/Nagelestock p62(b), Alamy/Peter Carroll p101(e), Alamy/Peter Casolino p61, Alamy/Rob Bartee p227 Alamy/Science Photos 101(a), Alamy/South West Images, Scotland p62(c), Alamy/Tony Clements p201 (t), Alamy/Travel & Landscape UK/Mark Sykes p148(t), Alamy/Wolfgang Kaehler p129(c), Alamy/Woodystock p224 (b); **Corbis**/Jens Buettner/epa p24 (cl), Corbis/Betmann p101(d), Corbis/Mimi Mollica p148; Getty Images/Axiom Photographic Agency p225 (r), **Getty Images**/Ted Spiegel p201(tr); **Punchstock**/Blend Images p192, Punchstock/Comstock p53 (c), Punchstock/Digital Vision p1 (tl), Punchstock/FStop p172, Punchstock/Imageshop p1 (tc); **Rex Features**/James Fraser p168, Rex Features/Jamies Jones p148 (r), Rex Features/Kubacsi/Phanie p42; **Sam Hallas** p101(b); **Science Photo Library**/Maximilian Stock Ltd p120; **Shutterstock** pp5, 31, 70, 148, 159, 224 (t).

Recordings produced by Leon Chambers at The Soundhouse, London.

Design by Kamae Design.

Contents

To the student

Who is this book for?

This book is for anyone preparing for the Cambridge Certificate in Advanced English (CAE) or Certificate of Proficiency in English (Proficiency/CPE) exams and covers the grammar needed for these exams. You can use it to support a CAE or Proficiency coursebook, for extra grammar practice on a general English language course, or with practice tests as part of a revision programme. You can use in it class or for self-study.

How do I use this book?

There are two ways to use this book. You can either start at Unit 1 and work through to the end of the book, or you can do the online Entry test to find out which units you need most practice in and begin with those. Go to www.cambridge.org/elt/grammarforcae.

What is in this book?

This book contains 25 units. Each unit is in four parts:

A: Context listening This introduces the grammar of the unit in context. This will help you to understand the grammar more easily when you study section B. It also gives you useful listening practice. Play the recording and answer the questions. Then check your answers in the Key.

B: Grammar Read through this section before you do the grammar exercises. **Start points** act as a brief reminder of grammar that you probably already know, and you should look at these before reading the more advanced explanations. Material likely to be relevant to students taking Proficiency is indicated with a bar in the margin.

C: Grammar exercises Write your answers to each exercise and then check them in the Key. You can refer back to section B when you are doing the exercises.

D: Exam practice Each unit has a writing task and one other exam task. These have been designed to give you practice in the grammar for that unit as well as helping you to get to know the different parts of the CAE and Proficiency exams. The Use of English tasks test the grammar presented in that unit, but they also test other areas of grammar (which are presented in the rest of the book). Tasks similar to those in the Proficiency exam are indicated with a bar in the margin.

Appendices

The Appendices give more information about some of the grammar points presented in the units. They include lists of verbs commonly found in particular grammatical patterns, and further examples of points explained in Section B.

The Key

The Key contains:
- answers for all the exercises. Check your answers at the end of each exercise.
- sample answers for all the writing tasks in the Exam practice section. Read these after you have written your own answer. Study the language used and the way the ideas are organised. Examples of the grammar points practised in the unit are highlighted in the sample answers.

The Recording scripts

There are recording scripts for the Context listening in each unit, and for the Exam practice listening tasks. Do not look at the script until after you have answered the questions. It is a good idea to play the recording again while you read the script.

The Entry test

The Entry test is available online at www.cambridge.org/elt/grammarforcae. You can do this test before using the book to help you choose what to study. Answer the questions and then check your answers in the online Key. This Key tells you which units are most important for you.

To the teacher

This book offers concise yet comprehensive coverage of the grammar students need to be successful in the Cambridge Certificate in Advanced English (CAE) and Certificate of Proficiency in English (Proficiency/CPE) exams. It can be used for self-study or with a class. It will be particularly valuable for revision, for students retaking one of the exams, and for candidates in classes where some students are not entered for the exam. Sections A, B and C are designed to be useful for all advanced level students whether or not they are entered for CAE or Proficiency.

The Entry test

The online Entry test can be used diagnostically as a means of prioritising the language areas to be covered, either for a class, or for individual students.

What is in this book?

A: Context listening This section is suitable for classroom use. Many of the tasks can be done in pairs or small groups if appropriate.

B: Grammar This section is designed for private study, but you may wish to discuss those parts which are particularly relevant to your students' needs.

C: Grammar exercises This section can be done in class or set as homework. Students can be encouraged to check their own work and discuss any difficulties they encounter.

D: Exam practice This section can be used to familiarise students with the task types found in the CAE and Proficiency exams, while offering further practice in the grammar for each unit. Each task is followed by a Grammar focus task. The Grammar focus task highlights how the grammar studied in the unit is used in the exam task. The book contains at least one task from most parts of the Reading, Writing, Use of English and Listening papers in the CAE and Proficiency exams. Although the tasks have the same format as those found in the exams, the content has sometimes been changed to reflect the focus on grammar found in this book. In addition, there are more tasks from the Use of English paper than the others because this paper tests grammar more than the others. The Writing tasks cover a wide range of the tasks which students may come across in the exams, including articles, essays, reviews and proposals. Tasks similar to those found in the Proficiency exam are indicated with a bar in the margin. The Writing hints offer extra support in the form of useful words and expressions.

In classes where there are students who are not entered for either of the exams, you might prefer to set Exam tasks as extra work for exam candidates only. Alternatively, you could set the tasks for all students, as a further opportunity to practise the grammar of each unit.

A Context listening

1 You are going to hear part of a radio phone-in programme. Before you listen, look at these pictures. What do you think the topic of the phone-in is?

2 (🔊 1) Listen and check whether you were right. As you listen, answer the questions.

Which of the callers (Karen, Dave, Beryl or Keith) ...

1 ... lost something on the train one day? ......*Beryl*......

2 ... travels to work by bus? ....

3 ... works at home permanently? ....

4 ... may buy a motorbike? ....

5 ... has always liked travelling by train? ....

6 ... used to catch the train at a quarter past seven in the morning? ....

7 ... is working at home temporarily? ....

8 ... has never owned a car? ....

3 (🔊 1) Listen again and fill in the gaps. Identify the tenses you used.

1 I ......*commuted*....... to London for over ten years.

2 I .... over an hour when they announced that the train was cancelled.

3 I .... at home happily for the last five years.

4 I .... late for work twice this week.

5 I .... of buying a motorbike.

6 I .... at home while our office block is being renovated.

7 I .... to her only a couple of times before then.

8 I .... travelling by train ever since I was young.

9 I .... to phone in to your programme for the last half hour.

10 Yesterday, I .... all my work by 2.30.

B Grammar

1 Simple and continuous tenses

present continuous
- *I'm working* at home while our office block is being renovated. (= temporary state)
- *I'm phoning* from the train. (= action in progress)

present simple
- Public transport *has* a number of advantages over driving. (= permanent state)
- I *catch* the train at 7.05 at the station near my home every morning. (= habit or regular event)

past continuous
- I *was travelling* home when the train broke down. (= action in progress at past point)

past simple
- I *sold* my car last week. (= completed past action)
- I *drove* to work for a couple of years. (= past situation that doesn't exist now)
- I *caught* the train every morning at 7.15. (= repeated past action)

We usually use simple tenses with verbs that describe an unchanging state rather than an action:
*I **love** trains.*
(▷See Appendix 1.1.)

⚠ We can use continuous tenses with state verbs to emphasise that a situation is temporary or untypical:
*I'm **appreciating** being able to get up later than usual.* (= emphasises that this is a temporary arrangement)
*Now that I work at home I **appreciate** being able to get up late.* (= suggests that this is now a more permanent arrangement)

With some verbs that describe mental states (e.g. *consider*, *understand*) and attitudes (e.g. *hope*, *regret*), continuous tenses suggest a process going on at the time of speaking, or emphasise that the process continues to develop:
*I'm **regretting** selling my car already.* (= emphasises that I have started to regret it and that this regret may grow)
*I **regret** selling my car.* (= describes an attitude that is unlikely to change)

Some verbs have different meanings when talking about states and describing actions:
*I'm now **thinking** of buying a motorbike.* (*think of* (action) = consider)
*Do you **think** that's a good idea?* (*think* (state) = asking about an opinion)
(▷See Appendix 1.2.)

We usually use the present simple with verbs that describe what we are doing as we speak:
*I **admit** that it can be frustrating at times.* (= I agree that it is true when I say 'I admit')
*I **predict** that increasing numbers of people will start working at home.*
(▷ See Appendix 1.3.)

We often use the past simple in a narrative (e.g. a report or a story) to talk about a single complete past action, and the past continuous to describe the situation that existed at the time:
*I **dropped** my purse while I **was getting** off the train.*
When we talk about two or more past completed actions that followed one another, we use the past simple for both:
*She **woke** me up and **offered** me a lift.*
When we talk about two actions that went on over the same period of past time, we can often use the past continuous or the past simple for both:
*I **was listening** to music while I **was driving** here.* or *I **listened** to music while I **drove** here.*

We usually use continuous tenses with adverbs such as *always, constantly, continually* and *forever* to emphasise that something is done so often that it is characteristic of a person, group or thing:
*I **was forever arriving** late for work.*

We can use either the present continuous or present simple to describe something we regularly do at a certain time:
*At 8 o'clock I'm usually **having** a leisurely breakfast.* or *At 8 o'clock I usually **have** ...*

We often use the present continuous or past continuous:
● to make an enquiry or a statement of opinion more tentative:
  *I'm **hoping** we've got Dave Jones on the line.* (= implies that the speaker is not sure whether Dave Jones is there)
● to make a request or an offer more polite:
  *Karen, **were** you **wanting** to say something?*

2 Perfect tenses

START POINT

present perfect
● *I've **lived** in Spain, and the trains are so much more reliable there.* (past situation relevant to the present)
● *I've just **sold** my car and so now I go to work by bus.* (recent action with consequences for the present)
● *I've **enjoyed** travelling by train ever since I was young.* (situation continuing until the present)
past perfect
● *This morning I'd **read** a couple of reports before I got off the train.* (past event before another past event)

We use the present perfect to talk about a situation that existed in the past and still exists now, and the past simple when the situation no longer exists:
*I've **commuted** to London every weekday for over ten years, and I actually enjoy it.*
*I **commuted** to London every weekday for over ten years before I started working at home.*

We use the present perfect to talk about a repeated action that might happen again:
I've arrived late for work twice this week so far.
and the past simple for a repeated action that won't happen again:
I arrived late for work twice this week. (= the working week is over; I won't arrive late again this week)

When we give news or information, we often introduce a topic with the present perfect and then give details with other past tenses:
The new high speed rail link between the north of England and the Channel Tunnel has opened. It took 15 years to build and cost nearly ten billion pounds.

When we use a time expression (e.g. *after, as soon as, before, when*) to say that one event happened after another, we can use either the past simple or past perfect for the event that happened first:
I'd read a couple of reports before I even got to work. or *I read a couple of reports ...*

3 Present perfect continuous and past perfect continuous

We use the present perfect continuous (*have been + -ing*) to talk about an action in progress in the past for a period until now, and which is either still in progress or recently finished:
I've been working at home for the last five years. (= action still in progress)
Sorry I'm late. I've been trying to find a parking place. (= action recently finished)

We often prefer the present perfect continuous to say how long the action has been in progress:
I've been trying to phone in to your programme for the last half hour.

⚠ We use the present perfect to talk about a completed action or series of actions when we are interested in the result:
I've called the bus company a number of times to complain.
They've bought new trains and have really improved the service.

We use the past perfect continuous (*had been + -ing*) to talk about an action in progress over a period up to a particular past point in time:
I'd been waiting over an hour when they announced that the train had been cancelled.
If we are not interested in how long the action went on, we often use the past continuous rather than the past perfect continuous:
I was waiting on the platform when they announced that the train had been cancelled.
rather than *I'd been waiting ...* (= there is no mention of how long the person was waiting.)

⚠ We use the past perfect when we say how many times something happened in a period up to a particular past time:
I'd spoken to her only a couple of times before then.

We don't usually use the present perfect continuous or the past perfect continuous to describe states:
I'd owned a car ever since I left college. (**not** *I'd been owning ...*)

C Grammar exercises

1 Complete this radio news report with the verbs given. Use these tenses – present simple, present continuous, past simple, past continuous – giving alternatives where possible. Sometimes you may need to change the order of the adverb and verb.

Emergency services were bombarded with phone calls from all over the north of England last night by people who **(1)** ....*reported*........ (report) seeing blue objects shoot across the sky. Mrs Linda Hayward **(2)** .... (drive) along the B456 road at the time.

'I usually **(3)** .... (come) along that bit of road at about ten. As I **(4)** .... (go) past the old barn, I **(5)** .... (see) a single bright blue light going across the road in front of my car. I **(6)** .... (stop) the car and **(7)** .... (watch) it for about fifteen minutes. It **(8)** .... (travel) quite slowly from east to west and then it suddenly **(9)** .... (disappear). Until now I never **(10)** .... (believe) in UFOs, although my son forever **(11)** .... (try) to persuade me that they **(12)** .... (exist). But now I **(13)** .... (think) that maybe he **(14)** .... (be) right.'

At the height of the panic, police stations **(15)** .... (get) around a thousand calls an hour from members of the public. Sergeant Ron Drake of the Ambledale police **(16)** .... (be) particularly busy. 'Between 10 and 11 o'clock we **(17)** .... (receive) around thirty calls. The callers said they **(18)** .... (see) a single blue light about as big as a car over the village. We now **(19)** .... (consider) searching the fields around Ambledale for any evidence left behind.'

Dr Bart Mastow, a lecturer in astronomy at Trumpton University **(20)** .... (offer) a simple explanation. 'The reports that **(21)** .... (come) in last night **(22)** .... (suggest) that it **(23)** .... (be) a meteor shower. This **(24)** .... (be) not unusual on a small scale, but last night's shower **(25)** .... (seem) to have been very large. In fact, we **(26)** .... (get) an increasing number of meteor showers, and my department currently **(27)** .... (research) possible reasons for this.'

But many witnesses to the events **(28)** .... (believe) that they **(29)** .... (observe) more than a meteor shower, and the Ministry of Defence **(30)** .... (say) that they **(31)** .... (take) the reports of UFO sightings very seriously.

2 Complete the sentences using the verbs in the box. Use the same verb in each pair of sentences. Use the present simple, present continuous, past simple or past continuous.

appear   attract   expect   hate   look   measure   see   ~~think~~

1 **a** I'm thinking........... about taking a gap year before I go to university and going travelling around South America.
   b A: Why's Terry having a party?
       B: I ....think............ it's his birthday.

2 **a** A: How did the cat get up into the tree?
       B: I .... he was chasing a bird.
   b A: Let me know when the post arrives.
       B: Why, ... you .... something important?

3 **a** A: Did you enjoy your time at boarding school?
       B: No, I .... every minute of it.
   b As the boat was thrown about by the huge waves, she looked across at Paul and wondered if he .... this, too.

4 **a** This month's special exhibition of South African art .... over 5000 visitors a day to the museum, whereas we normally only get about 2000.
   b As the home of William Shakespeare, Stratford .... tourists from all over the world.

5 **a** .... you .... that big house over there? It's my uncle's.
   b I split up with Alex when I found out that he .... someone else.

6 **a** A: What happened to your wrist?
       B: I .... the window for some new curtains when I fell off the ladder and sprained it.
   b I was given this pedometer for my birthday. You just hook it on your belt and it .... how far you walk during the day.

7 **a** A: What on earth are you doing down there?
       B: I .... for one of my earrings – it fell off and rolled under the bed.
   b A: Which course are you going to apply to?
       B: Well, this one on anthropology .... interesting.

8 **a** Our neighbour's cat .... at our door every morning, demanding to be fed.
   b Chris is incredibly busy. At the moment he .... in *Hamlet* at the Crescent Theatre.

3 Complete the sentences with an appropriate form of the verb given. Use the past simple, present perfect, past perfect and past perfect continuous tenses. Use each tense at least once in each group of four sentences, but give alternatives where possible.

1 *play*
   a We .....*have played*..... 35 matches so far this season, so we're all feeling pretty tired.
   b After the match, she admitted that she .... badly.
   c .... you .... rugby or football at the school you went to?
   d We .... really well all year, so it came as a big surprise when we were beaten by Wales last December.

2 *make*
   a We .... the right decision in emigrating to Canada in the mid-1990s.
   b Henson never thought about retirement. In fact, he .... a documentary film about the indigenous people of Chile when he died.
   c A: When did you realise that you .... a mistake in joining the army?
      B: When I was posted to Afghanistan.
   d Korean scientists believe that they .... a breakthrough in the fight against cancer by developing a technique for containing the disease. They reported their findings at the AAL conference in New York this week.

3 *eat*
   a The couple described how they .... in the dining room when the explosion destroyed the hotel.
   b My mother was a vegetarian, and as children we rarely .... meat.
   c I .... prawns a few times before last week without any ill effects, but the ones I had at the restaurant made me very sick indeed.
   d A: Would you like some of these cherries?
      B: Yes, please. I .... any fresh fruit for days.

4 *run*
   a Over the last year I .... workshops on creative writing in twelve colleges and universities.
   b She was breathing hard as if she ....
   c She .... only two marathons before breaking the world record in the Pan-African Games.
   d I was late for work so I .... most of the way.

4 Complete the sentences using either the present perfect or present perfect continuous form of the verb given. Sometimes both are possible.

1 Alice ....*has competed*.... *(compete)* in the London Marathon twice before, but hopes to achieve her best time this year.

2 Income from manufacturing exports still provides the largest proportion of the country's export earnings, but the proportion .... *(drop)* for many years.

3 The house .... *(belong)* to the Beecham family for over 250 years, but the present owner, Donald Beecham, is selling it.

4 Campbell .... *(serve)* a life sentence for murder since 1990, but his lawyers are arguing for an early release.

5 So far, attempts to rescue the climbers from the ledge where they camped during the storm .... *(fail)*.

6 A: I'd like a career where I can travel and meet people.
   B: .... *(consider)* becoming a tour guide?

7 A: .... *(swim)*? You look really exhausted.
   B: I am. I did fifty lengths of the pool.

8 A: Did you manage to get in touch with Tony?
   B: No, I .... *(try)* three times in the last hour, but he's always engaged.

9 A: Hello, Stannard's Plumbers. How may I help you?
   B: My hot water tank .... *(burst)* and my sitting room is flooded!

5 Choose the correct tense. Sometimes both are possible.

A: Good morning, Mr Davies. What can I do for you?

B: Well, doctor, **(1)** *I've been getting / I've got* some really bad headaches.

A: Okay. Can you tell me exactly when these headaches **(2)** *were starting / started*?

B: Oh, yes, I **(3)** *have remembered / remember* it vividly – it was on a Friday three weeks ago. I **(4)** *had been working / had worked* in front of my computer all week because I **(5)** *did / was doing* a job for an important client – **(6)** *I was working / I've been working* as a website designer for the last few years, you see. I **(7)** *had just finished / had just been finishing* when the pain started, and by the end of that day I **(8)** *was feeling / felt* really bad.

A: Okay. And how **(9)** *have you slept / have you been sleeping*?

B: Not very well, actually. Usually I'm asleep as soon as my head **(10)** *hits / is hitting* the pillow, but recently **(11)** *I've been having / I'm having* difficulty getting to sleep.

A: I see. Now, **(12)** *I'm noticing / I notice* that you wear glasses. **(13)** *Have you had / Were you having* your eyes tested recently?

B: No, I **(14)** *haven't had / didn't have* them tested for a couple of years, I suppose.

A: Okay, what **(15)** *I suggest / I'm suggesting* is that first you get your eyes tested. Then when you **(16)** *are working / work* at your computer, take frequent breaks to rest your eyes. If that **(17)** *hasn't solved / doesn't solve* the problem, come back and see me again.

This exercise tests grammar from the rest of the book as well as the grammar in this unit.

D Exam practice

Reading

You are going to read three extracts which are all concerned in some way with memory. Choose the answer **A**, **B**, **C** or **D** which you think fits best according to the text.

Being a hostage

(This extract is from a book called Bel Canto *by Ann Patchett. In the story so far, kidnappers in a Spanish-speaking country in Latin America have taken a number of people hostage. One of these is Mr Hosokawa, the Chief Executive Officer of a big Japanese company, Nansei. Mr Hosokawa loves opera, which has inspired him to try to learn Italian in the past. Another hostage, Gen, is Mr Hosokawa's translator.)*

But in this vast ocean of time Mr. Hosokawa could not seem to startle up any concern for Nansei. While he stared at the weather he never wondered if his abduction had affected stock prices. He did not care who was making his decisions, sitting at his desk. The company that had been his life, his son, had fallen away from him as thoughtlessly as a coin is dropped. He took a small spiral notebook from the pocket of his tuxedo jacket and, after inquiring as to the correct spelling from Gen, added the word *garúa*[1] to his list. Incentive was key. No matter how many times Mr. Hosokawa had listened to his Italian tapes in Japan he could remember nothing that was on them. No sooner had he heard the beautiful words, *dimora, patrono,* than they vanished from memory. But after only one week of captivity look at all the Spanish he had learned! *Ahora* was now; *sentarse,* sit; *ponerse de pie,* stand up; *sueño,* sleep, and *requetebueno* was very good, but it was always spoken with a certain coarseness and condescension that told the listener not that he had done well but that he was too stupid to merit high expectations. And it wasn't just the language that had to be overcome, there were all the names to learn as well, those of the hostages, those of the captors when you could get one of them to tell you his name. The people were from so many different countries that there were no easy tricks of association, no familiar toehold from which to pull oneself up. The room was full of men he did not know and should know, though they all smiled and nodded to one another. He would have to work harder to introduce himself. At Nansei he had made a point of learning the names of as many of his employees as was possible. He remembered the names of the businessmen he entertained and the names of their wives whom he inquired after and never met.

[1] *garúa* is the Spanish word for 'mist'

1 Mr Hosaka finds it easier to learn Spanish now than to learn Italian in Japan because
   A he didn't write down words in Italian.
   B he found it difficult to learn from tapes.
   C he now has more motivation to learn.
   D the captors and other hostages are good teachers.

2 Which of the following best explains why Mr Hosaka finds it difficult to learn the names of the captors and other hostages.
   A He has always been bad at learning people's names.
   B They have Spanish names.
   C He is not sufficiently motivated to do so.
   D They are not Japanese.

The purpose of memory

As Matthew Wilson, of the Picower Institute for Learning and Memory in Cambridge, Massachusetts observes, memory is like everything else in biology. It has evolved to serve a purpose and is honed for that purpose, which in this case is to react appropriately to the stimuli an animal meets in the environment by drawing on the experience of previous encounters. That is emphatically not the same as having a perfect memory for each of those encounters. Instead, memory should generalise from similar experiences and disregard the individual details.

And indeed that is most people's everyday experience. The elderly are notorious for remembering every detail of their childhood but being unable to recall what they did last week. Such inability to remember details is often regarded as a failing, whereas so-called eidetic (or photographic) memory is often admired by outsiders.

In Dr Wilson's view this perception is probably wrong. Indeed, an ideal memory would have generalised from experience to such an extent that individual events no longer need to be remembered at all; merely the appropriate response to the situation. So the fact that the elderly, who already have vast experience to draw on, do not waste precious storage capacity on adding things that will not aid their survival could well be the result of evolutionary adaptation rather than an indication of waning powers.

3 In what way, according to Matthew Wilson, are memory and everything else in biology similar?
   A They all adapt to changing circumstances.
   B They all originate in our animal instincts.
   C They all vary across individuals.
   D They are all far from perfect.

4 In Dr Wilson's view, why do older people remember fewer details of a recent situation than do younger people?

   A They have reduced ability to remember facts.

   B They do not have the brain capacity to store details.

   C They lose the ability to react to a stimulus.

   D They do not need to be able to remember details.

The myth that memory is perfect

One in four of us is susceptible to false memory syndrome. With prompting and coaxing, one in four of us can be led to believe that something has occurred in our past that, in fact, has no basis in truth. After the 1992 Amsterdam plane crash, a study showed that an impossible 66% of those interviewed claimed to have seen the event. Witness testimony is vulnerable to suggestibility and in particular there are differences of reliability with regard to age, race, presence of a weapon and duration of exposure to the evidence. Older people are more likely to pick someone from an identity parade. Own-race bias (ORB) means that the identification of someone of one's own race is more accurate than of someone of another race.

It can be seen that memory is a more malleable phenomenon than everyday sense would lead us to believe. This makes the 'truth' itself more fallible, particularly when it involves an individual drawing upon it. In order for us to survive and to lead balanced and healthy lives, we have become accomplished practitioners in false memory syndrome. Thankfully this is a very necessary part of everyday existence: a survival imperative. What would your life be like if you could remember everything?

5 In what way does the 1992 Amsterdam plane crash exemplify false memory syndrome?

   A People claimed they saw the plane crash in order to please the interviewers.

   B More people claimed to see the plane crash than actually did.

   C People's memories of the event were influenced by their age.

   D People don't quickly forget a traumatic event like this.

6 In the writer's view, memories are unreliable because

   A people are prejudiced against other races.

   B people only remember what they want to.

   C people are influenced by what others say and do.

   D people try to remember everything.

1

This is an extract from the first text. Without looking back at it, fill in the gaps using the past perfect or past simple of the verb in brackets.

But in this vast ocean of time Mr. Hosokawa could not seem to startle up any concern for Nansei. While he (1) ....stared......... *(stare)* at the weather he never (2) .... *(wonder)* if his abduction (3) .... *(affect)* stock prices. He (4) .... *(not care)* who was making his decisions, sitting at his desk. The company that (5) .... *(was)* his life, his son, (6) .... *(fall)* away from him as thoughtlessly as a coin is dropped. He (7) .... *(take)* a small spiral notebook from the pocket of his tuxedo jacket and, after inquiring as to the correct spelling from Gen, (8) .... *(add)* the word *garúa* to his list. Incentive (9) .... *(be)* key. No matter how many times Mr. Hosokawa (10) .... *(listen)* to his Italian tapes in Japan he could remember nothing that was on them. No sooner (11) .... *(hear)* the beautiful words, *dimora*, *patrono*, than they (12) .... *(vanish)* from memory. But after only one week of captivity look at all the Spanish he (13) .... *(learn)*!

Writing

You have recently read an article in an English language magazine aimed at young adults, which reported a survey finding that television was considered to be the most important invention of the last 100 years. You decide to write an article arguing that another invention has had as great an impact. Describe the invention and the impact it has had on our world, and say why you think it is a more important invention than television.

Write your **article** in **300–350** words.

This task gives you the chance to practise a range of tenses:
- past simple when talking about the impact of television
  Television brought films and news into people's homes.
- present perfect when talking about the impact so far of your chosen greatest invention
  The mobile phone has changed the way we conduct conversations.
- present simple to describe the characteristics of your chosen greatest invention
  Jet engines provide much more power than propellers.

The future

will, *be going to* + infinitive, *shall*; present tenses for the future; future continuous, future perfect and future perfect continuous; *be to* + infinitive; future in the past

2

A Context listening

1 Which of these activities would you like to do on a visit to the USA?

1 2 3

4 5 6

2 ⊙2 Jessica is doing a course in American Studies at a British university. As part of this programme she will spend her third year studying at a university in Los Angeles in California. Her friend, Kelly, wants to visit her while she is there. Listen to them talking about their plans. Which of the activities shown in Exercise 1 do they mention?

3 ⊙2 Listen again and fill in the gaps.

1 I *'m spending*............ a few days sightseeing in New York.

2 I .... in Los Angeles on the 20th.

3 I .... for my own place.

4 It .... a long time to catch up.

5 I .... up there if it's not too expensive.

6 .... you stop over anywhere on the way out?

7 When I come to see you, you .... in California for nearly six months.

8 You .... longer, won't you?

4 How many different ways of referring to the future have you used? ....

2

B Grammar

1 *will, be going to* + infinitive and *shall*

will
- *I think I'll fly directly to Los Angeles.* (= a decision made without planning)
- *Everyone says America's a great place – I'm sure you'll have a fantastic time.* (= a prediction based on opinion or experience)
- *I'll be 21 on 2nd January.* (= a fact about the future)
- *I'll meet you at the airport.* (= willingness)

be going to + infinitive
- *First I'm going to stay with Don and Suzanne.* (= a decision already made)
- *The cloud's building up. It's going to rain this afternoon.* (= a prediction based on outside evidence)

We can sometimes use *will* instead of *be going to* to make a prediction based on outside evidence, but when we do, we usually include an adverb:
The cloud's building up. It'll definitely rain / It's definitely going to rain this afternoon.

We can use *will* or *be going to* in the main clause of an *if*-sentence with little difference in meaning when we say that something is conditional on something else:
If I don't go now, I'll / I'm going to be late for my next lecture.
⚠ We use *will*, not *be going to*, when the main clause refers to offers, requests, promises and ability:
If my plans change, I'll let you know, of course. (= promise)
If you bring your tent, we'll camp on the coast for a few days. (= ability; 'we will be able to camp')

In formal contexts, we can use *shall* instead of *will* with *I* or *we*:
- in questions that ask about intentions:
  Shall I / we see you before you leave? (= Will I / we have the opportunity to see you?)
- in statements about the future, although *will* is more usual:
  When I finish my course I shall have some time to travel around America. or
  When I finish my course I will have some time ...

2 Present continuous and present simple for the future

present continuous
- *I'm spending a few days sightseeing.* (= event intended or arranged)

present simple
- *Lectures start on 27th July.* (= event as part of official schedule)

Compare the use of the present continuous for the future and *be going to*:
I'm flying on 15ᵗʰ July at ten in the evening. (= already arranged)
I'm going to fly up there if it's not too expensive. (= the speaker intends to fly but has not made the arrangements yet)

We tend to avoid *be going to go* and use the present continuous (*be going to*) instead:
Then I'm going to San Francisco. rather than *Then I'm going to go to San Francisco.*

We can't use the present continuous for future events which are outside people's control:
It's going to rain this afternoon. (**not** It's raining this afternoon.)

We can use either the present simple or *will* to talk about official arrangements:
The semester begins on 7ᵗʰ December. or *The semester will begin on 7ᵗʰ December.*
The present continuous is used in informal arrangements:
You're not staying with them the whole time, then? (= informal arrangement) (**not** You don't stay with them the whole time, then?)

We use the present simple, or sometimes other present tenses, to refer to the future in time clauses with a conjunction (e.g. *after, as soon as, before, by the time, when, while, until*); in conditional clauses with *if, in case, provided* and *unless*; and in clauses beginning with *suppose, supposing* and *what if*:
As soon as I book my tickets, I'll let you know. (**not** As soon as I will book ...)
It'll be good to know I can contact them in case I have any problems. (**not** ... in case I will have any problems ...)
What if I don't like it? (**not** What if I won't like it?)

3 Future continuous, future perfect and future perfect continuous

We use the future continuous (*will* + *be* + present participle) to talk about something predicted to happen at a particular time or over a particular period in the future:
I'll be studying really hard during the semesters.

We use the future perfect (*will* + *have* + past participle) to make a prediction about an action we expect to be completed by a particular time in the future:
By the time you come I'm sure I'll have got to know the city really well.

We use the future perfect continuous (*will* + *have been* + present participle) to emphasise the duration of an activity in progress at a particular point in the future:
When I come to see you, you'll have been living in California for nearly six months.

We can also use the future continuous, future perfect and future perfect continuous to say what we believe or imagine to be true:
Dad won't be using his car, so I'm sure it's okay to borrow it. (= an activity happening now or at a particular point in the future)
They'll have forgotten what I look like. (= an event that took place before now or before a particular point in the future)
My plane's been delayed. Don and Suzanne will have been waiting for me at the airport for hours. (= an activity continuing to now)

4 *be to* + infinitive

Be to + infinitive is commonly used:
- in news reports:

  *Extra lifeguards **are to be posted** at the beach after a shark was seen swimming close to the shore.*
- to talk about official plans, and rules or instructions:

  *Students **are to hand in** project reports at the end of semester two.* (active)
  *Project reports **are to be handed in** at the end of semester two.* (passive)

⚠ We only use *is / are / am to* + infinitive to talk about future events that people can control:
*The weather **will** still be warm even in winter.* (**not** ~~The weather is still to be warm.~~)

We often use *be to* + infinitive in *if*-clauses when we mean 'in order to':
*If she **is to get** a good grade in her project report, she needs to work on her statistics.* (= in order to get a good grade, she needs to work on her statistics)
Compare: *If she **gets** a good grade in her project report, she will be really surprised.*

5 Future in the past

A number of forms can be used to talk about a past activity or event that was still in the future from the point of view of the speaker:
*I **was going to see** an aunt in Seattle a couple of years ago, but I cancelled the trip because she got ill.* (= a plan that didn't happen)
*I knew I **would be feeling** awful by the end of the flight.* (= a prediction made in the past)
(▷See Appendix 2.)

We can use *was / were to* + infinitive and *was / were to have* + past participle to talk about the future in the past, particularly in formal contexts. With *was / were to* + infinitive we don't know whether the event actually happened unless the context makes this clear:
*First, I flew to New York and then I **was to go on** to Chicago.* (= we don't know whether the speaker went to Chicago or not)

⚠ *was / were to have* + past participle is used for things that were expected, but didn't actually happen:
*I **was to have visited** my aunt, but she was taken ill.* (= the visit didn't happen)

Unlike *is / are / am to* + infinitive (see B4 above), we can use *was / were to* + infinitive whether or not people can control the event:
*Helen left England for Australia in 1964 for what she intended to be a short visit, but it **was to be** 30 years before she returned to her home country.*

C Grammar exercises

1 Complete the sentences using the verbs in the box. Choose the most appropriate form.

miss / will miss	will have / am having
is going to melt / is melting	persuades / will persuade
will be enjoying / enjoys	~~am starting out / will start out~~
will be believed / is to be believed	is going to depart / departs
will agree / agrees	will rise / are to rise
see / are going to see	

1 A: Do you want to come out for a meal tonight?

B: I .m..starting..out.... early tomorrow morning – my flight's at six – so I don't think I'll come, thanks.

2 The next train for London .... from platform six at 16.07.

3 I .... some friends over for dinner on Saturday. Do you want to join us?

4 They reckon the Greenland ice sheet .... within a few years.

5 A: Gary doesn't want to come on holiday with us, then.

B: He says that now, but I'm sure Hannah .... him to change his mind.

6 By the middle of the week, temperatures .... to 30° C.

7 The striking workers have said that they will prevent finished goods leaving the factory until the management .... to their demand for improved working conditions.

8 I'm not sure when I'll be home tonight. Expect me when you .... me.

9 A: The coach leaves Oxford at exactly 5.00 from the bus station.

B: What if I .... it?

A: You'll have to take the train.

10 If the research .... , children now spend more time playing computer games than watching television.

11 A: It's Daniel's first week away at university. I wonder how he's getting on?

B: I'm sure he .... himself.

2 Choose the most appropriate future form. Sometimes more than one form is possible.

1 You'll freeze if .... you..go .... out dressed like that. Put on a warm coat!

(you'll go / you're going to go / you go)

2 When I retire next year, ... a lot of travelling around North America.
   (I'm doing / I do / I'm going to do)

3 A: Have you been in touch with Pat yet to say we can't come? You said you'd do it.
   B: Sorry, I forgot. .... her know tomorrow when I see her at work.
   (I'm going to let / I shall let / I'll let)

4 Look at that stupid cyclist. .... an accident.
   (He'll cause / He's going to cause / He causes)

5 A: What do you want done with this box?
   B: If you just leave it there, ... it upstairs when I go.
   (I'll take / I'm taking / I'm going to take)

6 A: What .... this evening?
   (are you doing / are you going to do / do you do)
   B: Oh, I don't know. Maybe .... watch a DVD.
   (I'm going to / I'll / I'm watching)

7 Please note that next week's concert .... at 7.00, not 7.30 as advertised
   in the programme.
   (is commencing / will commence / is going to commence)

8 Mr Kerr .... angry if you don't hand your homework in today.
   (is being / is going to be / will be)

9 A: Bob Dylan .... a concert in London next month.
   (will do / is doing / does)
   B: .... book some tickets?
   (Am I going to / Will I / Shall I)

10 The air tickets .... around a week to reach you.
   (shall take / will take / are taking)

11 The French oral tests .... next Monday.
   (are starting / will start / start)

12 When Guy .... 50, Gemma .... 18.
   (is / will be / is going to be)   *(is going to be / is to be / will be)*

13 If we get much more rain, the river .... its banks.
   (is probably going to burst / will probably burst / is bursting)

3 Complete the sentences using a future form of the verbs given. Use the same future form for all the sentences in each group. Use:

~~present simple~~   future continuous   *be to* + infinitive
be going to + infinitive   future perfect   present continuous
future perfect continuous

1 *get – go – terminate*
   a All change, please – this train ......*terminates*...... here.
   b What time *does our plane get* (our plane) to Athens?
   c The cat runs away from me as soon as I ....*go*............ near it.

2 *buy – have – need*
   a A: What are you going to town for?
      B: I .... some new shoes.
   b A: Jane's not looking very well.
      B: No, apparently, she .... a major operation.
   c A: I've made a list of the things you .... for the field trip to Iceland.
      B: Thanks, that's really helpful.

3 *negotiate – watch – work*
   a On April 1st next year I .... at the university for 25 years.
   b A: It's such a pity that Helen is away and can't watch the match with us. You know how much she loves tennis.
      B: I'm sure she .... it on TV in her hotel room.
   c The next statement from the trade union leaders is expected at ten o'clock this evening. By that time they .... with the employers for nearly 36 hours.

4 *come – do – support*
   a Justin's not feeling well, so he .... tonight after all.
   b Who .... (you) in the rugby world cup final next week, England or South Africa?
   c A: What do you think Susan .... at the moment?
      B: Oh, she'll still be in bed.

5 *create – launch – leave*
   a The computer firm Clark Campbell .... 300 new jobs at its assembly plant just outside Dublin.
   b All mobile phones .... outside the examination room.
   c The government .... an enquiry next week into allegations of corruption in the civil service.

6 *analyse – have – move*

    a The bank predicts that by the end of next year, over 80% of its customers .... to online banking.

    b Natasha .... her exam results by now. I wonder how she's got on.

    c My research is going rather slowly at the moment, but I'm certain by the end of the year all of my data ....

7 *go – have – make*

    a She .... a speech at the conference next week.

    b I .... out there – it's pouring with rain and I haven't got an umbrella.

    c We .... risotto for dinner. Is that okay with you?

4 Complete these texts using the future forms of the verbs in brackets. Give alternatives where possible. In some cases, you will need to use the future in the past.

THE NEWS IN BRIEF

A complete ban on tobacco advertising in the EU (1) comes / will come / is to come *(come)* into effect at midnight tonight. Initially, the ban (2) .... *(begin)* last October, but last-minute legal moves by the tobacco companies forced a delay. EU health ministers issued a statement welcoming the ban, and saying that it (3) .... *(reduce)* smoking-related disease significantly.

*   *   *   *   *

A Brazilian rocket has exploded after an engine ignited by mistake just days before its planned lift-off. The unmanned rocket (4) .... *(carry)* two satellites into space. A new launch (5) .... *(take place)* in March.

*   *   *   *   *

The Australian actress Niki Kardman (6) .... *(star)* in a film about the life of Princess Diana made by the director Baz Leeman. Ms Kardman said, 'When Baz said he (7) .... *(make)* a film about Diana's life and wanted to cast me, I jumped at the chance.'

*   *   *   *   *

The novelist Arnold Miller has died. Miller worked as a journalist in London during the 1960s before moving to Canada, where he (8) .... *(spend)* the rest of his life. He spoke exclusively to The Daily Reporter last month, in what (9) .... *(be)* his last major interview. A special report on his life and work (10) .... *(appear)* in next Friday's edition.

D Exam practice

Use of English

This exercise tests grammar from the rest of the book as well as the grammar in this unit.

Read the following texts on ageing. For questions 1–4 answer with a word or short phrase.
You do not need to write complete sentences.

A

Every revolution has a turning point – a time when the original impetus for change has run its course. History shows that this is often a vulnerable time. Opinion on where to go next is sharply divided. Indecision prevails at precisely the moment when decisive action is most essential. The longevity revolution is no exception. We know where we've come from and why, but we don't have a clear plan of where to go now. Ours has been a revolution from – from the terrible waste of life caused by premature death – not a revolution to. We are at our turning point now. The decisions we take in the next few years will have far-reaching consequences for the state of future society.

5

Two hundred years ago most people died before their time. Well, we fixed that. Rarely has a revolution succeeded so well. What we now experience are the deaths associated with old age, with degenerative conditions. Much of modern medicine is concerned with fighting these, pushing back the frontiers of survival further and further. But suddenly we are not so sure about where we are going and why. Many are the news stories trumpeting that we will soon all live to 130, 200 or 400 years, but what about the New Yorker cartoon that showed one old man saying to another, 'I hope I die before science makes me live to 150'.

10

15

The ambivalence of our attitudes reflects the confusion of rapid change. Not long ago the attainment of old age was hailed as a success. Ageing today is widely seen as a failure, unless you are as extremely old as Jeanne Calment. I remember being deeply struck by a remark from a former medical colleague whose research was on heart disease: 'There is nothing interesting about the ageing of the cardiovascular system,' he exclaimed. 'It just rots!' What, I wondered, did he feel was the point of his work? What, for that matter, is the point of mine?

20

1 Why, according to the writer, is this 'vulnerable time' (line 2) of particular significance?

2 What is meant in the context by the phrase 'The ambivalence of our attitudes', in line 17?

B

Ageing is a physical phenomenon happening to our bodies, so at some point in the future, as medicine becomes more and more powerful, we will inevitably be able to address ageing just as effectively as we address many diseases today. I claim that we are close to that point because of the SENS (Strategies for Engineered Negligible Senescence) project to prevent and cure ageing. It is not just an idea: it's a very detailed plan to repair all the types of molecular and cellular damage that happen to us over time. And each method to do this is either already working in a preliminary form (in clinical trials) or is based on technologies that already exist and just need to be combined. This means that all parts of the project should be fully working in mice within just ten years and we might take only another ten years to get them all working in humans.

When we get these therapies, we will no longer all get frail and decrepit and dependent as we get older, and eventually succumb to the innumerable ghastly progressive diseases of old age. We will still die, of course – from crossing the road carelessly, being bitten by snakes, catching a new flu variant etcetera – but not in the drawn-out way in which most of us die at present. So, will this happen in time for some people alive today? Probably. Since these therapies repair accumulated damage, they are applicable to people in middle age or older who have a fair amount of that damage.

I think the first person to live to 1,000 might be 60 already.

5

10

15

3 Which word in the first paragraph conveys the writer's certainty that ageing will be cured?

4 What opinion does the writer's use of 'ghastly' in line 12 convey?

Grammar focus task

Without looking back at the texts, add *will* and one of the following verbs to these extracts in the most natural places.

live   die   be able to   happen   get   have

1 We~will~ inevitably ~be able to~ address ageing just as effectively as we address many diseases today.

2 The decisions we take in the next few years far-reaching consequences for the state of future society.

3 Many are the news stories trumpeting that we soon all to 130, 200 or 400 years.

4 When we get these therapies, we no longer all frail and decrepit and dependent as we get older.

5 We still, of course.

6 So, this in time for some people alive today?

Writing

You are on the committee of an organisation called *Sport for Youth*, which encourages young people to become more involved in sports. The next annual conference will be held in your home town. Delegates have received a provisional programme, but you need to write a letter to them shortly before the conference giving them further details about the first day, and suggesting what they might do in the evening. Read the provisional programme and some notes you took at a recent meeting of the organising committee.

15th Annual Conference of 'Sport for Youth'
Provisional programme for Day 1

Registration –	all day
9.30	Opening talk by Peter Taylor
10.30–11.00	Coffee
11.30–1.00	Talks
1.00–2.00	Lunch
2.00–5.00	Talks
Evening free	

Note:

1 Registration desk opens at 8.30. Collect 'Welcome Pack' there

2 Peter Taylor's talk: 'The state of sport in schools'

3 Coffee & lunch in Avon Room

4 Certificate of Attendance in Welcome Pack

5 Internet access - computers in basement

Write a **letter** to delegates in **180–220** words.

Writing hints

This task gives you the opportunity to practise future forms:
- *will*
  Internet access will be available.
- present continuous for the future
  Peter is talking about sport in schools.
- present simple for the future
  The registration desk opens at 8.30.

3 Modals 1

ability; possibility; conclusions, willingness, habitual events;
necessity, deduction; 'not necessary'; obligation

A Context listening

1 Look at these newspaper headlines.
What do you think the stories are about?

School evacuation in South Wales

More air travel chaos looms

Sport the answer to obesity crisis

Borland link opened

2 [3a] Listen to a radio news summary and check whether you were right.

3 [3a] Listen again and fill in the gaps.

1 Air passengers ......*could be hit*...... badly today.

2 The cabin staff .... the new working conditions.

3 Firefighters .... the fire under control fairly quickly.

4 I think it .... of great benefit to the island.

5 There .... restrictions on the number of people moving here.

6 Schools .... a more active role in encouraging children to take up sports.

7 They .... their children whatever encouragement they can.

8 It .... warm, sunny and dry, with temperatures up to 22° C.

4 In which of the extracts do the words you have written refer to:

1 ability?   ......*3*......   4 possibility?   ....

2 necessity?   ....   5 prediction?   ....

3 obligation? ....

24

B Grammar

can / could
- *We'll get wealthy people from the mainland who **can** afford second homes.* (= general ability)
- *Before the bridge was built we **could** only get to the island by ferry.* (= general ability in the past)

may / could / might
- *Up to 100,000 people **may** experience delays.* (= it's possible this will happen)
- *Air passengers **could** be hit badly today.* (= it's possible)
- *It **might** be a number of months before the sports centre is back in operation.*
  (= it's possible this is true; less certain than *may* or *could*)

will / would
- *That **will** push up house prices.* (= prediction about the future)
- *If schools highlighted the importance of physical exercise, this **would** have a major positive impact on children's attitudes to sport.* (= prediction about an imaginary situation)

must
- *The cabin staff **must** accept the new working conditions.* (= a rule or order)
- *This negative attitude to sport **mustn't** be allowed to continue.* (= it's not allowed or not a good idea)

don't need to / needn't / don't have to
- *Parents **don't need to** / **needn't** be very interested in sport themselves.*
  (= it's not necessarily true)
- *I'm sure I **don't have to** spell out the chaos being caused in the airline industry.*
  (= it's not necessary)

ought to / should
- *Parents **ought to** / **should** give their children whatever encouragement they can.*
  (= obligation and recommendation)

1 *can, could, be able to:* ability

We can use *be able to* instead of *can* or *could*, particularly in more formal contexts:
*The hotels on the island **are able to** accommodate hundreds of visitors.* or
*The hotels on the island **can** accommodate ...* (less formal)

We use *be able to* to talk about ability on a specific occasion in the past:
*Firefighters **were able to** bring the fire under control fairly quickly.* (**not** ~~Firefighters could bring~~ ...)
⚠ We can use either *could* or *be able to* in negatives in the past:
*They **couldn't** / **weren't able to** prevent the fire damaging the school's sports centre.*

We usually prefer *can* or *could* with verbs of sense (e.g. *feel, hear, see, smell, taste*) and verbs of thinking (e.g. *believe, remember, understand*):
*I **can't** believe Mr Wade is being so confrontational.*

We use *be able to* in perfect tenses, *-ing* forms, infinitives, and after modal verbs:
*We've now **been able to** contact him.*
*The film star hates **not being able to** leave her house.*
*They've got **to be able to** adapt to change.*
*Parents **might be able to** help.*
⚠ We prefer *can* and *could* in passives:
*The news **can** be read on our website.*

To talk about a future ability, we use *will be able to*:
*Islanders **won't be able to** buy properties.*
⚠ We use *can* or *be able to* to talk about possible future arrangements and *can* (or more politely *could*) to ask for permission:
*The President **can't** / **is not able to** visit the country until next month.*
***Can** / **Could** I ask you what you think of the new bridge?*

2 *may, might, can, could*: possibility

To talk about a more general possibility of something happening we can use *can* or *may*:
*The temperature in the mountains **can** / **may** fall below freezing even at this time of year.*
We use *could* to say that something was possible in the past:
*It **could** be a very rough journey, too.*
We don't use *may* to ask questions about the possibility of something happening. Instead we use *could* or the phrase *be likely to*:
***Could** the negotiations finish today, do you think?*
*What time **is** the meeting **likely to** finish?*
Might is sometimes used in questions, but is rather formal.

We can use these modals in negative sentences, including those with words like *only* or *hardly*, to say that things are not possible or that it is possible that things are not the case:
*The company **can hardly** be described as a success.* (= it is not possible to describe it as a success)
*He **could never** be accused of being lazy.* (= it is/was not possible to accuse him of this)
*I think we should call off the strike, but other people **may** / **might not** agree with me.*
(= it's possible that people don't agree with me)

3 *will, would, used to*: conclusions, willingness, habitual events

We can use *will* to draw conclusions or state assumptions about things we think are true:
*No doubt you **will** have heard the news by now.*

We use *will (not)* to talk about (un)willingness or refusal to do something:
*The minister says he **will** resign if no solution is found.*
*We **will not** be bullied by management.*
*The computer **won't** let me print documents.*

We use *would* to talk about willingness in the future, in conditionals, and when we say that we are willing but unable to do something:
*Many people **would** be happy to pay higher taxes for better public services.*
*The minister **would** be pleased to accept the invitation if it were not for other commitments.*
⚠ We don't use *would* to talk about willingness on a specific occasion in the past:
David Wade agreed to meet the union representatives. (**not** ~~David Wade would agree~~ ...)

We can use *will* (present) and *would* (past) to talk about characteristic behaviour or habits, or about things that are true now or were true in the past:
*Some parents **will** actually discourage their children from taking up a sport.*
*Many passengers **would** get seasick during the crossing.*

We can use either *would* or *used to* to talk about things that happened repeatedly in the past:
*The crossing **would** / **used to** take over an hour at least.*
⚠ We don't use *would* to talk about past states:
*We **used to** be terribly isolated here because the ferry service was so bad.*
(**not** ~~We would be terribly isolated~~ ...)

4 *must, have (got) to*: necessity, deduction

We can use either *must* or *have to* to say that it is necessary to do something, although *have to* is less formal and is also preferred in questions:
*Schools **must** / **have to** play a more active role in encouraging children to take up sports.*

When we say that something was necessary in the past we use *had to*, not *must*:
*Up to 200 teachers and pupils **had to** be evacuated from a school in South Wales today.*
To say something is necessary in the future we use *will have to*:
*To stay in business we **will have to** cut our costs.*

We use *must* when we decide for ourselves that something is necessary or important:
*I **must** give you my email address.*
Have to suggests that someone else or an outside circumstance or authority makes something necessary:
*The council **has to** close two city centre car parks following a health and safety report.*

We usually use *must*, rather than *have to*, when we conclude that something (has) happened or that something is true:
*The bridge **must** have cost a fortune.*
In negative conclusions we use *can't* or *couldn't*:
*That **can't** be right, surely?* (**not** ~~That mustn't be right, surely?~~)

Sometimes we can use either *have to* or *have got to*, although *have got to* is more informal.
We use *have to* with frequency adverbs and with other modal verbs:
*Islanders normally **have to** queue for half an hour to get on the ferry.*
*The airlines will **have to** return to the negotiating table.*
If *have* is contracted (e.g. *I've*), then we must include *got*:
*They**'ve got to** be changed.* (**not** ~~They've to be changed.~~)
When we use the past simple we prefer *had to* rather than *had got to*:
*The manager seemed to be doing a good job. Why **did he have to** go?* (**not** ~~Why had he got to go?~~)

5 *didn't need to, didn't have to, needn't have*: not necessary

To say it was not necessary to do something in the past, we use *didn't need to* or *didn't have to*:
*He **didn't have to** wait long for a response.* (= he didn't actually wait long)
To show that we think something that was done was not necessary, we use *need not (needn't) have*:
*The event organisers expected the bad weather to affect ticket sales. However, they **need not have** worried, as every ticket was sold.* (= they worried but it was not necessary)

6 *should, ought to*: obligation

We can often use either *should* or *ought to* to talk about obligation (in giving advice and recommendations, saying what we think is a good idea and talking about responsibility):
*I think we **ought to** / **should** keep Borland for the islanders!* (= it's a good idea or I recommend this)
*The authorities **ought to** / **should** prosecute companies that cause pollution.* (= talking about responsibility)

We can use either *should* or *ought to* to say that something is likely because we have planned it or expect it to happen:
*The contractors say the road will take five years to complete, but they **should** / **ought to** be able to finish it faster.*
We use *shouldn't* rather than *oughtn't to* if something is unlikely:
*If you're in the south of the country, you **shouldn't** be troubled by any rain today.*

The use of *should* and *ought to* is for actions or events the speaker sees as desirable. Otherwise, an alternative to the modal is used. Compare:
*It **should** be sunny tomorrow.* but *You're **likely** to see an occasional shower.*

C Grammar exercises

1 **Choose the correct verb. Sometimes both are possible.**

1 Adult ladybirds *may* / *might* be black, red or yellow.
2 *We can* / *We'll be able to* get into the city centre in less than 20 minutes when the new railway line is finished.
3 I left Doncaster because I *wasn't able to* / *couldn't* find a job there.
4 A: We've had a parcel delivered. It's from New Zealand.
  B: Well, it *couldn't* / *mightn't* be from Ken. He's working in Australia at the moment.
5 A: I can't find my purse anywhere.
  B: *May* / *Could* you have left it in the restaurant?
6 Not so long ago, more than 20 species of fish *could* / *were able to* be found in this river.
7 A: Apparently, there's been an accident in the High Street.
  B: That *might* / *could* explain why the bus is taking so long.

8 A: Donna says she'll definitely pay the money back.
   B: I wish I *was able to* / *could* trust her.

9 This camera is a bit cheaper than the other one, although it *mightn't* / *can't* be as good, of course.

2 Alan is talking to Martha just before and after a job interview. Choose the correct verb. Sometimes more than one is possible.

Before
A: What time **(1)** *have you to* / *have you got to* / *must you* be there by?
M: 10.30.
A: You **(2)** *must* / *have to* / *have got to* be really nervous.
M: Terrified! But it doesn't matter, I know I won't get the job.
M: You **(3)** *haven't got to* / *mustn't* / *can't* be sure of that. You've got just the right experience and qualifications.
A: But I feel so tense. I **(4)** *can't* / *couldn't* / *mightn't* create a very good impression in the interview.
M: I'm sure you'll be okay. You **(5)** *should* / *must* / *ought to* be more positive.

After
A: I got it!
M: Congratulations! What **(6)** *had you got to* / *must you* / *did you have to* do?
A: Well, mainly I **(7)** *had got to* / *had to* / *must* tell them about why I wanted to work for the company.
M: And does the job sound good?
A: Fantastic. I'll **(8)** *have to* / *must* / *have got to* do a lot of travelling.
M: Well that **(9)** *oughtn't to* / *shouldn't* / *mustn't* be a problem for you.
A: Not at all, and I may **(10)** *must* / *have to* / *have got to* spend some time at their office in Barcelona.
M: Well, I think we should certainly go out for a meal to celebrate.
A: Good idea. But first I **(11)** *have to* / *'ve got to* / *must* call my parents and let them know. They'll be waiting to hear from me.

3 Choose the correct sentence ending. Sometimes both are possible.

1 I have to get up early tomorrow, so I
   (a) mustn't be too late going to bed tonight.
   b don't need to be too late going to bed tonight.

2 When we got to the station we found that the train was half an hour late, so we
   a didn't need to rush after all.
   b needn't have rushed after all.

3 The meeting will be quite informal, so you
   a don't need to wear a suit.
   b don't have to wear a suit.

29

4 Fortunately, he wasn't badly hurt in the accident, so he
  a needn't go to hospital.
  b didn't need to go to hospital.

5 Gwen has lost a lot of weight during her illness, so you
  a needn't look surprised when you see her again.
  b mustn't look surprised when you see her again.

6 The tennis courts are open to the public, so you
  a needn't be a member of the club to play here.
  b mustn't be a member of the club to play here.

7 The house was in good condition when I bought it, so I
  a didn't need to decorate before I moved in.
  b didn't have to decorate before I moved in.

8 As it turned out, the exam was quite easy, so I
  a didn't have to spend all that time revising.
  b needn't have spent all that time revising.

4 Match the sentence beginnings and endings, completing them with one of the verbs in the box. Use each verb once.

shouldn't   would   could   will be able to   used to   will   ~~wouldn't~~

1 I said I'd pay for her ticket but she   a cause dangerous driving conditions.
2 In just a few years from now everybody   b take me too long.
3 I still remember how they   c accept my offer.
4 Forecasters are warning that heavy snow   d play together so well as children.
5 Here's some really nice cheese that I don't think you   e watch TV on their computers.
6 We live in an old house that   f belong to a politician.
7 Writing my geography assignment   g have tasted before.

1 I said I'd pay for her ticket but she wouldn't accept my offer.
2 ....
3 ....
4 ....
5 ....
6 ....
7 ....

D Exam practice

This exercise tests grammar from the rest of the book as well as the grammar in this unit.

Listening

3b You will hear three different extracts. Choose the answer (**A**, **B** or **C**) which fits best according to what you hear. There are two questions for each extract.

Extract One

You hear two people on a radio programme discussing music education for children.

1 What do the two people agree about?
  A Young children should learn an instrument that needs a lot of concentration.
  B Children should learn an instrument when they are young.
  C It is important for young children to learn some music theory.

2 Why does the woman think the piano is not the best instrument for young children to learn?
  A It is not possible to play simple tunes on the piano.
  B Playing the piano can discourage children from learning another instrument.
  C Most young children are not mature enough to learn the piano.

Extract Two

You hear part of an interview with a rock climber.

3 In Ben's view, what is the best way to improve as a climber?
  A take the advice of other climbers
  B learn from the mistakes you make
  C watch more experienced climbers

4 Why does Ben prefer to climb with others when it is icy?
  A He can learn new techniques from them.
  B He gets nervous in icy conditions.
  C He lacks experience in icy conditions.

Extract Three

You hear part of an interview with a well-known restaurant critic called Amanda Downing.

5 According to Amanda, how do most waiters react when they realise she is a restaurant critic?
  A They give her special attention.
  B They get very nervous.
  C They give her free food or drink.

6 In what way, according to Amanda, are most restaurant owners completely wrong?
  A They think customers choose a restaurant only for its quality of service.
  B They misjudge customers' motivation for going to restaurants.
  C They think that they have different priorities to their customers.

Grammar focus task

Complete these extracts from the recordings. Two options are possible in each sentence.

1 As well as improving manual dexterity and concentration, it seems that it .... help emotional development, too. *(could / may / must)*

2 But a rather academic approach like that .... turn children off for life it they're not ready for it. *(ought to / will / can)*

3 But at the end of the day you .... learn independently, through trial and error. *('ve got to / should / 've to)*

4 When I was younger I .... do most of my climbing during summer holidays, and I haven't done much winter climbing. *(would / might / used to)*

5 You're such a household name, it .... be terrifying for staff when you go into a restaurant. *(must / should / could)*

6 It .... be considered unethical to accept a gift like that. *(could / would / 's got to be)*

Now listen again and compare your answers with what the speakers actually say.

Writing

You work for a large company based in a town centre. Most of the employees of the company drive to work. The director of the company has asked you to prepare a proposal on reducing car use by employees including:

- an outline of why it would be a good thing to reduce car use

- possible ways of achieving this

- problems in introducing changes

- your recommendations on what should be done.

Write your **proposal** in **300–350** words.

Writing hints

This task gives you the chance to practise modal verbs to:
- make recommendations
  The company should consider giving grants for staff to buy bicycles.
  The reliability of public transport needs to be improved.
- talk about the possible consequences of changes
  This would be a popular move among staff.
  This could decrease the use of private cars.

4

Modals 2

complex modal forms; *dare* and *need*; *had better*; *be allowed to*; *be supposed to*; other verbs with modal meanings

A Context listening

1 **⊙ 4** Listen to this extract from a radio drama. Two police officers are discussing a major art theft from the fourth floor of a modern art gallery. Which of these pictures a–f do the police officers discuss?

a

b

c

d

e

f

2 **⊙ 4** Listen again and match the sentence beginnings and endings.

1 Anybody trying to do that would
2 After that they might
3 So someone else must
4 Do you think he might
5 But of course, he might

6 I suppose he could
7 The driver must
8 The forensic team should

a have opened the door from the inside.
b be hiding some information from us.
c have been seen from the street below.
d have finished examining the building by now.
e have been expecting them and that he was part of the gang?
f have been lowered by rope from the roof.
g have been waiting nearby.
h be lying.

3 Which of the sentences in Exercise 2 include these grammatical patterns?

1 modal verb + *have been* + past participle .....1....... ....would have been seen................
2 modal verb + *have* + past participle ....
3 modal verb + *have been* + present participle ....
4 modal verb + *be* + present participle ....

B Grammar

1 *may / might / could* + *have* + past participle
may / might / could + *be* + present participle

*But of course he **might be lying**.* (**not** *But of course, he can be lying.*) (= now: it's possible he's lying)
*They **could have got** in through a window up on the fourth floor.* (= in the past: it's possible they got in)

With a future time reference we can use *may / might / could* + *be* + present participle and *may / might / could* + *have* + past participle to say it is possible that something will happen in the future:
*Ray's flight was cancelled, so he **may / might / could be arriving** much later than expected.*
*The thieves **may / might / could have left** the country by the time we get to the airport.*

We can also use *might / could* + *have* + past participle (not *may*) to criticise someone because they didn't do something we think they should have:
A: I told the head cleaner he could go home.
*B: You **might have asked** me first. I wanted to ask him a few questions.*

2 *may / might / could* + *have been* + present participle

We can use *may / might / could* + *have been* + present participle to talk about situations or activities that were possibly happening at a particular past time:
*Do you think he **might have been expecting** them?*

3 *would / will* + *have* + past participle

We use *would have* + past participle to talk about an imaginary past situation:
*People **would have seen** them from the street below.*
⚠ To show that we think a past situation actually happened, we use *will have* + past participle:
*If they smashed a window to get in, people living nearby **will** certainly **have heard** something.*

We can use *would have been able to* to talk about a possible past ability:
*You don't think they **would have been able to jump** from the block across the road, do you?*

4 *should / ought to* + *have* + past participle

We use *should / ought to* + *have* + past participle to talk about something that didn't happen in the past, particularly when we want to imply some regret or criticism:
*He must know that he **ought to have called** the police as soon as he found the door open.*
*We **should have been contacted** earlier.* (passive)

We can also use *should / ought to* + *have* + past participle to talk about an expectation that something happened, has happened, or will happen:
*The forensic team **should have finished** examining the building by now.*

5 *must / can't / couldn't* + *have* + past participle

START POINT

> *So someone else **must have opened** the door from the inside.* (active)
> *It **must have been opened** from the inside.* (passive)
> We can use **must have** + past participle to draw a conclusion about something in the past.

To draw a conclusion about a past event, saying that it was not possible, we use *can't have* + past participle or *couldn't have* + past participle:
*One man alone **couldn't have carried** all those paintings.* (**not** ... ~~mustn't have carried~~)

To draw a conclusion about something happening at a particular past time, saying that it was likely or certain, we use *must have been* + present participle:
*The driver **must have been waiting** nearby.*

6 *must have (had) to*

We can use *must have to* to say that we draw a conclusion based on what we know about a present situation:
*He **must have to know** the entry code, too.*
and *must have had to* to conclude something about a past situation:
*The robbers **must have had to bring** a van around to the front of the building.*

7 *must be* + present participle

We can use *must be* + present participle to draw a conclusion about something happening around the time of speaking. We can use *must be* + present participle or *must be going to* to draw a conclusion about something likely to happen in the future:
*I'll speak to the curator of the museum later. She **must be feeling** devastated.*
*They're taking the head cleaner to the police car. They **must be going to arrest** him.* or
*They **must be arresting** him.*

8 *dare* and *need*

START POINT

> *He gets annoyed easily, so I **daren't criticise** him.* / *A good car **needn't cost** a lot.*
> *She **dared** me **to jump** across.* / *We **need to talk** to them.*
> **Dare** and **need** can be used either as modal verbs (+ bare infinitive) or ordinary verbs (+ *to*-infinitive).

As modals, *dare* and *need* are mostly used in negative contexts. If *not* doesn't follow the verb, *dare* can be used either with or without *to*:
*But no one **would have dared (to) climb up** the outside of the building.*

⚠ We can't include *to* after *needn't*:
*We **needn't interview** everyone in the block.* (**not** ~~We needn't to interview~~ ...)

9 *had better*

We can use *had better* instead of *should / ought to*, especially in spoken English, to say that we think it is a good idea (or not) to do something:
*We**'d better find** out all we can about that guard as soon as possible.*
*We**'d better not go** in until the forensic team has finished.*
⚠ We use *should* or *ought to* when we talk about the past or make general comments:
*I **should / ought to** have phoned her earlier.*
*People living around here **should / ought to** support the police more.* (**not** ~~People living around here had better~~ ...)

10 *be allowed to*

We can use *could* or *was / were allowed to* to say that in the past someone had general permission to do something:
*Only the security guard **could / was allowed to** stay in the museum after it closed.*

To talk about permission on a particular occasion, we use *was / were allowed to* (**not** *could*):
*Although he had no ID, the man **was allowed to** enter the building.*
⚠ In negative sentences we can use either *could* or *was / were allowed to* when talking about permission in general or on particular occasions:
*They let reporters into the crime scene, but they **couldn't / weren't allowed to** take photos.*

11 *be supposed to*

We can use *be supposed to* to express a less strong obligation than with *should* or *ought to*. Using *be supposed to* often suggests that events do not happen as expected:
*The entry code **is supposed to be known** only by the security guard.* (= suggests that it was in fact known by others)

We can use *be supposed to* to report what people think is true:
*The building **is supposed to be** one of the most secure in the country.* (= people say it is.)
(**not** ~~the building should / ought to be~~ ...)

12 Other verbs with modal meanings

A number of other verbs are used with similar meanings to modal verbs:
*No one **is to** enter the building until the police give permission.* (= obligation – formal)
*Everyone present **was required** to give a statement to the police.* (= obligation)
*How did they **manage to** get in?* (= ability)
*We **have succeeded in** narrowing down the list of suspects.* (= ability)
*He **might be prepared** to tell us more.* (= willingness)
*The suspects **have refused** to co-operate.* (= unwillingness)
*From the evidence we have found, **it follows** that it was a carefully planned operation.* (= conclusion – formal)
*We can **conclude** that the paintings were stolen by professionals.* (= conclusion)

C Grammar exercises

1 Choose the correct verbs. Sometimes more than one is possible.

1 A: We *could / can / were allowed to* use the university's telescope to watch the comet last night.

   B: You *must have got up / must have had to get up / must have to get up* really early to see it.

2 I *didn't dare admit / didn't dare to admit / couldn't be admitting* that I'd dropped his laptop. He *will have been / would have been / can have been* so angry with me.

3 The weather forecast said it *might be raining / can be raining / could have rained* later, so *we'd better to / we ought to / we'd better* take an umbrella when we go out.

4 The work on repairing the bridge *must have started / is supposed to start / ought to start* next month, but there have been a lot of complaints about it. It's the height of the tourist season, so they *oughtn't to / couldn't / mustn't* have chosen a worse time to do it.

5 You *should / must / will* have been mad to jump off the wall like that. You *might / will / could* have broken a leg.

6 Kevin *can have known / must have to know / must have known* the brakes on the car weren't working properly. He really *should have warned / ought to warn / had better have warned* me when he sold it to me.

7 A: I'm afraid I spilt some coffee on the sofa this morning.

   B: You *can / may / might* have told me earlier! My parents will be home soon, and they'll be furious.

   A: But they *need never to / need never / mustn't have to* know. I bought this stain remover, and I'm sure it will get it clean.

8 There have been yet more delays in building our new office block. They *must / should / were supposed to* have finished by now, but I'm starting to think that I *could / might / can* have retired before it's built.

2 Complete the sentences using the verbs from the box in one of these forms:

have + past participle   *be* + present participle
have been + past participle   *have been* + present participle

| cause | change | find | make | ~~snow~~ | talk | wait | work |

1 A: The clouds are getting really dark.

   B: Yes, I think it could .....be snowing......... by morning.

2 A: So how did the explosion happen?

   B: They think it may .... by a gas leak.

3 A: You were born in Wooton, weren't you. It's supposed to be a lovely village.

   B: It certainly used to be, but it may .... – I haven't been there for years.

4 A: I rang Terry's doorbell twice, but there was no answer.

   B: He must .... in the garden.

5 A: Cutting those roses was so difficult. I've still got thorns in my hands.

   B: You might .... it easier if you'd been wearing gloves.

6 A: I thought we were meeting Les at the theatre.

   B: Yes, he should be here by now. I suppose he might .... for us inside the theatre.

7 A: That suit she was wearing must have cost a fortune.

   B: Do you think it might .... of silk.

8 A: When Kathy said 'He's really lazy', do you think she meant me?

   B: Well, she could .... about someone else, I suppose.

3 A group of geography students are going on a field trip to Iceland. Their teacher is talking about the arrangements. Rewrite the underlined parts using one of the words or phrases from the box. You need to add extra words in each case.

> allow   are to   compulsory   managed
> possibility of   recommend   refused   succeeded

" Unfortunately, the authorities **(1)** won't allow us to carry out fieldwork on the glacier. Apparently, because of weather conditions it's not safe at the moment. Instead, **(2)** we've been able to arrange a boat trip to study coastal features, and **(3)** we may see whales. So **(4)** you should bring a pair of binoculars if you can. You might also want to bring a camera, too. In past years, students have **(5)** been able to take some excellent photographs during our Iceland fieldwork. Let me remind you, however, that no portable stereos with external speakers **(6)** should be taken on the trip, although **(7)** you may bring an MP3 player if you want to. And finally, can you remember that **(8)** everyone must arrange their own private medical insurance for the trip. I'll check next week that everyone has done this ... "

1 *have refused to*

2 ....

3 ....

4 ....

5 ....

6 ....

7 ....

8 ....

4 Read these extracts from newspaper and magazine articles. Choose one phrase from each of the pairs in the box to complete the sentences.

> must have been going through / could have been going through
> could be facing / can be facing
> ~~could have been prevented / can have been prevented~~
> must have been / must have to be
> ought to give / ought to have given
> would not have been able to grow / will not be able to grow
> might be working / might have been working
> must get easier / must be getting easier

1 An enquiry into last year's explosion at the Amcon Refinery that killed 25 workers and injured hundreds more concluded that it ......*could have been prevented*...... if the refinery had installed a hazard warning system, as safety officers had recommended.

2 There is some evidence to suggest that Jonathan Myles .... as a secret agent during the 1960s, although even after the end of the Cold War this was never confirmed.

3 Andy Smith, chief executive of the Schools Examination Authority said: 'The newspapers claim that the improving results show that exams .... But we are absolutely certain that standards have remained the same.'

4 Although Arthur Rodway suffered from a long and painful illness, he never showed any sign of what he .... and continued to take on film roles until just a few months before his death.

5 Mr Wise will return to court in London on January 31st to hear his sentence, having been warned yesterday that he .... a long period in prison.

6 I interviewed Hemingway in the idyllic garden of his house in the south of France, with vineyards behind us and the clear blue sea in front. My first question was: 'You .... so disciplined to ignore all this and work. How do you continue to write so much?'

7 Lampard .... them the lead just before half time, but he shot straight at the goalkeeper, who made an easy save.

8 For centuries the flooding of the Nile was very important because, without it, the people .... crops in the dry desert. But global warming has changed the traditional patterns of agriculture in this part of the world.

D Exam practice

This exercise tests grammar from the rest of the book as well as the grammar in this unit.

Use of English

For questions **1–8**, complete the second sentence so that it has a similar meaning to the first sentence, using the word given. **Do not change the word given.** You must use between **three** and **six** words, including the word given. Here is an example **(0)**.

0 Those working with pre-school age children will probably find the course interesting.
INTEREST
The course is likely *to be of interest to* those working with pre-school age children.

---

1 During the winter I prefer watching football to playing it.
SOONER
During the winter I .... it.

2 Karen says it takes less than an hour to drive there, but I'm sure she has got it wrong.
MUST
Karen says it takes less than an hour to drive there, but she .... a mistake.

3 Students wishing to enrol on the course should complete all sections of the application form.
REQUIRED
Students wishing to enrol on the course .... in all sections of the application form.

4 She decided to move to a part-time job so that she could spend more time with her young children.
ORDER
She decided to move to a part-time job .... able to spend more time with her young children.

5 I really messed up the first question in the exam. I wish I had considered it more carefully before answering.
THOUGHT
I really messed up the first question in the exam. I should .... it more carefully before answering.

6 The factory has been able to reduce its CO_2 emissions by 50% in the last year.
SUCCEEDED
The factory .... back its CO_2 emissions by 50% in the last year.

7 It's a long walk home, so I advise you not to miss the last train.
BETTER
It's a long walk home, so .... the last train.

8 They didn't mention the subject of unpaid holidays until the end of the interview.
BRING
Not until the end of the interview .... the subject of unpaid holidays.

Look at your answers to the exam practice.

1 Which answer refers to something that didn't happen in the past? ....
2 Which answer draws a conclusion about something that happened in the past? ....
3 Which phrase could be replaced by *shouldn't* with a similar meaning? ....

Writing

Last year you went on an organised walking holiday for a week, walking along a long-distance footpath to a different hotel each night. A friend has written to you asking whether you would recommend the holiday that you went on and the company who organised it. Read the extract from your friend's letter and some extracts from the diary you wrote during your holiday. Write a letter to your friend saying what you thought about the holiday, how it could have been better, and whether you would recommend the holiday and the company.

Since you told me about your walking holiday, I've thought about doing the same. I enjoy walking a lot, although I'm not very fit. I'll be going on my own, so it would be good to meet some friendly people on the tour. I hope it won't be too expensive, though. I'm saving up to buy a car, so I don't have much money. Would you recommend the holiday? And what about the company you went with?
Love,
Martha

June 3rd
Beautiful scenery again, but really hard work in the hills. Struggled to keep up with rest of the people in the group.

June 4th
Exhausting walk again. Guide really knowledgeable – but got us lost again. Excellent lunch along the way – but v. expensive!

June 5th
Chatted more to others in group as we walked. Nice people! Hotel not ready for us when we got there. But great food again.

Write your **letter** in **180–220** words. Do not write any postal address.

This task gives you the chance to practise complex modal forms, particularly when you say how things might have been different:
It could have been better organised.
They should have warned us that it would be very expensive.
It might have helped if we had walked more slowly.

Nouns, agreement and articles

compound nouns and noun phrases; subject–verb agreement;
countable and uncountable nouns; articles

5

1 Nazim has applied to do a college course in Environmental Science. You are going to listen to part of his interview for a place on the course. What questions do you think the interviewer will ask?

2 ⊚ 5 Listen and check whether you were right.

3 ⊚ 5 Listen again and write one word in each gap to complete the compound nouns.

1 climate ......*change*...... 2 .... -making 3 rain ....

4 river .... 5 .... saving 6 lighting ....

7 .... scheme 8 the arms .... 9 mountain ....

Which of the following forms do each of the compound nouns take?

noun + noun ...*1*........ noun + -*ing* form .... -*ing* form + noun ....

4 Read these pairs of sentences from the interview. Explain the differences in meaning in the words in *italics*.

1 a There's been *a drought* there for a number of months, and river levels are low.
  b The main problem has been the effect of *the drought* on food supplies.

2 a And what are your plans for *the future*, after you've left college?
  b It's hard to imagine *a future* without farming in an area like that.

3 a And what are your plans for the future, after you've left *college*?
  b Have you got any questions about the course here at *the college*?

B Grammar

1 Compound nouns and noun phrases

START POINT

Common compound noun patterns:

noun + noun	-*ing* form + noun	noun + -*ing* form
climate change	*recycling scheme*	*energy-saving*

Some compound nouns are usually written as one word (e.g. **rainforest**), some as separate words (e.g. **climate change**), and others with a hyphen (e.g. **energy-saving**).

The first noun in a compound usually has a singular form, even if it has a plural meaning:
decision-making (**not** *decisions-making*)

Instead of a compound noun we can use:
- noun + 's + noun when the first noun is the user of the second noun:
  *a **women's clinic**, a **boys' school***
- noun + preposition + noun:
  *a **book about energy conservation**, a **book about grammar*** (*a grammar book* is also common)

We can sometimes use noun + 's + noun or noun + *of* + noun with a similar meaning:
*the **charity's aim*** or *the **aim of the charity***
⚠ We are more likely to use noun + 's + noun:
- when the first noun refers to a particular person or group of people or to talk about time:
  Mike's job**, **next year's field trip
⚠ We more often use noun + *of* + noun:
- with an inanimate second noun: *the **title of the CD***
- when we talk about a process or change over time: *the **destruction of the rainforest***
- with a long noun phrase: *Mike is **the brother of someone I went to school with**.*

We can use noun + *of* + 's or a possessive pronoun to talk about something that someone owns, or about a relationship:
*an old **jacket of Mike's**, a **friend of mine***
When we talk about a relationship between people, we can also use a noun without 's:
*She's a friend of my **mother's**.* or (less commonly) *She's a friend of my **mother**.*

Compounds often combine with other nouns or compounds to form longer combinations:
decision-making process, energy conservation scheme

2 Subject–verb agreement

Some nouns with a singular form, referring to a group (e.g. *government, class, department, team*), can be used with either a singular or plural form of the verb, although in formal contexts a singular verb is often preferred:
*The government **has** (or **have**) introduced some really interesting projects.*
(⊳See Appendix 3.1.)

44

We usually use a **singular verb**:
- when names and titles (e.g. of countries, newspapers, books, films) ending in *-s* refer to a single unit:
  *The Netherlands **has** begun to tackle the problem.*
- with a phrase referring to a measurement, amount or quantity:
  *Only a few miles **separates** the villages involved in the project.*
- after *percent* (also *per cent* or *%*) referring to a singular or uncountable noun: *10% of the country's energy **comes** from wind power.* But if *percent* refers to a plural noun we use a plural verb:
  *60% of people there **are** malnourished.*

We usually use a **plural verb**:
- with nouns that normally have a plural form: *congratulations, outskirts, clothes.* (▷ See Appendix 3.2.)
  ⚠ The following nouns ending in *-s* take a singular verb − *news, linguistics, mathematics, physics,* and *politics, statistics, economics* when they refer to the academic subject:
  *I noticed that statistics **is** included in the course.*
- after *a / the majority / minority of, a number of, a lot of, plenty of, all (of), some of* + a plural noun / pronoun:
  *The majority of people there **are** farmers.*
  ⚠ We use a singular verb with *the number of*: *The number of people suffering from malnutrition **is** increasing.*

When the subject of a sentence is complex, the following verb must agree with the main noun in the subject:
*Levels of income from the sale of handicrafts **have** increased.*
When the subject follows the verb, the verb agrees with the subject:
*Among the projects invested in by the government **is the use** of low-energy light bulbs.*

If the subject is a clause, we usually use a singular verb:
*Having responsibility for the whole project in the area **means** that ...*
⚠ If the subject is a *wh*-clause, we use a singular verb before a singular or uncountable main noun, and a plural verb before a plural main noun. Compare:
*What's needed now, though, **is** to expand **work** like this.*
*What is needed **are** more **schools**.*
(*What's needed **is** more schools.* would be acceptable in informal speech.)

3 Countable and uncountable nouns

START POINT

Many nouns in English are uncountable: they are not used with **a/an** or in the plural. For example: **advice, equipment, information.** (▷ See Appendix 4.1.)

Some nouns are used uncountably when we are talking about the thing in general or the general idea, but countably when we are talking about particular examples or particular types of the thing or idea:
*The charity's project has been **a success**.* (= a particular example of success)
*Financial **success** isn't everything.* (= success in general)
*You'd be able to get by with **a basic knowledge** of some statistical techniques.* but *The desire for **knowledge** is a fundamental human instinct.*
Other nouns like this include: *business, knowledge, sound.* Some of these (e.g. *knowledge*) are only used countably in the singular. (▷ See Appendix 4.2.)

Some nouns (e.g. *accommodation, speech, work*) have a different meaning when they are used countably and uncountably. Compare:
*She gave **a speech** about global warming.*
*Children usually develop **speech** in their second year.*
(➤ See Appendix 4.3.)

We use *a good / great deal of* and *amount of* before uncountable nouns:
*There's **a great deal of** interest in recycling in the country.*
*It's saving **an enormous amount of** our natural resources.*
⚠ Using these before a plural countable noun is incorrect and you should avoid it in exams. However, they are sometimes used in this way in informal contexts.

We use *a number of* before plural countable nouns:
*There's been a drought there for **a number of** months.*
and *plenty of* and *a quantity of* before either uncountable or plural countable nouns:
*There was **plenty of** opportunity for me to travel around the country.*
*I saw **a huge quantity of** trees being cut down.*

4 Articles

We use *the*:
- with singular, plural or uncountable nouns when we expect the listener or reader to be able to identify the thing or person referred to:
  It's a project run by a European charity.
  ***The** charity's aim ...*
- when a following phrase or clause identifies what particular thing we are talking about:
  ***the** climate in this region, **the** impact of climate change, **the** ecology of mountain environments*
- when we talk about things that are unique:
  *in one part of **the** world, the sky, **the** future; **the** first / next time; **the** only / main problem; **the** smallest improvement, **the** arms trade, **the** environment*
⚠ Some 'unique' nouns can be used with *a/an* when we describe a type or aspect of the thing. Compare:
*What are your plans for **the** future?* and *It's hard to imagine **a** future without farming in an area like that.*

We use *a/an*:
- when a singular countable noun is introduced for the first time into a spoken or written text:
  *He's the head of **a** project run by **a** European charity.*
- to talk about an unspecified person, thing or event:
  *I didn't have **a** shower for days.*
- to describe someone/something or say what type of thing someone/something is:
  *It's **a** beautiful country. It's **an** international organisation.*
- to say what a person's job is:
  *You think that as **a** politician, you'd be able to do this?*
⚠ We use *the* or no article to give a person's title or their unique position:
*He's **the** head of a project there.* or *He's head ...*
- in number and quantity expressions:
  ***a** month or so, **a** couple of weeks, half **an** hour, three times **a** year, 50 cents **a** litre, **a** huge number of, **a** bit*

We use no article:
- with uncountable and plural nouns when we talk generally about people or things rather than about specific people or things: *I've always been fascinated by **plants** and **animals**. They haven't had **rain** for months.*
- with some singular nouns referring to institutions (e.g. *school, college, hospital, prison, university, work*) when we talk about them generally. Compare: *after you've left college* and *the course here at the college*
- with countries:
  Brazil, Switzerland, Norway but *the Netherlands, the USA, the UK, the Philippines, the Gambia*

- with meals (e.g. *dinner, breakfast*), special times of the year (e.g. *Ramadan, Easter*), the names of months and days of the week (e.g. *in June*)
  ⚠ We use articles to talk about, for example, a particular meal: *We had **an** early dinner. It was **the** summer after my operation.*
- with *by* to talk about means of communication and transport: *by post / email / phone; by car / taxi / bus / plane / air / sea.* Compare: *We had to go by boat.* and *Sometimes we had to carry **the** boat.*
- (or *the*) with seasons: *I like to go skiing in winter* or *in the winter.*
  ⚠ We always use *the* when it is understood which particular season it is: *I'm going to Nepal in **the** summer.* (= next summer).

C Grammar exercises

1 **Choose the correct phrase. Sometimes both are possible.**

1 I don't like tomatoes, so I left them at *the side of the plate / the plate's side*.

2 Do you know Sue Lane? I was *a colleague of her / a colleague of hers* at Carbuild.

3 It was *the decision of Adam / Adam's decision* to take out the loan, so he has to take responsibility for repaying it.

4 I've seen two really good programmes on TV this week. The first was *a horror film / a film about horror*, and the second *a documentary about apartheid / an apartheid documentary*.

5 John is *someone I worked with in Malaysia's brother / the brother of someone I worked with in Malaysia*.

6 The average temperature of *the Earth's surface / the surface of the Earth* has fallen slightly over the last century.

7 He apologised without *the hesitation of a moment / a moment's hesitation*.

8 My house is by *a children playground / a children's playground*, so it can be quite noisy.

9 Did you know that I used to go to school with *a cousin of John Lennon / a cousin of John Lennon's*?

10 *The construction of the new library / The new library's construction* took so long that building costs were ten times higher than first expected.

11 When I got home I found that an envelope had been pushed through my *letters box /
letter box*. In it was *a congratulations card / a congratulation card* from Aunt Alice.

12 Jerry got into journalism when she was asked to do some *book reviews / books reviews*
for the local newspaper, and then she took over as the *crimes reporter / crime reporter*.

2 Nazim has been accepted on the Environmental Science course (see page 43). Read this
email he sent to a friend during a field trip. Fill in the gaps with a present tense form
of the verbs in brackets.

Hi Cathy,

Greetings from Nepal! I'm sending this from an internet café in a small town north of
Kathmandu. The town itself isn't very interesting, but the surroundings (1) .....*are*..... *(be)*
beautiful – I can see the Himalayas through the café window!

The lectures here are brilliant. The Politics and Ecology courses are great, but Economics (2)
.... *(be)* really difficult – although maths (3) ………. *(be)* certainly not my strong point!

I'm really learning a lot about the country and its environmental problems. Sixty percent of
Nepal's population (4) .... *(live)* in the mountainous parts of the country south of the
Himalayas, and the majority of these people (5) .... *(depend)* on growing crops and
keeping animals. The standard of living in Kathmandu and the other cities (6) .... *(have)*
risen a lot recently, and the number of people likely to move into the cities (7) ....
(be) expected to increase. It's a real problem here. *The Himalayan Times*, the local English-
language newspaper, (8) .... *(have)* just published a survey showing that most young
people would stay in their home villages if jobs were available.

I was planning on coming home at the end of June, but the college (9) .... *(have)*
arranged for a few of us to stay during the summer on a WWF conservation project in a region
in the north called Helambu – there (10) .... *(be)* just a few kilometres between the
village where I'll be working and the border with China. Among the various projects that have
been set up (11) .... *(be)* a scheme for producing biogas locally – that's gas produced
from plant and animal waste. Using biogas for cooking rather than wood (12) .... *(mean)*
less deforestation. All my living expenses (13) .... *(be)* being paid for by the WWF.
Maybe I'll travel around Nepal after. What I'm really hoping to see (14) .... *(be)* the tigers
in the Chitwan National park.

Hope all is well with you. I'll send more news when I can.

Nazim

3 Choose one word or phrase from each of the pairs in the box to complete the sentences. In some cases, both words or phrases are correct.

> advertising / advertisements   advice / tips   explosives / ammunition
> fresh fruit / vegetables   jobs / work   ~~meetings / foreign travel~~
> rubbish / empty bottles   salt / cups of coffee

1 Her job involves a good deal of ..... *foreign travel* ..... .
2 Make sure you eat plenty of ....
3 What I don't like about the magazine is the huge number of .... in it.
4 Many people should reduce the amount of .... they consume.
5 The Students' Handbook includes a great deal of .... on study skills.
6 The police discovered two rifles and a large quantity of .... in his apartment.
7 I have a huge amount of .... to do at the weekend.
8 I was shocked by the amount of .... left behind after the party.

4 Fill in the gaps using the words in the box. Use the same word to complete the sentences in each pair. Add *a / an* if necessary.

> competition   ~~conversation~~   importance   iron
> knowledge   paper   shampoo   time

1 a He lists his interests as reading, listening to music and good ..... *conversation* ..... .
  b It's very difficult to hold ..... *a conversation* ..... with Sarah because she keeps interrupting all the time.
2 a Customers have benefited from lower prices resulting from .... between the supermarkets.
  b A: I see you've bought a new bike. B: Actually, I won it in ....
3 a Our council is encouraging everyone to recycle ....
  b Professor Tench has recently published .... on her research.
4 a You can only tell whether you like .... by washing your hair with it a few times.
  b A: Do we need anything from the chemist's?
     B: Just .... and a tube of toothpaste.
5 a Don't leave the flower pot outside. It's made of .... and it will go rusty.
  b I burnt a hole in my trousers with ....

6 a Has there ever been .... when you've regretted moving to Australia?

   b Definitions of poverty have changed over ....

7 a When parents take an active role in schools, children see their parents placing .... on their education.

   b The manuscript is of great historical ....

8 a Humans are driven by the pursuit of ....

   b Living in Dublin gave me .... of Irish history.

5 **Add *a, an* or *the* to these texts where necessary.**

1 a   an   the (× 3)

My brother wasn't very good at taking exams and he left school at 16. At first he went to work in *the* construction industry. But he didn't enjoy it, so he took evening course in accounting. Eventually, he started company offering financial advice. He's now managing director, and it seems that company's doing really well.

2 a (× 3)   an   the (× 3)

A: Do you remember summer we went to Sweden? 1995, I think it was.

B: It was wonderful holiday, wasn't it? And so good to see Joakim again. I'll never forget picnic we had with him. There were huge number of mosquitoes.

A: Yes, I remember. And then when sun was going down there was amazing sky – bright orange.

B: And then his car broke down as we were going home, and we had to go back by bus.

B: No, we got taxi, didn't we?

A: Oh yes, that's right.

3 a (× 4)   the (× 5)

Linda has busy life as lawyer, but in her free time she really enjoys hiking. Most weekends she drives out into countryside and walks for few hours. She says she likes to forget about work, and she doesn't even take mobile phone with her. In summer she's going hiking in Philippines. She's never been there before, but friend she's going with knows country well.

D Exam practice

This exercise tests grammar from the rest of the book as well as the grammar in this unit.

Use of English

Read the text below and think of the word which best fits each space.
Use only **one** word in each space.

The origins of chess

A great **(0)** ..deal.. has been written about the origins of modern chess, and there

(1) .... still considerable debate about the subject. **(2)** .... theory

most widely accepted is that its earliest ancestor was Shaturanga, a game played in India from

around AD 600. **(3)** .... with modern chess, Shaturanga was played on a board

with 64 squares. Pieces such as Kings, Queens and Knights were able to move in different

ways with **(4)** .... aim of capturing other pieces and, at the end of the game, the

opponent's King. Unlike chess, it was played by four people, **(5)** .... with their own

army, the other main difference **(6)** .... the use of dice to decide which

piece moved each turn. Some chess historians believe that the game in fact derives

(7) .... a Persian game, Shatranj, the first references to which also

(8) .... from the sixth century. In Shatranj, the powers of the King to move and

capture pieces **(9)** .... more limited than in Shaturanga. **(10)** ....

there may be disagreement about its origins, it is generally accepted that chess in essentially

the form it is played today appeared in southern Europe around the end of the fifteenth century

and quickly spread **(11)** .... the continent. **(12)** .... this time,

the Queen had become the most powerful piece of all. Today, chess has become one of the

world's **(13)** .... popular games. It is played by millions of people both informally

and in tournaments, and **(14)** .... number of people playing online

(15) .... increasing with access to the Internet.

**Without looking back at the text, complete these sentences with *the*, *a* or –
(= no article). One sentence from each pair is based on the text.**

1 a Chess is played by millions of people both informally and in .... tournaments.

   b Of all .... chess tournaments I've competed in, this was the best organised.

2 a .... theory most widely accepted is that its earliest ancestor was Shaturanga.

   b There are many books written about .... chess theory.

3 a A great deal has been written about the origins of modern chess, and there is still considerable debate about .... subject.

   b The origins of chess is .... subject I know very little about.

4 a Its earliest ancestor was Shaturanga, ... game played in India from around AD 600.

   b The rules of .... game have changed little since the fifteenth century.

Writing

The Council wants to improve the sports facilities in your town. You have been asked to conduct a survey of the opinions of local people and prepare a report suggesting which facilities to focus on. In your report:

● say what sports are most popular among the people surveyed

● say what people think about the facilities available now

● suggest what new sports facilities should be provided to encourage interest in sports.

Write your **report** in **220–260** words.

This task gives you the chance to talk about:

● groups and organisations such as 'the public' and 'the council'. Remember with nouns like these you can use either a singular or plural form of the verb (*the council has / have spent a lot of money*), but make sure you use the same form consistently throughout your answer.

● percentages and parts of a group.
90% of funding comes from..., 10% of those questioned have...; a number / majority / minority of users have found that..., the number of users has fallen

Determiners and quantifiers

no, none, not a, not any; much, many, a lot of, lots of; all, both, whole; every, each; (a / the) few, little; less, fewer, much, many, etc. + (of)

A Context listening

1 You are going to listen to three people talking about running. Write down three benefits and three possible problems of taking up running as a hobby.

benefits: possible problems:

....

....

....

2 **⏼ 6a** Listen to three people giving their views on running. Which of the benefits and possible problems you have listed do the speakers mention?

3 **⏼ 6a** Listen again and fill in the gaps.

1 a Until then I did a bit of sport at school, but I didn't do ....*much*.......... outside school at all. *(Speaker 1)*

   b In fact, I suppose I didn't have .... interests. *(Speaker 1)*

2 a Now I run a few kilometres .... day. *(Speaker 2)*

   b You can be sure that .... one of us will have a really good time. *(Speaker 3)*

3 a Inevitably you get .... injuries, too – everyone gets aching muscles after a long run. *(Speaker 3)*

   b It's one of .... sports where no special equipment's needed. *(Speaker 2)*

4 a I certainly go out a lot .... during the winter. *(Speaker 3)*

   b But surprisingly I seem to have .... injuries now than when I was younger. *(Speaker 3)*

4 In which pair of sentences are the words you have written interchangeable? ....

6

B Grammar

1 no, none, not a, not any

> *No two pairs of running shoes are the same.* (= not any)
> *None of them like the thought of running long distances.* (= not any of)

We use *neither of* instead of *none of* when we talk about two people or things:
Neither of us did any exercise.

We don't usually use *not a / not any* in initial position in a clause. Instead we use *no* and *none of*:
None of the runners is under 60. (**not** ~~Not any of the runners~~ ...)

If it is clear from the context what is meant, we can use *none* without a following noun:
*I've had **none** so far.* (= no injuries)

2 much, many, a lot of, lots of

> *Did you do **much** running last winter?*
> *There could be **many** reasons for the current interest in running.*
> *I get **a lot of** satisfaction out of it.*
> *You get to meet **lots of** interesting people.*
> We use **much (of)** (+ uncountable noun) and **many (of)** (+ plural noun) particularly in negative sentences and in questions. In affirmative sentences we usually use **a lot (of)** or **lots (of)**. However, in more formal contexts we usually prefer **much (of)** and **many (of)**.

If it is clear from the context what is meant, we can use *much* and *many* without a following noun:
*I didn't do **much** outside school at all.*

We can use *much of* and *many of* to mean 'a large part of' or 'a large number of':
*I used to spend **much of** my free time sitting around.*
*I was in first place for **much of** the race.*

We can use *many* between *the* or a possessive pronoun (e.g. *my*) and a plural noun:
*I'm one of the **many** thousands of older people who now run regularly.*
*Even his **many** injuries didn't make him give up running.*

We usually use *many* rather than *a lot of* or *lots of* with time expressions (e.g. *days, minutes, months, weeks, years*) and 'number' + *of* (e.g. *thousands of dollars*):
*I spend **many** hours training.*
*Running clubs often have **many** hundreds of members.*

3 all, both, whole

All (of) my friends like watching sport on TV.
I suppose all exercise carries some risks.
I thought the whole event was brilliant.
Sometimes I go whole weeks without running.
By the time we got to the bus stop both of us were completely exhausted.

To make negative sentences with *all (of)* we usually use *not all (of)* rather than *all ... not*:
Not all the effects are positive. or *The effects are not all positive.* (not ~~All the effects are not positive.~~)
⚠ *None of* and *not all (of)* have different meanings:
Not all of them like the thought of running long distances. (= some of them do)
None of them like the thought of running long distances. (= not one of them does)

We usually put *all* after the verb *be* and after the first auxiliary verb:
Next spring we're all going to Madrid.
They could all have been Olympic athletes.
If there is no auxiliary, we usually put *all* before the verb:
We all went running together.
We sometimes use *all* after the noun it refers to:
My friends all think I'm crazy. or *All my friends think I'm crazy.*

To talk about two things or people we use *both (of)* in affirmative sentences or *neither (of)* in negative sentences:
We certainly both got a lot fitter. Both of us were completely exhausted.
Neither of us did any exercise. (not ~~Both of us didn't do any exercise.~~)

Before singular countable nouns we usually use *the whole* rather than *all (of) the*:
I thought the whole event was brilliant.
⚠ Before *day / week / night / month / summer*, etc. we prefer *all* rather than *the whole*:
After I've been sitting at my computer all day I can't wait to go out for a run.
I might go all week without a run.
⚠ We can use *all the* or *the whole* before *way* and *time*:
I was really surprised when I managed to run all the way. or *... the whole way.*

4 every, each

I go running on Wednesday and on Friday, and I try to run ten miles each day. or *... every day.*
Every one of us will have a really good time. or *Each one of us ...*
Before a singular countable noun, we use **each (of)** to talk about two or more things or people, and **every** to talk about three or more things or people. Sometimes we can use either **every** or **each** with little difference in meaning.

We use *every*:
- with *almost, nearly, practically, virtually* to emphasise we are talking about the group as a whole:
  Now I run **nearly every** day.
- to talk about events at regular intervals:
  every other kilometre, every single day, every few weeks, every six months:
  I go out running **every** couple of days.

We use *each*:
- when we talk about both people or things in a pair:
  I had to wear a bandage on **each** knee. or ... on **both** knees.
- as a pronoun:
  We were **each** given a medal for completing the 5km fun run.

5 (a / the) few, little; less, fewer (than)

START POINT

A **few of** my friends are quite good at team sports.
I seem to have **fewer** injuries now than when I was younger.
There is **little** evidence that running causes major problems.
You should eat **less** protein as you prepare for a race.
There's **not much** you can do about it.

Few (of) and little (of) are often rather formal. Less formally, we use phrases such as **not many** and **not much**.

We often use *a few* and *a little* to suggest that a small quantity or amount is enough, or more than we would expect:
He's won **a few** medals.
I've been starting to get **a little** pain in my knees.
In formal contexts, we often use *few* and *little* to suggest that a quantity or amount is not enough, or is surprisingly low:
Before I joined the club I had very **few** friends who lived nearby.

We can also use *the few* and *the little* followed by a noun to suggest 'not enough':
It's one of **the few** sports where no special equipment's needed.
I used **the little** time I had to prepare for the race.

In comparisons, we use *less* with an uncountable noun, and *fewer* with a plural noun:
I should eat **less** chocolate. You should eat **fewer** biscuits.
The opposite of both *less* and *fewer* is *more*:
I should eat **more** chocolate. You should eat **more** biscuits.

In conversation, some people also use *less (than)* before a plural noun referring to a group of things or people:
There were **less** than 20 competitors.
⚠ This is grammatically incorrect and would be marked wrong in a formal written exam. *Fewer (than)* should be used instead:
There were **fewer** than 20 competitors.

When we talk about a period of time, a distance or a sum of money, we use *less than*, not *fewer than*:
My aim is to complete the course and do it in **less than** six hours.

(▷ See Appendix 5 for information about subject–verb agreement when these and other determiners and quantifiers are used.)

6 *much, many, both, all, each, none, few, little + (of)*

We usually need to put *of* after these words when they are followed by a pronoun, a determiner or possessive form:

*We know that not **all of** us will finish the course. **Few of** the runners were under 65.*
__Many of__ Alice's friends are runners.

Informally after *both* and *all* we can leave out *of* before *the, these, those; this, that* (with *all*); possessive pronouns (e.g. *my, mine*) but not before *them, you, us; it* (with *all*):

*I've been running regularly **all of** my life.* or *I've been running regularly **all** my life.*
__Both of__ us decided to do more exercise. (**not** *Both us decided* ...)

C Grammar exercises

1 **Fill in the gaps using the correct form of the verb in brackets to form either the present simple or the present perfect. Sometimes both are possible.**

1 Next week, my work colleagues are doing a bike ride across France for charity. They won't cycle the whole way – they each ....*do*.............. *(do)* 30 kilometres a day and follow by car the rest of the time. That's just as well, because none of them .... *(be)* terribly fit. A number of people .... *(have)* already agreed to sponsor them, and they hope to raise a lot of money.

2 I think that everything .... *(be)* now ready for the party. One of my sisters .... *(have)* organised the drinks, and each of the people coming .... *(have)* agreed to bring some food.

3 I'm having trouble selling my house. Although a lot of interest .... *(have)* been shown in it – I've had lots of phone calls and visitors – the majority of potential buyers .... *(seem)* surprised at how small it is. And not everybody .... *(like)* the fact that there's no garden.

2 **Choose the correct option. Sometimes both are possible.**

1 The nuclear power station is in an earthquake zone, and it's worrying that there have been *a few* / *few* minor tremors here in the last couple of months.

2 There were four candidates in the election and *every* / *each* got about 5000 votes.

3 We didn't have snow once *all* / *the whole* winter.

4 The hurricane will go north of the city, so *little* / *a little* major damage is expected.

5 *We were all* / *We all were* astonished by her exam results.

6 She got a lot of feedback on the course, but *all of it wasn't* / *not all of it was* positive.

7 *Not all / None of* the seats in the carriage were taken, and I sat down by the window next to a man using a laptop.

8 Is there *less / fewer* caffeine in green tea than in coffee?

9 We are trying to preserve *few / the few* remaining areas of rainforest in the country.

10 These old bookshelves *will all be / all will be* replaced by cupboards.

11 It takes me *fewer / less* than 30 minutes to walk to work.

12 When I was in hospital, Martha visited me *each / every* single day.

13 Although the management said they were going to restructure the company, in fact they made *a few / few* changes.

14 Nowadays, *nearly every / nearly each* new car is fitted with airbags.

15 When I got on, *all of the / the whole* bus seemed to be full of screaming schoolchildren.

16 Did *your children all / all your children* go to university?

17 Usually he records other people's songs, but *few / a few* of the tracks on his latest album he wrote himself.

18 The company has *fewer / less* than 20 employees.

3 Complete the sentences using the pairs of words or phrases in the box.

> many / a lot of   no / not any   neither of / none of
> much / a lot of   not any of / none of   many / the many

1 a A KLM flight from Amsterdam overshot the runway at Heathrow Airport yesterday, but ....none of.......... the crew or passengers was hurt.

  b My parents came all the way to Sydney to see me, even though ....neither of.......... them likes flying very much.

2 a When you're in Prague, order a coffee in one of .... cafés around the Old Town Square, and watch the world go by.

  b Storms have been sweeping across .... parts of the country overnight.

3 a I hope you like the present. I put .... effort into finding just the right thing for you.

  b Among linguists, there is .... debate about the origin of the word 'quiz'.

4 a The new anti-malaria drug took .... years to develop.

  b I've got .... friends who live in London.

5 a The government has allocated two million euros to the project, but .... the money has been spent yet.

  b A: Have you been able to fix your car?

    B: No. It's .... the usual problems, so I'll have to take it to the garage.

6 a .... major damage was done to the building by the earthquake.

b I tried to organise a tennis competition at my college, but there was .... interest, so I gave up the idea.

4 Complete the newspaper article with one of these words or phrases. Use each word and phrase once.

all	~~all of~~	all (of)	both	both of	each of	every	~~few~~	few of
little	little of	many	many of	much	much of	none	none of	

'5 PORTIONS A DAY' FALLS ON DEAF EARS

Despite the government's '5 portions a day' recommendation to eat more fruit and vegetables, a recent study has found that **(1)**............_few_............ British teenagers are taking its advice. A thousand teenagers were questioned in the survey, **(2)**..........._all of_.......... them between the ages of 14 and 17. While **(3)**............................ said they knew about the campaign, **(4)**............................ the young people questioned, just 5%, said it had influenced their eating habits. In answer to the question 'How many pieces of fruit have you eaten in the last week?', an incredible 50% responded '**(5)**............................'.

Sam Brown, 15, and Sarah Goodall, 16, were among the young people who took part in the survey. **(6)**............................ them conceded that fruit and vegetables didn't figure greatly in their diets. Sam admitted: 'I don't eat **(7)**............................ fruit at all, maybe just an apple sometimes. I don't think **(8)**............................ my friends are different.' Sarah felt that the busy lifestyle of today's teenagers was partly to blame: 'I'm not into vegetables, and **(9)**............................ the time I'm too busy to eat fruit after dinner. I've got homework to do or friends to see.'

(10)............................ agreed that the government's campaign wouldn't affect what they ate. Sam said: '**(11)**............................ the posters and adverts are hard-hitting enough. Their message is just 'Eat fruit or veg with **(12)**............................ meal.' If they want teenagers to eat more fruit and vegetables, they've got to convince us that it's really important.'

(13)............................scientists have warned that failure to eat fruit and vegetable, particularly by young people, can lead to obesity, cancer and a host of other diseases. Professor Jess Adams from Queen's Hospital said: '**(14)**............................ the research points to a close relationship between levels of fruit and vegetable consumption and health, but surprisingly **(15)**............................ this research is reported in the press or on television. This means that the message is not getting across. The government tries to highlight the problem with its campaigns, but unfortunately there is **(16)**............................ sign that they have any long-term impact. Ultimately, however, it's up to **(17)**............................ us to think about what we eat and make healthy choices.'

D Exam practice

This exercise tests grammar from the rest of the book as well as the grammar in this unit.

Listening

(🎧 6b) You will hear a woman called Janet Naylor talking about her experience as a volunteer in Tanzania. Complete the sentences.

Janet can now do voluntary work because she is free of [＿＿＿＿＿＿＿ **1**] .

Most of Janet's friends were [＿＿＿＿＿ **2**] by her decision to volunteer.

Janet disagrees with people who say that she is [＿＿＿＿＿＿ **3**] the people she is trying to help.

Janet advised on a project to improve [＿＿＿＿＿＿ **4**] in a farming community.

The villagers had been dependent on [＿＿＿＿＿＿ **5**] from charities to survive.

The scheme aimed to make the villagers [＿＿＿＿＿ **6**] in agricultural production.

Janet's job was to help the villagers sell any [＿＿＿＿＿ **7**] crops.

Janet believes that the [＿＿＿＿＿ **8**] of the village have been changed dramatically by the scheme.

Grammar focus task

Complete the extracts from the talk using the words in the box.

all	few	less	many	~~much~~	whole

1 I've worked in marketing for ....much.......... of my life.
2 .... were impressed, I think, and a lot said that given the opportunity they'd like to do something similar.
3 I must say that not .... of them were so keen when I told them later about how basic the conditions were.
4 But a .... clearly disapproved of what I was doing.
5 The .... region was on the brink of starvation and handouts from charities were the only thing that kept people alive.
6 The scheme had been underway for .... than a year when I arrived.

Writing

The Principal of your college is concerned that many students have part-time jobs and that these are interfering with their studies. As the student representative on the staff–student committee, you have been asked by the Principal to interview 50 students and write a report of your findings. Here is his note outlining what he wants you to find out.

Thanks for agreeing to do the survey. I'm interested to find out:

- how many students have part-time jobs, what kinds of jobs they have, and how many hours a week they work
- what negative effect having a part-time job has on their studies
- what students think are the advantages of having a part-time job.

As you know, I'm thinking of putting a limitation on the number of hours students can work in part-time jobs. If you have any thoughts on whether this would be a good or bad idea, put them in the report.

Write your **report** in **220–260** words.

This task gives you the chance to practise determiners and quantifiers:
Many / Most / Few / All of the students ...; A few students said ...
less time for relaxation, fewer hours a week, most weeks, little work

Adverbs and adjectives

position of adverbs; *quite, rather, already, yet, still, even, only, really;*
position of adjectives; gradable adjectives; patterns after adjectives

A Context listening

1 You are going to hear an interview with an author. In the interview he mentions three countries. Look at these photos. Which countries do you think they show?

2 ⊙ 7 Listen and check whether you were right. Why is each of these countries important to the author?

3 Read these eight extracts from the interview. The words on the right have been removed. Put an arrow to show where you think the words came from.

1 I suppose I'd been a writer (always)
2 I left teaching and I started writing. (professionally)
3 I go back on every occasion. (possible)
4 I know how a book is going to end. (always)
5 I'm up at about 7.00 in the morning. (generally)
6 I prefer finding information from books. (as a rule)
7 I still speak Swedish. (quite well)
8 My mother was a gentle woman. (rather)
9 I'm sketching out the plot. (still)

⊙ 7 Listen again and check your answers.

4 Read these further extracts from the interview. Tick (✓) those where you can add *very* before the underlined adjective and put a cross (✗) where this is not possible.

1 Some of my close friends thought I was <u>mad</u> to give up my job. ✗
2 I rarely have a <u>clear</u> idea at the beginning of how the characters will develop.
3 I was <u>happy</u> to teach during the day.
4 It felt <u>fantastic</u> having my first book published.
5 I've just finished his <u>excellent</u> novel *Restless*.
6 I felt <u>bad</u> leaving the children.
7 There are a lot of <u>historical</u> links between Norway and the north of Scotland.
8 My mother was a rather gentle woman and always <u>even-tempered</u>.

B Grammar

1 Position of adverbs

There are three main positions for adverbs:
- front position:

Normally, I write for about six hours a day.
- mid position:

I usually start work by about 8.00. I'm generally up at about 7.00. I had never been to Norway before.

If my books hadn't been successful, I would happily have stayed in teaching. or *I would have happily stayed ...*
- end position:

He writes simply.

Many adverbs can go in any of these positions, depending on context or style:

Gradually, they grow into real people. or *They gradually grow into real people.* or *They grow gradually into real people.*

Some adverbs tend to appear in particular positions:
- *Always, never*; adverbs of indefinite frequency (*hardly ever, often, rarely, regularly, seldom*); and degree adverbs (*almost, hardly, nearly, quite, rather, scarcely*) are usually put in mid position:

   I rarely have a clear idea. I always know how a book is going to end.

- *Constantly, continually, regularly; absolutely, completely, entirely, greatly, perfectly* are usually put either in mid or end position, but not in front position:

   I greatly admire William Boyd. (**not** *Greatly I admire ...*)

- Adverbs of place (e.g. *upstairs*) and adverbs of definite time and frequency (e.g. *last January, monthly*) are usually put in end position.

- Adverbs of time or frequency consisting of more than one word (e.g. *as a rule, from time to time, every so often*) are usually put either in front or end position, but not mid position:

   As a rule, I prefer finding information from books. (**not** *I as a rule prefer ...*)

We avoid putting an adverb between a main verb and a direct object, or following an *-ing* form or *to*-infinitive:

I still speak Swedish quite well. (**not** *I still speak quite well Swedish.*)

I started writing professionally. (**not** *I started professionally writing.*)

I'd like to go back again. (**not** *I'd like to go again back.*)

In end position we usually put adverbs of place before adverbs of time:

I hadn't been to Norway before. rather than *I hadn't been before to Norway.*

2 quite, rather; already, yet, still; even, only; really

quite, rather

The usual position for *quite* is before *a / an* and an adjective, where it means 'moderately':

Elsa is quite a dominant figure.

Less often, *quite* is used between *a / an* and an adjective, where it means 'completely':
*It's a **quite** remarkable story.*

The usual position for *rather* is between *a / an* and an adjective. Less often, but with a similar meaning, *rather* is used before *a / an* and an adjective:
*My mother was a **rather** gentle woman.* or *My mother was **rather** a gentle woman.*

With a singular noun or *a lot of* but no adjective, *rather* must come before *a / an*:
*There was **rather** a shortage of teachers at the time.* (**not** ~~There was a rather shortage~~ ...)
*I had **rather** a lot of writing to do.* (**not** ~~I had a rather lot of writing to do.~~)

already, yet, still
Already can go in either mid or end position:
*I'd **already** decided that I wanted to write about a single-parent family.* or *I'd decided **already** that ...*
Yet is usually put in end position in negatives, questions and expressions of uncertainty:
*I don't know if I can tell you **yet**.*
Still usually goes in mid position:
*I'm **still** sketching out the plot.*

even, only
Even and *only* usually go in mid position, but if they refer to the subject they usually come before it:
*He can **even** speak Swedish. Sometimes **even** I'm surprised.*
***Only** my close family had read anything I'd written.*

really
The meaning of *really* can change according to its position in a sentence. Immediately before an adjective it means 'very'. In other positions it can mean 'actually' or 'in fact':
*I'd been feeling **really** tired.*
*My friends thought I was joking, but I **really** had decided to leave teaching.*

3 Position of adjectives

START POINT

*his **excellent** novel*   *his novel is **excellent***
Many adjectives can be used either before the noun they describe, or following the noun and a linking verb such as **be, become, feel** and **seem** that connects a subject with a word or phrase that describes the subject.

The following adjectives can be used **immediately** after a noun:
- many participle adjectives:
  *There'll be a lot of people **waiting** eagerly to get hold of it.* (= a lot of people who will be waiting)
  *Some of the geographical settings **used** in A Woman Alone are based on places I visited.*
  (= settings which are used in *A Woman Alone*)
- adjectives used after indefinite pronouns (e.g. *something, nothing*):
  *I really don't think it was **anything special**.*
  *There was **nothing extraordinary** about my first novel.*

Some participle and *-ible/-able* adjectives can be used either before or immediately after a noun, (e.g. *affected, alleged, applicable, available, possible, required, stolen, suggested*):
*I go back on every **possible occasion**.* or *... on every **occasion possible**.*

The following adjectives have different meanings when used in the different positions: *concerned, involved, opposite, present, proper, responsible*:
*And what about your **present writing project**?* (present = current)
*All the **people present** ...* (present = in that particular place)
(▷See Appendix 6.1.)

Many *-ible/-able* adjectives can only be used immediately after a noun when the noun follows a word such as *first, last, next, only* + superlative adjectives, or when extra information is given after the noun:
*It was the most difficult decision **imaginable**.*
*Elsa is a woman **susceptible** to periods of depression.*

4 Gradable adjectives

If an adjective is gradable, we can say that a person or thing can have more or less of the quality referred to (e.g. *ambitious, busy*). Gradable adjectives can be used with adverbs such as *extremely, slightly* or *very*:
somewhat ambitious, extremely busy, slightly different, very rich, pretty strong

If an adjective is non-gradable, we don't usually imagine degrees of the quality referred to (e.g. *huge, impossible*). To emphasise the extreme or absolute nature of non-gradable adjectives we can use adverbs such as *absolutely, completely* or *totally*:
absolutely huge, completely impossible, practically unknown, almost unique, totally useless

Some adjectives have both gradable and non-gradable uses:
- some (e.g. *common*) have gradable and non-gradable uses with different meanings:
  *Bardreth isn't a very **common** surname.* (gradable = frequent)
  *Elsa and my mother have certain **common** characteristics.* (non-gradable = similar)
  (▷See Appendix 6.2.)
- some (e.g. *diplomatic*) have gradable and non-gradable uses with only small differences in meaning between them:
  *You're being very **diplomatic**.* (gradable because it refers to the quality the person has)
  *He worked as the **diplomatic** correspondent of a national newspaper.* (non-gradable because it refers to the type of correspondent he is)
  (▷See Appendix 6.3.)

Some non-gradable adjectives (e.g. *actual, financial, medical, major*) are rarely used with a preceding adverb such as *absolutely* or *completely*:
*I'd expected to pay about £1000, but the **actual** cost was much higher.* (**not** *... the absolutely actual cost ...*)

⚠ Gradable adjectives can be used as non-gradable adjectives, and vice versa, when we want to give special emphasis or when we are being humorous:
*You've got £100 – wow, you're **virtually rich**!*
*It was my first proper meal for three days, and I felt **almost human** again.*

5 Patterns after adjectives

When an adjective comes after a linking verb, we can use a number of patterns after the adjective, including a *to*-infinitive or an *-ing* form:

*I was **unwilling to leave** teaching.*
*It felt **fantastic having** my first book published.*
*Some of my close friends thought I was **mad to give up** my job.* or *... **mad giving up** my job.*

Many adjectives can be followed by a *that*- clause, including some that can also be followed by a *to*-infinitive or an *-ing* form:

*I was **aware** that I needed rest.*
*I was greatly **relieved** that my subsequent books sold quite well.* or *... **relieved** to find ...*
*I felt **bad** that I was leaving the children* or *I felt **bad** leaving the children.*

(⊳See Appendix 7.)

C Grammar exercises

1 Complete the sentences by writing the words in brackets in the correct order. Give alternatives where possible.

1 Not wanting to wake the children, I climbed .the..stairs..quietly. . *(quietly – stairs – the)*

2 Most days I walk to work, but .... the car if the weather's bad.
   (I – sometimes – take)

3 She .... her parents. *(ever – hardly – visits)*

4 When I bumped into his car, he began .... at me. *(angrily – shout – to)*

5 Ken thinks we should sell our car and buy bikes instead, and .... with him. *(absolutely – agree – I)*

6 Natalie is on a working holiday in New Zealand. She .... and should be home at the end of June. *(last – left – week)*

7 .... for a meal after work to catch up on news. *(go – occasionally – we)*

8 Have you been .... ? *(before – Sweden – to)*

9 We .... to see a film. *(go – out – seldom)*

10 As I walked out of the room, she .... *(loudly – singing – started)*

2 Complete the sentences using the adjectives in the box. Use the same adjective in each pair of sentences. If possible, include the adverb given in brackets.

> (severely) critical   (very) genuine   (rather) odd   (highly) original
> (extremely) particular   (thoroughly) professional
> (somewhat) technical   (pretty) wild

1 a She's *extremely particular* about what she eats, and never touches processed food at all.

  b There are so many hotels in the city to choose from. Why did you go for that ......*particular*...... one?

2 a The launch of the space shuttle has been delayed due to a .... fault.

  b The operating instructions were .... and difficult to understand.

3 a The vase is a .... antique, not a recent copy.

  b I'm sure Melanie wouldn't lie to you – she's a .... person.

4 a After protests on the streets, the government had to reconsider its .... decision to double the tax on petrol.

  b He's admired around the world for his .... style of guitar playing.

5 a She is a dedicated teacher, ... and hard-working.

  b I couldn't fix my computer myself, so I had to get some .... help.

6 a As soon as I'd eaten the oysters, I had a .... feeling in my stomach.

  b All the houses on this side of the street have .... numbers.

7 a The strike comes at a .... time for the company, which has just invested in a major new factory.

  b The report was .... of the Principal's management of the college, and she was forced to resign.

8 a The disease was passed on to chickens by .... birds.

  b It's a .... area of moorland, a long way from roads and settlements.

3 Complete the sentences with a *to*-infinitive or *-ing* form of the verb in brackets. Give alternatives where possible.

1 When the phone rang she was busy ....*doing*.......... her homework. *(do)*

2 When I see pictures on TV of the flooding near the coast, I'm thankful .... inland. *(live)*

3 You're welcome .... as long as you like. *(stay)*

4 It was terrible .... her so ill. *(see)*

5 My teacher's rather old and he's inclined .... asleep during lessons. *(fall)*

6 I never felt comfortable .... in the same office as Theresa. *(work)*

7 As soon as you're ready .... , I'll call for a taxi. *(leave)*

8 You should take the job. You'd be foolish .... an offer like that. *(turn down)*

9 I felt terrible .... to help them. *(not to be able)*

10 When the weather's very cold it's difficult .... my car. *(start)*

11 Maria's already lent me a lot of money and I feel awkward .... her for more. *(ask)*

12 Certain newspapers are always quick .... the government if anything goes wrong in the country. *(blame)*

13 The trains have narrow doors, and it's awkward .... on and off. *(get)*

14 I felt bad .... her to do all the clearing up after the party. *(leave)*

4 Choose the correct position for the adjectives and adverbs in these conversations. Sometimes both are possible.

1 A: It says on the website that the film starts at 6.20. But there'll be adverts before, so **(1)** I imagine the ~~proper~~ film (proper) won't start until 6.45. Shall we meet about half six?

B: Fine. And is Lucy coming?

A: **(2)** I haven't *yet* heard back from her *yet*. I think she's coming, although I know **(3)** she's had a *really* bad cold *really*. I've got her a ticket. Unfortunately, **(4)** the only *available* seats *available* were right at the back, and **(5)** I still had to pay *quite* a *quite* ridiculous price for them.

2 A: Sorry to bother you, madam, but we're just making a few enquiries. **(1)** Have you seen *unusual* anything *unusual* in the street over the last 24 hours?

B: Well, I was a bit surprised to see Mr Jones going in and out of his house last night. Normally, **(2)** *only* I *only* ever see him early in the morning.

A: And Mr Jones lives where exactly?

B: **(3)** He's the *living* man *living* in **(4)** the *opposite* house *opposite* – number 35.

A: Could you describe him for me?

B: **(5)** He's *rather* a *rather* tall man, in his mid thirties, with blond hair.

3 A: So which way are we driving across the mountains?

B: I downloaded some information from a travel website, but **(1)** the *given* instructions *given* aren't very helpful.

A: Why not?

B: Well, **(2)** the *suggested* route *suggested* takes you up the narrowest and **(3)** steepest *imaginable* road *imaginable*, and **(4)** there are *rather* a *rather* lot of hairpin bends on it. I'm used to driving in mountains, but **(5)** *even* I *even* would be worried about driving along that road.

D Exam practice

This exercise tests grammar from the rest of the book as well as the grammar in this unit.

Use of English

For questions **1–6**, think of **one** word only which can be used appropriately in all three sentences. Here is an example (0).

0 It's going to be difficult to finish the work by the deadline, but I'm sure I'll ....*manage*........ it.

I run most aspects of the business myself, but I have an accountant to ....*manage*........ the financial side.

That box looks really heavy – can you ....*manage*........ to lift it by yourself?

---

1 West Nile Virus is a potentially fatal infection, and the mosquito .... is becoming increasingly widespread.

Jason wasn't in the house when the window was broken, so he couldn't be ....

Any .... employer will take steps to ensure the safety of their workers.

2 Harry should have been here ages ago, and I'm .... that he might have got lost.

There was a mistake in the maths paper, but the students .... will be allowed to take the examination again.

The academic writing classes are open to all students, but we are particularly .... to help students from overseas.

3 Tony Austin's performance was a highly .... mix of songs, poetry and stories.

My .... plan was to drive to Greece, but I eventually decided it was too far.

There is a copy in an art gallery in St. Petersburg, but the .... painting was lost many years ago.

4 School sports day will be held on Thursday July 1st, or Friday July 2nd in the .... that the weather is bad on Thursday.

Tonight's match is the first .... to be held in the stadium since its reopening.

We only expected about a hundred people at the meeting, but in the .... the hall was completely full.

5 When the Socialists were elected to power, it was a .... moment in the history of the country.

The company director refused to resign, even though the report was .... of his performance.

Recent research has shown that diet is .... to the prevention of many types of cancer.

6 Sarah didn't come into work this morning, but she seemed .... well when I saw her last night.

I .... understand your objections, but I still think we should accept the recommendations.

He always seems to have .... combed hair, even when the wind is blowing!

Grammar focus task

1 Look again at the adjectives you have written in the sentences in question 3 and 5. In which are they used as gradable adjectives and in which are they used as ungradable adjectives? ....

2 Look again at the adverb you have written in the sentences in question 6. In each sentence, decide whether other positions are possible for this adverb.

Writing

You have seen this announcement in the *English Language Learning Magazine*.

English Language Teacher of the Year Award
Write and tell us why your language teacher should win.
Tell us a little about his or her background.
Say why you think he or she is an outstanding teacher.
Say how he or she has helped you to learn.
The writer of the winning entry will receive a £250 prize and the winning teacher will be presented with a trophy.

Write your **competition entry** in **220–260** words.

Writing hints

The task gives you a chance to practise gradable and non-gradable adjectives:
● usually non-gradable − *essential, excellent, fascinated, necessary, outstanding, perfect*
● usually gradable − *angry, entertaining, enthusiastic, helpful, patient*
If you use a gradable adjective, consider using an adverb such as *exceptionally, highly, immensely, rather, really, very*.

Comparison

comparative and superlative forms of adjectives and adverbs; comparisons with as ...; comparisons with so ..., too ..., enough

8

A Context listening

1 You are going to hear four friends discussing where to go on holiday. They have already decided to go to Greece, either to Athens or the island of Corfu. What are the advantages of going to each place?

2 🎧 8 Listen to the discussion. How many of the advantages you identified do they mention?

3 🎧 8 Listen again and complete these extracts by writing three words in each sentence.

1 If we don't decide soon, it'll be ....*too*........ ....*late*........ ....*to*........ get anywhere to stay.

2 They all look pretty good, and they're right next to ....
.... beach .... the island.

3 It says in my guidebook that there are reasonable hotel rooms for ....
.... 40 euros a night.

4 It was .... holiday I've ever had.

5 And it would be .... being in a city.

6 It's still supposed to be a really beautiful place, so we'll want to see ....
.... we can.

4 How are the comparative and superlative statements formed?

B Grammar

1 Adjectives and adverbs: comparative and superlative forms

START POINT

*Accommodation would be **cheaper** in Athens.*
*It's probably the **cheapest** hotel in Athens.*
*I want to come home **more relaxed** and **healthier/more healthy**.*
*The walking tour in France was the **healthiest/most healthy** holiday I've had.*
*It will be **more expensive** to get to Corfu than Athens.*
*It's the **most expensive** flight that day.*

There are exceptions to the comparative and superlative forms illustrated above.

We usually add *-er/-est* to one-syllable adjectives.	However, we use *more/most* ● before past participle adjectives: *I want to come home **more relaxed**.* ● before *fun, real, right, wrong*: *It'd be **more fun** to go to Corfu.*
We can usually add *-er/-est* or put *more/most* before two-syllable adjectives.	However, we always use *more/most* with ● participle adjectives: *It was **the most boring** holiday I've ever had.* ● adjectives ending *-ful* or *-less*: *It would be **more peaceful** than being in a city.* ● *afraid, alert, alike, alone, ashamed, cautious, complex, direct, exact, famous, frequent, modern, special, recent:* *I'm **more afraid** of flying than travelling by boat.* *The Parthenon is one of the **most famous** buildings in the world.*
We usually put *more/most* before three- or more syllable adjectives.	However, we can add *-er/-est* to ● *unhappy, unhealthy, unlikely, unlucky, unsteady, untidy:* *I came back feeling **unhealthier** than when I went away.* or *I came back feeling **more unhealthy** ...*

We can use a sentence with two comparatives to say that as one thing changes, another thing also changes:
*The **longer** we leave it, the **more expensive** it's going to be.*

We can use *less/least* as the opposite of *more/most* with all adjectives, including one-syllable adjectives:
*Hotels in Corfu are quite cheap – although **less cheap** than they used to be.*
*It was the **least expensive** flight I could find.*
⚠ In informal contexts we usually prefer *not as ... as* rather than *less than*:
*It's probably **not as** unspoilt **as** some of the other Greek islands.*

The forms and uses of comparative and superlative adverbs are similar to those of adjectives, although most adverb comparatives and superlatives are formed with *more* and *most* rather than *-er/-est*:

*We could live **more cheaply** in Athens.*
***Most importantly**, we need to book our flights soon.*

Common adverbs which take *-er/-est* include *hard* and *fast*.

2 Superlatives: special cases

> **START POINT**
>
> *That's the most convenient **of** the flights from London ...*
> *It's one of the most famous buildings **in** the world.*
> *They're right next to the best beach **on** the island.*
>
> After a superlative we usually use **of** before plural words and **in** or **on** before singular words for places or groups.

For emphasis we can put an *of*-phrase at the beginning of the sentence:
***Of the flights from London**, that's the most convenient ...*

In informal contexts we sometimes leave out *the* after a linking verb (see page 64), particularly when the superlative is at the end of a sentence:
*Which one's **cheapest**?*

⚠ We can't leave out *the* when we go on to say what group of things is being compared:
*That's **the most convenient** of the flights from London ...*

When *most* + adjective is used without *the, most* means something like 'very':
*The route he took was **most odd**.*

3 Comparisons with *as ...*

> **START POINT**
>
> *Isn't Corfu likely to be **as hot as** Athens at that time of the year?* (= equally hot)
> *Getting to Corfu is just **as easy as** getting to Athens.* (= equally easy to get to)

Before the first *as* we can use words and phrases such as *about, almost, just, just about, nearly,* and informally *not anything like, nothing like, nowhere near, not nearly* to indicate the degree of similarity:
*The heat is **nowhere near as bad as** people say.*

In negative forms we can use *not as* in informal contexts, or less commonly *not so*:
*Corfu is certainly **not as quiet as** it used to be.* or *... **not so quiet as** it used to be.*

We use *as much / many as* or *as little / few as* to say that a quantity or amount is larger or smaller than expected:
*There are reasonable hotel rooms for **as little as** 40 euros a night.*
*There are **as many as** 12 flights a day to Athens from London.*

We also use *as much / many as* with a noun phrase, a clause, or the words *ever, possible*, and *usual*:
*We want to see **as much as possible**.*

We can put a singular noun between an adjective and the second *as*:
*We want **as cheap a flight as** possible.*
⚠ Notice that we use *a/an* in front of the noun.

The negative form of sentences like this can use either *not as* or *not such*:
*Getting there is **not as big a problem** as you might think.*
*That's **not such a bad idea**.*
⚠ Notice that we use *not as* + adjective + *a/an* + noun but *not such a/an* + adjective + noun.

as + clause
We can use a clause after *as* to compare two situations:
*Maybe we could hire a car, **as we did last year**.*

In writing and formal spoken contexts, *as* can act like a relative pronoun:
*The fee will be £35, **as was agreed** at our last meeting. (= which was agreed)*

In formal contexts we can sometimes invert the subject and verb after *as* (and also *than*) in comparisons:
*They travelled by train, **as did my brother**. or ... **as my brother did**.*

as or *like*
When followed by a noun, *as* is used to describe the job or role of someone, or the function of something, and *like* is used to say that one person or thing is similar to another:
*My friend Mark used to work there **as** an English teacher.*
*Sounds **like** a good deal.*

4 Comparisons with *so ..., too ..., enough*

Comparative clauses with *so, too* and *enough* are followed by clauses beginning *that* or *to*-infinitive.

so + adjective + *that*- clause
*It gets **so hot that** a lot of people leave the city.*
More formally we can use *so* + adjective + *as* + *to*-infinitive with a similar meaning. Compare:
*The difference in price is **so small as to not** be worth bothering about. (formal)*
*The difference in price is **so small that** it's not worth bothering about. (informal)*

too + adjective + *to*-infinitive
*If we don't decide soon, it'll be **too late (for us) to get** anywhere to stay.*

adjective + *enough* + *to*-infinitive
*It's **easy enough to get** into the centre from there.*
In formal contexts we can use *sufficiently* before adjectives to express a similar meaning to *enough*:
*I'm not **sufficiently familiar** with the city to act as your guide. or I'm not **familiar enough** ...*

C Grammar exercises

1 Complete the sentences with an appropriate comparative or superlative form of the adjectives in the box. Give alternative forms where possible.

> alert   close   ~~common~~   concerned   deep   handsome   harmful   magnificent
> narrow   poor   respected   sad   thrilled   unhealthy   venomous

1 Redbacks are among the _commonest / most common_ spiders in this part of the country. Unfortunately, they're also the ....

2 The road seemed to be getting .... as we drove .... into the forest.

3 I know coffee isn't good for me, and certainly .... than tea, but I'm at my .... early in the morning after a couple of cups of coffee, and I would find it difficult to give it up.

4 It was the .... I had ever come to a fully-grown elephant, and I was terrified. But even then I realised that I was in the presence of one of the .... creatures on earth.

5 The head of Presto Stores argued that without supermarkets to provide cheap and fresh food, we would all be .... and ....

6 When Diana saw Nick at the party, she thought he was the .... man she had ever seen and went over to speak to him. But she soon realised that he was .... with looking good than talking to her.

7 I couldn't have been .... when Professor Hackman agreed to meet me to discuss my research. He's one of the .... scientists in his field. But I was .... than angry when he phoned to say that he couldn't meet me after all. I realise that he's a very busy man.

2 Complete the sentences using the words given in comparative or superlative forms. You may not need to use all the words. Give alternatives where possible.

1 It may not be **(a)** _the most beautiful part of the city_ to live in, but it's certainly **(b)** ....

    a *beautiful - city - in - most - of - part - the - the*
    b *cheapest - the*

2 Harold was **(a)** .... the three Stevens brothers, and he became perhaps

(b) ....

a *in - the - of - oldest*

b *artist - famous - generation - his - in - of - most - the*

3 I think Richard should run first in the relay. He's **(a)** .... , and probably

(b) ....

a *in - of - the - team - the - youngest*

b *fittest - the*

4 We were staying in **(a)** .... , but the airline lost our luggage and we had
to spend the first couple of days wearing old jeans and T-shirts. It was

(b) ....

a *exclusive - hotel - island - most - of - on - the - the*

b *embarrassing - most - the*

3 **Complete the sentences in these radio news stories. Choose the correct or more likely option in each pair. Sometimes both are possible.**

With just a few days before the general election, as **(1)** .... *many* .... (*many / much*)
as 100,000 people have demonstrated in the capital of Manistan as attacks on opposition
candidates have continued. When voters were asked about their intentions in a recent
opinion poll, as **(2)** .... (*little / few*) as 10% said they would be voting. This
is seen as a protest against the way in which the ruling party has conducted its campaign.
However, a government spokesperson claimed that the figure of 100,000 demonstrators
was 'inaccurate', as **(3)** .... (*were the poll findings / the poll findings were*).

President Clarke has claimed that thanks to recent medical advances, malaria could be
eradicated worldwide within as **(4)** .... (*little / few*) as ten years. In a speech
to the World Health Organisation, she said that a cheap vaccine against malaria is just
around the corner, **(5)** .... (*as it is / as is*) a cure for hepatitis B. She called
on developed countries to invest **(6)** .... (*as much / so much*) as possible so
that they can have the maximum impact on those most affected in poorer countries.

The former Formula One world champion Carl Nielsen left hospital today just six
weeks after his horrific crash in the Monaco Grand Prix. Speaking to reporters outside his
home, he said that damage to his back was not as **(7)** .... (*serious a problem /
a serious problem*) as first thought, and he hoped to return to as **(8)** ....
(*normal life / normal a life*) as possible. But there is **(9)** .... (*not such a / not
a such*) positive outcome for the spectator who was hit by debris from Nielsen's car. He is
said to be still in a critical condition.

A 64-year-old man who works **(10)** .... *(like / as)* a school crossing warden has become the country's biggest ever lottery winner. Mark Johns from London said that the win had come at the perfect time for him. He said: 'I'm not **(11)** .... *(so / as)* young as I was, and I can now look forward to a comfortable retirement.'

4 Match the pairs of sentences. Rewrite each pair as one sentence using *so* + adjective + *that*-clause.

1 I was exhausted.	a It can easily fit into your shirt pocket.
2 Adam is tall.	b He has to bend down to get through doorways.
3 The job offer was very good.	c The building had to be evacuated.
4 The comet is very bright.	d The actors couldn't make themselves heard.
5 The traffic outside the theatre was very loud.	e It can be seen with the naked eye.
6 The camera is very small.	f I couldn't turn it down.
7 The results were awful.	g Our teacher made us take the test again.
8 The fire was serious.	h I couldn't go any further.

1 *I was so exhausted that I couldn't go any further.* ....

2 ....

3 ....

4 ....

5 ....

6 ....

7 ....

8 ....

5 Four of the sentences in Exercise 4 can be written using either *too* + adjective + *to*-infinitive or adjective + *enough* + *to*-infinitive. Find them and rewrite them.

1 *I was too exhausted to go any further.* ....

2 ....

3 ....

4 ....

D Exam practice

This exercise tests grammar from the rest of the book as well as the grammar in this unit.

Reading

Read the three texts below and decide which answer (**A**, **B**, **C** or **D**) best fits each gap.

Cycling is good news – so what's stopping us?

The government's recent campaign, encouraging us to leave our cars at home and get on our bikes, has had some success, with a slight increase **(1)** .... the numbers cycling to work. We all now know the benefits – cyclists have **(2)** .... health problems than non-cyclists, and they don't damage the environment. But we won't become a nation of cyclists until we **(3)** .... two major barriers. First, exhaust fumes in heavily congested streets can be as **(4)** .... to the lungs as cigarette smoke. So we must have more cycle lanes separating cars and bikes. Second, bikes need to be used for everyday transport. Cycling in many cities has been cornered by enthusiasts who weave in and out of traffic, ignore the lights, trespass on pavements and shout abuse at cars that **(5)** .... their progress. Only when British commuters emulate their French, German and Scandinavian counterparts and use bicycles to go about their business in their everyday clothes **(6)** .... large numbers start pedalling.

1 A on	**B** of	**C** in	**D** to
2 A fewer	**B** smaller	**C** less	**D** lower
3 A prevent	**B** reduce	**C** beat	**D** overcome
4 A risky	**B** bad	**C** unhealthy	**D** damaging
5 A interfere	**B** impede	**C** counter	**D** restrain
6 A must	**B** should	**C** will	**D** may

Why do birds eat seeds?

Powered flight requires fuel. For birds, that fuel is food; and since flight demands that bulk and weight should be **(7)** .... to a minimum, the more compact and powerful that fuel is, the **(8)** .... Seeds have both those qualities. The nourishment they contain is there to enable a developing seedling to build a stem and leaves so that it can start to manufacture food on its own **(9)** .... , but that same nourishment can also feed birds and it is so rich and so conveniently packaged that many birds eat little else. **(10)** .... it is of no benefit to a plant to have its seeds destroyed in the stomachs of birds, many plants armour their seeds to prevent that **(11)** .... Birds, in response, have evolved special tools and strategies to ensure that they can continue to plunder this valuable food supply that **(12)** .... their needs so well.

From The Life of Birds, by Sir David Attenborough

7	**A** kept	**B** managed	**C** maintained	**D** controlled
8	**A** greater	**B** better	**C** lighter	**D** higher
9	**A** accord	**B** account	**C** way	**D** terms
10	**A** Although	**B** While	**C** Despite	**D** Since
11	**A** happening	**B** appearing	**C** following	**D** proceeding
12	**A** becomes	**B** agrees	**C** suits	**D** pleases

Reflexology

By walking barefoot across the open countryside, early man was inadvertently enjoying the benefits of reflexology, a therapeutic form of foot massage. Both ancient Chinese and Egyptian cultures practised foot massage **(13)** .... the aim of improving general health, but it was not **(14)** .... the early twentieth century that reflexology reached the West. Reflexologists believe that specific points on the feet **(15)** .... to areas of the body, and that these areas can be stimulated by applying gentle pressure to the soles of the feet. Some doctors have criticised reflexology, pointing in particular to the short **(16)** .... of training programmes. **(17)** .... , it is possible to gain a qualification in reflexology with as little as six months of home study. However, many thousands of people **(18)** .... to have enjoyed improvements to their health from reflexology, especially in reducing levels of stress.

13	**A** in	**B** by	**C** with	**D** to
14	**A** to	**B** in	**C** until	**D** before
15	**A** correspond	**B** match	**C** complement	**D** equal
16	**A** course	**B** duration	**C** time	**D** continuation
17	**A** Arguably	**B** Definitely	**C** Actually	**D** Certainly
18	**A** believe	**B** insist	**C** say	**D** claim

Grammar focus task

These sentences are based on the texts. Without looking back, complete the sentences with the comparative and superlative forms.

1 Exhaust fumes in heavily congested streets can be ......as...... .....damaging...... to the lungs ......as...... cigarette smoke.

2 For birds, food is fuel and .... compact and powerful that fuel is, the ....

3 Seeds are .... rich and .... conveniently packaged .... many birds eat little else.

4 It is possible to gain a qualification in reflexology with .... six months of home study.

Writing

Your college has asked you to write an information sheet for students on effective study skills. Information should be included on managing your time, how to read difficult books, and remembering information.

Write your **information sheet** in **220–260** words.

Writing hints

This task gives you the chance to use comparative and superlative forms:
more difficult than, easier to remember than, a more efficient method, the most popular methods, it's better to
You can also use comparisons with *as ... as*:
as often as possible, not as difficult as ...
Useful language
study periods, timetable, reading strategies, visual images

Verb patterns 1

verbs with two objects; verb + object + adjective; verb + reflexive
pronoun; verb + *each other* / *one another*

A Context listening

1 You are going to listen to part of an introductory lecture in
a course on first language learning. Do you know what your
first words were? Or the first words of a child you know?

2 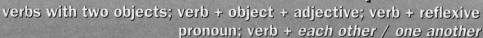 9 The lecturer tells the students about the first five
lectures in the course. Here are the titles of these lectures.
Listen and number them in the order they will take place.

Language learning problems: what and why?   ....

Listening and learning: the interrelationships   ....

Early communication: parents and play   ....

Patterns of communication: learned behaviour?   ....

Private conversations: talking to toys   ....1.......

3 9 Listen again and fill in the gaps.

- I recently **(1)** ..... *bought my two-year-old daughter a cuddly elephant* ....., and it has
become the 'person' she talks to each morning lying in bed.

- The first stage of interactive play might be a child **(2)** ....
or **(3)** ....

- A broken toy handed to a parent with an 'Aaa' might mean **(4)** '...................................'.

- **(5)** .... is a similarly important part of this
process of listening and understanding.

- Dr Jackman will be **(6)** .... in detail in later
talks.

4 Which of the following patterns do the phrases you have written have?

1   verb + person / people + thing(s)   ....1,............

2   verb + thing(s) + *for* + person / people   ....

3   verb + thing(s) + *to* + person / people   ....

5 Decide whether the phrases in Exercise 3 could be rewritten using the other patterns.

1   ✓ bought my two-year-old daughter a cuddly elephant

    ✓ bought a cuddly elephant for my two-year-old daughter

    ✗ ~~bought a cuddly elephant to my two-year-old daughter~~

81

B Grammar

*Interactions between infants will often **copy** parental speech.* (transitive)
***Fetch** me your hat.* (transitive)
*Infants are keen to **interact** with others.* (intransitive)
Some verbs (transitive verbs, e.g. *copy*) are followed by an object. Some of these verbs can be followed by two objects (e.g. **fetch**). Usually the first object (the indirect object) is a person or group of people and the second object (the direct object) is a thing.
Some verbs (intransitive verbs, e.g. **interact**) are not followed by an object, and can't have a passive form.
(▷See Appendix 8.1–8.3.)

1 Verbs with two objects

After many verbs with two objects, we can reverse the order of the objects if we put *for* or *to* before the indirect object:
*I recently bought **my two-year-old daughter a cuddly elephant**.* or
*I recently bought a cuddly elephant **for** my two-year-old daughter.*
*A child might offer **their** mother some food.* or
*A child might offer some food **to** their mother.*
We often use this pattern to focus particular attention on the indirect object or when the indirect object is much longer than the direct object:
*She lent the book **to** one of the students who asked for some additional reading.* (**not** ~~She lent one of the students who asked for some additional reading the book.~~)

We use *for* + indirect object with verbs such as *build, find* and *get*:
*Go to the toy box and find the car **for** me.* or *Go to the toy box and find me the car.*
We use *to* + indirect object with verbs such as *give, offer* and *show*:
*She gave a toy **to** me.* or *She gave me a toy.*

We can use either *for* or *to* + indirect object with verbs such as *play, read* and *write*.
Often there is a difference in meaning:
*I couldn't find her email address, so I had to **write** a letter **to** her.*
*She was too young to write herself, so I **wrote** the letter **for** her.* (= instead of her)
Sometimes the meaning is very similar:
*Reading stories **for** / **to** young children is an important part of this process.*

Some verbs with two objects cannot have their objects reversed with *for* / *to*, including *ask*, *guarantee* and *refuse*:
*Most parents **ask themselves the question**: 'Did they copy that from us?'* (**not** ... ~~ask the question for / to themselves~~ ...)
(▷See Appendix 8.4–8.6.)

If the direct object is a pronoun, we usually use direct object + *for* / *to* + indirect object:
*I bought it **for** my daughter.*   *Give it **to** me.*
▲ While *I bought my daughter it* and *Give me it* might be heard in informal speech, this pattern is usually considered to be bad style and should be avoided in writing.

Some verbs can only have two objects in the pattern direct object + *for* / *to* + indirect object:
- *for* (These verbs include *collect*, *fix* and *mend*.)
  Mend this for me. (**not** ~~Mend me this.~~)
- *to* (These verbs include *describe*, *explain* and *mention*.)
  Dr Jackman will be describing this process to you in detail. (**not** ~~Dr Jackman will be describing you this process in detail.~~)
  (▷ See Appendix 8.4 (ii) and 8.5 (ii).)

2 Verb + object + adjective

Some verbs (e.g. *believe, consider, prove*) can be followed by an object + adjective:
*We might consider **first language learning natural** ...* (object = *first language learning*; adjective = *natural*)
This is usually considered rather formal. Less formal alternatives can be made with verb + object + *to be* or verb + *that-* clause:
*We might consider first language learning **to be** natural ...* or *We might consider **that** first language learning is natural ...*
(▷ See Appendix 8.7.)

3 Verbs + reflexive pronouns

START POINT

*Let me introduce **myself**. I'd like to talk about what I call 'private' conversations – children talking to **themselves**.*
When the subject and the object of a sentence refer to the same person or thing, we use a reflexive pronoun as the object rather than a personal pronoun. The reflexive pronouns are: **myself, yourself, herself, himself, itself, ourselves, yourselves, themselves**.

After some verbs we can use a reflexive pronoun or leave it out with little difference in meaning. These include *acclimatise ... to, adapt ... to, (un)dress, hide, move, prepare ... for, shave* and *wash*:
*As my three year-old daughter **dresses (herself)**, she likes to talk.*
We include the reflexive pronoun for emphasis. In this example, we might include *herself* to emphasise that she dresses without help.

Some verbs commonly used with reflexive pronouns can have different meanings when used with a personal pronoun. These include *apply, compose, distinguish* and *explain*:
*When a child is **applying herself** to painting a picture ...* (= working hard at it)
*She took some sunscreen and **applied it** to her arms and legs.* (= spread it on)
(▷ See Appendix 8.8.)

A few verbs are very often used with a reflexive pronoun followed by a particular preposition: *busy ... with, distance ... from, pride ... on*:
*When children appear to be **busying themselves with** their toys ...*
(▷ See Appendix 8.9.)

Some verbs are rarely or never used with a reflexive pronoun in English, but often are in other languages. These include *complain, concentrate, get up, get hot, get tired, lie down, meet, relax, remember, sit down,* and *wake up*:

From the moment they wake up ... (**not** ~~From the moment they wake themselves up~~ ...)

With verbs followed by direct object + preposition + indirect object we usually use a personal pronoun, not a reflexive pronoun, as indirect object:

*Parents sometimes hide an object behind **them**.* (**not** ~~Parents sometimes hide an object behind themselves.~~)

⚠ If we need to make it clear that the subject and indirect object refer to the same person, we use a reflexive pronoun. Compare:

*Maria didn't buy the teddy bear for **her**.* (her = could mean either Maria or someone else)
*Maria didn't buy the teddy bear for **herself**.* (herself = Maria)

4 Verbs + *each other / one another*

Compare the use of verbs with reflexive pronouns and *each other / one another*:

*Sue and Ken blamed **themselves** when their daughter broke her arm.* (= they said it was the fault of both of them)
*Sue and Ken blamed **each other / one another** when their daughter broke her arm.* (= Sue said it was Ken's fault and Ken said it was Sue's fault)
(▷ See Appendix 8.10.)

With some verbs (e.g. *agree, coincide, play*) we have to use the preposition *with* before *each other / one another*:

*It is wonderful to see two small children **playing with each other** peacefully.*
(▷ See Appendix 8.11.)

After the verbs *embrace, fight, hug, kiss, marry* and *meet* we can use *each other* or *(with) one another*, but this can be omitted:

*Two small children at a nursery school might **hug (each other / one another)** when they meet.*

For emphasis we can separate *each* and *other*:

*If their language is more developed, they might **each blame the other** for a broken toy or a spilt drink.*

C Grammar exercises

1 Describe each situation using *They + verb + (with) + each other.* Choose from the verbs in the box.

> agree   blame   compete   disagree
> know   miss   ~~resemble~~   respect
> trust   work

1 We look alike.
............They resemble each other............

2 You were right!
....

3 I always like to be better than you!
....

4 I admire your character.
....

5 I believe that you're honest.
....

6 I'm sorry you're not here.
....

7 We met 20 years ago.
....

> *Speech bubble:* We look alike.

8 We're employed in the same office.
....

9 It was your fault.
....

10 You were wrong!
....

2 Complete the sentences using the pairs of objects in the box. Give all possible word orders, adding prepositions where necessary.

> some apples / me   your car / you   some chocolate / myself
> a £10 gift voucher / me   a favour / you   your glass / me
> how to print out a document / me   those letters / you   a lot / you
> the mistake / the manager   ~~a seat / me~~   them / you   some water / you

1 I'll be a bit late getting to the concert tonight. Can you save
..............a seat for me / me a seat.............. ?

2 I'm on a diet, so I'm trying to cut down on sweets, although I do allow
.... after dinner.

3 I have to go past the postbox on my way home. I'll post
.... , if you like.

4 I haven't eaten any fruit all week. Can you buy
.... when you're at the supermarket?
I'll pay .... when you get back.

5 A: Can I ask .... ?
B: Of course.
A: Can you show .... ?

6 I'm sure they could repair ....
at Smallwood's garage. They're very good there, but it would probably cost
....

7 In my local supermarket I noticed a sign saying 'Two for the price of won!' I pointed
out .... , and a week later she sent
.... to say 'thank you'.

8 A: Can you pass me the water, please?
B: Give .... and I'll pour
....

3 **Complete the sentences by adding an appropriate personal or reflexive pronoun,
an adjective from box A and an ending from box B.**

A

| fit   guilty   incapable |
| independent   lucky |
| responsible   unable |

B

| of the murder   for its collapse   to play again |
| of the Soviet Union   to sing |
| to be alive   of maintaining order |

1 After undergoing a minor operation on her throat, she found
.... herself unable to sing ....

2 Although the police didn't have hard evidence against Karl Stevens, they still believed
....

3 The police officers lacked experience in crowd control and proved
....

4 After all his injury troubles, Marcuson has now pronounced
....

5 When I looked at the damage to my car in the crash, I considered
....

6 Mary Wallis had been the company's CEO for five years and the board of directors held ....

7 In 1991, Estonia declared ....

4 Complete the sentences with a personal pronoun, a reflexive pronoun or a reflexive pronoun + preposition. Sometimes a pronoun may not be necessary. Write the reflexive pronoun in brackets if it can be omitted.

1 When the police came to arrest him, Thomson hid ....(himself)........ under the floorboards until they had gone.

2 He had always prided .... his physical fitness, so it surprised him when he found it so difficult to acclimatise .... walking in the mountains.

3 Sarah came in carrying a big box of chocolates. At first I thought they were for me, but she said she'd bought them for .... because she'd had such a bad day at work. So I had to content .... a couple of rather boring biscuits.

4 I tried to prepare .... the interview by looking at the company's website and familiarising .... their range of products.

5 Thanks for taking the children to the zoo last week. They enjoyed .... enormously. I'm looking forward to having lunch with you on Thursday. Shall I meet .... outside the restaurant at about 12.30?

6 My father had broken his arm and couldn't shave .... , so I had to do it for him. I found it really difficult and had to concentrate .... hard.

D Exam practice

This exercise tests grammar from the rest of the book as well as the grammar in this unit.

Use of English

For questions **1–8**, complete the second sentence so that it has a similar meaning to the first sentence, using the word given. **Do not change the word given.** You must use between **three** and **six** words, including the word given. Here is an example (**0**).

0 If there is a fire, you must not use the lift to leave the building.

EVENT

<u>In the event of a fire</u>, you must not use the lift to leave the building.

---

1 Nina was driving the car at the time, but I don't think the accident was her fault.
RESPONSIBLE
Nina was driving the car at the time, but I don't hold .... the accident.

2 Jack has such a vivid imagination, it is possible that he invented the whole story.
MADE
Jack has such a vivid imagination that he might .... the whole story.

3 I had only just got home when the phone rang.
SOONER
No .... the phone rang.

4 Although Karen and Mark have very different personalities and interests, they seem to have a good relationship.
ALONG
Although Karen and Mark have very different personalities and interests, they seem to .... another very well.

5 I hadn't seen Martha for over 20 years, but I didn't find it difficult to recognise her at the airport.
DIFFICULTY
I hadn't seen Martha for over 20 years, but I had .... her at the airport.

6 She is proud of being able to write clearly.
ABILITY
She prides .... to write clearly.

7 Once Dr Smithers had given us a clear explanation of the procedure, we were able to go ahead with the experiment.
EXPLAINED
Once Dr Smithers had .... , we were able to go ahead with the experiment.

8 The government has banned all exports to the country except for food and medicine.
EXCEPTION
The government has banned all exports to the country .... food and medicine.

1 The answer to question **6** includes the pattern verb + reflexive pronoun + preposition.

Which prepositions usually go with the following verbs in the same pattern?

disguise   *disguise herself as*
impose   organise   brace   acclimatise   distance
console   familiarise   establish   tear away   busy

2 The answer to question **7** includes the pattern verb + direct object + *to* + indirect object.

Which of these verbs can also be followed by direct object + *to* + indirect object?

prove   ✓ *prove it to me*
fetch   collect   owe   offer   build
point out   repair   choose   hand   introduce

Writing

Your friend has applied for the post of editor of a weekly newsletter for members of staff in a large company, and you have been asked to write a letter of reference for him or her. Include information about your friend's relevant experience and the skills and characteristics that make him or her suitable for the job. Here is an extract from the job advertisement.

LETTSCO STAFF NEWSLETTER EDITOR

Applications are invited for the post of editor of the weekly newsletter for the 1000 staff members of Lettsco.

Duties will include interviewing people for articles and writing brief reports of latest developments in the company.

The person appointed will have excellent communication and administrative skills.

Write the **letter of reference** in **220–260** words.

Writing hints

The task gives you the chance to practise using verbs with two objects and verbs followed by an object and adjective:
She gave me the opportunity to retrain ...
She had to write reports for the company ...
She explained the procedures to her colleagues ...

I always found her helpful ...
I consider her suitable for the post ...

10 Verb patterns 2

verb + *to*-infinitive / -*ing*; verb + (object) + bare infinitive; verb + object + *to*-infinitive / -*ing*; verb + object / possessive + -*ing*; other patterns after verbs

A Context listening

1 🔊 **10** Listen to part of an interview from a radio travel programme. The reporter is talking about his recent visit to the island of Lombok in Indonesia. Which of these problems did the reporter encounter on his trip?

> seasickness   shark attack   passport left at home   volcanic eruption
> hurricane   missed flight   stung by jellyfish   missed boat

2 🔊 **10** Listen again and fill in the gaps.

1 I'd been so anxious to get into the taxi that I.d. *forgotten to pick* it up.

2 It .... to Bali and then taking a ferry to Lombok.

3 We were .... outside the harbour for hours.

4 A number of people .... to the coral reefs off the northwest coast.

5 When I was younger I used to .... in the sea.

6 As it swam past I .... me across the stomach.

7 I really .... me so well.

8 As we .... the amazing sunset, it was almost possible to believe it.

9 I .... the camera in my mobile phone, but the quality was pretty poor.

10 I .... that the Lombok people are very kind.

11 I .... for a few more days, but I didn't have time.

3 Notice that in each space in Exercise 2 you have written two verbs, and that the second verb has either a *to*-infinitive or an -*ing* form.

1 In three of these sentences you could use the other form of this verb and still have a correct sentence. Which three? ....

2 In only one of these three would the sentence have a similar meaning with either a *to*-infinitive or an -*ing* form. Which one? ....

B Grammar

I **managed to find** a friendly taxi driver.
I **considered staying** for a few more days.
I **couldn't get** out of the way.
When two verbs are used together, the second verb is in either a **to**-infinitive, an **-ing** or a bare infinitive form.
(▷ See Appendix 9.)

1 Verb + *to*-infinitive / *-ing*

Some verbs can be followed by either a *to*-infinitive or an *-ing* form with little or no difference in meaning:
I **started to scream**. or I **started screaming**.
Other verbs like this include: *begin, not bother, cease, continue.*
⚠ We normally avoid using two *-ing* forms together:
I was **beginning to feel** quite at home there. (**not** I was beginning feeling ...)

After the opinion verbs *hate, like, love* and *prefer* we can use either a *to*-infinitive or an *-ing* form with little difference in meaning.
However, we prefer a *to*-infinitive when we say we do something regularly. Compare:
When I was younger, I used to **hate to swim** in the sea. (= implies regular swimming)
When I was younger, I used to **hate swimming** in the sea. (= implies swimming in general)

After *would* (*'d*) with *hate, like, love* or *prefer*, we use a *to*-infinitive, not an *-ing* form:
I'**d love to think** that it could avoid a huge expansion in visitors.

Some verbs can be followed by either a *to*-infinitive or an *-ing* form but the meaning of the verb is different:
I **came to realise** that the Lombok people are very kind. (= talking about a gradual realisation)
It **came swimming** towards me. (= saying that something swam in your direction)
(▷ See Appendix 10.)

We use an *-ing* form after a verb with a preposition:
I **put off going** home for as long as possible.
⚠ We use an *-ing* form after *to* when *to* is a preposition:
I'd really been looking forward **to staying** at the Hotel Sanar in Mataram.

In negative sentences, the position of *not* can influence meaning. Compare:
I regretted **not** speaking the local language. (= I didn't speak the language and regretted it)
I **didn't** regret speaking the local language. (= I spoke it and didn't regret it)
I was told **not** to exercise. (= they said I shouldn't exercise)
I **wasn't** told to exercise. (= they didn't say I should exercise)

2 Verb + (object) + bare infinitive

When *let* and *make* have an object, this is followed by a bare infinitive:
*They **made us wait** outside the harbour for hours.*
⚠ We use a *to*-infinitive after a passive form of *make*:
*We **were made to wait** outside the harbour for hours.*

We can also use *have* + object + bare infinitive when we say that we caused someone to do something:
*I **had him wait** for me while I went swimming.*

When the verbs of perception *feel, hear, notice, observe, overhear, see, watch* have an object, this is followed by an *-ing* form or a bare infinitive:
*I **felt** it **stinging** me across the stomach.* or *I **felt** it **sting** me across the stomach.*
*I sat on the beach and I **watched** the sun **setting**.* or *I **watched** the sun **set** and then went home.*
We usually prefer an *-ing* form when the action is in progress or we want to emphasise that it continued for some time, and a bare infinitive when an action is complete or we want to emphasise that it lasted for a short time.

We use a bare infinitive in certain idiomatic phrases with *dare, make, let* and *hear*:
*I **dare say** you're tired after your journey.* (= I think this must be true)
*I had to **make do** with a less luxurious hotel.   I had to **let go** of the rope.*
*He **let slip** that he hadn't got a driving licence.   I **heard tell** there were sharks around.*
(▷ See Unit 4 for more on *dare*.)

After *help* we can use either a bare infinitive or *to*-infinitive:
*Some of the villagers **helped carry** me back to my taxi.* or
*Some of the villagers **helped to carry** me back to my taxi.*

3 Verb + object + *to*-infinitive / *-ing*

After some verbs we have to include an object before a *to*-infinitive in active sentences:
*A number of people **had encouraged** me **to go** to the coral reefs off the north-west coast of the island.*
Other verbs like this include: *advise, persuade, tell.*
(▷ See Appendix 9.4.)

Some verbs can't include an object before a *to*-infinitive:
*I **decided to go** ahead.*
Other verbs like this include: *agree, guarantee, refuse.*
(▷ See Appendix 9.1.)

With some verbs we have to include the preposition *for* before an object + *to*-infinitive:
*I **arranged** for the taxi **to collect** me.*
Other verbs like this include: *advertise, apply, campaign, pay, wait.*
(▷ See Unit 24 for more on prepositions after verbs.)

Some verbs are only followed by an *-ing* form when they have an object:
*I **saw** the jellyfish **coming** towards me.*
Other verbs like this include: *feel, find, hear*.
(▷ See Appendix 9.5.)

4 Verb + object / possessive + *-ing*

Some verbs can be followed either by an object or, more formally, a possessive form:
*I really appreciated **them** looking after me so well.* or
*I really appreciated **their** looking after me so well.*
Other verbs like this include verbs of (dis)liking (*appreciate, detest, (dis)approve of, (dis)like, enjoy, hate, love, object to*) and verbs of thinking (*forget, imagine, remember, think of*).
⚠ We can only use a possessive form to talk about a person or a group of people:
*The experience with the jellyfish was awful. I'll never **forget it swimming** towards me.*
(**not** ... *its swimming towards me*)
We don't use a possessive form if the object is complex:
*I really enjoyed **Arun and his sister** showing me around.* (**not** ... *Arun('s) and his sister's* ...)

5 Other patterns after verbs

The *to*-infinitive can also have perfect, passive, and continuous forms.

Verb + *to have* + past participle
We use forms of the perfect infinitive to talk about an event that happened earlier or is complete:
*The Sasaks **are thought to have** originally **come** to Lombok from India or Burma.*

This is particularly used to talk about actions that did not happen or may not have happened:
*I **was supposed to have arrived** on the 14th October.*
*I **was supposed to have been flying** from London to Singapore.*
*The mountain's **thought** by some **to have been created** by the god Batara.*

Verb + *having* + past participle
We use the perfect *-ing* form to emphasise that one action happens before another:
*I really **regret not having taken** my camera with me.*
This form is most often used with the verbs *admit, deny, forget, recall, regret,* and *remember*.

Verb + *to be* + present / past participle
Future actions can also be indicated using the continuous infinitive (verb + *to be* + present participle) and the passive infinitive (verb + *to be* + past participle):
*I **hope to be going** back again.*
*More flights to the island **are expected to be introduced** next year.*

C Grammar exercises

1 Choose the correct answer. Sometimes more than one option is possible.

1 The President *has urged people vote* / *has urged to vote* / *has urged people to vote* 'Yes' in tomorrow's referendum on joining the European Union.

2 After Arthurs injured his knee last year, a number of specialists *advised him to give up* / *advised to give up* / *advised him giving up* football, but he is still playing as well as ever.

3 As we entered the art gallery, we *were not asked to use* / *were asked not to use* / *were asked to not use* flash photography.

4 Despite the likely opposition from local residents, the council *has suggested widening* / *has suggested to widen* / *has suggested widen* the main road going through the village.

5 A video recording from a security camera at the bank was used in Thomas's trial. It clearly *showed pointing* / *showed him pointing* / *showed him to point* a gun at the cashier.

6 If you have any questions, please write to me at the above address. I can't *guarantee you to reply* / *guarantee to reply* / *guarantee you replying* immediately, but I will certainly write back before the end of the month.

7 'You can lead a horse to water but you can't *make it drink* / *make it to drink* / *make it drinking*.' (a proverb)

8 We really *appreciate you help* / *appreciate you helping* / *appreciate your helping* us move house.

9 I've decided to look for a new job as I *enjoy not sitting* / *don't enjoy to sit* / *don't enjoy sitting* in front of a computer all day.

10 Now that Kevin has bought a house in Edinburgh, I will have to *advertise for someone to share* / *advertise someone sharing* / *advertise someone to share* my flat with me.

2 Complete these texts using each verb in the appropriate form. If necessary, add a preposition and/or object before the verb.

A | be   have   sack   steal   talk |

“ I think it's fair to say that Jim Thompson wasn't liked in our company and when he was made sales manager, many of us objected to (1) ....*his being*........ promoted. Over the next few weeks, things just got worse. When we walked past his office, we often heard (2) .... to his friends on the phone. Then one of my colleagues caught (3) .... some money from the cash box. Eventually, a group of us went to the Managing Director of the company and demanded (4) .... Thompson dismissed. But despite our objections, the MD said that he wasn't prepared (5) .... his own son! ”

B   capture   call   eat   escape   get

KEEPERS CRITICISED AFTER BEAR ESCAPE

When a bear broke out of its cage at Dudland Zoo last week and climbed a nearby tree, there wasn't much the zookeepers could do. They failed **(1)** .... it with the large net they had, and then just had to wait **(2)** .... hungry. They put some honey, the bear's favourite food, inside its cage, and eventually the bear came back and began **(3)** .... it.

Since then, there has been a lot of criticism of the zoo staff by local residents. Mo Baker, 41, of Sea Street said: 'I accept that keepers couldn't have done much to prevent **(4)** .... , but they didn't even bother **(5)** .... the police.'

The director of Dudland Zoo has said that an enquiry into the escape is now under way.

C   collect   do   get   have   say   see

Hi!

Do you remember **(1)** .... that you wanted a recent photo of me? Well, here it is. Yes, it's not very flattering, but you know how I hate **(2)** .... my photo taken. Can't wait **(3)** .... you again in July. Until then, you'll have to make **(4)** .... with this photo! Btw, let me know when your flight gets in and I'll get Jenny or Tom **(5)** .... you from the airport.

Must go. We're off to the cinema tonight, so I have to hurry **(6)** .... dinner ready. Will email again soon.

Love,

Luis

3 Complete the sentences with phrases from the box. Use a *to*-infinitive, bare infinitive or *-ing* form of the verb (including perfect, passive, and continuous form).

argue with him	be a successful businesswoman	be here an hour ago
cause by a virus	get more exercise	go at the weekend
have her around	be killed in the earthquake	pay for both of us
shout at anyone	~~take a couple of paracetamol~~	talk on my mobile

1 If your headache doesn't go soon, try .... *taking a couple of paracetamol* ....

2 The Department of Health has just launched a campaign to encourage people
....

3 Around 2000 people are believed ....

4 Ray's invited me over for a meal on Wednesday after work, but I'd prefer
....

5 I didn't want to speak to James, so when he walked past I pretended
....

6 He had such a bad temper that no one dared ....

7 They say that Mark can be quite aggressive, but personally I've never heard him
....

8 She started life as a teacher, but went on ....

9 I hope nothing's happened to Emily. She should
....

10 When the waiter brought the bill, Alice discovered she'd left her purse at home,
so I ended up ....

11 Now that Laura has gone away to college, I really miss
....

12 Last week's problems with the computer system at the university are thought
....

This exercise tests
grammar from the
rest of the book
as well as the
grammar in
this unit.

D Exam practice

Reading

Read the following magazine article. In items 1–7 that follow, choose the best answer, **A**, **B**, **C** or **D**.

My life as a human speed bump

Giving up a car has not been quite the liberating experience that George Monbiot had hoped.

Seventeen years after giving up my car, I still feel like a second-class citizen. I am trying to do the right thing, but the United Kingdom just isn't run for people like me. Take our bus services. My home city, Oxford, has invested massively in a park-and-ride scheme: buses shuttle people into the centre from car parks on the periphery. At first I thought this was a great idea. Now, having stood for what must amount to weeks at bus stops, watching the full double deckers go by every couple of minutes without stopping, I realise it's not just the roads which have been monopolised by drivers, but also the public transport system.

Or take the bike lanes. Most consist of lines painted on the road where it is wide and safe, which disappear as soon as it becomes narrow and dangerous. One of them, in Oxford, has been gravelled, which shows that the people who designed them have never ridden a bicycle. When we asked for a bike lane on one of the city's busiest streets, the council chose instead to narrow the street and widen the pavements, in the hope that the bicycles would slow down the cars. The cyclists, perversely reluctant to become human speed bumps, started travelling down the pavement.

Now there is almost nowhere reserved for people like me. Out of political cowardice, councils and the police have given up enforcing the law. Preventing people from parking on the pavement would mean cutting the number of parking places, as the streets are otherwise too narrow. Though they cannot complete a sentence without using the words "sustainable development", this action seems impossible for our councillors to contemplate. In one part of Oxford they have solved the problem by painting parking places on the pavement. Since my daughter was born, and I have started pushing a pram, I have been forced to walk in the middle of the road. In one respect this makes sense: the pavements are so badly maintained that she will only sleep when she's being pushed down the smooth grey carpet laid out for the cars.

My problem is that by seeking to reduce my impact on the planet, I joined a political minority that is diminishing every year. As car ownership increases, its only remaining members are a handful of eccentrics like me, the very poor and those not competent to drive. None of these groups wield political power. Our demands are counter-aspirational, and therefore of little interest to either politicians or the media.

Now, to my horror, I find I am beginning to question even the environmental impact of my 17 years of abstinence. It is true that my own carbon emissions have been suppressed. It is also true that if everyone did the same thing the total saving would be enormous. The problem is that, in the absence of regulation, traffic expands to fill the available space. By refusing to own a car I have merely opened up road space for other people, who tend to drive more fuel-hungry models than I would have chosen. We can do little to reduce our impacts on the environment if the government won't support us.

There are some compensations, however. About three or four times a year I hire a car. When I stop at motorway service stations, I am struck by the staggering levels of obesity: it appears to be far more prevalent there than on trains or coaches. People who take public transport must at least walk to the bus stop. The cyclists among us keep fit without even noticing.

Being without a car in Oxford has forced me to embed myself in my home town. It throws me into contact with far more people than I would otherwise meet. There are a couple of routes which make cycling a real pleasure: the towpath along the Thames, for example, takes me most of the way to the station. But overall, as far as self-interest is concerned, I would struggle to claim that giving up my car was a wholly positive decision.

1 The writer's view of the Oxford park-and-ride scheme is that
   A the large volume of cars prevents it from operating effectively.
   B it has been an unqualified success.
   C it has suffered from insufficient investment.
   D it has become too popular.

2 The writer thinks that cyclists started travelling down the pavement in one of Oxford's busiest streets because
   A the council put speed bumps in this street.
   B the pavement is very wide.
   C there is no bike lane in this street.
   D in the bike lane cyclists are too close to cars.

3 In what way does the writer believe that Oxford city council has shown 'political cowardice'?
   A It is reluctant to prevent cars parking on pedestrian areas.
   B It doesn't want cyclists on the city's roads.
   C It has narrowed some roads to discourage cyclists from using them.
   D It has a policy of sustainable development.

4 According to the writer, the 'political minority' that he is part of
   A is becoming poorer.
   B has little political influence.
   C consists of people who can't drive.
   D includes people who act in a strange way.

5 In paragraph 5 the writer suggests that the effect of his actions has been to
   A discourage the government from giving support.
   B lower maintenance standards for pavements.
   C create more room on the road for other cars.
   D encourage others to drive bigger cars.

6 The writer's observations at motorway service stations suggest to him that
   A car drivers are more overweight than public transport users.
   B people who own cars are thinner than people who hire them.
   C people who use public transport don't get enough exercise.
   D cyclists ride bikes in order to keep fit.

7 According to the writer, being without a car in Oxford
   A has been a completely positive experience.
   B has increased the number of people he knows.
   C has forced him to stay at home more.
   D has been a complete mistake.

Grammar focus task

These are extracts from the text. Without looking back, fill in the gaps with either a bare infinitive, *to*-infinitive or *-ing* form of one of the following verbs.

| cut | ~~do~~ | enforce | narrow | push | question | reduce | travel |

I am trying (1) ....*to do*.......... the right thing, but the United Kingdom just isn't run for people like me.

When we asked for a bike lane on one of the city's busiest streets, the council chose instead (2) .... the street and widen the pavements, in the hope that the bicycles would slow down the cars. The cyclists, perversely reluctant to become human speed bumps, started (3) .... down the pavement.

Out of political cowardice, councils and the police have given up (4) .... the law. Preventing people from parking on the pavement would mean (5) .... the number of parking places, as the streets are otherwise too narrow.

Since my daughter was born, and I have started (6) .... a pram, I have been forced to walk in the middle of the road.

My problem is that by seeking (7) .... my impact on the planet, I joined a political minority that is diminishing every year.

Now, to my horror, I find I am beginning (8) .... even the environmental impact of my 17 years of abstinence.

In which of these would it be possible to use either form? ....

Writing

Each year, senior citizens from the local community are invited to look around your college, to meet and be entertained by students, and to have refreshments. After this year's visit you were asked to write an article for the college newsletter. Tell readers about the event and encourage other students to get involved next year. Use the information in the programme and the quotations from some of the visitors to write your article.

Senior Citizens' Visit July 15th

Programme

2.00	Visitors arrive. Welcome speech from Principal
2.00–2.30	Guided tour of college by students
2.30–3.30	Concert by students (music, drama, dance)
3.30–4.30	Coffee / tea & cakes. Students and senior citizens in groups
4.30	End of visit

Excellent. I hope we can come for a longer visit next year. Could tour groups be smaller?

The entertainment was superb. The dancing, in particular, was very professional. Rock band a bit noisy, though!

The cakes made by the students were first class.

Lovely to talk to young people about their lives. They were very interested in what life was like for us when we were young, too.

Write your **article** in **180–220** words.

Writing hints

This task gives you the chance to practise using verbs followed by either an *-ing* form or a *to*-infinitive:

We can't wait to come back!
We enjoyed hearing about their experience.

Some might have to be used with an object:

We appreciated them looking after us.
We encouraged the visitors to join in.

Relative clauses 1

defining and non-defining relative clauses; relative pronouns; other words beginning relative clauses; prepositions in relative clauses

11

A Context listening

1 You are going to hear part of a commentary about the story of radio from an audio-guide in a museum of science and technology. Before you listen, look at these pictures. What do you think the commentary is about?

vacuum tubes

Hertz's experiment

wireless telegraph

a ☐   b ☐   c ☐   d ☐   e ☐

2 🔊 11 Listen to the commentary. Number the pictures in the order they are mentioned.

3 🔊 11 Listen again and fill in the gaps.

1 He devised an experiment ....*in which*.......... a spark jumped across a gap in a metal ring when a sparking coil was held a few metres away.

2 For most people, however, it is the Italian Guglielmo Marconi .... name is mainly associated with the development of radio.

3 The first public demonstration of the power of radio came in 1901, ... Marconi announced that he had received a transmission from across the Atlantic.

4 There are just a few of the 'wireless telegraphs' the factory produced left in the world, an example .... you can see in Case 2.

5 Radio waves could not carry speech until a method had been developed .... the low-frequency waves produced in a microphone could be combined with high-frequency radio waves.

6 In Britain, the popularity of radio increased until 1952, ... four out of five households owned one.

4 What do the words you have written refer to?

1 He devised **an experiment** ....*in which*.......... a spark jumped across a gap in a metal ring when a sparking coil was held a few metres away.

B Grammar

1 Defining and non-defining relative clauses

START POINT

*The old photograph **that you can see ahead of you** shows Marconi at Signal Hill.* (defining relative clause)
*The story of radio probably begins with Heinrich Hertz, **who was the first to produce radio waves in a laboratory**.*
(non-defining relative clause)
Relative clauses give more information about someone or something referred to in the main clause.
Defining relative clauses specify which or which type of person or thing we mean.
Non-defining relative clauses simply add extra information about a noun.

We put a relative clause as close as possible to the noun it refers to:
*There are just a few of the 'wireless telegraphs' **the factory produced** left in the world.* rather than
*There are just a few of the 'wireless telegraphs' left in the world that **the factory produced**.*

Some relative clauses refer back to the whole idea in the previous clause, not just the previous noun. Most of these begin with *which*:

*The owner of the old radio claims that it is in excellent condition – **which** is obviously not the case.*

2 Relative pronouns

Adding information about people
- defining relative clause (subject pronoun):

  subject
  pronoun

  *There were many people **who** doubted that Marconi would ever succeed.*
  (Or informally: *There were many people **that** doubted ...*)

- defining relative clause (object pronoun):

  object
  pronoun   subject

  *Augusto Righi was an Italian physicist **who** Marconi studied with in the 1890s.*
  (Or informally: *an Italian physicist **(that)** Marconi studied with.*)
  (Very formally: *Augusto Righi was an Italian physicist **whom** Marconi studied **with**.*)

- non-defining relative clause (subject pronoun):
  *The story of radio probably begins with Heinrich Hertz, **who** was the first to produce radio waves in a laboratory.*

- non-defining relative clause (object pronoun):
  *Augusto Righi, **who** Marconi respected greatly, guided his research.*
  (Very formally: *Augusto Righi, **whom** Marconi respected greatly, guided his research.*)

⚠ *Whom* is now used only in very formal styles, mostly in writing.

Adding information about things or animals

- defining relative clause (subject pronoun):
  *The invention **that** made this possible was the vacuum tube.*
  More formally: *The invention **which** made this possible ...*

- defining relative clause (object pronoun):
  *The model (**that**) you can see in Case 1 shows how this works.*
  More formally: *The model **which** you can see ...*

- non-defining relative clause (subject and object pronoun):
  *Marconi opened a 'wireless telegraph' factory in England, **which** employed around 50 people.*
  *Marconi's 'wireless telegraph' factory, **which** he set up in England, employed around 50 people.*
  ⚠ Although some people use *that* here, it is grammatically incorrect and should be avoided in written exams.

In both defining and non-defining relative clauses we can often use *who, that* or *which* with collective nouns referring to groups of people (e.g. company, *government, orchestra*):
*The company **who/which/that** made the first radios was set up by Marconi.*

3 Other words beginning relative clauses

We often use *when* after a noun referring to a time, or words such as *day, period, time*:
*The first public demonstration of the power of radio came **in 1901**, **when** Marconi announced that he had received a transmission from across the Atlantic.*
More formally, we can often use a preposition + *which*:
*It was **a period during which** they met very infrequently.* or *... **a period when** ...*
Less formally, we can use *that* or no relative pronoun in defining relative clauses:
*I can still remember **the time (that)** I first watched television.* or *... **the time when** ...*

We often use *why* after *reason*:
*You can probably guess **the reason why** radio began to lose some of its popularity.* or informally *... **the reason (that)** radio began to lose ...*

We often use *where* after a noun referring to a location, or words such as *case, condition, example, experiment, instance, point, process, situation, system*:
*Move now to room 36, **where** you can find information and displays.*
*Marconi's goal was to find a system **where** telegraphic messages could be transmitted.*
More formally, we can use preposition + *which*:
*He devised an experiment **in which** a spark jumped across a gap in a metal ring.*

We use *whereby* (or a preposition + *which*) in formal contexts to mean 'by which way or method':
*Technology is the process **whereby** / **by which** humans modify nature to meet their needs and wants.* or less formally *... the process **where** ...*

We use *whose + noun* to talk about something belonging to or associated with a person, town, country, or organisation:
*For most people, however, it is the Italian Guglielmo Marconi **whose name** is mainly associated with the development of radio.*

In formal uses, noun + *of which* can sometimes replace *whose* + noun:

*Project Geneva is a computing project, **the purpose of which** is to analyse very large amounts of data on environmental change.* or
*Project Geneva is a computing project **whose purpose** is to analyse large amounts of data on environmental change.*

4 Prepositions in relative clauses

START POINT

*These early radio systems could only be used for Morse code, **in which** each letter of the alphabet is represented by a combination of dots and dashes.* (= These early radio systems could only be used for Morse code. In Morse code, each letter of the alphabet is represented by a combination of dots and dashes.)

A preposition usually comes before the relative pronoun in formal styles:
*In 1901 Marconi made the announcement **for which** he will always be remembered.*
⚠ After a preposition we usually use *whom* rather than *who* in formal styles:
*Augusto Righi, **with whom** Marconi studied in the 1890s, was a physicist.*
*Augusto Righi, **whom** Marconi studied **with** in the 1890s, was a physicist.*

A preposition usually comes later in the clause in less formal styles:
*In 1901, Marconi made the announcement **which** he will always be remembered **for**.*
*Augusto Righi, **who** Marconi studied **with** in the 1890s, was a physicist.*

We can use *of which* and *of whom* (or very informally *of who*) after *all, both, each, many, most, neither, part, several, some, a number* (e.g. *one, two, the first, the second, half, a third*) and superlatives:
*Radio entertainers, **many of whom** became household names, were highly paid.*

We can use a preposition, usually *from*, with *where* and *when*:
*Marconi set up a transmission station in Cornwall, **from where** the first transatlantic radio message was sent.*

A number of common prepositional phrases are used in non-defining relative clauses with *which*. These include: *in which case, at / by which time, as a result of which*:
*In Britain, the popularity of radio increased until 1952, **by which time** four out of five households owned one.*

C Grammar exercises

1 Match the sentence halves and join them with one of the words in the box.

when   ~~where~~   whereby   which   whose   why

1 The new factory will be located in an area

2 The photograph reminded him of the time

3 Any complaints should be sent to the Broadcasting Regulator,

4 The journalists have reached an agreement

5 I couldn't see any reason

6 The university has introduced an initiative in

a job it is to maintain standards in television programmes.

b he used to live in New York.

c talented students can complete their degree in only two years.

d Maude should be offended by my letter.

e there are high levels of unemployment.

f they will be paid for a minimum 35-hour working week.

1 *The new factory will be located in an area where there are high levels of unemployment.*

2 Underline all the possible relative pronouns that can complete each sentence. ('−' means that the sentence is correct with no relative pronoun.) If there is more than one possible answer, decide which one(s) are less formal.

1 The new drug should be of benefit for anyone .... suffers from severe hay fever.

A <u>who</u>   B −   C which   D <u>that</u>

'that' is less formal than 'who' here

2 Did the committee .... took the decision on the new housing estate meet local protestors?

A −   B which   C who   D whom

3 The wallpaper, ... is available in a number of colours, is based on an eighteenth-century design.

A which   B that   C −   D who

4 Howard Stevens was one of the artists .... Carlson worked with in his youth.

A whom   B −   C which   D who

5 Conservationists have called for a programme to eliminate the rats ....
are killing seabirds on the island.

    A that   B –   C which   D whom

6 A government spokesperson, ... did not wish to be named, said that
there had been a major disagreement between the Prime Minister and the Finance
Minister.

    A which   B that   C who   D –

7 Were the coins .... he dug up worth a lot of money?

    A who   B –   C that   D which

8 He was survived by his wife Mary Trotter, ... he married in 1936.

    A whom   B that   C –   D who

3 **Complete these sentences with an appropriate preposition.**

1 There were many excellent matches in the World Cup, the best ......*of*...........
which, in my view, was France against Brazil in the semi-final.

2 There were criticisms of the way .... which the election was conducted.

3 Celebrations begin at nine o'clock, ... which time a huge bonfire will be
lit.

4 We climbed to the top of the mountain, ... where it is possible to see
three countries.

5 She has recently published a collection of short stories, most .... which
first appeared in the *London Literary Magazine*.

6 They showed enormous kindness to me, ... which I will always be
grateful.

7 We will soon notify you of the date .... when the goods will be
despatched.

8 He was married in 1253 to a woman named Purcelle, ... whom nothing
more is known.

9 The train drivers are threatening to strike next week, ... which case I'll
have to work from home.

10 We're trying to speed up the process .... which decisions are made in
the company.

4 Match information from A and B to write definitions of the words and phrases below. Use a relative clause in your definition.

A

A political system.

A Muslim doctor.

A narrow piece of wood at the end of a swimming pool.

A piece of equipment like a lift.

Housing for old and ill people.

Women's narrow trousers.

An early period in human history.

A person or company.

B

They end just below the knee.

People can move food in it between the floors of a building.

People made tools and weapons only out of stone then.

Their job is to organise the sending of goods from one place to another.

Help can be given there if it is needed.

Parties are represented in parliament according to the number of people who vote for them.

They use traditional methods to treat people.

People can dive from it.

1 Sheltered accommodation is *housing for old and ill people in which / where help can be given if it is needed.*

2 A diving board is ....

3 Capri pants are ....

4 A shipper is ....

5 A *hakim* is ....

6 A dumb waiter is ....

7 The Stone Age is ....

8 Proportional representation is ....

D Exam practice

This exercise tests grammar from the rest of the book as well as the grammar in this unit.

Use of English

Complete the following article by writing one word only in each space.

Origami

Origami is the art **(0)** ......*of*...... paper folding, the aim of **(1)** .... is to make objects using folds and creases. In general, these objects begin with a square sheet of paper, **(2)** .... sides may be different colours, and this is usually folded without cutting. The origins of origami are disputed, **(3)** .... believing that it began in Japan, others that it originated in China, from **(4)** .... it was taken to Japan in the seventh century. It may also have developed independently in the West. **(5)** .... is undisputed is that it reached its greatest development in Japan. Origami was mostly a traditional art carried **(6)** .... for amusement, but it has also been put **(7)** .... practical use, such as producing boxes, mats and umbrellas. It is also used in studying the principles **(8)** .... design. Probably the most famous modern origami artist was Akira Yoshizawa, **(9)** .... died in 2005. He pioneered origami as **(10)** .... creative art, as well as devising a symbolic method of representing paper folding. This allows enthusiasts worldwide to copy his models from books, **(11)** .... if they do not speak Japanese.

(12) .... all, he created more than 50,000 models, only a few hundred designs **(13)** .... which were shown in his books. In 1998, he was one of the exhibitors at the Louvre in Paris for **(14)** .... was probably the greatest exhibition of origami **(15)** .... seen.

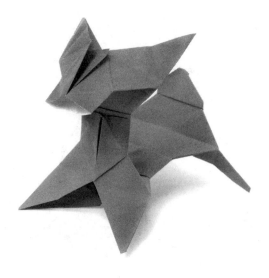

Grammar focus task

Without looking back at the text, write the two sentences as one, including a relative clause.

1 Origami is the art of paper folding.

  The aim of origami is to make objects using folds and creases.

  Origami is the art of paper folding, the aim of which is to make objects using folds and creases.

2 In general, these objects begin with a square sheet of paper.

  The sides of these sheets of paper may be different colours.

3 Some believe that origami originated in China.

  It was taken to Japan in the seventh century.

4 Probably the most famous modern origami artist was Akira Yoshizawa.

  Akira Yoshizawa died in 2005.

5 Akira Yoshizawa created more than 50,000 models.

  Only a few hundred designs were shown in his books.

Writing

At a recent meeting of your college student committee, there was a discussion of fundraising for good causes. Here is an extract from the minutes of the meeting.

5   *Any other business*

5.1   Daphne Jones noted that college students raised over £4,500 for a number of good causes last year (including Oxfam, UNICEF, people with visual impairment, homeless people), but that the maximum raised for any one good cause was only £520. She suggested that next year one particular good cause should be identified, and all funds raised should go to this.

5.2 After discussion it was decided to ask students to write proposals. Students should:
- identify a good cause and say why they would like the college to support it
- suggest what fundraising activities might be done
- say what part they will play in the fundraising process.

The college student committee will select the best proposal and choose the student to be in charge of fundraising.

You decide to write a proposal for them. Write your **proposal** in **300–350** words.

Writing hints

The task gives you the chance to practise using nouns followed by relative clauses:
a company which might agree to sponsor us ...
The reason why I am suggesting this charity is ...
a charity, the aim of which is ...; a fundraising activity in which ...

Useful language
a contribution, a sponsored event / walk / swim, sponsorship, proceeds from the sale,
a charity event / concert / appeal

A Context listening

1 You are going to hear an interview with a food photographer. Which of these items do you think she uses in her work and what for?

2 🔊12 Listen and check whether you were right.

3 🔊12 Listen again and write what the speakers actually said.

belonging

1 When I was quite young – 10 or 11 – I started using an old camera <u>which belonged</u> to my father.

2 It was easy to find a photographer <u>who wanted</u> to take an assistant for no pay!

3 She was really the first person <u>who encouraged</u> me to take up food photography.

4 I was the youngest person in the competition <u>who won</u> any of the major categories.

5 The biggest problem is the heat <u>that is produced</u> by the lights.

6 The food in photographs <u>which are used</u> to illustrate cookbooks and magazine articles isn't always entirely authentic.

7 Personally, I prefer food <u>that is not made</u> of cardboard!

8 I generally have with me a spray bottle <u>which contains</u> glycerine mixed with water.

9 We use cotton wool balls <u>that have been soaked</u> in water.

4 Look at your answers for Exercise 3. In which did the speakers use:

1 a present participle (*-ing* form)? ...1?..........

2 a past participle (*-ed* form)? ....

3 a *to*-infinitive? ....

B Grammar

1 Participle clauses

*I started using an old camera **belonging** to my father.*
*The food in photographs **used** to illustrate cookbooks and magazine articles isn't always entirely authentic.*
*And then we put in some material **to substitute** for the food.*
We can often reduce a defining relative clause so that it begins with a present participle (**-ing**), past participle
(**-ed**), or **to**-infinitive. Usually we do this to sound less formal.

-ing clauses correspond to defining relative clauses with an active verb, and *-ed* clauses
correspond to defining relative clauses with a passive verb:
*The editor **working** on the cookbook or magazine is often there, too.* (= The editor who is
working ...)
*A challenge **facing** food photographers is how to keep food looking fresh.* (= A challenge which
faces ...)
*The big problem is the heat **produced** by the lights.* (= ... the heat that is produced ...)
*Personally, I prefer food **not made** of cardboard!* (= ... food which is not made of cardboard.)

Verbs which are not normally used in continuous forms may be used in reduced relative *-ing*
clauses. We use:
*This spray bottle **contains** glycerine mixed with water.* (**not** ... *is containing* ...)
However, we can say:
*I generally have with me a spray bottle **containing** glycerine and water.*
Other verbs like this include *belong to, comprise, consist of, constitute, equal, own, possess,*
resemble, result from, surround.

It is not always possible to use a reduced form of a relative clause.
● We can't use a reduced form when the first verb in the relative clause is a modal verb:
   *A technique that **might** be used in photographing meat is to use a glycerine spray.*
   *Food that **can't** be frozen is particularly difficult to photograph.*
● We can't use an *-ing* reduced form when we are talking about a single, completed action.
   Compare:
   *Sometimes the chef **who created** the dish in their restaurant comes to the studio.* (**not** ... *the chef*
   creating the dish ...)
   *The chef **preparing** the food today works in a well-known restaurant.* (= The chef who is
   preparing the food today ...)

In written English particularly we can use a reduced relative clause beginning with –
● *being* + *-ed* to emphasise that a situation is continuing or will happen in the future:
   *There was a major photography competition **being held** in Paris.* (= ... which was being held in
   Paris)
   *The work **being shown** in next month's exhibition is all by young French photographers.*
   (= The work which will be shown ...)
● *to be* + *-ed* to talk about a future event:
   *A food stylist prepares the food **to be photographed**.* (= ... which will be photographed)

Reduced relative clauses can also be used instead of non-defining relative clauses, particularly in written English:

*Her photographs, **taken** in her studio in California, have appeared in magazines across the world.* (= ... which were taken in her studio in California ...)

*My parents – **not having much money** – rarely took us to restaurants.* (= ... who didn't have much money ...)

These are usually written between commas or dashes.

2 *to*-infinitive clauses

We often use a *to*-infinitive clause instead of a relative clause after:

● a superlative + noun (phrase):
  *I was the youngest person in the competition **to win** any of the major categories.*
● the *first / second* etc. + noun (phrase):
  *She was really the first person **to encourage** me to take up food photography.*
● *the only / the next / the last / another / one* + noun (phrase):
  *By the time we photograph the food, it's completely cold. The only thing **to do** in that case is to create steam from elsewhere.*

to-infinitive clauses can sometimes replace relative clauses with modal verbs:

*We have a number of techniques **to help us**.* or
*We have a number of techniques **that can help us**.*

Often we can use an active or passive *to*-infinitive clause with little difference in meaning:

*The **only thing to do** in that case is to create steam from elsewhere.* or
*The only thing **to be done** in that case ...*

3 Adjective phrases

Adjectives and adjective phrases can be used after nouns with a meaning similar to a relative clause. Often the adjective is followed by a *to*-infinitive or a preposition, or is used with an adverb:

*It was easy to find a photographer **willing to take** an assistant for no pay!* (= a photographer who was willing to take an assistant for no pay)

*It's a job **difficult for** even a skilled photographer.* (= a job which is difficult for even a skilled photographer)

*Glycerine's a liquid, **completely colourless**, that's often used to sweeten food.* (= a liquid which is completely colourless)

A few adjectives (e.g. *affected, available, present*) can be used alone after a noun with a meaning similar to a relative clause:

*We use cardboard or any other material **available**.* or *... material **which is available**.*
(▷See Unit 7, B3.)

4 Prepositional phrases

We can give additional information about a thing or person using a prepositional phrase. Often these have a meaning similar to a relative clause:

*The vegetables **around** that succulent piece of meat could be made from plastic.*
(= The vegetables which are around ...)

113

C Grammar exercises

1 Match sentences 1–7 with sentences a–g. Write two new sentences using the same information. In the first use a relative clause, and in the second use a reduced relative *-ing* or *-ed* clause.

1 Some jewellery has been stolen from Buckingham Palace.

2 The Internet is bringing about a degree of cultural change.

3 All the passengers have been released from hospital.

4 People can expect to pay over 100 euros.

5 Our teacher came hurrying into the room.

6 Is that woman your sister?

7 Barton Green will be the location of the new sports stadium.

a Such change has not been seen for centuries.

b It is situated five miles from the city centre.

c They were injured in the train crash.

d It belongs to the Queen.

e They want tickets for the cup final.

f She is playing the piano.

g She was carrying a huge pile of textbooks.

1+d

Some jewellery which / that belongs to the Queen has been stolen from Buckingham Palace.
Some jewellery belonging to the Queen has been stolen from Buckingham Palace.

2 Use the information in the boxes to complete these newspaper extracts. Use reduced relative clauses beginning with an *-ing* or *-ed* form, *being* + *-ed* or *to be* + *-ed*. If a reduced relative clause is not possible, use a relative clause + relative pronoun (e.g. *which*).

1 The government has brought in new legislation
affecting Britain's 5.4 million dog owners. . From next year
all dogs will have to be tagged with tiny electronic chips
....

| It will affect Britain's 5.4 million dog owners. |
| They will hold information about the dog's owner. |

2 The inquiry into the wreck of the oil tanker *Patricia*,
..........................., has produced its final report. The report,
..........................., is thought to show that the captain was
mainly responsible for the collision with a smaller vessel.

| It sank off the south-west coast in 2007. |
| It is to be published tomorrow. |

3 The road bridge .... will not now be completed
until next January, nearly four years behind schedule, after
yet another accident on the site. A section of the bridge
.... fell from the cranes ....,
causing major damage to parts already completed.

| It is being built across the River Neem at Walden. |
| It was being lowered into position. |
| They were lifting it. |

4 Demonstrators .... against the play *Global Strife* at the Crest Theatre in London, claiming it to be 'anti-religious', have succeeded in preventing it being performed. The theatre management, ..., cancelled last night's performance. On Thursday, a number of demonstrators .... caused damage to the theatre and terrified members of the audience.

They have been protesting.
They were advised by police that security could not be guaranteed.
They broke through police lines.

5 Researchers in New Zealand are developing a new drug .... A group of 20 elderly people .... were given the drug over a two-year period, and results showed a significant slowing down in memory decline. The drug, ..., will now be tested on a larger group before being made more widely available.

It might prevent memory loss in older people.
They were suffering from dementia.
It is derived from a plant. The plant is found only in New Zealand.

3 **Complete the sentences with phrases from the box. Use a *to*-infinitive clause, an adjective phrase or a prepositional phrase. Make changes and additions as necessary.**

ring today about the car	announce large-scale redundancies
very similar to Romanian	you should contact the human resources manager
pass the French exam	look at the environmental effects of nuclear power
take part in the London Marathon	the south side of the city
would be happy to help out	~~orbit the Earth~~

1 In 1962, John Glenn became the first American .... to orbit the Earth ....

2 If you want to find out if there any job vacancies in the company, the person

....

3 The government has set up yet another enquiry ....

4 It was really expensive living in the centre, so we've just bought a flat

....

5 You won't have to organise the party yourself. I'm sure there'll be a lot of people

....

6 At 91, Abraham Weintraub is the oldest competitor ever

....

7 The state language of Moldova is Moldovan, a language

....

8 Out of my entire class, I was the only student ....

9 With fewer cars being sold around the world, Nisda has become the latest car company ....

10 You're the tenth person .... I'm sorry, but it's already been sold.

4 Underline the eleven relative clauses in this newspaper article. Then, where possible, rewrite the relative clauses as reduced relative clauses.

Monitors to cut home electricity use

Monitors <u>which show the real-time cost of electricity</u> use are to be provided free of charge to homes across the UK in an effort to slow down climate change. Under the new government proposals, from next year electricity suppliers will have to provide the devices – which have cut power use by up to 6.5% in Canada – to all customers who want them. Domestic appliances which are left on unnecessarily are estimated to waste £900 million of electricity a year.

Traditional electricity meters are usually kept out of sight in cupboards. However, the monitors, which use microchip technology and a digital display, are intended to be placed in full view as a constant reminder of the electricity that is being used in a house at any given moment.

The Environment Secretary said: 'People want to do their bit to help protect the environment as well as save money, and visual display units that are provided free of charge will help people do both.' A spokeswoman for the Electricity Consumer Council said it supported any plan that would give customers access to free monitors. The shadow environment secretary said: 'Although it is an interesting and welcome measure, there are still many details that should be considered, not least the reliability of these meters.'

However, the Energy Retail Council has criticised the proposal, saying that it did not go far enough. In a statement, their chief executive said: 'We had hoped the government would recommend the introduction of 'smart meters' – which communicate electricity consumption to both the customer and the energy supplier – rather than meters that are only able to do half the job.'

1 showing the real-time cost of electricity use .

2 ....

3 ....

4 ....

5 ....

6 ....

7 ....

8 ....

9 ....

10 ....

11 ....

D Exam practice

This exercise tests grammar from the rest of the book as well as the grammar in this unit.

Reading

Read the following extract from a novel and answer questions **1–7**.

The letter

The letter came one Saturday at the end of April, when Imogen Doody was retrieving balls from the canteen roof. This was part of her job as caretaker, and the whole process represented an ongoing battle between her and the entire male population of the school. She knew they threw them up on purpose, but she had to remain one step ahead. Once she had the balls in her possession, she could confiscate them for a fortnight. It was a hot day, even hotter on the roof, so she was anxious to get down as soon as possible.

She could see the postman walking up the path from the main school building. Patrick Saunders, an odd man – the children called him Postman Pat. He ambled and stopped to talk to anyone who was interested, which meant his delivery times were unreliable. She remained where she was on the edge of the flat roof, not wanting to be seen, unwilling to talk to him. From her high position, she could see that he was nearly bald, and there were clusters of dark freckles on his head, brown against the unconvincing wisps of his pale hair. She didn't like this glimpse of his frailty. It made her feel sorry for him, and she knew she wouldn't be able to express that sympathy.

He rang twice, and kept shifting his bag from one shoulder to the other while he waited. Doody resented this. Why should she have to worry about his aching back? He chose to be a postman.

She threw down a ball – orange, soggy, in need of new air – and he jumped. He squinted up at her through the fingers of his free hand, and she was pleased that he couldn't see her properly.

'Why are you ringing the bell?'

He waved a letter at her. 'I've got this.'

'You can put letters through the letter-box. Get it? Letters – letter-boxes.'

He shrugged and turned away. 'Please yourself. It's registered post.'

'Hang on,' she called, and came down the ladder. He was waiting for her at the bottom.

'It's not addressed to you.'

Doody scowled at him. She put her hands into her pockets and pulled out a handful of small balls, multi-coloured and very bouncy. She dropped them, and they scattered in all directions. Their bouncing continued until they settled cheerfully into drains, corners, dips in the Tarmac, delighted with their miraculous escape. 'So you ring the doorbell twice to give me a letter that you're not going to give me?'

'It's your address, but it says Imogen Hayes.'

She tried to take it from him, but he moved it out of her reach. 'That's me. How many Imogens do you know?'

'So why's the name different? Is it your undercover name?' He looked pleased with himself.

'Yes,' she says. 'I'm a Latvian sleeper. Waiting to be activated. Perhaps that's what you've got there. My orders.' Anything would be more interesting than the reality of her present life. She reached for the letter, but he moved it away again.

Anger was brewing inside her, bubbling away ominously, but she wanted the letter, so she made herself speak in a calm manner. 'It's my maiden name. I was Imogen Hayes a long time ago. Now I'm Imogen Doody. Mrs Doody to you.'

He gave in. He was looking very uncomfortable, with beads of sweat on his top lip, his feet shuffling. She snatched the letter out of his hand and he didn't resist. 'You have to sign for it.'

She took his pen and signed the electronic screen he put in front of her. Should she offer him a cold drink?

If he'd done his job properly, he wouldn't have been standing so long in the hot sun.

'Thanks!' she shouted at his retreating back.

He didn't turn round. He let himself out of the gate and plodded heavily past the blue iron railings of the school. He was stubborn, but too pedestrian for a real argument.

Doody was pleased to have had the last word, and the fact that it had been a gracious word made her feel even better. She decided to make herself a glass of lemonade before opening the letter.

1 In the first paragraph we learn that Imogen
   A resents a certain aspect of her job.
   B secretly intends to throw the balls away.
   C will need to return the balls to their owners eventually.
   D is upset by the attitude of the boys at the school.

2 Imogen feels sorry for the postman when she sees him coming up the path because
   A he is showing signs of age.
   B he walks slowly.
   C she thinks he is lonely.
   D the children tease him.

3 Why does the postman find it hard to see Imogen when he looks up?
   A His backache makes it difficult for him to stand up straight.
   B His eyesight is poor.
   C She is hiding from him on the roof.
   D The sky behind her is very bright.

4 The postman suggests that the surname on the letter is Hayes rather than Doody because
   A Imogen is using a false name.
   B the letter writer has made a mistake.
   C Imogen changed her name when she married.
   D Imogen has done something illegal.

5 Imogen decides not to offer the postman a cold drink because
   A she wants to open the letter quickly.
   B she is annoyed that he made her sign for the letter.
   C she doesn't want to talk to him any longer.
   D she convinces herself that he doesn't deserve it.

6 The writer suggests that the reason the postman avoids an argument with Imogen is that
   A he wants to get out of the heat.
   B he knows he wouldn't win.
   C he is angry with Imogen.
   D he is late in delivering his letters.

7 What do we learn about Imogen from the text?
   A She doesn't like to talk about her feelings.
   B She finds it difficult to express her feelings in a positive way.
   C She is satisfied with her life at present.
   D She is reluctant to get into conversation with people.

Without looking back at the text, can you remember exactly how the relative clauses in these extracts were reduced?

1 She could see the postman, who was walking up the path from the main school building.
   She could see the postman walking up the path from the main school building

2 ... there were clusters of dark freckles on his head, which were brown against the unconvincing wisps of his pale hair.

   ....

3 She put her hands into her pockets and pulled out a handful of small balls that were multi-coloured and very bouncy.

   ....

4 I'm a Latvian sleeper who is waiting to be activated.
   (Note: A 'sleeper' here means a spy who only becomes active a long time after they are put in place by their organisation or country.)

   ....

Writing

The tourist board of your country is preparing a new brochure for overseas visitors which includes a section with the title *Holidays by the sea*. You have been asked to contribute a piece about a seaside holiday resort. You should include information about:

● what people can do during a holiday there
● types of accommodation available
● the advantages of a seaside holiday over one in the countryside or a city.

Write your contribution to a **brochure** in **220–260** words.

This task gives you the chance to practise using participle clauses to give more information about nouns:
a beach situated nearby, events held every year, shops selling fresh fish, boats sailing past

Useful language
breathtaking, superb, glorious, magnificent; coastline, coastal scenery, estuary, windsurfing

Adverbial clauses
adverbial clauses including time clauses, contrast and concession clauses, reason clauses, purpose and result clauses

1 Sarah and Don are being interviewed about their eating habits. Before you listen, here are some definitions of words and phrases used in the interview. What do you think they are? Check your answers in the Key.

1 Food with substances added to it to preserve it or to give it a new colour or taste.

2 A meal cooked before you buy it so that you only have to heat it before eating.

3 A combination of the correct quantities and sorts of food eaten every day.

4 The process of getting the right sorts of food and drink in order to keep you healthy.

2 ⊕13 Listen and complete the sentences 1–10 using the phrases a–j. Add a word or phrase to link each sentence.

1 At the weekend I like to make something myself *so as not to eat processed food all the time*

2 We'll usually go out to eat ....

3 She also talked to me about the food she made ....

4 If I get hungry, I'll eat some fruit, ...

5 I don't eat much for breakfast ....

6 I have to get out by 7.30 ....

7 Sometimes I get up in the night and have a snack, ...

8 I was absolutely exhausted ....

9 I don't have the opportunity to go shopping ....

10 It's very hard to put a healthy diet into practice ....

a at school I'd buy a bar of chocolate

b none of us likes cooking

c I know it's bad for me

d I know all about the theory

e catch my bus

f I'm always in a rush

g I had to run for the bus yesterday

h I'd learn about diet and nutrition

i I'm working

j ~~eat processed food all the time~~

3 Look at the word or phrase you wrote in sentence 5 in Exercise 2. What other word or phrase you wrote has a similar meaning? What about in sentence 7?

B Grammar

1 Adverbial clauses: general

START POINT

*I seem to eat less healthily **as I get older**.*

***Although I'd like to eat more fresh food**, I don't have time to prepare meals in the evenings.*

An adverbial clause is a type of subordinate clause, linked to a main clause. It adds extra information to the main clause about such things as time, reason or purpose. Most adverbial clauses begin with a conjunction (e.g. **as**, **although**) and can come before or after the main clause.

An adverbial clause must be connected to a main clause; we can't use it as a separate sentence:

*I don't eat much for breakfast **because I'm always in a rush**.*

(**not** ~~I don't eat much for breakfast. Because I'm always in a rush.~~)

We only use one conjunction to connect an adverbial clause and a main clause:

(**not** ~~Because I'm always in a rush, so I don't eat breakfast.~~)

2 Time clauses

We don't use *will* in a clause with a time conjunction (e.g. *before*, *until*, *when*) to talk about a future action or an action that is completed before another in the main clause:

*I'd like to have something more substantial **before** I **leave** home in the morning.* (**not** ~~... before I will leave home in the morning~~.)

***When** I've written* up the research, I'll let you have a copy. (**not** ~~When I will have written up the research, ...~~)

START POINT

*I generally have a sandwich and a packet of crisps **as / when / while** I'm sitting at my desk.*

We can use **as, when** or **while** to talk about something that happens when something else takes place.

As can sometimes mean either 'because' or 'during the time that':

*I opened the window **as** I was cooking.* (= *... because I was cooking* or *... while I was cooking*)

We use *when* (not *as* or *while*) at the beginning of an adverbial clause which:

- refers to a point in time:

  *I remember once I was eating some sweets in my bedroom **when** my mother walked in.*

- describes the circumstances in which the event in the main clause happens:

  ***When** I get home late, I take a ready meal out of the freezer.*

- refers to a past period of our lives:

  ***When** I was younger, my mother used to keep an eye on what I ate.*

- talks about 'every time' something happens:

  ***When / Whenever** I've had one of those ready meals, I feel hungry by the time I go to bed.*

We prefer *as* to say that when one thing changes, another thing changes at the same time:
*Of course, **as** I put on weight, it gets more and more difficult to exercise.* (rather than ... *when / while I put on weight*)

We use *as* or *when* to highlight the moment that something happens:
***As / When** I turned the corner, the bus was just pulling up and I had to run to catch it.* (**not** ~~While I turned~~ ...)

3 Contrast and concession clauses

We use *although* or, less formally, *though* to say that there is a surprising contrast between what happens in the main clause and the adverbial clause:
*Sometimes I get up in the night and have a snack, **although** I know it's bad for me.*
or to introduce a clause (a concession clause) that suggests the opposite of the main clause:
***Although** I don't enjoy cooking, I prepare a meal for myself every evening.*

We can use *though* at the end of a clause:
*In some ways, it's better now, **though**.* (**not** ... ~~it's better now, although.~~)

We can use *while* with a meaning similar to *although*. The *while* clause can't follow the main clause:
***Although** I'd like to spend more time over breakfast, it's just impossible.* or ***While** I'd like to spend ...* (*While* is usually more formal than *although*.)

We can use *despite the fact that / in spite of the fact that* or *despite / in spite of + -ing* with a similar meaning to *although*:
***Despite the fact that** I know all about the theory of a healthy diet, it's very hard to put it into practice.* or
***In spite of the fact that** I know ...*
***Despite (my) knowing** all about the theory of a healthy diet, it's very hard to put it into practice.* or ***In spite of (my) knowing** ...*

We can use *while* or *whereas* to say that there is a contrast with something in the main clause. The *while / whereas* clause may come before or after the main clause:
*If I got hungry at school, I'd buy a chocolate bar, **whereas** nowadays I'll eat some fruit.* or *... **while** nowadays ...*
***Whereas** nowadays I'll eat some fruit, at school I'd buy a chocolate bar.* or
***While** nowadays ...*
We can use *whilst* as a more formal alternative to *while*.

(▷ See Unit 14, B3 for *even if* and *even though*.)

4 Reason clauses

*I must be eating too much **because** I've been getting a bit overweight recently.*
***Because** it's so easy to buy ready meals from the supermarket, it makes me quite lazy.*
*I have to get out by 7.30, **so** I really don't have time.*

A very common way of giving a reason or explanation for something, particularly in speech, is to use an adverbial clause with **because**. A clause beginning **so** is also often used to express a similar meaning.

*Most recipes in magazines are no use to me **because of** the time they take.*

The preposition **because of** can also be used before a noun or noun phrase to give a reason for something.

Formal alternatives to *because* are *as*, *since*, and *for*:
*She made a particular effort **because** / **since** / **as** I was often ill as a child.*
*She taught me with great patience **for** I was often inattentive.*
For is now considered old-fashioned.

Informal alternatives to *because* are *seeing that* and *seeing as*:
*We'll usually go out to eat **seeing that** / **as** none of us likes cooking.*

In formal contexts we can also use clauses beginning with *inasmuch as* (also written *in as much as*) and *in that*, which clarify what has been said by adding detail:
*I'm quite a good cook **inasmuch as** I can easily follow most recipes.* or *... **in that** I can follow most recipes.*
*I think that's true, **in that** I ate more regularly then.* or *... **inasmuch as** I ate more regularly then.*

5 Purpose and result clauses

To talk about the purpose of an action we can use *in order / so as* + *to*-infinitive:
*I have to get out by 7.30 **in order to catch** my bus.* or *... **so as to catch** ...*
Informally, it is more common to use a *to*-infinitive to express the same meaning:
*I have to get out by 7.30 **to catch** my train.*

In negatives we prefer to use *in order not / so as not* + *to*-infinitive rather than *not* + *to*-infinitive:
*I like to make something myself **so as not to** / **in order not to** eat processed food all the time.*
However, in contrastive sentences we can use *not ... to*-infinitive, *but ... to*-infinitive:
*I buy ready meals **not to eat** well, **but to eat** quickly.* or
*I buy ready meals **not in order** / **so as to** eat well, but **in order** / **so as to** eat quickly.*

We also use *in order that* and *so that* to talk about a purpose:
*She also talked to me about the food she made **in order that** I'd learn about diet and nutrition.* or
less formally *... **so (that)** I'd learn about ...*

We often use modal verbs after *in order / so that*:
*It'll be interesting to read the results of the research **so that I can** see how typical my diet is.*
*She also talked to me about the food she made **so that I'd** learn about diet and nutrition.*

C Grammar exercises

1 **Complete the sentences with** *as, when* **or** *while*. **Give all correct or likely alternatives.**

1 You wouldn't think it now, but ....*when*............ I was very young I used to have curly, brown hair.

2 Did you see her hands shaking .... she spoke? She must have been so nervous.

3 It's more and more important for business people to speak foreign languages .... business becomes increasingly international.

4 How old were you .... you got married?

5 .... the structure of the novel might at first appear chaotic, in fact it is very carefully organised.

6 I was so tired last night, I must have gone to sleep .... my head hit the pillow.

7 .... my children get older, I find they get even fussier about the food they eat.

8 She always brings a bunch of flowers .... she comes to visit.

9 .... I sat down to take my maths exam, I realised I'd forgotten to bring my calculator with me.

10 Put the whole tomatoes into a saucepan of boiling water, switch off the heat, and drain after a few minutes. .... they are cool enough to handle, peel them carefully.

11 .... the level of pesticides in the potatoes is well below the legal limit, the public have been advised to avoid eating them for the time being.

2 **Match clauses 1–7 with clauses a–g, and write two new sentences, one beginning** *Although* **... and the other using** *Despite* **... -ing. Put the clauses in the more likely order.**

1 people were still swimming in the river
2 sales of cigarettes have actually increased
3 she fell heavily at the start of the race
4 we were eventually only a few minutes late
5 the alarm went off when the house was broken into
6 we had never spoken to each other
7 she helped a number of passengers out of the crashed coach

a nobody bothered to call the police
b we lived in the same village
c smoking is now banned in public spaces
d she was badly hurt herself
e we got lost on the way
f there were plenty of warning signs
g she went on to finish second

1 + f

Although <u>there were plenty of warning signs, people were still swimming in the river</u>

Despite <u>there being plenty of warning signs, people were still swimming in the river</u>

3 Complete the sentences using a phrase from A and an ending from B.

A	B
in order that	she could get to the concert on time
so as not to	the front wheel is smaller than the back
in that	it's so poorly paid
seeing that	~~some broken tiles could be repaired~~
	damage its roots
	larger planes can land there
	she's so fit
	they are carnivorous
	be overheard

1 The swimming pool had to be emptied <u>in order that some broken tiles could be repaired</u>.

2 People here don't put much effort into the job ....

3 My bike is unusual ....

4 You need to lift the plant carefully ....

5 Pitcher plants are unique ....

6 The runway is going to be extended ....

7 She'll probably recover from the illness quickly ....

8 She left work early ....

9 We spoke very quietly ....

4 Choose the correct or more likely options in these texts.

A

Hello Alison

I couldn't contact you this **(1)** *morning because* / *morning. Because* we had a power cut here. Sorry.

Thanks for the invitation to lunch tomorrow. I'm not sure I'll be able to make it, **(2)** *though* / *although*. **(3)** *In spite of that* / *In spite of the fact that* we've got extra staff at work, we're struggling to meet the deadline to finish writing the software. This means I've got a huge amount of work to do **(4)** *before I go* / *before I will go* on holiday at the end of the week. I feel really guilty **(5)** *seeing* / *seeing that* this is the second time this year I've had to turn down your invitation.

Hope to see you in the near future.

Regards,

Ros

B

'I'm sorry I'm not here to take your call. Please leave a message after the tone and I'll get back to you as soon as I can.'

'Hello, Robert, it's Martha. I'm afraid I have to cancel our meeting tomorrow. My father's just phoned to say my mother's been taken ill. **(1)** *Because of / Because* it sounds quite serious, **(2)** *I'll have to / so I'll have to* take time off to go and see her. I may be away for a few days, but I'll have my laptop with me **(3)** *while / whilst* I'm there **(4)** *so as I can / so that I can* do some work. When **(5)** *you will get / you get* the chance, give me a ring and we'll sort out another time to meet. Bye for now.'

C

(1) *Inasmuch as / Inasmuch that* advertising is their major source of revenue, the mass media seek to appeal to as large an audience (with as much purchasing power) as possible. However, in recent years popular newspapers have had declining advertising income **(2)** *despite the fact that / despite that* sales have increased. They need, therefore, to find alternative sources of income **(3)** *not to / in order not to* fail as profit-making enterprises. One possibility is to offer competitions, which readers pay to enter. **(4)** *Whereas / Although* a number of newspapers have done this, most have now withdrawn this activity. It has been found that relatively small amounts of revenue are raised overall **(5)** *as / for* the administrative costs of running a competition are substantial.

D Exam practice

Use of English

Read the text below and think of the word which best fits each space. Use only **one** word in each space. There is an example at the beginning **(0)**.

This exercise tests grammar from the rest of the book as well as the grammar in this unit.

The Spanish way of life

The inhabitants of this very varied country have **(0)** .....few..... things in common **(1)** ....
for a natural sociability and a zest for living. Spaniards commonly put as **(2)** .... energy into
enjoying life as they do into their work. The stereotypical *mañana* (leave everything **(3)** ....
tomorrow) is a myth, but time is flexible in Spain and many people bend their work **(4)** ....
as to fit in with the demands of their social life whenever they can, instead of letting **(5)** ....
be ruled by the clock. The day is long in Spain and Spanish has a word, *madrugada*, for the time
between midnight and dawn, **(6)** .... city streets are often lively.

Spaniards are highly sociable **(7)** .... that they like nothing better than spending leisure time
in the company of others. In many places people still go out in the evening for the *paseo*, and
the streets are crowded **(8)** .... strollers at this time. Eating is invariably communal and big
groups often **(9)** .... up for dinner. Not **(10)** .... , Spain has more bars and restaurants
per head than any **(11)** .... country.

Traditionally, the state in Spain has been very inefficient at providing public services, although
this has improved in the last 20 years. The Spanish have therefore always relied **(12)** ....
their families and personal connections, rather than institutions, in **(13)** .... to find work or
seek assistance in a crisis. This attitude has sometimes **(14)** .... to a disregard for general
interests – such as the environment – if they come into **(15)** .... with private ones.

Without looking back at the text, can you remember which conjunctions are used to connect these clauses?

1 Many people bend their work .._so as to_.. fit in with the demands of their social life .... they can.

2 Spaniards are highly sociable .... they like nothing better than spending leisure time in the company of others.

3 The state in Spain has been very inefficient at providing public services, ... this has improved in the last 20 years.

4 The Spanish have therefore always relied on their families and personal connections, rather than institutions, ... find work or seek assistance in a crisis.

Writing

The editor of your college / workplace newsletter sent you this note:

Hello

Would you like to do a review for the magazine of a couple of DVDs that you've seen recently? Take two of the same genre (e.g. comedy, thriller, documentary). Say what the films are about, and why you like them and would recommend them. Also say what makes them different.

Let me know what you think!

Thanks,

Alan

Write your **review** of the DVDs you have chosen in **220–260** words.

This task gives you the chance to practise writing sentences including adverbial clauses:
- to describe the films
  Before she came to the village, she travelled throughout Europe
  She marries him despite disliking him at first.
- to give your opinion of the films and why you recommend them
  While I don't usually enjoy his performances, he was terrific as the President.
  I can't wait until she appears in her next film.

Conditionals 14

real and unreal conditionals; *if … not* and *unless*; *even if* and
even though; *if only* and *wish*; other conditional expressions

A Context listening

1 Look at these photos of places where wild animals can be seen. Which places are
shown here?

a

b

c

2 🔊 **14a** Listen to part of a radio discussion programme where three people are being
interviewed about the opening of a new zoo. Which speaker or speakers (M̲ark, D̲ebbie,
or W̲endy) make these points?

1 Only rich people have the opportunity to see wild animals in their natural
environment. M. and W

2 Captive breeding programmes are important in preserving wild animals. ....

3 Animals may suffer when they are being taken to zoos. ....

4 Many animals now in zoos were born there. ....

5 It is unacceptable to keep animals in cages or small enclosures. ....

6 Safari parks haven't always looked after animals well. ....

7 The main purpose of zoos and safari parks is to make money. ....

8 Game reserves need to be supported by governments in developed countries. ....

3 🔊 **14a** What word or phrase did the speakers use to link these ideas? Listen again if
you are not sure.

1 we didn't have zoos + most people would never see wild animals in real life ......if.......

2 we expand captive breeding + many more animals will die out ....

3 wild animals are born in a zoo + it's still cruel to keep them in a small enclosure
....

4 I'm all in favour of safari parks + the animals are well looked after ....

5 they say they are concerned about the welfare of animals + they are still businesses
mainly out to make a profit ....

6 developed countries put money into these reserves + species will be preserved ....

B Grammar

1 Real and unreal conditionals

Conditional sentences may suggest that an event or situation is:

- **real** – it is true, generally happens, has happened or is likely to happen
- **unreal** – it is imaginary or untrue, did not happen or is not likely to happen.

Real conditionals

*If there **is** a health problem, vets **deal** with it quickly.*

*Before safari parks were opened, **if** people wanted to see lions and giraffes, they **had** to go to a zoo.*

*If we **don't provide** safe havens for animals, many **will die** out.*

Unreal conditionals

*If they **were** in the wild, they **would have** more space to roam free.*

*If we **had introduced** captive breeding programmes sooner, we **would have prevented** the extinction of a number of animals.*

Real conditionals

We can use a wide variety of other patterns in the *if*-clause and the main clause:

*If we**'re going to protect** animals in Africa, we**'ll need** to invest much more money in game reserves.*

*If we **close** zoos, we **might deprive** people of the opportunity of seeing wild animals.*

*If you **think** closing down zoos will improve the chances of survival of endangered species, you**'re making** a big mistake.*

We don't usually use *will* in the *if*-clause:

*If they**'re not eaten** by the larger animals first, they'll be killed by visitors' cars.* (**not** ~~If they won't be eaten~~ ...)

⚠ We can use *will* when we talk about a *result* of something in the main clause:

*Certainly we should have captive breeding programmes **if** it **will** help save species.* **or**

*... **if** it **helps** save species.*

or when we want to show that we strongly disapprove of something:

A: That zookeeper was really annoyed with me.

*B: Well, **if** you **will** throw stones at the animals, it's not surprising!*

Unreal conditionals

We can use modals other than *would* in the main clause:

*If we'd introduced captive breeding earlier, animals now extinct **might** have survived.*

We don't usually use *would* in the *if*-clause:

*If we **had** more funding, we would be able to do even more educational work.* (**not** ~~If we would have more funding~~ ...)

⚠ We can use *would* when we talk about a desired outcome:

*If it **would** remove some of the concerns of Save the Animals, they could be involved in drawing up plans for the new zoo.*

Mixed conditionals

We can sometimes vary the basic types of conditionals by mixing the tenses:

***if** + past tense, **would have** + past participle*

*If it **wasn't** so expensive, we **would have opened** many more safari parks around the country.* (= it is very expensive, so we didn't open any more)

***if** + past perfect, **would** + bare infinitive*

*If game reserves **had been set up** earlier, there **would** now **be** fewer animals in danger of extinction.* (= game reserves were not set up earlier, so more animals are in danger of extinction)

In formal contexts we can use *were* instead of *was* in the *if*-clause:

*If it **were** not for zoos, most people would never see wild animals.* or less formally ... **was** *not for* ...

⚠ We prefer to use *were* in the expression *If I were you* ... giving advice.

We can use *if ... were + to*-infinitive rather than *if* + past simple to talk about imaginary future situations:

*If the government **were to ban** zoos, it would put captive breeding programmes at risk.* or
*If the government **banned** zoos ...*

⚠ We don't usually use this pattern with state verbs (e.g. *belong, doubt, know, understand*):

*If we **understood** more about animal behaviour we would be in a better position to protect them.* (**not** ~~If we were to understand more about~~ ...)

if and politeness

In addition to indicating conditions, *if*-clauses are also used to tell or ask people to do things in a polite way:

If I could just get a word in here ...
If you'll wait here, I'll fetch the manager.
If I could just have your attention for a moment ...
Mark Archer, if I could come to you first ...

2 *if ... not* and *unless*

Unless we expand captive breeding, many more animals will die out. or *If we don't expand...*

In real conditional sentences, we can often use either **unless** or **if ... not** when the meaning is 'except if'.

We usually use *if ... not* but not *unless*:

● when we say in the main clause that an event or action in the *if*-clause is unexpected:

*I'll be surprised **if** we **don't** get permission to build the zoo.*

- usually in questions:
  *How will children learn about wild animals **if** they do**n't** see them in zoos?*
- when the meaning is similar to 'because ... not' rather than 'except if':
  ***If** developing countries do**n't** have the money to establish nature reserves, more developed countries must offer help.*
- in unreal conditional sentences:
  ***If** we did**n't** have zoos, most people would never see wild animals.*

We use *unless* but not *if ... not* when we introduce an afterthought:
*We must have zoos if we want children to learn more about wild animals – **unless** their parents are rich enough to go on holiday to Africa, of course.*

3 *even if* and *even though*

We can use *even if* to mean 'whether or not' and *even though* to mean 'despite the fact that':
***Even if** wild animals are born in a zoo, it is still cruel to keep them in a small enclosure.*
(= whether or not animals are born in a zoo)
***Even though** they say they are concerned about the welfare of animals, they are still businesses mainly out to make a profit.* (= despite the fact that they say they are concerned)

4 *if only* and *wish*

We can use *if only / wish* + past simple to say that we want a present situation to be different, and *if only / wish* + past perfect to say that we regret a past event:
*I **wish** the situation **was / were** different.* or *If only the situation **was / were** different.*
***If only** we **had acted** sooner.* or *I **wish** we **had acted** sooner.*

We can use *if only / wish* + *would* to criticise someone, to say that we want someone to change their behaviour or that we want something to change:
*I **wish** Debbie Hall and the people in Save the Animals **would** read the scientific research on the value of zoos.*
⚠ We can't say ~~I wish I would~~:
I wish I worked in a zoo. or *I wish I could work in a zoo.* (**not** ~~I wish I would work~~ ...)

5 Other conditional expressions

A number of other expressions are used at the beginning of conditional clauses:
*I'm all in favour of safari parks **provided (that) / providing (that)** the animals are well looked after.*
*So / **As long as** developed countries put money into these reserves, species will be preserved.*
*I'm willing to support the proposal **on condition that** animals are kept in large enclosures.*
***In the event of** the alarm sounding, visitors should leave the zoo by the nearest exit.*
***Supposing** the proposal is rejected, what will you do then?*
*An alarm will sound **in case of** animals escaping from the safari park.*
*We must protect natural habitats, **otherwise** more animals will become extinct.*
***But for** the existence of zoos, many people would never have seen wild animals.*

C Grammar exercises

1 Rewrite each sentence, beginning the new sentence with *If ...* . Keep the meaning of the new sentence as close as possible to the meaning of the original sentence.

1 I don't have a reliable car, so I probably won't drive to France.

If I had a reliable car I would probably drive to France.

2 With a student card you can get a discount at the bookshop.

3 You can borrow my laptop for the evening as long as you promise to bring it back tomorrow.

4 By using more efficient light bulbs, there could be a 5% reduction in electricity consumption.

5 I wasn't promoted, so I didn't have to move to our head office in Madrid.

6 You'll have to leave the house by 7.00 to catch the 8.30 train.

7 I didn't know you were a vegetarian, otherwise I wouldn't have cooked lamb for dinner.

8 I didn't study hard, and that's why I have such a poorly paid job now.

2 Complete the sentences using a word or phrase in the box and the verb in brackets.

even if   even though   if   unless

1 I didn't tell my parents I was coming to a night club. ....*If they knew*.... where I was, they'd be really annoyed. *(know)*

2 It's so cold, it would be surprising .... we .... snow tonight. *(not get)*

3 Malcolm looked at some of my recent paintings, but .... he .... them he didn't show it. *(like)*

4 She didn't seem at all tired .... she .... all day. *(drive)*

5 The town hall is a beautiful old building. It would be a great shame .... it .... to be pulled down. *(be)*

6 I haven't lost any weight .... I .... lots of exercise. *(do)*

7 .... you .... David Mitchell's first novel, I'm sure you'll like this one, too. *(enjoy)*

8 .... it .... soon, there will still be water rationing in this part of the country. *(rain)*

9 I could pick you up at about eight, and we could go to the party together –
.... you .... to go on your own, of course. *(prefer)*

10 Where shall we go .... the restaurant .... open tonight?
(not be)

11 .... a buyer .... be found for the company, it is likely to
close by the end of the week. *(can)*

12 Miles has announced that .... he .... to be beaten in
tomorrow's tennis final, he will not consider retiring from the sport. *(be)*

13 The latest opinion poll suggests that .... the election ....
to be held today, the ruling party would again have a huge majority. *(be)*

14 He's a very good mechanic, ... he .... any formal
qualifications. *(not have)*

3 **Match the sentence beginnings and endings, joining them with one of the words or
phrases from the box. Sometimes more than one word or phrase is possible.**

| in the event of | on condition that | but for | in case | providing | otherwise |

1 I'll be in my office just before the exam

2 Aid must reach the refugees before the rainy season starts,

3 The demonstrators arrested were allowed to go free

4 Car airbags were designed to prevent chest injuries to the driver

5 He would have gone on working until he was 65

6 We should get to the airport by 5.00

a they remained outside a ten-mile zone around the nuclear power station.

b the traffic isn't too heavy on the motorway.

c a head-on collision.

d anyone has any last-minute questions.

e his poor health.

f many thousands will die.

1 +d *I'll be in my office just before the exam in case anyone has any last-minute questions.*

2 ....

3 ....

4 ....

5 ....

6 ....

4 Choose the correct verb forms in these conversations. Sometimes both are possible.

1

A: I feel terrible.

B: Well, if you **(1)** *will stay* / <u>*stay*</u> out until three in the morning, what do you expect?

A: I don't think I'll go to school today.

B: But supposing they **(2)** *phone* / *would phone* to find out where you are? What shall I tell them?

A: Okay, I'll go – if it **(3)** *will make* / *makes* you happy.

2

A: Grandad, before you blow out the candles, you've got to make a wish.

B: Well, I wish I **(1)** *had bought* / *would have bought* a house with a smaller garden. It's a lot of hard work to look after it.

A: And what else are you going to wish for?

B: I wish I **(2)** *have* / *had* more energy to play with my grandchildren.

A: And anything else?

B: I suppose I wish I **(3)** *was* / *would be* a young man again.

A: And have you got any more wishes?

B: Yes, I wish you **(4)** *stopped* / *would stop* asking me questions and let me eat my birthday cake!

3

A: You're still here! I thought you'd left this morning.

B: If it **(1)** *didn't snow* / *wasn't snowing* so much, **(2)** *I'd have left* / *I'd leave* ages ago.

A: But it wasn't snowing this morning. If **(3)** *you'd got up* / *you got up* earlier, you **(4)** *could get* / *could have got* there easily.

B: Okay, okay. I'll go now.

A: No, you shouldn't drive if it **(5)** *will be* / *is* dangerous.

B: Right, I'll stay here then!

D Exam practice

This exercise tests grammar from the rest of the book as well as the grammar in this unit.

Listening

14b You will hear five short extracts in which people are talking about cooking. While you listen you must complete both tasks, but you will hear the five extracts twice.

Task One

Choose from the list **A–H** the person who is speaking.

A a nurse

B a retired person   Speaker 1 ☐

C a student   Speaker 2 ☐

D an author   Speaker 3 ☐

E a lawyer   Speaker 4 ☐

F a teacher   Speaker 5 ☐

G a lorry driver

H an unemployed person

Task Two

Choose from the list **A–H** what each speaker is expressing.

A admiration for people who can cook well

B a pride in his or her cooking ability   Speaker 1 ☐

C a reluctance to cook   Speaker 2 ☐

D a criticism of current trends in cooking   Speaker 3 ☐

E a desire to learn to cook   Speaker 4 ☐

F a wish to try food from other countries   Speaker 5 ☐

G an awareness of his or her poor diet

H a dislike of unfamiliar food

Complete these sentences using one of the phrases, a or b. Sometimes both are possible.

1 Dinner isn't a time to talk and relax, _unless I've got_ friends round.
  a unless I've got   b if I haven't got
2 .... the place I'm going to, I'll generally take food from home.
  a Unless I know   b If I don't know
3 My mum did all the cooking .... away.
  a unless she was   b if she wasn't
4 .... so busy, I'd certainly like to cook more.
  a Unless I was   b If I wasn't
5 I might work through from 8 in the morning to 3 in the afternoon without a break
  – .... and then I might go out for a walk.
  a unless the sun's shining   b if the sun isn't shining

Writing

As part of a study project you have been asked to write an essay on the impact of the growth of the urban population. Read the instructions.

> You should write an essay with the following title:
>
> ## THE GROWTH OF CITIES: PRESENT AND FUTURE CONSEQUENCES
>
> In your essay, you should –
> - explain why people move to urban areas from the countryside
> - discuss some of the consequences of this trend
> - give your view on what is likely to happen in the future.

Write your **essay** in **300–350** words.

This task gives you the chance to practise conditional clauses:
If people live in the countryside, they may find it difficult to travel to hospitals.
If more jobs aren't provided in the countryside, people will continue to move to cities.
Unless better housing is built in cities, people will have a poorer quality of life than in the countryside.
Governments need to make rural areas more attractive by improving health and educational facilities; otherwise, cities will continue to grow.

Participle, *to*-infinitive and reduced clauses

Participle clauses including present participle (*-ing*) clauses, past participle (*-ed*) clauses, participle clauses after conjunctions and prepositions, *to*-infinitive clauses, reduced clauses

A Context listening

1 🎧15 Sam Green has taken three months off work to do a sponsored walk through Italy raising money for charity. Each week he sends an article to his company for its newsletter. Listen to two of his colleagues talking about Sam's latest article. Which of the problems does Sam talk about?

1  2  3

4  5  6

2 Complete the sentences 1–6 using the phrases a–f.

1 Because I had fallen over a number of times,

2 Because I was exhausted by a difficult few days,

3 Before I left Naples,

4 After I had left the sprawl of the city behind me,

5 When I opened up my sleeping bag,

6 After I had been woken up by a scratching sound,

a I walked up into the hills.

b I found a large rat trying to get into my backpack.

c I was only interested in finding a bed for the night.

d I discovered a scorpion.

e I was feeling thoroughly miserable.

f I bought yet more walking socks.

3 🎧15 Listen again and write down what Sam actually said.

Having fallen over

1 Because I had fallen over a number of times …

B Grammar

1 Participle clauses: general

Walking into each village, I was met by a pack of unfriendly dogs.
Found mainly in the south of the country, scorpions in Italy can give a nasty bite but are rarely dangerous.
Having spent a couple of hours exploring Amalfi, I'm now ready for an excellent Italian dinner.
Participle clauses are more common in writing, and are often used to express ideas in an economical way.

The implied subject of a participle is usually the same as the subject of the main clause:
Snarling aggressively, the dogs were pretty terrifying at first. (= the dogs were snarling and the dogs were pretty terrifying)

In careful speech and writing we avoid a participle clause when the subjects are different:
Snarling aggressively, I kept away from the dogs.
In this example, the writer is trying to say that the dogs were snarling and he kept away from them. However, it sounds as if he was snarling! The more accurate alternative is:
The dogs were snarling aggressively, so I kept away from them.

In formal English, a participle clause can sometimes have its own subject, which is often a pronoun or a noun phrase including a pronoun:
*Scorpions in North Africa, **some measuring** up to 20 centimetres, can kill adults.*

When we use *not* in a participle clause it usually comes before the participle:
*Not **wanting** to carry my backpack any further, I went to the first hotel I came across.*

2 Present participle (*-ing*) clauses
We can use a present participle clause to talk about something that takes place at the same time as, or just before, an action in the main clause:
Opening up my sleeping bag, I discovered a scorpion.

A present participle clause can be used to give background information:
Living mainly in warm climates, scorpions have existed for over 400 million years.
and after quoted speech, to say what someone was doing while they were talking:
*'Wait for me here,' said Frank, **running** out of the house.*

Present participle clauses can also be used to talk about a reason or result:
Arriving in Amalfi early in the afternoon, I had time to look around the town.
(= because I arrived in Amalfi early in the afternoon)

3 Past participle (*-ed*) clauses
We can use a past participle clause to talk about reasons and conditions:
Made from the softest leather imaginable, they are as comfortable as a pair of slippers.
(reason = because they are made from the softest leather imaginable)
Sold in Britain, the boots would have cost a lot more. (condition = if they were sold in Britain)

Past participles combine with forms of *be* and *have* to create passives and perfect forms:
Having fallen over a number of times, I was feeling thoroughly miserable. (= I was feeling thoroughly miserable because I had fallen over a number of times)
We can use either *having + -ed* or a present participle with a similar meaning to describe consecutive events. However, *having + -ed* emphasises that the action in the participle clause is complete before the action in the main clause begins:
Having climbed to the top of the hill, I could see all the way to the Mediterranean. or *Climbing to the top of the hill, ...*
Being made so welcome at the hotel, I was reluctant to leave. (= because I was made so welcome)
Having been woken up by a scratching sound, I found a large rat trying to get into my backpack. (= after I had been woken up)

4 Participle clauses after conjunctions and prepositions

We can use a present participle clause after a number of conjunctions and prepositions, including: *after, before, by, in, on, since, when, while, with, without, unless, until*:
Before leaving Naples, I bought yet more walking socks. or less formally *Before I left Naples, I bought yet more walking socks.*
We can also use *with* (or informally *what with*) to introduce a reason for something in the main clause. Notice that a subject has to come between *with* and *-ing*:
With Naples being such a busy city, I was surprised to find a hotel room so easily.
What with sleeping badly, and some very steep hills to walk over, it was quite a relief to get to Amalfi this afternoon. (= because I had slept badly)

In formal contexts we can use a past participle after *(al)though, as, if, once, when, while, unless* and *until*:
Walking through Italy was a fantastic experience, but if asked, I'm not sure I'd do it again.
or *... but if I was asked ...*

5 *to*-infinitive clauses

We can use a clause beginning with a *to*-infinitive to talk about purpose, result or condition:
I walked up into the hills to avoid the long trek around the coast. (= purpose)
I got to the hotel early, only to find that I couldn't check in until later. (= result)
To hear him grumbling last week, you'd think he was about to get on the next flight home. (= if you had heard him grumbling)

6 Reduced clauses

We can sometimes use a 'reduced' clause beginning with a conjunction or adjective, but with no verb. Reduced clauses are usually fairly formal:
While in Naples, I did what all visitors do. or *While I was in Naples, ...*
Exhausted by my walk, I went straight to bed. or *Because I was exhausted ...*

C Grammar exercises

1 Match the pairs of sentences. Rewrite each pair as one sentence starting with a participle clause in an appropriate form.

1 She swam strongly.

2 Colin got out from under the car.

3 I can't speak Portuguese.

4 Manchester United are favourites to win again.

5 I was shown how to use the software.

6 I hadn't eaten or drunk anything for hours.

7 She began to read her speech.

8 The two letters were sent in 1406 to the French king.

a I found it easy to design my own website.

b He was covered in oil.

c I was starting to feel a bit faint.

d They have already beaten Real Madrid twice this year.

e She put on her glasses.

f They were written in Latin.

g She was able to cross the river in just a few minutes.

h I found travelling in Brazil difficult.

1 + g *Swimming strongly, she was able to cross the river in just a few minutes.*

2 Read this extract from a blog about a visit to London. Rewrite the underlined parts using a participle clause, *to*-infinitive or reduced clause.

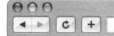

While in London

(1) While I was in London I just had to go to the British Museum. There's so much to see and I only had time to spend a few hours there. First, I went to the collection of clocks and watches. **(2)** When I saw the pocket watches, I was reminded of the old watch my grandfather used to wear. I don't think I ever saw him without it. Then I went to the Money Gallery. They've got an incredible collection of coins, **(3)** and some of them are over 2000 years old. Next stop was the Chinese collection. **(4)** Because I'd lived in Hong Kong for so many years, I was very interested in this. Some of the jade objects were stunning. **(5)** After I looked at the Chinese collection, I had hoped to see the Mexican collection. Unfortunately, **(6)** when I got there I found that it was closed. **(7)** Because I'd spent the whole morning walking around the museum, I decided that I wanted to do something very different in the afternoon. So I went to the London Eye **(8)** in order that I could get a bird's-eye view of the city. **(9)** When they are looked at from the top of the Eye, some of the biggest buildings appear quite small – even St. Paul's Cathedral, across the river. After that, **(10)** because I was tired from all the walking, I went back to my hotel room and slept for a couple of hours **(11)** before I went out to have dinner.

15

3 In these sentences, is the subject of the participle and the main clause the same (S) or different (D)? If it is different, rewrite the sentence correctly.

1 Painted bright yellow, I could see the signs clearly from a distance. ......*D*......
Because the signs were painted bright yellow, I could see them clearly from a distance.

2 Hearing a noise from one of the bedrooms, I quietly climbed upstairs. ....

3 Laughing at her new hat, Kate looked really angry with me. ....

4 Kept in the fridge, the cheese should stay fresh for weeks. ....

5 Holding her umbrella tightly, she went out into the storm. ....

6 Talking to each other in the library, I asked them to keep quiet. ....

7 Caught in traps put on the riverbed at night, many fishermen depend on crayfish for their livelihood. ....

8 Worried that Judy hadn't arrived, I decided to phone her home. ....

4 Complete each sentence using one of the words in the box and an appropriate form of the verb in brackets. Use either an *-ing*, an *-ed* or *being* + *-ed* verb form.

although	before	if	once	since	while	with	without	~~unless~~	until

1 ......*Unless*...... otherwise ......*stated*......, all software contained on the CD is for demonstration purposes only. *(state)*

2 .... my book on the European Union, I interviewed more than a hundred members of the European Parliament. *(research)*

3 .... no longer .... in the day-to-day running of the business, Mr White retains a keen interest in its development. *(involve)*

4 .... Defence Minister, he was head of the army for five years. *(make)*

5 .... her parents, she took their car and drove into town. When they found out, they were furious. *(ask)*

6 Not .... school had anyone told me to 'sit down and be quiet'. *(leave)*

7 The virus doesn't have serious effects, but ...., it remains in the body for life. *(catch)*

8 .... the wind .... hurricane force, ships have been advised to head for land. *(reach)*

9 I slept deeply .... by a fire engine going past the house. *(wake)*

10 .... guilty, she could face ten years in prison. *(find)*

D Exam practice

This exercise tests grammar from the rest of the book as well as the grammar in this unit.

Use of English

Read the text below. Use the word given in capitals at the end of some of the lines to form a word that fits in the gap in the same line. There is an example at the beginning **(0)**.

Instincts and learned behaviour

To survive, an animal has to be able to do certain things as soon as it is

born or it hatches. **(0)** .... *Governed* .... by its genes, some parts of an   **GOVERN**

animal's behaviour are innate. This kind of behaviour is vital for a young

animal, **(1)** .... it recognise danger and food. But animals   **HELP**

need also to adapt their behaviour as they gain experience, and most show

some degree of learning, even insects. Butterflies are **(2)** ....   **INSTINCT**

attracted to coloured flowers, and have a built-in preference for particular

colours, but they **(3)** .... learn to adapt these preferences   **READY**

on the basis of their experience. This **(4)** .... to learn makes   **ABLE**

the animal's behaviour much more **(5)** .... to changing   **ADAPT**

environments. A butterfly that couldn't learn to change its flower colour

preference would quickly die of **(6)** .... if there were no   **STARVE**

flowers of the preferred colour around.

A bird will recognise its mother very early in its life. Having

(7) .... what she looks like, chicks are then able to avoid   **LEARN**

making **(8)** .... approaches to other potentially dangerous   **ADVISE**

birds in the community. Mammals often have an even greater degree of

(9) .... care, some staying with their mother even until her   **PARENT**

next offspring is born. Not all animals have the same opportunities to learn,

however, and those that are not looked after by their parents have to be

(10) .... from the start.   **DEPEND**

Look back at the text. Find:

1 two sentences that include a participle clause with a present participle *(-ing)* form of the verb

....

....

2 two sentences that include a participle clause with a past participle *(-ed)* form of the verb

....

....

3 one sentence that includes a *to*-infinitive clause

....

Writing

Your English club magazine is producing a special issue focusing on novels by women authors. Write a review of a novel you have enjoyed by a woman author. Give a brief outline of the plot, say what you particularly enjoyed about it, and say why you would recommend it to other readers.

Write your **review** in **220–260** words.

This task gives you the chance to practise using present participle clauses and past participle clauses to:

- summarise the action in the novel
  Set in an Italian village, the novel ...
  Living alone, she found that she was ...
  With his family facing starvation, he decided to ...
- give your opinion
  Having read the novel twice, ...
  Although written over a hundred years ago, the novel still ...

A Context listening

1 You are going to hear Joe Simpson, head of the Norton Wildlife Trust (NWT) encouraging some residents of Norton to volunteer for some local projects. Before you listen, look at these pictures and identify the activities.

1

2

3

4

5

6

2 🔊16 Listen to the talk. Which of the activities are mentioned?

3 🔊16 Listen again and decide whether these statements are true (T) or false (F).

1 The NWT owns Norton Marsh. ....T........

2 Broadstone Park is now a wilderness. ....

3 The NWT gets its money from the Montague family. ....

4 Initially, the most important task is clearing overgrown plants and trees. ....

5 NWT volunteers are invited to barbecues. ....

6 One of the jobs that volunteers can do is publicise the NWT. ....

7 Only members of the NWT can work on the project. ....

8 The NWT was given the Marsh by Mr Reynold's brother. ....

9 Volunteers can usually get a lift to the Marsh. ....

4 🔊16 Listen again and complete these extracts with the words you hear.

1 I can guarantee .... and we organise barbecues and other social events.

2 We will be very grateful for ....

3 Nine o'clock is ...., on Saturday and Sunday mornings.

4 Just come along to the Marsh and we'll show you ....

5 Can I ask ....?

5 Look at your answers to Exercise 4. What words begin each clause you have written?

B Grammar

What you've told us is very interesting. (= The *information* is very interesting.)
*You've probably also heard **that the Marsh has been given to the NWT to look after**.* (= You've probably also heard this *report*.)
*Nine o'clock is **when we usually** meet.* (= Nine o'clock is *our usual meeting time*.)
A noun clause functions in a sentence in a similar way to a noun (e.g. **information, report**) or noun phrase (e.g. **our usual meeting time**). Noun clauses usually begin with **that** or a wh-word (e.g. **how, what, when, where, which, who, why**; also **whether, whatever**).

1 *that-* noun clauses

In informal contexts we often leave out *that* at the beginning of a *that-* noun clause:
*It's also good to know **that** they're helping the environment.* **or** *... to know they're helping ...*
*I can guarantee **that** you'll make a lot of new friends.* **or** *I can guarantee you'll make ...*

We usually use *the fact that* (rather than *that*):
● when the noun clause is subject:
   ***The fact that** you're not a member of the trust makes no difference.* (**rather than** *That you're not a member of the trust makes no difference.*)
● after a preposition or after verbs such as *change, face* and *overlook*:
   *We have to **face** (up to) **the fact that** we don't have enough resources at the moment.*
(▷ See Appendix 11.1.)

Depending on meaning, we can use words like *argument, assumption, belief, claim, idea, notion,* and *view* instead of *fact*:
***The idea that** it's all hard work is just wrong.*

2 *wh-* noun clauses

When a *wh-* noun clause follows certain nouns (e.g. *example, problem*), we often have to include *of* before the *wh*-word:
*We'd like to follow the **example of what** they've done at Broadstone Park.*
(▷ See Appendix 11.2.)

Some verbs (e.g. *advise, teach*) must have an object before the *wh-* word:
*I'll be happy **to advise you** when to come.*
(▷ See Appendix 11.3.)

Noun clauses beginning *how* are commonly used after certain verbs (e.g. *decide, know*):
*It's entirely up to you to **decide how** much time you can give.*
(▷ See Appendix 11.4.)

We can use a *wh-* noun clause, but not a *that-* noun clause, after a preposition:
*If you've got any questions about **what I've said so far**, I'd be happy to answer them.* (**not** *... about that I've said so far ...*)

We can also use noun clauses beginning with *whatever* (= anything, or it doesn't matter what), *whoever* (= the person/group who, or any person/group who), or *whichever* (= one thing or person from a limited number) to talk about things, people or times that are indefinite or unknown:

*We will be very grateful for **whatever** time people can spare.*
*You can phone **whoever** is in charge of arranging lifts on the weekend you want to come.*

Rather than a *wh-* noun clause, we can often use a noun or pronoun which has a meaning related to the *wh-* word:

***Why** most people volunteer is that they want fresh air and exercise.* or
***The reason** (why/that) most people volunteer ...*
*Clearing the vegetation is **what** is urgently needed.* or
*Clearing the vegetation is **something** which/that is urgently needed.*

Other words used in this way include *the place* (rather than *where*), *the time* (rather than *when*), *the way* (rather than *how*) and *somebody/someone* (rather than *who*).

3 *whether* and *if*

We can use *whether* as the *wh-* word in a noun clause when we talk about possible choices. *Whether* has a similar meaning to *if*:

*I can't remember **whether** it runs on Sundays.*

Notice the difference between sentences with *whether-* and *that-* noun clauses:

*I didn't know **whether/if** the bus service has been cancelled.* (= it may or may not have been cancelled)
*I didn't know **that** the bus service had been cancelled.* (= it was cancelled; now I know)

In rather formal contexts, particularly in writing, we can use *as to* with a meaning similar to 'about' or 'concerning' before a *whether* noun clause:

*There was some debate **as to whether** he could legally give us the land.*

We use *whether*, not *if* –
- before *or not*:
  *I don't know **whether or not** I'd be able to come on a regular basis.*
  ⚠ However:
  *I don't know **whether/if** I'd be able to come on a regular basis **or not**.*
- before a *to*-infinitive:
  *I can't make up my mind **whether to help** on Saturdays or Sundays.*
- usually after a preposition, and also after the verbs *advise, choose, consider, debate, discuss, enquire, question*:
  *You can think **about whether** you'd like to be involved.*
  *You can **choose whether** you want to work indoors or outdoors.*
- in a clause acting as a subject or complement:
  ***Whether you help with the outdoor or indoor work** depends on you.* (= subject)
  *What I'm not clear about is **whether we can get a lift to the reserve**.* (= complement)

C Grammar exercises

1 Read these comments by a resident, a fire officer and a climate change expert about a recent flood. Complete each text with *that* or *the fact that*.

Nobody really thought **(1)** ....that............ flooding this bad would happen again, but as the river level rose, we had to face up to **(2)** .... we'd have to leave our home. Personally, I blame the fire service. **(3)** .... it's been raining heavily here for five days should have meant that they were better prepared to help us.

I really feel **(4)** .... some of the criticisms of my fire officers are unfair, although **(5)** .... today is a public holiday did mean that many of our staff weren't here to help with the rescue. However, we warned residents yesterday **(6)** .... they might have to evacuate their houses with little notice, and the difficulty in evacuating people from their houses wasn't helped by **(7)** .... they wanted to take large amounts of personal belongings with them.

We can't ignore **(8)** .... climate change is going to increase the risk of flooding, and a number of studies have suggested **(9)** .... winter river levels throughout the country will be much higher than in the past. Unfortunately, the situation in this area is complicated by **(10)** .... so many trees have been cut down on the hills around here and rainwater flows more quickly into the rivers. So there's a real possibility **(11)** .... serious flooding could now happen here every winter.

2 Read this extract from the blog of an American woman living in Paris. Complete the text using a word from Box A and a phrase from Box B.

A

how   if   the way
what   when   where
whether   whichever
who   whoever   ~~why~~

B

the light shines through them   I'd make it
the cathedral was built   to take a guided tour
designed the cathedral   they managed to do that
direction you approach it   ~~it was built there~~
conditions were like for the builders   wrote that
the building materials came from

I rented a car yesterday and drove about 50 miles from Paris to Chartres. The area around Chartres is very flat. That's probably the reason **(1)** why it was built there . It dominates the landscape from **(2)** .... At first, I wasn't sure **(3)** .... of the cathedral. I'm pretty independent and like to wander around on my own. But this time I decided to go for it, and I'm really glad I did – the guide was excellent! She talked a lot about **(4)** .... – it was begun before 1200 – and told us **(5)** .... Some of the stone was transported from hundreds of miles away – I'll never understand **(6)** .... **(7)** .... isn't known. Apparently in those days architecture was a cooperative effort by the stonemasons working on the site. She also gave us some idea of **(8)** .... It sounds like an incredibly hard life. I thought the stained-glass windows were awesome. I was so impressed with **(9)** .... and creates patterns on the cathedral floor. After the tour, I looked again at my guidebook and noticed that it mentioned the 'easy climb' up the north tower, so off I went. But **(10)** .... must have been super-fit. For me it was a long, exhausting climb, and there were times when I didn't know **(11)** .... The magnificent view was certainly worth the effort when I got to the top, but be warned!

3 Match the sentence beginnings and endings, joining them with *whatever, whoever* or *whichever*.

1 Mr Phelps has resigned as managing director, and it will be a difficult job for

2 I must have that painting, and will pay

3 The police have said that to protect the public they will take

4 I've bought this armchair that adjusts itself to the body shape of

5 We've got lots of cakes, so just choose

6 At the first modern Olympic games in 1896, athletes could wear

7 Houses next to the river are at risk of flooding,

8 Both the number 45 and 47 buses go into town, so get on

a is sitting in it.

b side they are on.

c replaces him.

d action is necessary.

e it costs.

f comes first.

g one you want.

h they wanted to.

1+c Mr Phelps has resigned as managing director, and it will be a difficult job for whoever replaces him.

4 Complete the sentences using the notes in brackets and *where, what, when, why* or *how*. Add any other words necessary.

1 Our Maths teacher made the exam quite easy for us. In our last lesson he gave us some **(1)** examples of what would (examples / would) be in the paper, and he **(2)** .... (told / questions) to answer.

2 A: There's a job advert here for a train driver. Do you think I should go for it?

B: But **(3)** .... (know / to drive) a train?

A: No, but I'm sure they'll be able **(4)** .... (teach / to do). I might send for an application form.

3 When I got to hospital, a nurse took me into a room and **(5)** ....
(showed / to sit). I was very anxious **(6)** .... (would happen / next) and **(7)** .... (asked / the doctor) would be coming.

4 A: Remember **(8)** .... (time / were) in London and our wallets and train tickets were stolen?

B: I certainly do. Then we had **(9)** .... (problem / to get back) to Manchester without tickets or money.

A: **(10)** .... (reason / mention) now is that the man who gave us the money to get home is on the front of today's paper. He's wanted for robbing a bank!

D Exam practice

This exercise tests grammar from the rest of the book as well as the grammar in this unit.

Use of English

For questions **1–12**, read the text below and then decide which answer (**A, B, C** or **D**) best fits each space. There is an example at the beginning (**0**).

Homework: how useful is it?

Homework is an (**0**) ....B.... part of school life in most countries around the world. However, there is still considerable debate among teachers about (**1**) .... homework has a significant educational value. On the one side are those who (**2**) .... that it takes too much time away from other (**3**) .... useful activities. On the other are those who see homework as reinforcing school lessons so that concepts will not be forgotten. (**4**) .... is often neglected in this debate is the role of parental involvement and (**5**) .... or not the child's home provides support for effective homework. Middle-class families regularly spend time helping with homework by providing facilities and being interested. These are the same families who can (**6**) .... other educational experiences like overseas holidays and weekend museum visits. Parents in low-income families often don't have the time to make homework a priority or aren't able to afford a computer or additional books. (**7**) .... money they have goes on the basic necessities of life – accommodation, food, clothing and heating. Their children are more (**8**) .... to spend weekends doing part-time jobs or playing on the street. However, the (**9**) .... that only middle-class parents support their children's education is quite obviously wrong. Not (**10**) .... well-to-do parents give the support they should, and some parents living in the most impoverished circumstances (**11**) .... find the time and energy to involve themselves in their children's homework. In general, (**12**) .... , the family's economic status is a major factor in determining the value of homework.

0	**A** ingrained	**B** established	**C** allowed	**D** accustomed
1	**A** if	**B** that	**C** whether	**D** supposing
2	**A** tell	**B** describe	**C** claim	**D** propose
3	**A** more	**B** most	**C** such	**D** much
4	**A** Whatever	**B** Which	**C** That	**D** What
5	**A** whether	**B** why	**C** whatever	**D** if
6	**A** show	**B** propose	**C** bring	**D** offer
7	**A** Whichever	**B** That	**C** Whatever	**D** Which

8	**A** likely	**B** possible	**C** especially	**D** like
9	**A** fact	**B** concept	**C** idea	**D** reason
10	**A** each	**B** all	**C** any	**D** every
11	**A** imaginable	**B** imagining	**C** imagined	**D** imagine
12	**A** therefore	**B** consequently	**C** however	**D** then

Grammar focus task

There are six noun clauses in the text on page 151. Find and underline them.

Writing

Read this extract from a letter to a newspaper.

Write a letter to the newspaper saying whether you agree or disagree with David Wallace's opinion and why, and saying what you believe should happen in the future.

> Dear Editor
>
> Many recent letter writers have called for the rapid expansion of renewable energy. I agree that the burning of fossil fuels is a major cause of global warming and climate change and needs to be phased out. But renewable energy sources like solar and wind power will never provide enough energy to allow us to reduce our dependence on coal and oil or enable developing countries to expand their industries. Only nuclear power can do this.
>
> David Wallace
> Melbourne, Australia

Write your **letter** in **300–350** words. Do not write any postal address.

Writing hints

This task gives you the chance to practise using noun clauses:

The issue of what to do with nuclear waste needs to be resolved.
He overlooks the fact that technology is advancing rapidly.
No one knows whether renewable energy sources will ever provide sufficient electricity for our needs.
He is quite correct in saying that nuclear power is the only realistic option.

Useful language
carbon neutral, hydro / wind / solar / tidal / geothermal energy

1 Which of these do you think learner drivers find most difficult?

> reversing around corners overtaking parking
> starting on a hill getting into the correct lane
> changing gear driving at night
> using the rear-view mirror

2 🔊 17 Listen to Marie and Sam talking about their experiences of learning to drive. Which of the things in Exercise 1 were particular problems for them?

3 🔊 17 Listen again. In what order does Marie mention these advantages of being taught by a professional instructor?

a he passed on useful tips ....

b he was always encouraging ....

c he used a dual-control car .....1.....

d he could tell when she was ready to take her test ....

In what order does Sam mention these advantages of being taught by his mother?

e she was calm most of the time ....

f he got lots of time to practise ....

g she knew a quiet place to practise ....

h he didn't have to pay for lessons ....

4 What words or phrases are used to connect these ideas?

1 I stalled in the middle of the road + my instructor stayed completely cool ...*even if*...

2 I had the mirror positioned + I couldn't judge where the back of the car was ....

3 it was disappointing to have replacement instructors + the replacements were patient and helpful ....

4 it's expensive to have driving lessons + I would recommend it ....

5 my mum doesn't have a professional qualification + she has lots of experience ....

6 I didn't do anything stupid + she stayed calm ....

B Grammar

1 Sentence connectors and conjunctions: general

> **START POINT**
>
> *My mum used to come and collect me from college in the car and I'd drive home.* **What's more**, *she'd let me drive when we went shopping.*
>
> A sentence connector (e.g. **what's more**) links one sentence with another.
>
> *My mum taught me to drive* **because** *I couldn't afford to pay for driving lessons.*
>
> A conjunction (e.g. **because**) links clauses within a single sentence.
>
> (▷ See Appendix 12.)

To link two clauses, we use only one conjunction, not two:
Although it's expensive having driving lessons, I'd really recommend it.
(**not** ~~Although it's expensive having driving lessons, but I'd really recommend it.~~)

We usually put a comma between clauses linked by a conjunction:
As long as I didn't do anything stupid, she stayed pretty calm.
⚠ When *because* or *while* (referring to time) begin the second clause in a sentence, we don't need a comma.

Sentence connectors usually come at the beginning of a sentence and less often at the end or in another position. The only ones that can't come at the beginning are *too* and *as well*:
*You can spend a lot more time practising, **as well**.*

We usually put a comma after a sentence connector at the beginning or end of a sentence:
*My mum thought I was ready to take my driving test. **However**, I failed first time.*
*There are lots of advantages in having your parents teach you. There's the cost, **for instance**.*
When a sentence connector comes elsewhere in a sentence, punctuation is more variable.

⚠ Sentence connectors can be used to link clauses in a sentence if the clauses are joined with *and*, *but*, *or*, *so*, or a semi-colon (;), colon (:), or dash (–):
*My instructor was very experienced **and, as a result**, he had lots of useful tips to pass on.*
*Having a professional teach you to drive is best; **however**, it can be very expensive.*

2 *before, until* (conjunctions)

Sometimes we can use either *before* or *until* with little difference in meaning:
*She wouldn't let me drive on busy roads **before/until** I could control the car well.*
⚠ We use *until*, not *before*, to highlight that an action continues to a particular time and then stops:
*I just carried on having lessons **until** my instructor said I was ready to take the driving test.*

3 *hardly, no sooner, scarcely* (conjunctions)

After *hardly* and *scarcely* the second clause usually begins with *when* or *before*; after *no sooner* it begins with *than* or *when*:

*We'd **hardly** driven out of our road **before** we were shouting at each other.*
*I'd **no sooner** passed my test **than / when** my friends started asking me for lifts.*

We often use a past perfect in the clause with *hardly*, *no sooner* or *scarcely* and a past simple in the other.

(▷ For word order in sentences with *hardly*, *no sooner* and *scarcely*, see Unit 21.)

4 *first(ly), at first; last(ly), at last* (sentence connectors)

We use *first* or *firstly* to label the first point in a list and *last* or *lastly* to label the final point. We use *at first* to indicate that there is a contrast between two past situations, and *at last* to show that something happened later than hoped or expected. Often *at last* suggests annoyance or some inconvenience that results from the delay:

***Firstly**, cars like the one I learnt in have dual controls.*
***At first**, I couldn't get the hang of this at all.*
*I passed my driving test **at last**, after taking it five times.*

⚠ We don't use *at last* to label the last point in a list:
*First, I had to practise starting on a hill ... **Finally / Lastly**, the instructor made me reverse around a corner.* (**not** ~~At last, the instructor made me reverse ...~~)

5 *however*

However is often a sentence connector, but can also be used:
● as an adverb when it is followed by an adjective, adverb or *much / many*:
   *My instructor never got annoyed, **however** badly I was driving.* (= despite how badly)
● as a conjunction when it means 'in whatever way':
   ***However** I had the mirror positioned, I just couldn't judge where the back of the car was.*

6 *even so* (sentence connector), *even though* (conjunction)

Even so has a meaning similar to *however*. We use it to introduce a fact that is surprising given what has just been said:

*He was great and I didn't want to be taught by anyone else. **Even so**, I always found the replacements very patient and helpful.*

We use *even though* to say that a fact doesn't make the rest of the sentence untrue:
***Even though** she doesn't have a professional qualification, she's got lots of experience to pass on.*

7 *on the other hand, on the contrary* (sentence connectors)

We use *on the other hand* when we compare or contrast two statements. We sometimes introduce the first statement with *on the one hand*:

*It may be that the quality of the tuition is better with a professional driving instructor. **On the other hand**, it's cheaper if your parents teach you.* **or**
***On the one hand,** it may be that the quality of the tuition is better with a professional driving instructor. **On the other (hand)**, it's cheaper if your parents teach you.*

On the contrary is used similarly, but emphasises that we reject the first statement and accept the second:

*Some people say that it's more expensive to be taught by a driving instructor than a friend or relative. **On the contrary**, it works out cheaper.*

8 Prepositions commonly confused with conjunctions and connectors

⚠ These are prepositions, and **can't** be used as conjunctions or sentence connectors:

*As **well as** being calm and patient, he was always very encouraging. (**not** ~~As well as he was calm and patient~~ ...)*

***Apart from** the cost of insurance, I think it's much better to be taught by your parents. (**not** ~~Apart from the insurance costs were high~~ ...)*

*I think there's a lot of other good things about having your parents teach you, **besides** saving money. (**not** ... ~~besides you can save money~~)*

*I'd recommend professional driving lessons **despite / in spite of** the expense. (**not** ... ~~despite / in spite of they are expensive~~)*

*The lesson was cancelled **due to** the heavy rain. (**not** ... ~~due to it was raining heavily.~~)*

*We used to stop driving at some point **during** the lesson, and he would ask me how I felt I'd improved. (**not** ... ~~at some point during we were having the lesson~~ ...)*

C Grammar exercises

1 Match the items, joining them with the conjunction or sentence connector given. Write either one or two sentences, as appropriate. There may be more than one way of joining the sentences.

1 Amy was on the phone for hours	a it's a public holiday
2 she always finds time to talk to students	b such a move would be controversial
3 the restaurant's closed next Monday	c we got onto the motorway
4 he's a seismologist	d I noticed she'd been crying
5 tuition fees have been increased	e he studies earthquakes
6 we travelled much faster	f the number of applications has fallen
7 the government is being urged to build more nuclear power stations	g his shoes were black
8 he was wearing the same clothes as me	h how busy she is

1 (*later*)   Amy was on the phone for hours. Later, I noticed she'd been crying.

2 (*no matter*)   ....

3 (*because*)   ....

4 (*that is to say*)   ....

5 (*as a result*)   ....

6 (*once*)   ....

7 (*however*)   ....

8 (*except that*)   ....

2 **Choose the correct word or phrase. Sometimes both are possible.**

1 She isn't very interested in science subjects. *On the contrary / On the other hand*, she really loves studying history.

2 There are a number of problems with your suggestion. *At first / Firstly*, it's very expensive. Then there is the question of getting planning permission.

3 I had *hardly / scarcely* stepped through the door when the telephone rang.

4 He walked quickly down the corridor *before / until* he reached the last door.

5 My aunt was followed into the room by my two nieces and three nephews. *Lastly / At last* came my uncle, carrying all the suitcases.

6 I knew I had the right qualifications and experience for the job. *Even though / Even so*, I felt very nervous as I walked in to face the interview panel.

7 At college I had only two tutorials a week, but this didn't mean I had nothing to do the rest of the time. *On the contrary / On the other hand*, I studied at least six days a week.

8 I didn't know anything about your illness *before / until* your mother mentioned it.

9 Once he'd done the washing up and got the children to bed, Matt sat down in front of the fire. *Lastly / At last* he had some time to himself.

10 There was a loud bang. *At first / Firstly*, she thought it was thunder. Then she realised it must have been an explosion.

11 *Even though / Even so* the snow had stopped falling, it was still freezing cold.

12 We had *no sooner / hardly* started driving than the children said, 'Are we there yet?'

3 Complete the sentences using a word from box A and a phrase from box B.

A

> consequently   in case
> in contrast   ~~meanwhile~~
> otherwise   whereas
> while   unless

B

> she's looking for a new flat   it isn't very heavy
> there's a power cut   in Marketing they get an hour
> the weather's bad   we'll have to walk miles to the bridge
> I prefer Italian   ~~my parents are letting me borrow theirs~~

1 I'm saving up to buy my own car. *Meanwhile, my parents are letting me borrow theirs.* .

2 I always keep some candles in the house ....

3 My husband adores Chinese food, ...

4 The boat is made entirely of fibreglass. ....

5 We should be able to wade across the river; ....

6 Your sister can stay with us ....

7 The lunch break in the Personnel Department is 30 minutes.

....

8 We're planning on having a picnic in the park ....

4 Complete these extracts from emails. Choose from the words and phrases in the boxes.

A

> ~~although~~   at first   because   because of   despite
> during   even so   even though   firstly   while

I'm in Jamaica for a week. (1) ....*Although*........ it's a work visit, I've had a few days free,
so I decided to have a go at windsurfing (2) .... I'm here. I'd never tried it
before (3) .... I'm not a very good swimmer.
(4) .... I found it really difficult to stay upright, but it wasn't long until I
was going quite fast. (5) .... , I didn't go far from the beach.

B

> as well   as well as   before   even though   hardly
> in addition   in spite of   no sooner   until   what's more

The weather here is terrible. (1) .... heavy rain, we've had gale force winds.
(2) .... the bad weather, we're doing a lot of walking. Yesterday was typical.
When we got up it was wet – of course – and we decided to wait (3) ....
the rain stopped. The sun came out by midday and we set off for Wicklow Hill. We had
(4) .... started to climb than it began pouring down! (5) .... ,
the wind was so strong, we were almost blown over. But we still got to the top!

D Exam practice

Use of English

Read the text below and think of the word which best fits each space. Use only **one** word for each space. The exercise begins with an example (**0**).

This exercise tests grammar from the rest of the book as well as the grammar in this unit.

Psychology: the science of the mind

Psychology is the study of the mind, by far the (**0**) ....most.... sophisticated machine
(**1**) .... Earth. But how can (**2**) .... as inaccessible as the mind be studied? Even
(**3**) .... we were to open someone's skull and look inside, we would only see the brain, not
the mind in action. (**4**) .... we cannot observe the mind directly, it controls everything we
do. Therefore, psychologists study human behaviour in (**5**) .... to discover (**6**) .... the
mind works. The behaviour (**7**) .... interests them ranges from simple acts such as feeding,
to much more complex skills (**8**) .... language. Psychologists measure behaviour, and often
use statistics to show that (**9**) .... they find is reliable evidence and not just down to chance.
The scientific knowledge gained from this research is then used by practising psychologists. For
example, clinical psychologists – (**10**) .... make up the largest group of specialists – help
people with emotional problems (**11**) .... with their difficulties. Research findings are not
only used by psychologists, but also by other professionals who are concerned (**12**) .... the
ways people interact – doctors, teachers and judges, to name just a (**13**) .... A substantial
body of psychological knowledge has been built up since the nineteenth century. Nevertheless, the
enormous complexity of the mind (**14**) .... that there will always be more to learn about it,
(**15**) .... much research is undertaken.

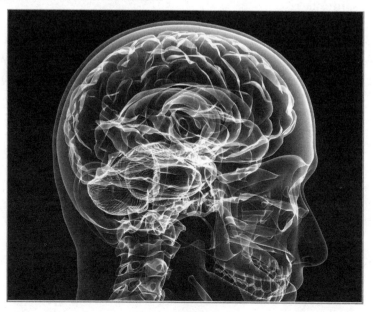

Without looking back at the text, complete the sentences with connecting words or phrases.

1 .... Even if .... we were to open someone's skull and look inside, we would only see the brain, not the mind in action.

2 .... we cannot observe the mind directly, it controls everything we do. ...., psychologists study human behaviour .... discover how the mind works.

3 A substantial body of psychological knowledge has been built up since the nineteenth century. ...., the enormous complexity of the mind means that there will always be more to learn about it, ... much research is undertaken.

Writing

You have been invited to write an article for an international student magazine, *The World Today*, about healthy eating. The article should explain:

- the principles of healthy eating
- why healthy eating is important
- what the consequences are of not eating healthily.

Write your **article** in **220–260** words.

This task gives you the chance to practise using words and phrases that connect ideas within and across sentences:
although, in order to, as well as; therefore, consequently, in addition, above all

Useful language
essentially, it is of particular significance for, it is particularly important, by eating well, can lead to, might result in

The passive

using the passive; active and passive verb forms; passive
forms of verbs with two objects; *get* + past participle;
get / *have* + object + past participle

18

A Context listening

1 You are going to hear an interview with a government minister talking about crime
statistics. Before you listen, look at these newspaper headlines and match them with
the crimes they refer to.

a burglary

b firearm offences

c street crime

d car crime

e vandalism

1 **STREET ART SPRAYED IN CAPITAL**

2 **More kids attacked in mobile thefts**

3 **GUN CONTROLS FAILING, SAYS POLICE CHIEF**

4 **Gang linked to 500 break-ins**

5 **VEHICLE THEFT COST £800M**

2 ⓹18 Listen to the interview. Which crimes are mentioned?

3 ⓹18 Listen again. According to the minister, are these statements true or false?

1 The chance of being a victim of crime has fallen by 40% in the last ten years.   ....T....

2 Peter Miles appointed a new head of the police service.   ....

3 The government has spent a lot of money on CCTV.   ....

4 The government copied the *Make Amends* scheme from another country.   ....

5 More people get mugged now than ten years ago.   ....

6 More people sell drugs now than ten years ago.   ....

7 The figures in the report are completely accurate.   ....

8 Violent crime is on the increase.   ....

4 ⓹18 Listen again and complete these extracts with the exact words used in the
recording.

1 Yes, indeed, I was delighted when I .... the figures.

2 This has meant that a much higher proportion of offenders .... during
the last ten years than ever before.

3 People .... less graffiti in city centres, for example.

4 These .... a particular target for street robbers.

5 Well, it's certainly true that more people .... selling drugs.

6 If I can give a personal example, my house .... only last week.

Are the verbs you have written in an active form or a passive form?

B Grammar

1 Using the passive

*The government **has published** a report today.* (active: focus on *the government*)
*A report **has been published** by the government today.* (passive: focus on *a report*)
(▷ See Appendix 13.1 for the main passive verb forms and Unit 23 for passives with introductory **it**,
e.g. *It is claimed that ...*)

We often use passive verbs
- when the agent (the person or thing that performs the action) is not known:
  *My house **was broken into** only last week.*
- when the agent is 'people in general':
  *The details **can be found** at the back of the report.* (= anyone can find these details)
- when the agent is unimportant, or is obvious:
  *A much higher proportion of offenders **have been arrested**.* (= the agent is clearly the police)
- when we don't want to say who the agent is:
  *It may be that some minor mistakes **were made** in collecting the figures.* (= she might not want
  to say who was responsible for the mistakes)
- to describe procedures or processes, focusing on what was done rather than who did it:
  *The figures **were collected** over a ten-year period.*
- to avoid repeating the agent in a description or narrative:
  *The police have made good use of CCTV. **It's been introduced** into many city centres.* rather than
  The police have made good use of CCTV. The police have introduced it into many city centres.

In informal contexts we often use active sentences with a subject such as *people, somebody/
someone, something, we, they* or *you* even when we do not know who the agent is. In more
formal contexts we often use a passive to avoid mentioning an agent:
*People **are seeing** less graffiti in city centres.* or more formally *Less graffiti **is being seen** ...*

Some verbs describing states (e.g. *have, become, seem*) are not usually made passive:
*Other countries **have** a similar policy.* (**not** ~~A similar policy is had by other countries.~~)
⚠ Other verbs describing states can be passive (e.g. *intend, know, own*):
*Our latest poster campaign **is intended** to reassure people.*
(▷ See Appendix 13.2 and 13.3.)

2 Active and passive verb forms

Compare these passive forms of active verb patterns.

Active	Passive
*They **started to keep** records ten years ago.* (▷ See Appendix 13.4.)	*Records **started to be kept** only ten years ago.*
*This figure is expected to fall as **they start using** new technology to trace stolen phones.* (▷ See Appendix 13.5.)	*This figure is expected to fall rapidly as **new technology starts being used** to trace stolen mobiles.*

They **made** them **repair** the damage.
(▷ See Appendix 13.6.)

People found guilty of vandalism **are made to repair** the damage they've caused.

The police **caught** them **selling** drugs.
(▷ See Appendix 13.7.)

More people **were caught selling** drugs.

We **expect** the figure **to fall** rapidly.
We **want** the crime rate **to fall** still further.
(▷ See Appendix 13.8 and 13.9.)

This figure **is expected to fall** rapidly.

Other verbs in this pattern have no passive:
(**not** ~~The crime rate is wanted to fall still further.~~)

Perfect forms are also possible:
More people **claim to have been** the victims of crime.
More people **have been caught selling** drugs this year than ever before.
This figure **is expected to have fallen** by next year.

Most passives with modal verbs are formed with modal + *be* + past participle or modal + *have been* + past participle:
The reason for this **can be found** in the huge increase in the number of mobile phones.
Some of the fall **might have been caused** by lower rates of reporting. (past)

3 Passive forms of verbs with two objects

START POINT

I was delighted when our crime statistics department **gave me the figures**. (active)
I was delighted when I **was given the figures** by our Crime Statistics Department. (passive) or
I was delighted when **the figures were given (to) me** by our Crime Statistics Department. (passive)
(▷ See Unit 9.)

Verbs followed by object + complement in the active have one passive form:
Attitudes to committing crime have changed significantly since Peter Miles **was appointed** head of the police service.
(▷ See Appendix 13.10.)

4 *get* + past participle; *get / have* + object + past participle

START POINT

It's true that more people **get mugged** today than they did ten years ago. or ... **are mugged** ...
People think more carefully about committing a crime if they know they **might get caught**. or ... **might be caught**.
Particularly in speech, we can use **get** + past participle instead of **be** + past participle.

Get + past participle is most commonly used to talk about events we see as unwelcome (e.g. *get mugged*). However, we can also use it with events the speaker sees as positive:
When we **got elected** ten years ago ...

We don't use *get* + past participle with verbs describing states:
*He **was known** to be a highly effective senior police officer.* (**not** ~~He got known to be~~ ...)

We can use either *have* + object + past participle or (more informally) *get* + object + past participle:
- to say that someone arranges for someone else to do something for them:
  *Virtually every person in my road **has had**/**got** a burglar alarm **fitted** recently.*
- to say that something unexpected, and usually unpleasant, happens to someone:
  *I **had** my TV and stereo **taken**.* or very informally *I **got** my TV and stereo **taken**.*

We can use a reflexive pronoun with *get* (not *have*) to suggest that the subject was responsible for the event:
*People will think more carefully about committing a crime if they know they're going to **get themselves arrested**.*

C Grammar exercises

1 **Complete these texts with the appropriate form, active or passive, of the verb.**
   A
   Acupuncture **(1)** has been practised.. *(practise)* in China for over 3000 years, and today
   it **(2)** .... *(widely use)* alongside conventional medicine. In traditional
   Chinese medicine, no symptom **(3)** .... *(view)* in isolation. Instead, the
   body and the mind **(4)** .... *(evaluate)* together. The goal of acupuncture
   (5) .... *(be)* to create harmony in the body by restoring the flow of
   Qi (pronounced 'chee'). This **(6)** .... *(consider)* to be the life force
   involved in all body functions. Qi **(7)** .... *(collect)* in the organs and
   (8) .... *(travel)* through energy channels in the body. Acupuncturists
   (9) .... *(believe)* that diseases **(10)** .... *(occur)* when the
   circulation of Qi **(11)** .... *(prevent)*, whether by injuries, heat, cold or other
   factors. By redirecting the flow of Qi, acupuncture can **(12)** .... *(help)* cure
   disease.

B

The first mobile phones **(1)** .... *(construct)* in Stockholm in the 1950s – but were not very mobile! They could only **(2)** .... *(use)* in cars because the receiver and transmitter **(3)** .... *(weigh)* over 40 kilos and had to **(4)** .... *(carry)* in the boot. But technology **(5)** .... *(advance)* so quickly that by the 1990s mobiles could **(6)** .... *(hold)* in the hand and people talking on their mobiles **(7)** .... *(become)* a familiar sight everywhere from trains to restaurants. Of course, not everyone welcomed mobiles, and in the mid-1990s their use **(8)** .... *(ban)* from many schools to prevent children using them in classrooms. Even recent research which **(9)** .... *(suggest)* that prolonged exposure to emissions from mobiles might be a health hazard **(10)** .... *(not discourage)* their use, and analysts now **(11)** .... *(predict)* that by 2025, 95% of all electronic communication **(12)** .... *(conduct)* by mobile phone.

2 Write passive sentences with a similar meaning to the first. Start with the word(s) given and use the verb in italics. In some cases, the passive is not possible.

1 They *paid* him a million dollars to appear in the film.
   He was paid a million dollars to appear in the film.

2 His name is Robin, but his friends *call* him Bobby.
   His name is Robin, but ....

3 Dr Davies *demonstrated* the procedure to us in the chemistry lab.
   We ....

4 The managing director *will announce* the news to staff later today.
   The news ....

5 They have *offered* me a new job in Hungary.
   I ....

6 People *saw* him push the goalkeeper just before he scored.
   He ....

7 The medical staff *have* declared the surgery a complete success.
   The surgery ....

8 We *watched* the rescuers pull the man from the sea.
   The rescuers ....

9 My English teacher *suggested* the idea to me.
   I ....

10 My uncle *bought* me this necklace when he was in Zimbabwe.
   This necklace ....

3 Complete the conversations using the pairs of verbs in the box. Use *be* + past participle, *get* + (object) + past participle, or *have* + (object) + past participle. Add the object in brackets where this is supplied and give alternatives where possible.

own – break into   ~~rob~~ – steal   cut – clean   catch – infect   wake up – throw out

1 A: Did you hear about Natasha?

   B: What happened?

   A: She _was / got robbed_ on her way to college.

   B: No! Is she okay?

   A: Yes, she's fine, but she .... *(her handbag)*

2 A: You're looking tired.

   B: I .... early by my neighbour's dog.

   A: Don't they keep it inside at night?

   B: Usually, yes, but I think it must .... because it was barking so much.

3 A: James looked different somehow.

   B: He'd .... *(his hair)*

   A: Yes, and I think he'd .... It looked much smarter! *(his jacket)*

4 A: What an amazing house!

   B: It .... by Jason Norman. You know, the rock singer.

   A: I know him, yes.

   B: The problem is, he's never there, and it keeps ....

5 A: What happened to your coat?

   B: I .... on some barbed wire as I was climbing over a fence. I hurt my arm, too. *(it)*

   A: Ouch. That looks nasty. You ought to go to the doctor. It might ....

4 **Rewrite the underlined part of the sentence using a passive form where possible. If it is not possible, write 'No passive'.**

1 When <u>they invited Malcolm to give</u> the main presentation at the conference he was delighted and wrote immediately to accept.

   Malcolm was invited to give ....

2 During our military training <u>they made us run</u> five kilometres before breakfast.

   ....

3 Sandra felt that the pay and conditions at Trimco were unsatisfactory, and <u>many of her colleagues seemed to support her</u>.

   ....

4 <u>We wanted Barbara to come</u> to the party.

   ....

5 I still have only a very vague memory of the explosion. I <u>remember someone asking me</u> to leave the building because there was a gas leak, but not much after that.

   ....

6 She was really unhappy <u>that they hadn't picked her</u> for the team.

   ....

7 Although at first the children were frightened by Mr Jennings' strictness, after a few weeks <u>most of the children in the class came to like him</u>.

   ....

8 <u>They caught him trying</u> to break into an expensive sports car.

   ....

9 More than anything else, our cat <u>likes people tickling him</u> behind the ears.

   ....

10 My children impressed me yesterday. They did all the washing and ironing <u>without anyone asking them</u>.

   ....

11 <u>Someone heard her remark</u> that Nicholas was too old for the job.

   ....

12 Henry performed badly in the last match, and <u>we need him to play better this week</u>.

   ....

13 <u>People expect over 100,000 demonstrators to march</u> through the capital in protest against the government's decision to go to war.

   ....

D Exam practice

This exercise tests grammar from the rest of the book as well as the grammar in this unit.

Reading

You are going to read a newspaper article. Six paragraphs have been removed. Choose from the paragraphs **A–G** the one which fits each gap **1–6**. There is one extra paragraph which you do not need to use.

Alexander McCall Smith: Terrible Orchestra?

Bestselling author Alexander McCall Smith explains why he started a band for useless musicians

There are two emotions a parent can feel when watching the school orchestra perform. One is pride – the most common emotion in the circumstances – and the other is envy. Wouldn't it have been great fun to be in a school orchestra and now… it's too late. Or is it?

1

These musical islands are full of amateur orchestras, but most of these are really rather good. We wanted something that would cater for those who really were very weak players, those who might have got as far as Grade 4 on their instruments and hovered around that level for years. So we formed the Really Terrible Orchestra in Edinburgh, a city known for having a number of fine amateur orchestras. The name was carefully chosen: what it said was what you would get.

2

Those who joined generally lived up to the name. Some, though, stood out for their musical weakness. One cello player some years ago even had the notes played by the open strings written in pencil on the bridge of the instrument. Another – a clarinetist – had had only three or four lessons and could not go above the middle B flat. He played only the bottom notes, and not very well.

3

Our heads turned, we decided to hold a concert at the Edinburgh Festival Fringe. The important thing about the Fringe is that anybody can perform, with the result that there are always a certain number of appalling performances which attract tiny audiences.

4

The fortunes of the orchestra continued to improve, even if its playing did not. We presumed to make two CDs, which somehow got into the hands of radio stations abroad. We have now been played more than once by the Australian Broadcasting Corporation, by the Canadian Broadcasting Corporation, and by National Public Radio in the United States.

5

Even if the orchestra never gets to New York, that will be enough. Of course New York was where the famous Florence Foster Jenkins would appear, at the Carnegie Hall, and torture her audience with her terrible singing. Perhaps it's ready for an orchestra that will live up to her.

6

Which makes one wonder: what is it that makes people want to listen to a group of extremely bad musicians torturing a piece that most of them cannot play? Is there something about failure and its cheerful acceptance? Whatever it is, there's certainly something quintessentially British about it. And the orchestra does a very fine 'Land of Hope and Glory' – a semitone flat.

A The response was overwhelming, particularly from clarinetists. I suspect that a very high proportion of the population is exposed to the clarinet at some stage and that British attics are crammed full of forgotten clarinet cases. Many of these were dusted off for the first meeting of the Really Terrible Orchestra, as were various other instruments. We appointed a professional conductor, Richard Neville Towle, a well-known Edinburgh musician and founder of the ensemble Ludus Baroque, and we began to rehearse. The result was cacophony.

B The Really Terrible Orchestra, however, was an immediate hit. The concert sold out well in advance, as it has done every year since, attracting an audience of more than 500 people, some not actually related to the players.

C 'We are pretty awful,' admitted one of the bassoonists. There is a very wide range of playing abilities, she added, noting that she herself had only passed Grade 3, the examination normally taken by 11-year-old British schoolchildren.

D Eight years ago my wife and I decided that we would do something about never having played in the school orchestra. We are both very challenged musicians: at the time she played the flute – hesitantly – and I played the bassoon – extremely incompetently.

E Now what has become the world's most famous amateur orchestra is about to perform in London. The Cadogan Hall is the site of this imminent musical disaster, and all 800 tickets vanished in a trice.

F An orchestra needs to perform, and we decided to hold a concert. Wisely, we took the view that the audience should be given a glass of wine, or even more than a glass, before the concert. This assisted their enjoyment and understanding of our idiosyncratic performance. Virtually every piece we played was greeted with shouts of applause and a standing ovation.

G The orchestra's fame spread. Earlier this year the *New York Times*, for a mention in which many professional musicians would sell their souls, devoted a quarter of a page to an article about the Really Terrible Orchestra. A few days after the appearance of the article the orchestra's chairman, Peter Stevenson, received an approach from the same New York impresario who had first taken the Beatles to the US.

Without looking back at the text, complete the sentences with an appropriate form (active or passive) of the verb in brackets.

1 Eight years ago my wife and I .... that we would do something about never having played in the school orchestra. *(decide)*

2 I suspect that a very high proportion of the population .... to the clarinet at some stage ... *(expose)*

3 We .... a professional conductor, Richard Neville Towle, ... *(appoint)*

4 This .... their enjoyment and understanding of our idiosyncratic performance. *(assist)*

5 Virtually every piece we played .... with shouts of applause and a standing ovation. *(greet)*

6 ... there are always a certain number of appalling performances which .... tiny audiences. *(attract)*

7 The concert .... well in advance, as it has done every year since, ... *(sell out)*

8 We have now .... more than once by the Australian Broadcasting Corporation, ... *(play)*

9 Now what .... the world's most famous amateur orchestra is about to perform in London. *(become)*

Writing

The following extracts are taken from letters to a national newspaper on the subject of the importance of university education. You decide to write a letter responding to the points raised and giving your own views.

... University shouldn't be for the rich elite alone. Students from all backgrounds should be encouraged to go. ...

... The country doesn't need large numbers of university-educated students. Over the next few years we are likely to see more and more graduates who are unemployed or who work in unskilled jobs. ...

... Your correspondent Mr Smithers (12th July) is wrong. It is actually in *everyone's* interest to contribute to universities. Universities need money, and this must come from the whole of society. ...

... Creating a pool of university-educated people contributes enormously to our economic development and to producing knowledgeable leaders of our society. ...

Write your **letter** in **300–350** words. Do not write any postal addresses.

Writing hints

This task gives you a chance to practise using a variety of passive forms:
are learned, are expected to pay, are being asked to fund, are being educated, will be left behind

Useful language
graduate (verb), a graduate, skilled / unskilled jobs, I am writing in response to, the opinion was expressed

19

Reporting

structures in the reported clause – *that-* clause, *to-*infinitive and *-ing*; verb tense in reporting; modal verbs in reporting; reporting questions; *should* in *that-* clauses; present subjunctive

1 If you lived close to an airport, what problems would you be most concerned about?

2 ⊙ 19a There are plans to expand the small airport near the village where Kath and James live. Kath has been to a meeting to discuss the plans, and she tells James about it. Listen to their conversation. Identify three advantages and three problems of the airport expansion that were mentioned at the meeting.

3 ⊙ 19a Listen again and complete these extracts with the words you hear.

1 They ....*told us that*.... the expansion would create 2000 jobs directly.

2 They .... a growing number of people in the local area supported the expansion.

3 They .... us informed about future developments.

4 They .... there and look at the plans in detail.

5 She .... the airport authorities were not telling the truth.

6 She .... to our local politicians with our objections.

7 She also suggested inviting the Minister for Transport to hear our complaints. I .... to her.

4 Put the past tense verbs you have written in one of the columns according to the pattern that follows them. Which one of the verbs can also be followed by one of the other patterns?

verb + *that-* clause	verb + *to-*infinitive	verb + object + *that-* clause	verb + object + *to-*infinitive
		told	

B Grammar

START POINT

We often report in our own words what people think or
what they have said:

> There will be a
> public enquiry.

Reporting clause ⟶ ⟨*Mr Kelly announced*⟩ ⟨*that there would be a public enquiry.*⟩ ⟶ Reported clause
with reporting
verb

1 Structures in the reported clause: *that*- clause

Reporting verbs can be followed by a number of structures in the reported clause. The most
important ones with *that*- clauses are given below. (⯈ See Appendix 14.)

- verb + *that* (⯈ See Appendix 14.1.)

  *Sue **reckoned that** the expansion would damage tourism.*
  *I **agree that** the plans will change the area.*
- verb + object + that (⯈ See Appendix 14.2.)

  *He **convinced me that** noise wouldn't be a problem for us.* (**not** ~~He convinced that noise wouldn't~~
  ~~be a problem for us.~~)
- verb + (object) + *that* (⯈ See Appendix 14.3.)

  *She **warned (us) that** the airport authorities were not telling the truth.*

Compare the use of *tell* and *say* in the reported clause:

*They **told us that** the expansion would create around 2000 jobs.* (*tell* + object + *that*)
*They **said (to us) that** it might increase tourism in the region.* (*say* + (*to* + object) + *that*)

- verb + *that* or verb + object + *to*-infinitive (⯈ See Appendix 14.4.)

  *I **found that** his reassurances were quite convincing.* or more formally
  *I **found his reassurances to be** quite convincing.*
- verb + (*to / with* + object) + *that* (⯈ See Appendix 14.5.)

  *They **admitted (to us) that** they're not sure exactly how many people it will attract.*
  *I **agree (with the anti-expansion group) that** the plans will change the area.*

We often leave out *that* in informal contexts, particularly with the most common reporting
verbs (e.g. *reckon, say, tell, think*). However, we don't usually leave it out if the *that*- clause
doesn't immediately follow the verb:

*Sue **reckoned (that)** the expansion would actually damage tourism.*
*I **agree** with the anti-expansion group **that** the plans will change the area.*

2 Structures in the reported clause: *to*-infinitive and *-ing*

These are the most important structures with a *to*-infinitive or *-ing* form in the reported clause:

- verb + *to*-infinitive (▷ See Appendix 14.6.)
  I've decided to wait and see what happens next.
- verb + object + *to*-infinitive (▷ See Appendix 14.7.)
  They encouraged us to go to the village hall.
- verb + (object) + *to*-infinitive (▷ See Appendix 14.8.)
  I expected them to be confrontational. or
  I expected to hear more objections.
- *verb + to*-infinitive or *verb + that* (▷ See Appendix 14.9.)
  They promised to keep us informed. or *They promised that they would keep us informed.*
- verb + object + *to*-infinitive or verb + object + *that* (▷ See Appendix 14.10.)
  She advised us to write to our local politicians with our objections. or
  She advised us that we should write to our local politicians with our objections.
- verb + *-ing* or verb + *that* (▷ See Appendix 14.11.)
  She suggested inviting the Minister for Transport to hear our complaints. or
  She suggested that we should invite the Minister for Transport (**not** *She suggested to invite* ...)

3 Verb tense in reporting

START POINT

When reporting, we often change the tense that was in the original.
'The airport authorities are not telling the truth.' → *She warned that the airport authorities were not telling the truth.*
'We carried out the trial flights last month.' → *Mr Kelly said that they had carried out the trial flights last month.* or *Mr Kelly said that they carried out* ...

We don't usually change a past perfect verb:
'We had hoped for more support.' → *He said they had hoped for more support.*

We can use a present tense verb for a situation that still exists when we report it:
James said he's worried about the nuclear power station on the coast. or *... said he was worried ...*

We usually use a past tense in the reporting clause. However, we can use the present simple to report current news or views, what is always said or what many people say:
I hear that Boeing 737s will be landing there.
Everyone I've spoken to thinks it's awful.

4 Modal verbs in reporting

A modal verb in the original sometimes changes in the report.
- *will* changes to *would*, *can* to *could*, and *may* usually changes to *might*:
  'It may increase tourism in the area.' → *They said it might increase tourism in the region.*

However, if the situation we are reporting still exists or is in the future, modals don't change if there is a present tense verb in the reporting clause:

'We'll be displaying copies of the plans in the village hall.' → They **say** they**'ll** be putting copies of the plans in the village hall.

We can use either form if there is a past tense verb in the reporting clause:

*'The expansion **will** create 2000 jobs.'* → They **told** us that the expansion **will** / **would** create around 2000 jobs.

- *shall* changes to *would* to talk about the future, and to *should* to report suggestions, recommendations and requests for advice:
  *'I **shall** decide later.'* → He said he **would** decide later.
  *'What **shall** we do next?'* → He asked what they **should** do next.
- *must* doesn't change or changes to *had to* when it is used to say it is necessary to do something:
  *'You **must** look at the plans before making any decisions.'* → He said I **must** / **had to** look at the plans before making any decisions.
  Had to is more natural in speech.
- *could, should, would, might, ought to* and *used to* don't usually change in the report:
  *'We **ought to** write to our local politicians.'* → She suggested we **ought** to write to our local politicians.

5 Reporting questions

'What are your views on this?' → They asked **what** our views were. **or** They asked (for) our views.
'Have you got any more questions?' → They wanted to know **if** / **whether** we had any more questions.
(▷ See Unit 16 on the choice between **whether** and **if**.)

The usual word order in the reported *wh-*, *if-* or *whether-* clause is the one we would use in a statement, and we don't use a question mark or the *do* auxiliary:

'How exactly will it boost tourism?' → I asked how exactly it would boost tourism.
'Where did you get your figures from?' → She asked where they had got their figures from.

We can use a negative form of *do* to report a negative question:

*'Why **don't** you want the airport to expand?'* → He asked why I **didn't** want the airport to expand.

If the original question begins *what, which* or *who*, followed by *be* + complement, we can put the complement before or after *be* in the report:

'Who's Sue Ray?' → He asked who Sue Ray was. **or** He asked who was Sue Ray.

To report a question with *should* asking for advice or information, we can use a *to*-infinitive:

*'What **should** we do to protest?'* → Someone asked Sue what **to do** to protest. **or** ... what we **should** do to protest.

⚠ We don't use a *to*-infinitive to report a *why* question:

'Why should we believe them?' → She wanted to know why we should believe them. (**not** ~~She wanted to know why to believe them.~~)

6 *Should* in *that-* clauses; the present subjunctive

We sometimes use *should* + bare infinitive or *should* + *be* + past participle (passive) in a *that-*clause to report advice, orders, requests and suggestions about things that are desirable or need to be done:

*I suggested **that** she **should contact** our MP.* (= suggestion)
*She demanded **that** we **should be shown** the details of the flight paths.* (= order)
*They urged **that** the expansion plans **should not be rejected**.* (= advice)

⚠ We don't use this pattern to report statements with other functions:
She warned us that the airport authorities were not telling the truth. (= warning) (**not** ~~He warned us that the airport authorities should not be telling the truth.~~)

In formal contexts, we can often leave out *should* and use only the bare infinitive or *be* + past participle (the present subjunctive):

*I suggested that she **contact** our MP.*
*They urged that the expansion plans **not be rejected**.*
(▷ See Appendix 14.12.)

C Grammar exercises

1 Complete the sentences with an appropriate form of the reporting verbs in the box. Add a preposition or pronoun if necessary.

> check   claim   commiserate   emphasise   explain
> grumble   persuade   reassure   reveal   whisper

1 Before I parked my car outside Frank's house, I ....*checked with*..... him that this would be okay.

2 It took a long time to feed all the customers, and by the time we got around to the last ones they .... that their food was cold. But I just ignored their complaints.

3 I know that Philip enjoys his work as a gardener, but when he .... to be the best job in the world, I wasn't sure whether he was being serious or not.

4 The company hadn't paid me for the work I'd done for them, but when I phoned, they .... that a cheque was on its way.

5 Carlson didn't want to speak to the police yet. He didn't want to .... anyone that he knew who the murderer was until he had concrete evidence.

6 When Teresa handed me the report she said that it was only a first draft. She .... that it should remain confidential until the statistics had been verified.

7 Just before I stood up to make my speech, my friend Jenny came up close and
   .... me that my shirt was hanging out at the back.

8 Terry said that he was going to re-paint the car himself, but I managed to
   .... that this was a bad idea and that he should get it done
   professionally.

9 When I heard about her disastrous job interview, I phoned Martha to
   .... her.

10 At first, the security guard stopped me going in, but when I .... him
    that I had an appointment with someone in the building, he let me through the
    barrier.

2 Stephen is an engineering student who has applied for a job when he leaves university.
Complete these extracts from Stephen's letter of application using the notes in
brackets. Use a *that-*, *to*-infinitive or *-ing* clause in your answer and give alternatives
where possible.

Dear Mr Clarke,

I am writing with reference to the post of Senior Research
Engineer advertised in Engineering Monthly. I assume
(1) that the post is / the post to be (*the post*) still vacant.
My supervisor, Professor Ken Newton, has advised
(2) .... (*apply*) and has assured **(3)** ....
(*my research*), which is described in detail in the attached papers,
will be of interest to you.
I expect **(4)** .... (*complete*) my PhD by the end of
the year, and I propose **(5)** .... (*publish*) the findings
of my research soon afterwards. I believe **(6)** ....
(*my qualifications and experience*) appropriate for the post.
I hope **(7)** .... (*hear*) from you in the near future.

Yours sincerely,

Stephen Finch

Stephen Finch

Stephen got an interview, but wasn't offered the job. Complete his account of the interview to his supervisor.

'They asked **(8)** .... (*explain*) the main purposes of my research.
I **(9)** .... (*tell*) I was working on a new hydrogen fuel cell. I admitted
(10) .... (*have problems*) in the early stages of the work. They were very
helpful. They suggested **(11)** .... (*look at*) Chris Hume's work at the University
of Harford. They agreed **(12)** .... (*me / my research*) has many practical
applications. They even invited **(13)** .... (*visit*) their laboratories if it would
help in my research.

Although they didn't offer me the job, they recommended **(14)** .... (*write*)
to them again after I've finished my PhD, and in the meantime they agreed
(15) .... (*contact*) if any other similar jobs come up. Of course, they couldn't
guarantee **(16)** .... (*offer*) a job in the future, but they were very encouraging.'

3 **Change the sentences into reported speech. Give alternative tenses where possible.**

1 'I broke my leg when I was skiing.' → She said ..(that) she broke / had broken her leg.. ..when she was skiing. .

2 'It's going to rain later today.' → He thinks .... later today.

3 'Why don't you walk to school any more?' → She asked me ....

4 'I don't think this is my coat.' → She didn't think ....

5 'Diane can speak six languages.' He said ....

6 'Are you going to college next year?' → She asked .... next year.

7 'You must set the alarm when you leave the house.' → She said ....

8 'Who was your favourite teacher when you were at school?' → She asked me
.... when I was at school.

9 'Where have I left my handbag?' → She couldn't remember ....

10 'I'm playing football this afternoon.' → He said .... yesterday afternoon.

11 'I won't be able to give you a lift after all.' → He said .... , so I'll have to
take a taxi.

12 'How much do you earn?' → He wanted to know ....

13 'We might go to France again in the summer.' → She mentioned .... in
the summer.

14 'What shall I do with this painting?' → He wanted to know ....

4 The organisation *Stop Poverty!* campaigns for more aid and fairer trade for developing countries. Report these items from a speech made by its leader.

Use a *that-* clause which includes, if possible, a present subjunctive.

> 1 ~~Double aid!~~

> 2 Cancel the debt of African nations!

> 3 Millions of people are being cheated of a proper living!

> 4 Focus aid on basic healthcare and education!

> 5 The current trading rules are not fair!

> 6 Allow poorer countries to trade as equals!

> 7 Don't rewrite trade rules to favour richer countries!

> 8 Help developing countries to expand their own industries!

> 9 *Stop Poverty!* is to launch a new public awareness campaign!

1 She proposed *that aid be doubled* .
2 She demanded ....
3 She argued ....
4 She recommended ....
5 She said ....
6 She urged ....
7 She insisted ....
8 She advised ....
9 She announced ....

D Exam practice

This exercise tests grammar from the rest of the book as well as the grammar in this unit.

Listening

(🎧 19b) You will hear two professional photographers, Alan and Maggie, talking about various aspects of their work. Decide whether the opinions are expressed by only one of the speakers or whether the speakers both express the opinion.

Write   **A**   for Alan,

         M   for Maggie,

or   **B**   for Both.

---

1   Studio photography is more predictable than landscape photography.

2   Careful preparation can make people look unnatural in photographs.

3   Photographers have to be good communicators.

4   Not having a formal training can be an advantage.

5   I welcome criticism of my photographs.

6   Digital technology has had a negative impact on photography.

Grammar focus task

In these extracts from the discussion, are either of the alternative endings also correct? Write 'yes' or 'no' next to each option.

1   My art teacher suggested *that I go along.*
   a ... me to go along.
   b ... that I should go along.

2   I encourage *them to look at the location in a different way.*
   a ... that they look at the location in a different way.
   b ... to look at the location in a different way.

3   Cartier-Bresson claimed *that photography is a way of life.*
   a ... photography to be a way of life.
   b ... it that photography is a way of life.

4   It's great when people consider *that an exhibition of mine is a success.*
   a ... it that an exhibition of mine is a success.
   b ... an exhibition of mine to be a success.

5   A colleague of mine persuaded *me to switch to a digital camera.*
   a ... that I switch to a digital camera.
   b ... to switch to a digital camera.

Writing

Your company sent five senior managers to a language school in Britain this year to improve their English. Read this message from your Director, on which you have made some notes, and the comments made by the managers. Use this information to write a report for your Director.

Weekend trips interesting (e.g. London, Oxford). Evening social events arranged by students.

Excellent teaching. Course too short.

Now that the managers are back from their English course, I'd like you to get some feedback from them. Can you please prepare a report covering:

Stayed with local families. Very friendly. Food awful!

- quality of the teaching and accommodation
- social activities
- problems

3 weeks too short (even with 25 hours of tuition per week).

Add your recommendation on whether we should repeat the exercise with the same school next year. Was it good value for money?

Had to pay for books, weekend trips, etc. Expensive.

Thanks.

School disorganised e.g. Kept changing our classrooms.

3 weeks.

£780 per person per week.

Write your **report** in **180–220** words.

Writing hints

This task gives you the chance to practise reporting, particularly in sentences with *that-* clauses:

The managers said that the teaching was excellent.
One participant complained that the food wasn't very good.
Some participants noted that the school was rather disorganised.

20

Substitution and ellipsis

*one/ones; so + auxiliary verb + subject; **neither, nor, not ...**
either; do so; leaving out words after auxiliary verbs and after **to***

A Context listening

1 You are going to listen to two college friends talking about adventure holidays. What activities are shown in these pictures?

2 〔 20a〕 Listen to the conversation. Which of these items does Alison advise Ben to take with him?

air tanks for scuba diving   cooking equipment for camping   a face mask
insect repellent   leather trainers   a life jacket   plastic trainers
a sleeping bag   a snorkel   a sun hat   a tent

3 〔 20a〕 Listen again. Change these sentences to show exactly what Alison or Ben said.

                     one

1 I went for the ~~adventure holiday~~ based in Brisbane.

2 One of the local organisers met me at the airport.

3 They should provide all the equipment.

4 But you don't have to be a very good swimmer.

5 Preferably plastic trainers.

6 By the end of the holiday I was exhausted, but I was very fit!

7 You'll certainly need some insect repellent.

8 I don't imagine you'll need to take a tent and cooking things.

B Grammar

Substitution

1 *one / ones*

They do diving holidays in quite a few places. I went for the **one** *based in Brisbane.* (**one** = *diving holiday*; one replaces a singular countable noun or a noun phrase)
Take a couple of pairs of old trainers – preferably plastic **ones**. (**ones** = *trainers*; ones replaces a plural noun)

We don't usually use *one / ones*:
- to replace an uncountable noun. Instead we use *some*:
  Don't forget insect repellent. You'll certainly need **some**. (**not** ... ~~need one.~~)
- to talk about a specific item. Compare:
  Do you know anyone who's got a sleeping bag? I was hoping to borrow **one**.
  Have you still got your sleeping bag? Can I borrow **it**? (= a particular sleeping bag)
- after *the*, unless it is followed by an adjective:
  'Are these your trainers?' 'No, **the leather ones** *are mine.'*
  or unless there is a descriptive phrase after *one / ones*:
  They had a number of adventure holidays on offer, and I chose **the one that was cheapest**.
  I went for **the one based in Brisbane.**
- after a possessive adjective (e.g. *my*). Instead we prefer a possessive pronoun (e.g. *mine*), or a phrase with an adjective:
  You can borrow **mine**. *or You can borrow* **my old one.** *rather than You can borrow my one.*
  ⚠ *one / ones* is sometimes used after a possessive adjective in informal speech.

We don't usually use *ones* on its own to replace a noun phrase. Compare:
'You'll need trainers.' 'Okay, I'll bring **some**. *or I'll bring some* **old ones**.' (**not** ~~I'll bring ones.~~)

We can either include or leave out *one / ones* after *which, whichever*; superlatives; *either, neither, another, each* (but not *every*); *the first/second/last; the other; this, that, these, those*; and often after colour adjectives:
'I can't decide whether to go on the adventure holiday to Thailand or Australia.' 'I'm sure you'll enjoy **whichever (one)** *you go on.'*
Get your own facemask. Buy **the best (one)** *you can afford.*
I've had three holidays with TransWorld Adventures, but **the first (one)** *was the best.*
I've got these two sleeping bags, but **this (one)** *is rather dirty.* (*these ones* and *those ones* are only used in informal speech.)
We had two small boats to practise sailing in. One was green and the **other (one)** *was red. I used to sail in the* **green (one)**.

2 *so* + auxiliary verb + subject; *neither, nor, not ... either*

START POINT

'Was diving as difficult as you expected?' 'Perhaps even more so.' (**so** = *difficult*; replaces an adjective)
TransWorld Adventures provides all the equipment – at least I presume so. (**so** = *TransWorld Adventures provides all the equipment*; replaces a clause)

We can use *so* instead of a clause after certain verbs to do with opinions (e.g. *expect, suppose, think*), but not after others (e.g. *accept, know, be sure*):
*'Will I be met at the airport?' 'I **expect so**.'*
'Apparently, the mozzies are really bad at that time of year.' 'I've heard that, too.' (**not** *I've heard so, too.*)
(▷ See Appendix 15.1.)

Some verbs are commonly used before *not* or in *not ... so* in short, negative replies:
*'You won't need a sleeping bag if it's really hot.' 'I **suppose not**.'* or *'No, I **don't suppose so**.'*
Other verbs like this include: *appear, seem; believe, expect, imagine, think*. (With the last four verbs we prefer *not ... so* in informal contexts):
*'Do you think I'll need to take a tent and cooking things?' 'I **don't imagine so**.'* or formally
*'I **imagine not**.'*

Before *not* we can use *be afraid* (= showing regret), *assume, guess, hope, presume, suspect*:
*'Do they offer any holidays in Africa?' 'I**'m afraid not**.* (**not** *I'm not afraid so.*)

We can use *so* + pronoun + auxiliary verb in a short answer to say that we can see that something is true, now that we have been told, particularly if it surprises us:
*'It mentions a holiday in Tasmania here on their website.' 'Let's see ... **So it does**.'* (= I can see it now that you have told me)
*'It says on their website that they run a holiday in Tasmania.' '**Yes**, it does. I noticed that this morning.'* (= I knew that before you told me) (**not** *So it does.*)

We can use *so* in a similar way (implying 'I knew before you told me') in short answers with verbs such as *appear* (after *it*), *believe, gather, hear, say, seem, tell, understand*:
*'Apparently the mozzies are really bad, particularly at the time of year you'll be going.' '**So I've heard**.'*

We can use *so* + auxiliary verb + subject to say that a second person does the same thing as the person already mentioned. In the negative we use *neither, nor*, or *not ... either*:
*'I'd like to go to Tasmania.' '**So would I**.'*
*'I'm not really a very good swimmer.' 'No, **neither am I**.'* or *'**Nor am I**.'* or *'I**'m not either**.'* or
*'I**'m not** a very good swimmer **either**.'*

3 *do so*

We can use a form of *do so* to replace a verb and the word or phrase that follows it to complete its meaning:

*When asked whether they intended to offer holidays in Africa, TransWorld Adventures said they had no plans to **do so**.* (*do so* = offer holidays in Africa)

*He planned to go to Australia this year, but now that he has lost his job he has little chance of **doing so**.* (*doing so* = going to Australia)

We can use *do so* where the verb describes an *action*, but avoid it with verbs that describe states and habitual actions:

*We went down the river by boat, and saw a lot of wildlife while **doing so**.*

*Some people didn't enjoy the hard work, but I **did**.* (**not** ~~but I did so~~ ...)

Do so is mainly used in formal contexts. Less formally, we use *do it* or *do that* with a similar meaning:

*We put up our tents by the side of the river. We **did that** at about four o'clock every afternoon.* **or** formally *We **did so** ...*

We use *do* (rather than *do so*) in informal English, especially after modals or perfect tenses:

*'Do they provide all the equipment?' 'They **should (do)**.'*

*'Could you have gone to Thailand instead?' 'Yes, I **could have (done)**.'*

⚠ We can often leave out *do*.

4 Ellipsis: leaving out words after auxiliary verbs and after *to*

START POINT

'Have you decided yet?' 'Yes, I have.' (= Yes, I have decided.)

A lot of people go to the Great Barrier Reef when they're in Australia. Were you able to? (= Were you able to go to the Great Barrier Reef?)

We often leave out or change verbs to avoid repeating them.

(▷ See Appendix 15.4.)

We can sometimes use *to* instead of a clause beginning with a *to*-infinitive when it is clear what we are talking about:

*I'd certainly like to go back to Australia. I hope **to** next year.* (= to go back to Australia)

We can use *to* or leave it out:
- after verbs such as *agree, promise, start*:
  *I want to read a lot about Australia before I go. I've **started (to)** already.*
  (▷ See Appendix 15.2.)
- after most nouns (e.g. *idea, opportunity*) and adjectives (e.g. *frightened, willing*) that can be followed by a *to*-infinitive clause:
  *I've always wanted to go, but I've never had the **chance (to)** before.*
  *I hope they don't ask us to swim if there are sharks around. I'd be **afraid (to)**.*
  (▷ See Appendix 15.2.)

- after *want* and *would like* in *if*-clauses and *wh*-clauses:
  *We must talk about it more. You can come over whenever you'**d like (to)**.*
  We don't use *to* after *like*:
  *You can come over whenever you **like**.*

We can use *to* but we can't leave it out:
- after verbs (e.g. *expect*, *mean*, *need*) which must have a complement:
  *You can borrow mine if you **need to**.*
  (▷ See Appendix 15.3.)
- after a negative:
  *You don't have to sail on your own if you do**n't want to**.*

When *have (got)* is a main verb in the first clause or sentence, we can often use either *have (got)* or *do* to avoid repetition in the following clause or sentence:
*Have you got a sleeping bag? I'm sure you **have**.* (= I'm sure you have got a sleeping bag.) or *I'm sure you **do**.* (= I'm sure you do have a sleeping bag.)
⚠ When *have* is followed by a noun to describe an action (e.g. *have a shower, have a shave, have a good time*) we usually use *do*:
*I wasn't really expecting to **have a good time**, but I **did**.*

When we use the verb *be* in the previous sentence or clause, the *to*-infinitive form of *be* is repeated in the next:
*'I**'m** not a very good swimmer.' 'You don't have **to be**.'* (**not** ~~You don't have to.~~)

C Grammar exercises

1 **Read the underlined parts of these dialogues. Cross out the words which can be left out.**

1 A: What was wrong with Sue?
  B: She was frightened, or at least she appeared <u>to be ~~frightened~~</u>.

2 A: You should have asked me. I could have given you a lift into town.
  B: Thanks, but I didn't like <u>to ask you</u>. I know how busy you are.

3 A: Has Sarah eaten anything today?
  B: No, I don't think she has <u>eaten anything today</u>.

4 A: My grandmother would have been shocked by all the changes in the village.
  B: Yes, I'm sure she <u>would have been shocked</u>.

5 A: Don't forget we're going out tonight. Can you leave work early?
  B: Okay, I'll try <u>to leave work early</u>.

6 A: Jackie's a vegetarian, isn't she?
  B: I'm not sure. I think she <u>might be a vegetarian</u>.

7 A: Why don't you come on holiday with us?
  B: I can't afford <u>to come on holiday with you</u>.

8 A: We could get to the island across the new bridge.
   B: But it hasn't been opened yet.
   A: I thought it <u>had been opened</u>.

9 A: I hope I get promoted this time.
   B: You certainly deserve <u>to get promoted</u>. You work really hard.

10 A: I didn't know you were getting married.
   B: Sorry. I thought you <u>did know I was getting married</u>.

2 **Replace the underlined word(s) with *one* or *ones* where possible. If it is possible to omit *one* or *ones*, put the words in brackets.**

1 A: Do you want one of these sweets?   B: Are there any green <u>sweets</u> *(ones)* left?
   B: No, they've all gone.

2 A: It's about time we got some new curtains.
   B: Okay, well, let's go out and buy <u>some new curtains</u>.

3 A: Which of these dresses do you think I should wear tonight?
   B: Actually, I like the <u>dress</u> you're wearing.

4 A: Have you spent all that money?   B: What money?
   A: The <u>money</u> you were given for your birthday.

5 A: I know it's muddy outside, but shall we go out for a walk?
   B: But I haven't got any wellies.   A: You can wear my old <u>wellies</u>.

6 A: To get to your house, do I take the first or second turning?
   B: You can take either <u>turning</u>.

7 A: Why did you buy those green apples?
   B: They were the cheapest <u>apples</u> I could find.

8 Have you seen the car keys? I can't find <u>the car keys</u> anywhere.

9 The mirror is like the <u>mirror</u> my parents have got in their sitting room.

10 This glass has got a crack in it. Have you got another <u>glass</u>?

11 I dropped my brother's mobile phone and had to buy him a new <u>mobile phone</u>.

12 A: Does this button turn the camera on?
   B: No, you want the <u>button</u> in the middle.

13 We've got chocolate biscuits or these <u>biscuits</u>. Which <u>biscuits</u> would you prefer?

3 Complete the sentences where possible with *so*, *do*, *do so* or *so do*, using an appropriate form of *do*. If it is not possible, suggest an alternative.

1 She stood up slowly, and was obviously in pain as she .... did so ....

2 A: Miller played really badly, didn't he?

   B: But .... the rest of the team.

3 A: Incredible storm last night. Look – the wind's blown that old tree down.

   B: .... it has. What a great shame!

4 A: Are you going to Spain again for your holidays?

   B: I might .... , I haven't decided yet.

5 Louise will be meeting us at the airport. At least, I hope ....

6 A: Apparently, Adam's dropped out of college.

   B: Yes, I'd heard .... , too.

7 A: They say it's going to snow tomorrow.

   B: .... I gather.

8 We do more or less the same job, but he earns much more than I ....

9 A: I see Jessica's sold her old car.

   B: .... she has. She told me she couldn't afford to run it any longer.

10 A: We can take a short cut if we wade across the stream.

   B: What's the point of .... ? The bridge isn't far.

11 He has yet to win a tournament, but he came close to .... in Monaco.

12 A: Do you really think she'll lend you the money?

   B: I'm sure ....

13 Megan loves horse riding, and .... Jim.

14 A: Great film, wasn't it?

   B: .... it was.

4 Improve this email by making changes to avoid repetition.

Hi Chris

I tried phoning you earlier, but you must have been out. But I just have to tell somebody about the terrible day I've had …

It started badly and got worse! When I got up the kitchen was flooded – I'd left the freezer door open! I've never ~~left the freezer door open~~ before. By the time I'd finished mopping up all the water, it was getting late. I was going to take my big handbag to work, but I was so rushed I picked up my small handbag by mistake, leaving my purse behind, so I didn't have any money. Luckily, I bumped into Bob at the station and he was able to lend me some money. My office key was also still at home, so when I got to work I had to borrow an office key.

Then I had to get to an important meeting. Our company is hoping to do some business with a Japanese firm. My boss thinks we have a good chance of signing a deal soon, but I don't think we have a good chance of signing a deal soon. I thought the meeting was on the fourth floor – in fact, I was certain it was on the fourth floor. But it had been rearranged and nobody had bothered to tell me. So I was 20 minutes late. I wasn't very happy, and my boss wasn't very happy either. To make matters worse, I'd been hoping to run through my presentation over breakfast, but I'd had no time to run through my presentation over breakfast. So my talk went really badly. Afterwards, my boss said she was disappointed with the way the meeting went. But I was disappointed with the way the meeting went, too.

After such a dreadful day, I was hoping I'd have a quiet evening, but I didn't have a quiet evening. When I got home I found that my cat had knocked over some glasses – you remember the beautiful old Swedish glasses that my parents gave me? I wonder if I'll be able to replace them? I don't expect I'll be able to replace them.

The only good thing is that it's the weekend. Come over whenever you want to come over. In fact, are you able to come over tomorrow? If you're not able to come over tomorrow, how about Sunday? Or are you still too busy decorating the house? I hope you're not too busy decorating the house. But give me a call and let me know.

Love,

Beth   x

done that

D Exam practice

Listening

This exercise tests grammar from the rest of the book as well as the grammar in this unit.

20b You will hear part of a radio interview in which David Evans, a chef in a British school, is talking about his work. Choose the answer (**A**, **B**, **C** or **D**) which fits best according to what you hear.

1 What was the students' initial reaction to the food they were served?
   A They didn't like being the subjects of an experiment.
   B They would rather have eaten traditional British food.
   C They were not sure whether it was good or bad.
   D They felt that it was an adventure for them.

2 According to David, why do some students have difficulty in accepting the 'restaurant system'?
   A They are uncomfortable eating meals with adults.
   B They are not used to having meals with others.
   C They don't like talking about food.
   D It takes too long to be served their food.

3 What main role do the staff play in the school restaurant?
   A They check that students are eating their meals.
   B They learn about the students' home lives.
   C They deal with students' complaints about the food.
   D They help students learn about a balanced diet.

4 According to David, where does most of the food served in the restaurant come from?
   A anywhere that can provide fresh ingredients
   B the school grounds
   C all over the world
   D suppliers close to the school

5 In David's view, which of his previous jobs prepared him best for his work as a school chef?
   A teacher
   B manager
   C waiter
   D cook

6 Why does David think that his approach could be difficult to introduce in other schools?
   A Many students are resistant to change.
   B Not all students see healthy eating as important.
   C Other schools don't see healthy eating as a priority.
   D Parents would be unwilling to accept it.

1 Complete these extracts from the interview by writing one word in each space.

1 Some people thought she'd be crazy to go ahead with the plan, but she was
......determined...... to.

2 I think it was quite adventurous for them to try what they saw as unusual, the kinds of foods they normally wouldn't have the opportunity to eat at home, or wouldn't .... to.

3 We've also got a small herb garden behind the science block. Students can help with this if they're .... to.

4 Interviewer: And do you think the approach to food you've taken here could be adopted in any school?
   David: No, I don't think all schools would be .... to.

5 But any school could take some steps to make students aware of the importance of healthy eating. I'd certainly .... them to.

2 In which of these is it possible to omit *to* after the word you have written and leave a correct sentence? ....

Writing

Your college has money to spend on improving the buildings and facilities. The Principal has asked each class to suggest how the money should be spent, and your class has decided it would like the library to be extended, more books to be bought and the resources (e.g. computers) to be upgraded. Write a proposal to the Principal outlining the benefits of your proposal.

Write your **proposal**, which may include headings, in **220–260** words.

When you give the consequences of a proposal you can use phrases such as *Doing so*, *In doing so*, and *By doing so* to avoid repetition:
An expanded library could be used as a classroom. Doing so will provide additional teaching space for the school.
Computers with Internet access should be bought. By / In doing so, the college can improve the research facilities at the college.

21 Word order and emphasis
fronting; cleft sentences; inversion; inversion in conditional sentences

A Context listening

1 Which of these qualities and characteristics might people use in describing you?

application	confidence	dedication	enthusiasm	loyalty	modesty
determined	efficient	formidable	patient	persuasive	reliable

2 🎧 21 Listen to this speech made in honour of Maria Adams, a music teacher. Which of these qualities and characteristics does the speaker use to describe her?

3 🎧 21 Listen again and say whether these sentences are true or false. If a sentence is false, say why.

1 Maria was a violinist before she became a conductor. ....T......

2 In the *Music in Schools* project the council gives children musical instruments. ....

3 Musicians are not paid to take part in the *Music in Schools* project. ....

4 Children in city schools now have to pay for their music lessons. ....

5 Maria helps children go to other countries to play music. ....

4 🎧 21 These ideas are expressed in a different way by the speaker. Listen again and write down exactly what he said.

1 We first met in the mid-1990s.
   It was in the mid-1990s that we first met. ....

2 She sees making music as a fundamental part of a child's development.
   ....

3 The way she calmly and clearly argued her case impressed us most.
   ....

4 I have rarely met anyone with such passion for their beliefs.
   ....

5 The council has tried to make changes to the *Music in Schools* project a number of times in order to save money.
   ....

6 The council backed down only after Maria threatened to withdraw her support from the project.
   ....

What difference do you notice between the sentences given and the ones you have written?

B Grammar

1 Fronting

We can emphasise a particular part of a sentence by moving it to the front of the sentence, changing the usual word order:

She sees making music as a fundamental part of a child's development. → *Making music she sees as a fundamental part of a child's development.* (fronting of object)
Maria had been writing to me for some weeks. → *For some weeks Maria had been writing to me.* (fronting of adverbial)
She resisted this. → *This she resisted.*

2 Cleft sentences

It's among children from poorer backgrounds that the Music in Schools project has had most impact. (emphasising *among children from poorer backgrounds*)
What impressed us most was the way she calmly and clearly argued her case. (emphasising *the way she calmly and clearly argued her case*)

An *it* cleft has the structure *it* + *is / was* + emphasised part + relative clause. The relative pronoun can be *that, which, who* or no relative pronoun. *When* and *where* are used only in informal English:
It was in the mid-1990s *that we first met.* or informally *... when we first met.*

A sentence with a *wh-* cleft usually has the structure *what-* clause + *is/was* + emphasised part. Sometimes we use *all* instead of *what*:
What she was suggesting was *that members of the YCO would volunteer their services.*
All she ever wanted to do *as she was growing up was play the violin.* (= the only thing she ever wanted to do)

⚠ After the *what-* clause we usually use a singular form of *be* (*is* or *was*). However, informally, a plural form (*are* or *were*) is sometimes used before a plural noun:
What she hopes to see is/are *children who enjoy a wide range of musical styles.*
We can sometimes put a *wh-* cleft at the end:
The way she calmly and clearly argued her case *was what impressed us most.*
The Music in Schools project *is what came out of our meeting.*

To emphasise an action we can use a *wh-* cleft with *what* + subject + form of *do* + form of *be* + *(to)* + infinitive:
What she did was (to) convince *us of the value of a musical education.*
To emphasise a whole sentence we can use a *wh-* cleft with *happen*:
What's happened *as a consequence* *is* *that music has become established as an important part of the national curriculum.*

3 Inversion

*In front of the committee **sat Maria**.*	= verb + subject
*Seldom **did she raise** her voice.*	= **do** + subject + verb
*Never **have I heard** such a persuasive speaker.*	= auxiliary + subject + verb

} = inversion of normal word order

Word order is inverted after certain words and phrases when these are put at the beginning of a sentence or clause in order to emphasise them. This kind of inversion is found mainly in formal speech and writing.

Inversion occurs after words and phrases with a 'negative' meaning:

- the negative adverbs *never (before)*, *rarely*, *seldom*; *barely / hardly / scarcely...when / before*; *no sooner ... than*; *nowhere*; *neither*, *nor*:
  __Rarely have I met__ anyone with such enthusiasm.
  __No sooner had Maria walked__ through the door than she started to talk about her proposal.
  I hadn't met Maria before, and __nor had the other members of the committee__.
  (▷ See also Unit 17 B3.)
- *only* + a time expression (e.g. *after*, *later*, *then*) or a prepositional phrase:
  __Only after__ Maria threatened to withdraw her support __did the council back down__.
- the prepositional phrases *at no time*, *on no account*, *under / in no circumstances*; *in no way* (or *no way* in informal language):
  __At no time has she__ ever __accepted__ payment for her educational work.
  She argued that __under no circumstances should children__ from poorer backgrounds be made to pay for music lessons.
- certain expressions with *not*: *not only*, *not until*, *not since*, *not for one moment*, *not once*, *not a* + noun:
  __Not only has she persuaded__ YCO members to give up their time, but she has also encouraged visiting musicians to give free concerts in schools.
- *little* with a negative meaning:
  __Little did she realise__ when she set up the project that it would be so influential.

Inversion also occurs after:

- prepositional phrases of place or movement, and adverbs describing direction of movement (most common in spoken and written narrative):
  __Into the committee room walked Maria.__ (= Maria walked into the committee room)
  __Along she came__ to present her proposal. (= She came along to present her proposal)
  verbs describing place and movement which are commonly used with inversion include: *be, come, fly, go, hang, lie, live, march, roll, run, sit, stand, swim, walk*
  we don't usually invert subject and verb when the subject is a pronoun:
  *Into the committee room **she walked**.* (**not** ~~Into the committee room walked she.~~)

- time sequence adverbs such as *first*, *next*, *now*, *then* with *be* or *come*:
  *And **then came an invitation** to be a special adviser to the government on music education.*
  If there is a comma (or an intonation break in speech) after the adverb, normal word order is used:
  Then, an invitation came from the government. (**not** ~~Then, came an invitation~~ ...)

- *so* + adjective ... *that*, emphasising the adjective:
  ***So successful has Music in Schools been, that** those involved in music education around the world have visited the city to see the project in action.*

- *such* + *be* ... *that*, emphasising the extent or degree of something:
  ***Such was her understanding of music education that** the government wanted to draw on her expertise.* (= Her understanding of music education was such that ...)

4 Inversion in conditional sentences

In formal or literary English, we can use clauses beginning *were*, *should* and *had*, with inversion of subject and verb, instead of a hypothetical conditional:
***Were she ever to leave** the orchestra, she would be greatly missed.* (= If she left ... or If she were to leave ...)
***Were he here** tonight, I know that he would want to express his thanks personally to Maria.* (= If he was / were here tonight ...)
***Should you need** any more information about Music in Schools, please feel free to contact me.* (= If you need ...)
***Had Maria not been** around, music education in most schools in this country would have practically disappeared.* (= If she had not been around ...)

In negative clauses with inversion, we don't use contracted forms:
***Had** Maria **not** set up the Music in Schools project ...* (**not** ~~Hadn't Maria set up the Music in Schools project~~ ...)

C Grammar exercises

1 Write a new sentence with a similar meaning to the original. Emphasise the information underlined using an *it* cleft or a *wh-* cleft at the beginning of the sentence. Sometimes both are possible.

1   I want you to <u>hold the cat tightly while I put on this collar</u>.
What I want you to do is hold the cat tightly while I put on this collar.

2   She announced she was going to join the air force <u>at her eighteenth birthday party</u>.
....

3   A: So how did you get the car out of the mud?
B: We <u>asked a farmer to pull us out with his tractor</u>.
....

4   A: Would you like a glass of champagne?
B: No, thanks. I really wanted <u>a cup of tea</u>!
....

5   A: What do you think's wrong with the car?
B: <u>The clutch cable could</u> have broken.
....

6   A: How on earth did you break your nose?
B: <u>I wasn't looking where I was going and walked into a lamppost.</u>
....

7   This huge bunch of flowers arrived for me this morning. I don't know <u>who sent them</u>.
....

8   <u>My parents</u> must have given Colin my telephone number.
....

9   The research shows <u>a link between salt intake and rates of heart disease</u>.
....

10 <u>His nervous laugh</u> made me think he was lying.
....

2 Match the sentence halves. Write new sentences with a similar meaning starting *Should* ..., *Had* ... or *Were* ....

1 If you require further details,   a she might have made a full recovery.

2 If today's match has to be postponed,   b the insurance covers a full refund.

3 If anyone had been looking at Martha when the police arrived,   c please contact our public information office.

4 If taxes were to be increased further,   d there would be a huge public outcry.

5 If the doctors had operated sooner,   e we would not have begun the climb.

6 If I were president,   f it will be replayed next week.

7 If your flight is cancelled,   g they would have noticed the expression of panic on her face.

8 If heavy snow had been forecast,   h I would introduce three-day weekends.

1 + c If you require further details, please contact our public information office.

Should you require further details, please contact our public information office.

3 Complete the sentences with appropriate words. Use three words only in each sentence.

1 I thought the insurance policy would pay my hospital fees. At no time *was I told / was I informed* by the company that it did not cover skiing injuries.

2 Seldom .... piano playing of such maturity from someone so young. I'm very impressed indeed.

3 He felt someone bump against him on the crowded bus, but only later .... that his wallet had been stolen.

4 I found the old bracelet while I was walking along the beach. Little .... then that I had made one of the most important archaeological discoveries of recent years.

5 Not since Philip and Gary Neville last played in 2004 .... two brothers in the England football team.

6 I asked her to describe her attacker, but only after several minutes .... me.

7 No sooner .... into bed than his flatmate started playing his drums.

8 The Atlantic crossing took eight days. I was in Harriet's company on several occasions, but not a word .... to me until near the end of the journey.

9 Remember that the gas fire is dangerous and on no account .... it on.

4 Rewrite the underlined parts of the conversation, emphasising the word(s) in italics. In each case use fronting, a cleft sentence or inversion.

A: I hear you and Anna didn't have a great holiday on the island.

B: No, not really, although
(1) we liked *the island* a lot.
(2) *The hotel* was the real problem.

A: Why? What was wrong with it?

B: Our room was just awful. The shower only had cold water, the air conditioning didn't work and sparks came out of the light switches when you turned them on.

A: Didn't you complain?

B: Oh, yes. We phoned the reception desk as soon as we found there were problems. **(3)** The hotel porter came *along*, looked around the room, and said he would send someone to sort things out. **(4)** He went *away* and an hour later **(5)** a man walked *in* carrying just a screwdriver. We left him to it, and went and had a swim in the pool. But when we got back, nothing had changed. By this time Anna was getting quite annoyed, so she went down to reception to complain. **(6)** They told her *there* she was just being fussy. And **(7)** she got really furious about *that*. She insisted on seeing the manager, and demanded that something should be done.

A: And was it?

B: Well, we had a steady stream of workers coming into the room after that. **(8)** An electrician came *first* and then the next day a plumber. But none of the problems got fixed. **(9)** It took them *three days* to decide that we needed another room.

A: You must have been fed up with the hotel by that time.

B: I think **(10)** *the attitude of the staff* annoyed me most – they really just didn't care. **(11)** I have *never* seen such a total lack of interest from people who are supposed to be providing a service. **(12)** No one apologised *once* the whole time we were there ...

1 the island we liked a lot

2 ....

3 ....

4 ....

5 ....

6 ....

7 ....

8 ....

9 ....

10 ....

11 ....

12 ....

D Exam practice

This exercise tests grammar from the rest of the book as well as the grammar in this unit.

Use of English

Complete the second sentence so that it has a similar meaning to the first sentence, using the word given. **Do not change the word given.** You must use between **three** and **eight** words, including the word given. Here is an example (0).

0 He always calls his house his 'castle'.
   REFERS
   He always refers to his house as his 'castle'.

---

1 The islanders are proud of the cheese they produce and they also like tourists to try the local honey.
   TAKE
   Not only .... the cheese they produce, they also like tourists to try the local honey.

2 I was grateful to them for letting me stay with them while I was in London.
   APPRECIATED
   I .... up while I was in London.

3 She hated publicity so much that she never gave any interviews to the media.
   HER
   Such .... of publicity, that she never gave any interviews to the media.

4 We expected to be told, but in fact nobody explained why he left the company so suddenly.
   DEPARTURE
   We expected to be told, but in fact no .... the company.

5 During her illness, she realised that the only choice she had was to take early retirement.
   ALTERNATIVE
   During her illness, she realised that there .... to take early retirement.

6 The President had only just been elected when the opposition party called for his resignation.
   VOTED
   No sooner .... the opposition party called for his resignation.

7 I'm sure she would do an excellent job if she ever became head of department.
   WERE
   I'm sure she would do an excellent job .... head of department.

8 It is distinctly possible that I will get promoted in the near future.
   OF
   There is a .... promoted in the near future.

Look at your answers to the exam task.

In which three of the sentences you have written are there examples of inversion?

....

Writing

The editor of your college magazine sent you this note.

> Hi!
>
> Would you be interested in writing a short article on global warming? We want something that talks about what young people can do as individuals to slow down global warming, what they should be asking their governments to do, and what the consequences of not preventing global warming are likely to be.
>
> Thanks,
>
> Anita

Write your **article** in **220–260** words.

The task gives you a chance to practise:

- cleft sentences

  What we have to do is change the way we live; It's in our everyday lives that we can make changes.

- word order after phrases such as *Not only, Not until, Never before, Only then*

  Only then will governments make changes.

Useful language

climate change, renewable energy, recycling scheme, fossil fuels

A Context listening

1 You are going to listen to a radio news report. Look at the pictures. What do you think the report is about?

2 🔊 22 **Listen and check whether you were right. As you listen, number these events in the order the reporter mentions them.**

a Two power stations were built close to Lake Taal. ....

b People were evacuated from around Lake Taal. ....

c The Taal volcano erupted and around a hundred people were killed. ....

d Scientists found that the temperature of Lake Taal was increasing. ....

e The Taal Emergency Strategy was introduced. ....

f A state of high alert was declared. ....

g The Taal volcano erupted and over a thousand people were killed. ....1.......

3 🔊 22 **Listen again. Complete each extract from the news report with a noun in the first space and a preposition in the second.**

1 The ......*breakdown*...... ......*in*...... communication cost at least a hundred lives.

2 There has been an .... the number of people living close to the lake.

3 The .... the power stations would leave thousands of homes and businesses without electricity.

4 There was also a dramatic .... the level of radon gas in the soil.

5 Their concerns increased with the .... thousands of dead fish.

6 Two days ago the .... around 30,000 people began.

4 Write new sentences with similar meanings to those in Exercise 3. In each case, use a verb related to the noun in the first space.

1 *Communication broke down and this cost at least a hundred lives.*

B Grammar

1 Nominalisation

*There has been **an increase** in the number of people living close to the lake.* or *The number of people living close to the lake **has increased**.*

We can sometimes use a noun or noun phrase for an idea usually expressed by a verb. This process is referred to as nominalisation.

Nominalised forms can also be used instead of other parts of speech:

***The danger** of the situation made it necessary to bring in the army to oversee operations.* or
*The situation was so **dangerous** that it was necessary to bring in the army to oversee operations.*

or more complex stretches of language:

*Evacuees will remain in temporary accommodation for **the duration of the emergency**.* or *Evacuees will remain in temporary accommodation for **as long as the emergency continues**.*

An adverb modifying a verb changes to an adjective in a nominalised form:

*Scientists noticed **a sudden rise** in the temperature of the lake.* or
*Scientists noticed that the temperature of the lake **had risen suddenly**.*

Noun phrases in nominalised forms are commonly made up of two nouns with a preposition:

*The industrial **development of** the area has increased the number of people living near the lake.*
*There was also a dramatic **rise in** the level of radon gas in the soil.*

We use nominalisation for a number of reasons:

● to avoid mentioning the agent (the person or thing that performs the action); for example, if we want to be impersonal or to make the agent less important. Compare:

*Two days ago **the authorities began to evacuate** 30,000 people.* (agent = the authorities)
*Two days ago **the evacuation** of around 30,000 people **began**.* (no agent mentioned)

● to express two clauses more concisely as one clause:

***The building of two power stations** just a few kilometres away was strongly criticised by environmentalists.* or ***Two power stations were built** just a few kilometres away. This was strongly criticised by environmentalists.*

This is particularly a feature of a formal style such as in academic writing and newspapers to give a different focus to the sentence. Compare:

***The provision** of temporary shelter in a safe location for those displaced is the army's top priority.* (New, important information is usually placed at the end of the sentence. The focus here is on 'the army's top priority'.)

*Temporary shelter in a safe location for those displaced **is being provided**, and this is the army's top priority.* (no particular focus)

2 *do, give, have, make, take* + noun

We can sometimes use a form with *do / give / have / make / take* + noun instead of a verb:
*The authorities **took** immediate **action**.* or *The authorities **acted** immediately.*
***The decision was made** to evacuate an area of 5 km around the entire lake.* or
***It was decided** to evacuate an area of 5 km around the entire lake.*

Often, the *do / give / have / make / take* + noun patterns are less formal than using a verb alone:
*When my mother was ill, I had **to cook** for the family.* (more formal)
*I had **to do** all **the cooking** last week because Mum was away.* (less formal)
Common informal alternatives include:
do + *the cooking, the gardening, the ironing, the shopping, the washing-up*
give + *a call, an explanation, a hug, a kiss, a look, a ring, a shout, a sigh, a warning, a welcome*
have + *a chat, a drink, a fall, a feeling, a guess, influence, a look, respect, a rest, a shower, a sleep,
a talk*
take + *action, aim, a (deep) breath, a decision, a (quick) glance, a look, shelter, a shower, a walk*
make + *an arrangement, an assumption, a comment, contact, a decision, a discovery, progress, a
recommendation, a start, use (of)*

C Grammar exercises

1   **Make these conversations more informal where possible, replacing the parts in italics
with appropriate *do / give / have / make / take* + noun forms.**

 1   A: Have you **(1)** *washed up* yet?
   B: I've **(2)** *started* on it. But there's such a lot to do, and you know how much I hate it.
   A: Well, I'm going outside to **(3)** *work in the garden*.
   B: **(4)** *Shout* if you need any help.
   A: No, thanks. You just concentrate on the washing-up!

   1   *done the washing-up*   3   ....

   2   4   ....

 2   A: Well, I've **(1)** *decided*. I'm going to apply for a job at Raggs.
   B: Good for you. I **(2)** *feel* you'd really get on there.
   A: I've **(3)** *arranged* to see their head of personnel next Friday.
   B: And how will you tell Terry you're thinking of leaving the company?
   A: Well, it won't be easy, but I suppose I'll just have to **(4)** *breathe deeply* and
     (5) *explain to him* why I want to go.

   1   4   ....

   2   5   ....

   3   ....

3 A: Did you (1) *talk with* Natasha about the holiday?
  B: Yes, I (2) *called* last night and we (3) *chatted* about it then.
  A: And how did she react when you said we weren't going with her?
  B: She just (4) *sighed* and said 'That's okay'. But she was obviously upset.

  1 .... 3 ....
  2 .... 4 ....

4 A: I'm exhausted. I'm going to (1) *shower* and (2) *rest* before we (3) *cook*.
  B: I'm pretty tired, too. I'll (4) *look* at what's in the freezer, or maybe we could eat out?

  1 .... 3 ....
  2 .... 4 ....

2 Rewrite the sentences to remove the agent. Use a nominalised form of the underlined verb and make any other changes needed.

1 The government <u>released</u> the prisoners unexpectedly.
2 They <u>organised</u> the conference very professionally.
3 Spectators <u>turned out</u> in huge numbers for the match.
4 The army <u>withdrew</u> the troops immediately.
5 We need to <u>shake up</u> top management for the company to be successful again.
6 The banks <u>increased</u> interest rates for the third time in two months.
7 They <u>agreed</u> on extra funding for the project.
8 The prisoners <u>broke out</u> of the jail during a power cut.
9 The companies <u>announced</u> the merger last week.
10 They <u>decided</u> to postpone the race at the last moment.

1 *The release of the prisoners was unexpected. / There was an unexpected release of prisoners.*

3 Rewrite each sentence using a nominalised form at the beginning. Leave out the agent.

1 After scientists identified the HIV virus in the mid-1980s, there were enormous efforts to produce a vaccine.
  The identification of the HIV virus in the mid-1980s led to / resulted in enormous efforts to produce a vaccine.

2 John is obsessed with cars, and this started when he was quite young.
  ....

3 The government has expanded the nuclear power programme, but this has been criticised by opposition politicians.
  ....

4   The petrol companies have reduced the price of petrol, which is good news for drivers.

   ....

5   The council abolished parking charges in the city centre, and as a result shops have reported increased business.

   ....

6   Parent organisations are demanding healthier food in schools, and this results from growing concerns about childhood obesity.

   ....

7   The train will depart half an hour late because of engine problems.

   ....

8   A new college principal has been appointed, and staff may leave as a consequence.

   ....

4   **Complete the extracts from newspaper articles using the information in the box. In each sentence, use a nominalised form.**

> ~~valuable books have disappeared~~   people have responded to its recruitment drive
> the English spelling system is complex   people are strongly resisting increased taxation
> the damage to property is extensive   the situation is threatening animal and plant species

1   Detectives were last night questioning a man about the disappearance of a number of valuable books. from the National Library over recent months.

2   'The teaching method we have developed acknowledges .... , and guides children towards a better understanding in carefully controlled stages.'

3   Hospitals will launch another bid to fill 40 more vacancies with experienced nurses. Last night the Health Minister said .... was 'excellent', with 7000 calls in two days.

4   Chinese remedies are rooted in 4000 years of tradition, but growing Western interest in alternative medicines has increased .... Products confiscated by environmental officers included some using the root and seedpods of a rare orchid.

5   The extra public spending will need to be paid for and, with borrowing ruled out, that can only mean putting up taxes. Given .... , this could undermine the government's chances of being re-elected.

6   Residents of the south coast are beginning to return to their homes after the recent severe flooding. However, ... means that some will be living in temporary accommodation for many months.

D Exam practice

This exercise tests grammar from the rest of the book as well as the grammar in this unit.

Reading

You are going to read five reviews of popular science books. Answer the questions by choosing from the reviews (**A–E**). The reviews may be chosen more than once.

Which review mentions … ?

1   a recent technological development that has become important for many people

2   scientists who had the ability to imagine the future accurately

3   an ability to think in general terms

4   the unexpected effects of scientific developments

5   a scientist who began an area of scientific investigation important today

6   experiments conducted over a long time with great attention to detail

7   an author's view that some people are likely to disagree with

8   explanations that are basic and undeveloped

9   someone whose most influential work was done in the early part of their life

10   a book aimed both at people who approve of technology and those who don't

11   scientific investigations whose value was only later understood

12   a book that both entertains and makes the reader think

13   an author who combines practical experience with an ability to write well

14   a skill that people are born with rather than learn

15   a book criticising scientists for making exaggerated claims

A   *A Monk and Two Peas* by Robin Marantz Henig

The work of an Augustinian monk from Brno laid the foundations of the science of genetics. Gregor Mendel was born in what is now the Czech Republic in 1822 and entered the monastery at the age of nineteen. In the mid-1840s he began to conduct a series of experiments with pea plants grown in the monastery garden and he continued these for twenty years. Over this period, by crossing pea plants which had clear differentiations in height, colour etc and by carefully logging the results, Mendel was able to formulate the basic principles behind heredity. Mendel's work was only published in obscure journals, he was eventually led away from science by administrative duties at the monastery and it was only some years after his death that the significance of his work was appreciated. Mendel's life was a quiet one, but a very important one to the science of the twentieth century. *A Monk and Two Peas* tells the story very well, explaining clearly Mendel's experiments and drawing out their significance.

B *The Maths Gene* **by Keith Devlin**

For those who are mathematically challenged it's an attractive notion that everybody possesses a latent talent for maths and that it is just a question of finding the right key to access it. Devlin, despite the title of his book, is not suggesting that there is a gene for maths that the Human Genome project might identify but he is saying that we have a natural ability to do maths, that it exists in everybody and there are sound evolutionary reasons why this is the case. The ability to do maths, clearly, means an ability to handle abstract ideas and relationships and this provides advantages in evolutionary terms. As human language emerged, so also did a new capacity for abstraction and this formed the foundations on which mathematical thought has been built. Some readers might find Devlin's account of the evolution of language debatable but his ideas about the nature of our mathematical powers and his practical suggestions about how to improve them are constantly stimulating.

C *Why Things Bite Back* **by Edward Tenner**

Subtitled 'Technology and the Revenge of Unintended Consequences', Tenner's book is an entertaining look at the myriad ways in which advances in science and technology seem to recoil against us. What we gain on the roundabouts we lose on the swings. Antibiotics promise release from the perils of major diseases and end up encouraging microorganisms to develop resistance to them. Widespread use of air conditioning results in an increase in the temperature outdoors, thus requiring further cooling systems. American Football safety helmets become more efficient but this heralds an increase in more violent play and injuries actually rise. Tenner mounts up the evidence in a book designed to appeal to technophile and technophobe alike. And remember, the disaster at Chernobyl was triggered during a safety test. Ironies like that just aren't funny.

D *The Undiscovered Mind* **by John Horgan**

How close are we to a full understanding of the workings of the human brain and of human consciousness? If you listened to, and believed, many of those working in the neurosciences, you would imagine that answers lay just around the corner. Not so, according to John Horgan, former journalist on *Scientific American* and author of *The End of Science*, another witty and provocative examination of the pretensions of some scientists. To all the important questions about the mind – what processes in the brain allow us to see, hear, learn, remember, reason, etc – only the most rudimentary answers have been offered. A unified theory of consciousness, far from being just within our grasp, seems a long way off. Our attempts to heal the troubled mind are equally hampered by a lack of true understanding. Using the same mixture of sharp, informative prose and incisive pen portraits of many of the people involved that characterised *The End of Science*, Horgan has produced another immensely readable study of science, its practitioners and their all too human hubris.

E *A Brief History of the Future* **by John Naughton**

So rapidly has the Internet become an integral part of many people's lives that it is easy to forget that only a few years ago it was known to the general public, if at all, as a playground for nerdy academics and that it is one of the most astonishing of all man's inventions. John Naughton, fellow of Churchill College, Cambridge and regular journalist on *The Observer* and other newspapers, has been on the net for many years himself and is the ideal person to write a history of what he calls this 'force of unimaginable power'. Starting with three little-known visionaries at MIT in the 1930s, Naughton traces the story through the engineers like Tim Berners-Lee who realised their vision, and on into what the future may hold. Written with the skill one might expect from a fine journalist and informed with the knowledge of an engineering professor, this is among the first histories of the net but is likely to remain among the best for some time to come.

Grammar focus task

Nominalised forms often have the pattern noun phrase + *of* + noun phrase. In six of the following extracts from the reviews the preposition that fills the gap is *of*. Without looking back at the reviews, find the two exceptions. What preposition is used in these?

1 a full understanding ..... the workings of the human brain

2 the foundations ..... the science of genetics

3 advances ..... science and technology

4 the significance ..... his work

5 the knowledge ..... an engineering professor

6 widespread use ..... air conditioning

7 an increase ..... the temperature outdoors

8 a lack ..... true understanding

Writing

A new out-of-town shopping centre has been built near your town. It includes over a hundred shops, restaurants and a cinema. You work for your town council. You have been asked to write a report on the impact of the centre on transport, on the environment, on people's shopping habits and on shops and recreational facilities in the town centre.

Write your **report** in **300–350** words.

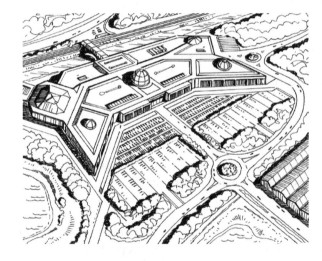

Writing hints

The task gives you a chance to practise nominalised forms:
the aim of the report, the construction of the out-of-town shopping centre, the increase in traffic

Useful language
*environmental impact, transport facilities, ease of access / easy access,
a significant negative / positive impact*

A Context listening

1 Liz is planning on moving out of her family home and buying her own apartment. What
are the advantages and disadvantages of living in a town centre or on the edge of a town?

2 ⓐ 23 Listen to the conversation. Which of the advantages and disadvantages you
thought of do Liz and her parents mention?

3 ⓐ 23 Listen again. Do these statements refer to the town apartment (T) or the out-of-
town apartment in Canley (C)?

1 It's been on the market for a long time. ....T......

2 It's obvious why they've been having problems selling it. ....

3 It really shocked me to see how bad it was. ....

4 It's about 15 kilometres from there into the centre. ....

5 There's bound to be a regular bus service from there. ....

6 There's no special parking area for the apartments. ....

7 There's that lovely little river that runs nearby. ....

8 You couldn't even fit a chest of drawers in there. ....

9 The rooms in it are quite dark and that made it feel cramped. ....

10 There is expected to be a lot of interest in the property. ....

4 Look again at the sentences in Exercise 3. Underline all the examples of *it* or *there*.
Some of the examples of *it* and *there* refer back to a thing or a place that has been
previously mentioned. Which ones are they? What do they refer back to?

1 It's been on the market for a long time.
   It refers to the town apartment.

209

B Grammar

1 Introductory *it* as subject

*'It struck me that the Canley apartment might be quite noisy with that busy road nearby.' 'But **it**'s in such a lovely location.'* (it refers back to the noun phrase *the Canley apartment*)

*If **it**'s possible, I'd like to go back and look at the Canley apartment again.* (it refers forward to *going back and looking at the Canley apartment again*)

It's going to be hard to choose between them. (introductory it as grammatical subject)

*Living in town would make **it** so much easier to get to work.* (introductory it as grammatical object)

Introductory *it* as subject is commonly used:

- to talk about weather, time, distance and to describe situations:

   It's raining again.   *It's five o'clock.*   *It's quiet in this part of town.*
   It's about 15 kilometres from the Canley apartment into the centre.

- as an alternative to a *that-*, *wh-*, *-ing* or *to*-infinitive clause as the subject of the sentence:

   It's a pity that the town apartment is so small. rather than
   That the town apartment is so small is a pity.
   It's obvious why they've been having problems selling it. rather than
   Why they've been having problems selling it is obvious.
   It's certainly an advantage being able to walk to work. rather than
   Being able to walk to work is certainly an advantage.
   It really shocked me to see how bad it was. rather than
   To see how bad it was really shocked me.

   It is more usual to use introductory *it* in these contexts, although in formal language the alternative with a *that-*, *wh-*, *-ing* or *to*-infinitive clause as subject is often used.

In writing, we don't usually use introductory *it* as an alternative to a noun as subject:
The town apartment is more expensive. (**not** ~~It is more expensive, the town apartment.~~)
However, this is quite common in informal speech in order to clarify what is being talked about:
*It'd be good to live near work, but **it**'s more expensive, the town apartment.*

We often follow introductory *it* with *be* + adjective / noun, but other patterns are possible:
it + verb + *to*-infinitive clause **It might help to run** through the pros and cons.
it + verb + object + *to*-infinitive clause **It shocked me to see** how bad it was.
it + verb + *that-* clause **It appears that** they're having trouble selling the apartment.
it + verb + object + *that-* clause **It struck me that** the Canley apartment might be quite noisy.
(▷ See Appendix 16.1.)

In formal contexts, a common way of reporting what is said by an unspecified group of people is to use *it* + passive verb + *that-* clause or *it* + passive verb + *wh-* clause:
It is said that the cost of accommodation in the town centre will rise. or less formally
They say that the cost of accommodation in the town centre is going to go up.

It was explained how difficult it is to prevent flooding in the area.
or less formally *They explained how difficult it is to prevent flooding in the area.*
(▷ See Appendix 16.2.)

2 Introductory *it* as object

We can use *it* as the object of a verb in a number of patterns:
- verb + *it* + *that-* / *if-* / *wh-* clause
  *I wouldn't **like it if** I had to get up at 6 o'clock.*
  *I couldn't **believe it when** the agent said the decoration was 'in good condition'.*
- *would appreciate* + *it* + *if-* clause
  *I **would appreciate it if** you could send me further details of the apartment.*
- verb + *(it)* + *that-* clause
  *We've just got to **accept that** neither of the apartments is perfect.* or informally
  *We've just got to **accept it that** neither of the apartments is perfect.*
- verb + *it* + adjective + *that-* / *wh-* / *to-*infinitive clause
  *The owner didn't **make it clear whether** they were included in the price.*
  *I **think it** highly **unlikely that** the seller will reduce the price.* (formal)
  *I **think it**'s highly **unlikely** ...* (informal)
- *leave* / *owe* + *it* + *to* somebody + *to-*infinitive
  *I think we should **leave it to** the estate agent **to talk** to the owner about whether carpets and curtains are included.*
- verb + *it* + *as* + adjective + *that-* / *if-* / *wh-* clause
  *I **see it as essential that** there should be somewhere to park*
  (▷ See Appendix 16.3.)

3 *There*

START POINT

There's a bus stop just outside the apartment block.
There are lots of new apartments being built in the city centre.

There + be is used to introduce new information, saying that a person or thing exists, happens, or is found in a particular place.

Because we use *there* to introduce topics, the noun after *there + be* often has an indefinite or non-specific meaning, so we often use *a/an*, no article, *any(one)* + noun or *some(thing)*, *no(body)*:
There's a car park behind the Canley apartment block (**not** ~~There's the car park behind the Canley apartment block.~~)
There's something about parking in the information the estate agent gave us.

⚠ We can use *there* with a definite noun when we treat information as already familiar to the listener / reader:
*If I ever bought a car, **there**'s the problem of parking at the town apartment.*

211

We use *there*, not *it*:
- to say or ask if people or things exist or are found in a particular place:
  There's nowhere to park. (**not** ~~It's nowhere to park.~~)
  Was **there** a dishwasher in the kitchen? (**not** ~~Was it a dishwasher in the kitchen?~~)
- to introduce information about quantities and amounts:
  There's a big grassy area at the back of the block.   **There** wasn't much space in the bathroom.

There + be is often followed by:
- noun + *that- / wh- / -ing / to*-infinitive clause
  There's a chance (**that**) he might include carpets and curtains.
  There are plans **to build** new apartments not far from the one we looked at.
- *bound / certain / (un)likely / supposed / sure + to be*
  There's **bound to be** a regular bus service from there.

There is often followed by *is*, *are*, *was* or *were*. However, also common are:
- *there* + auxiliary / modal verb + *be*
  There must be someone we know who would redecorate it.
- *there* + *seem / appear* + *to be*
  There seem to be good and bad aspects of each apartment.
- *there* + passive reporting verb + *to be*
  There is expected to be a lot of interest in the property.
  Reporting verbs commonly used in this pattern include *estimate, expect, find, reckon, report, say, think*.
- verb + *there* + *to be*
  I wouldn't expect **there to be** many people interested in buying the apartment. **or**
  I wouldn't expect many people to be interested ...
- *there* + *arise / emerge / exist / follow / remain / take place*:
  During the 1990s **there emerged** a tendency for young, well-paid people to buy apartments in the town centre.
- *there* + *being*:
  The bus service was withdrawn, **there being** so few passengers using it.
  This pattern often introduces a reason and is used mainly in formal writing.

If the noun after *there* is singular or uncountable, the verb is singular; if the noun is plural, the verb is usually plural (although *there's* is often used in informal speech):
There's a supermarket within walking distance.
There are so many things to think about. **or** informally **There's** so many things ...
If a noun phrase after *there* consists of two or more nouns in a list, we use a singular verb if the first noun is singular or uncountable, and a plural verb if the first noun is plural:
There was just a bed, a small wardrobe and some bookshelves.
There were just some bookshelves, a bed and a small wardrobe. **or** informally
There was just some bookshelves ...

4 Common expressions with *it's no* and *there's no*

It's no wonder they've been having problems selling the apartment; it's in a very poor condition.
There's no hurry to decide.
(▷ See Appendix 16.4.)

C Grammar exercises

1 Rewrite the underlined parts of the sentences where possible, beginning with *there*.

> *There are some tickets left*

1 <u>Some tickets are left</u> for the concert. Do you want to go?

2 I thought I heard voices, but when I opened the door <u>nobody was in the room</u>.

3 Jack's having a party this weekend even though <u>his birthday isn't until next month</u>.

4 <u>The first balloon voyage across the Atlantic Ocean was</u> in 1978.

5 You can find plenty of second-hand bookshops in town. In fact, <u>one is opposite the railway station</u>.

6 I knew that <u>my keys were</u> somewhere in the house, but I couldn't find them.

7 <u>Only ten places are available</u> on the course, so I'm going to apply as soon as possible.

8 When I opened the fridge I found that <u>no milk was left</u>.

9 When I got to his office I could hear that <u>Dr Jones was on the phone</u>, so I waited outside.

10 <u>Would anyone</u> like to volunteer?

11 <u>My hands were shaking</u> as I walked into the exam room.

12 <u>Something was on the radio</u> this morning about using weeds as cooking ingredients.

2 Add either *it* or *there* to each sentence as appropriate.

1 When the weather is dry, _{it} is estimated that 150,000 people cycle to work in the capital.

2 Fraser has said he will retire from football if is thought to be no chance of his ankle injury healing in the foreseeable future.

3 Is a swimming pool at the hotel we're staying at?

4 Worried me to see Heather looking so thin.

5 In December 1944 took place a secret meeting between the countries' leaders.

6 Although took hours of practice, I eventually managed to play a simple tune on the saxophone.

7 Most people had left the party and I decided that was time I went home, too.

8 The scientists said that is very little evidence that mobile phone use has any adverse effect on health.

9 How far is from Paris to Berlin?

10 They travelled by bus, being no railway line in that part of the country.

23

3 Complete the sentences using an expression with *it's no* or *there's no* and one of the words from the box. Add any other words necessary.

> chance   doubt   good   harm   hurry   longer   need   secret   ~~wonder~~

1 A: The opinion polls don't look good for President Broom, do they?

   B: Well, he's raised income tax three times in the last year and over a million people are unemployed. ...It's no wonder... he's so unpopular.

2 A: If only I'd warned Ken about the bad weather.

   B: .... blaming yourself for the accident. He knew it was stupid to go walking in the hills when there was a risk of heavy snow.

3 A: Apparently, Jean's looking for a new job.

   B: .... that she's thinking of leaving. She's been telling everyone about the jobs she's applied for.

4 A: Do you think your sister would lend us her car?

   B: Well, ... asking her. She can only say 'no'.

5 A: If we run, we might just get the 9.00 train.

   B: No, ... catching it now. Let's have a coffee and wait for the 9.30.

6 A: Mark's hoping to become a professional tennis player.

   B: .... that he's very talented, but I don't think he's hard-working enough to be successful as a professional.

7 A: I'm really sorry I missed the meeting.

   B: .... to apologise. We didn't discuss anything particularly important.

8 A: We used to spend hours playing in the river when we were children.

   B: But it's so polluted now that .... possible to swim in it safely.

9 A: Come on, we'll be late. The film starts at 7.30, doesn't it?

   B: .... There's always lots of adverts on before the main film starts.

4 Complete the conversations by reordering the words in brackets. If necessary, add *it* or *there*.

1 A: Why did you move out of the flat?

   B: My flatmates were constantly shouting at each other, and I hate it when people argue. all the time. *(argue – hate – people – when)*

2 A: Do you think you've got a chance of getting the job?

   B: Not really, but.......................... put in an application, does it? *(doesn't – hurt – to)*

3 A: Hello, I've got an appointment with Dan Jackman. What room is he in?

 B: I'm sorry, but .... the name of Dan Jackman here. *(by – is – nobody)*

4 A: Did you find your car keys eventually?

 B: Yes, ... I'd left them at home. *(out – that – turned)*

5 A: Has Jackie had an accident or something?

 B: What makes you think that?

 A: I .... limping. *(noticed – she – that – was)*

6 A: Do you think the concert will be a sell-out?

 B: No, I .... many people there at all. *(be – don't – expect – to)*

7 A: So as a classroom assistant, what do you do exactly?

 B: Well, I .... to help the weaker pupils keep up with the rest of the class. *(as – my – role – see)*

8 A: Did you phone and let your parents know about the car crash?

 B: No, I .... them until they got home from work tonight. *(best – not – tell – thought – to)*

9 A: Did I tell you I'd be leaving early in the morning?

 B: Yes, you .... that you'd got a meeting to get to. *(had – me – mentioned – to)*

10 A: Will you be able to email me from the hotel?

 B: Yes, I .... access in every room. *(Internet – think – is)*

11 A: Have we got any eggs?

 B: I know Tasha made an omelette for lunch, but .... in the fridge. *(be – left – might – some)*

12 A: Oh, great, lemon sorbet! My favourite.

 B: I .... you liked it. *(remember – saying – that – you)*

13 A: The forecast says it's going to be much cooler tomorrow. Not very good for our walk.

 B: Actually, ... it's chilly. I don't like walking in hot weather. *(I – if – prefer)*

14 A: So, Professor Kent, what was the most interesting part of your recent trip to Uganda?

 B: Undoubtedly, it was being able to see mountain gorillas, although .... only 600 or so left in that part of Africa. *(are – be – thought – to)*

D Exam practice

This exercise tests grammar from the rest of the book as well as the grammar in this unit.

Use of English

For questions **1–5**, think of **one** word only which can be used appropriately in all three sentences. Here is an example (**0**).

0 He may be nearly 90 years old, but in no ....way..... does his enthusiasm for life appear diminished.

The company is on its ....way..... to becoming the world's largest producer of satellite dishes.

She bought me a bunch of flowers by .....way.... of an apology for getting annoyed with me.

---

1 Early summer is without .... the best time to visit the island.

All the tickets have been sold, so there's no .... of rearranging the concert at this stage.

We were nearly at the end of the meeting before the .... of redundancies was brought up.

2 She is never .... with just passing an exam; she always wants an excellent mark.

Jamie's a very responsible boy, so I'm quite .... to let him look after the children.

If the salt .... of food is very high, I try to avoid it.

3 They became increasingly .... about their daughter as she continued to lose weight.

I left there early as I was .... to avoid the heavy traffic during the rush hour.

My parents were .... that I should settle down and find a job.

4 There are .... to be fewer than 4000 tigers surviving in the wild in India.

It's an interesting idea, but I wouldn't have .... it was very practical.

The nearest village was five miles away, but he .... nothing of walking there to do his shopping.

5 We first met on May 21st 1997 which, by .... , happened to be my 21st birthday.

Mr Turner claimed that it was mere .... that he sold his share of the company the day before it was declared bankrupt.

Perhaps it is no .... that poets often seem to lead very troubled lives.

Grammar focus task

Look again at the sentences in 1–5. Find all the examples of *it* and *there*.

1 In which are introductory *it* or *there* used to introduce new information?

2 Which refer to a place or to something mentioned previously?

Writing

You have received this note from your boss. Read it and the other information and write your proposal. Say what was wrong with last year's conference and suggest a suitable location and time for the conference this year.

The time has come to organise the sales conference again. Can you do it this year, please? As you know, it's always in the spring, and it's usually for 3 days in the middle of the week. But we could do it differently – we could make it shorter, or we could hold it at the weekend. And where do you suggest? Last year we had it at a conference centre in the country, but I don't think that was very popular. Could you ask staff for their views and let me have a proposal, please.

Thanks,

Wouldn't be popular. Especially people with children.

No! Very boring. Nowhere to go.

Staff views

Where?		When?		How long?	
Conference centre in country	5%	February	40%	2 days	90%
Conference centre in town	70%	March	40%	3 days	10%
In company headquarters	25%	April	20%		

Write your **proposal** in **180–220** words.

Writing hints

The task gives you the chance to practise sentences with introductory *it* and *there* to:
● report the views of staff members
   It appears that most staff members ...
   There is a strong preference for ...
● make your recommendations
   It is important to consider ...
   There would be overwhelming support for ...
   I think it vital that ....

24

Complex prepositions and prepositions after verbs

complex prepositions; verb + preposition – common patterns;
phrasal verbs: word order

A Context listening

1 Dan is flying tomorrow afternoon to visit his friend Jess in the south of France. What do you know about this part of France?

2 ⓐ **24a** Listen to their telephone conversation. Which of these instructions best represents the advice Jess gives to Dan?

1 Take a taxi from the airport to Montpellier station. Take the bus from Montpellier to Perpignan. Take a taxi from Perpignan station to the hotel. Eat at Café Mathis on Wednesday evening. Be in the hotel foyer at two o'clock on Thursday afternoon.

2 Take the bus from the airport to Montpellier station. Take the train from Montpellier to Perpignan. Walk from Perpignan station to the hotel. Eat at Le Metropole on Wednesday evening. Be at Café Mathis at two o'clock on Thursday afternoon.

3 Take a taxi from the airport to Montpellier station. Take the train from Montpellier to Perpignan. Walk from Perpignan station to the hotel. Eat at Le Metropole on Wednesday evening. Be in the hotel foyer at two o'clock on Thursday afternoon.

4 Take a taxi from the airport to Montpellier station. Take the train from Montpellier to Perpignan. Take a taxi from Perpignan station to the hotel. Eat at Café Mathis on Wednesday evening. Be in the hotel foyer at two o'clock on Thursday afternoon.

3 ⓐ **24a** Listen again and write the exact words from the recording. The number of words you should write in each space is given.

1 I'm really sorry, but I've messed ......up...... (1) ....our plans....... (2) for tomorrow.

2 So I won't be able to pick .... (1) .... (1) at the airport after all.

3 I've found .... (1) .... (3) from the SNCF website ...

4 You'll need to buy a ticket before you get .... (1) .... (2).

5 ... when you've checked .... (1) .... (2), I suggest you get a meal there.

6 I'll sort .... (1) .... (2) when I pick you up on Thursday afternoon.

7 Relax on Thursday morning and walk .... (1) .... (1).

4 In which of the extracts can you reverse the order of the words in the first space and the words in the second space?

B Grammar

1 Complex prepositions

Prepositions can be either simple (one word) or complex (two or more words):
*I'm really, really sorry **about** this.*
*The bus will only take you **as far as** the main square.*
(⊳ See Appendices 17.1 and 17.2.)

Some complex prepositions have a meaning similar to a simple preposition:
*I wasn't able to reschedule the meeting, **in spite of** my efforts.* (= despite)
*All the people **in front of** me had been queuing for a long time.* (= before)

2 Verb + preposition: common patterns

START POINT

*Don't forget to **bring** your camera **with** you.*
*I **insist on paying** your hotel bill.*
After some verbs a preposition is needed to link the verb to what follows. If the preposition is followed by a second verb, the verb must be an **-ing** form.

- verb + object + prepositional phrase: (⊳ See Appendix 18.1.)
  *I tried to **reschedule** the meeting **for next week**, but it's just impossible.*

- verb + preposition + object + preposition + object: (⊳ See Appendix 18.2.)
  *She **complained to** the company **about** the unreliability of their bus service.*

- verb + preposition + -ing: (⊳ See Appendix 18.3.)
  *Don't **worry about getting** lost.*

- verb + object + preposition + -ing: (⊳ See Appendix 18.4.)
  *I'd **advise** you **against catching** the bus.*

- verb + preposition + subject + -ing: (⊳ See Appendix 18.5.)
  *You can **depend on the train running** on time.*

3 Phrasal verbs: word order

START POINT

*I've **booked** you **into** a hotel not far from the station.*
book into is a transitive, two-word phrasal verb. The object here is *you* and the particle is *into*.
*While you're strolling around, **look out for** Café Mathis.*
look out for is a transitive, three-word phrasal verb. The object here is *Café Mathis* and the particles are *out* and *for*.
*Something's **come up** at work.*
come up is an intransitive phrasal verb. There is no object.

Some phrasal verbs can be used transitively or intransitively with the same meaning:
*Feel free to **call me back** if there's anything that's not clear about tomorrow.*
***Call back** later.*
(▷ See Appendix 19.1.)

Others have different meanings when they are used transitively and intransitively:
*I've **looked up** the online timetable and it appears that the last train from Montpellier to Perpignan is at 21.51.* (transitive verb = I've found the information)
*The weather has been bad over the last week, but it seems to be **looking up** now.*
(intransitive verb = improving)
(▷ See Appendix 19.2.)

With most phrasal verbs, the object can go before or after the particle:
*I'll **sort out the bill** when I pick you up on Thursday morning.* or
*I'll **sort the bill out** when I pick you up on Thursday morning.*
(▷ See Appendix 19.3.)

⚠ With these verbs we tend to put the object after the particle if the object is long:
*You might want to **take down** some of the information I'm going to give to you.* rather than
*You might want to **take** some of the information I'm going to give to you **down**.*
and we always put the object before the particle if the object is a pronoun:
*I won't be able to **pick you up** at the airport after all.* (**not** ~~I won't be able to pick up you at the airport after all.~~)

⚠ If the object consists of two or more items connected with *and*, it can occur before or after the particle even if one or both of the items is a pronoun:
*When I'm next in London I'll **look you and your wife up**.* or
*... I'll **look up you and your wife**.* (look up = go and see them)

With some phrasal verbs, the object must go after the particle(s):
*When you've **checked into the hotel**, I suggest you get a meal there.* (**not** ~~When you've checked the hotel into ...~~)
(▷ See Appendix 19.4.)

With a few phrasal verbs the object must go between the verb and the particle:
*Although she was the youngest in the class, she used to **order the other children about**.*
(**not** ... ~~she used to order about the other children.~~)
(▷ See Appendix 19.5.)

A few three-word phrasal verbs have two objects, one after the verb and the other after the particles:
*I'll **take you up on your offer** to buy me a meal.* (verb = *take up on*; objects = *you* and *your offer*)
(▷ See Appendix 19.6.)

C Grammar exercises

1 Complete the sentences using the notes in brackets. Use an appropriate tense for the verb. If two word orders are possible, give them both.

1 Sam sings really well. He takes after his father (*take / his father / after*).

2 I decided it was time to .... (*throw / some of my old exercise books from school / away*).

3 Sarah got really angry during the meeting, and eventually she .... (*gather / her papers / up*) and stormed out.

4 I .... (*bump / Cherie / into*) in town. She said she'll phone you later.

5 A: Have I got everybody on the list now?

   B: No, you .... (*leave / Dave's name / out*).

6 I really can't .... (*tell / the twins / apart*), they look so similar.

7 I don't suppose there's any way we can .... (*talk / you / leaving college / out / of*), is there?

8 You should really try and .... (*get / some food / down*), even if you're not hungry.

9 Our neighbours are so inconsiderate. Last night they .... (*wake / me and my husband / up*) at three o'clock in the morning playing loud music.

10 The new shop has loads of computers on show so that you can .... (*try / them / out*) before buying.

11 A: You don't think Gary was telling the truth, then?

   B: No, I think he .... (*make / the whole story / up*).

2 Complete the sentences using a complex preposition which includes the word in brackets and followed by a sentence ending from the box.

> their ability to pay   their health   a cut in their salaries   a strict protein-only diet
> an apology   the train driver   cream   his wishes   the 10,000 predicted
> an excellent art gallery   30th September   a terrorist attack

1 The workers got extra paid holiday in exchange for a cut in their salaries . (*exchange*)

2 The concert attracted only 2,000 people .... (*against*)

3 The pudding recipe's very rich, isn't it? Do you think I could use yogurt .... ? (*place*)

4 I think healthcare should be available to all people, ... (*irrespective*)

5 The city has drawn up plans for the evacuation of thousands of people .... (event)

6 She's lost a lot of weight recently, ... (thanks)

7 Although he didn't spend much of his life in Ireland, he was buried there .... (accordance)

8 My parents want to move somewhere out of the city .... (sake)

9 It may be only a small town, but it has an interesting natural history museum .... (along)

10 He was a bit bad-tempered with me last week, so he gave me a box of chocolates .... (way)

11 The road will be closed for major repairs .... (effect)

12 The crash was found to be the result of negligence .... (part)

3 Complete these extracts from a radio news report by expanding the notes in brackets. Choose appropriate forms for the verbs and add prepositions and pronouns where necessary.

1 Police have appealed to witnesses for information (appeal / witnesses / information) about the fire which has led to the closure of the main east coast rail line at Crewbury. A factory next to the line was burned down yesterday, causing major damage to the track. Rail passengers are currently being .... (advise / use) the line.

2 In the first interview given by the Foreign Minister since newspapers reported that she personally approved illegal arms sales, she .... (dismiss / the reports) 'completely untrue'. She went on to say that the accusation would not .... (prevent / do) her job, and that she intended to continue in her post.

3 Ten youngsters between the ages of 12 and 16 met the Prime Minister today after they competed in the World Youth Maths Challenge. The Prime Minister .... (congratulate / achieve) excellent results in the competition. He said that they .... (benefit / take part) the After School Maths scheme set up by the government to encourage young people's enthusiasm for the subject.

4 The Food and Agriculture Minister, Sheila Davies, ... (quarrel / European counterparts) the issue of fish conservation. During a discussion on the decline in fish stocks, Ms Davies got into a heated argument, which .... (end / walk) out of the meeting.

5 Senior environmental scientists have called on the government to act immediately to .... *(protect / the country)* the effects of rising sea levels by building additional coastal defences. However, a spokesperson from the Environment Department said that the government wouldn't .... *(rush / invest)* substantial amounts of money on coastal defences when these might not provide a long-term solution.

4 Add the missing prepositions to this letter.

Dear Jodi,

Sorry I haven't been in/ touch you for such a long time, but it's been a busy few months.

Earlier this year I heard that my great-aunt had died. Apart seeing her a couple of times at my parents' house, I didn't really know her. So you can imagine my surprise when I found she'd left me a cottage along some money in her will!

When I saw the cottage, I just fell in love with it. It's close a beautiful little village, and looks out the sea. My great-aunt used it as a holiday home, and I've decided to do the same. Unfortunately, it's been badly looked, so I've had to spend most weekends this year sorting the place.

I knew it was need some work, and at first I thought I could get away giving it a quick coat of paint. But I soon realised it was a much bigger job. There were holes in the roof, and the window frames were so rotten some of the panes of glass were danger falling out.

I was walking around the village one Saturday, wondering what best to do, when who should I run but Barney Adams. Do you remember him from school? As luck would have it, he now works in the village as a builder and decorator. We got talking, and he said he'd come and look the house. Naturally, I took him up his offer! He got really enthusiastic about it. He talked me replacing all the windows, and he's put in a new central heating system place the old coal fires. I've had to prevent him extending the kitchen, which he was keen to do! He's checked the roof, and fortunately that doesn't need replacing. Thanks Barney, the house is now looking brilliant, and comparison other builders, he doesn't charge very much.

The next project for me is to clean the mess in the garden, as it's completely overgrown. If you want to come and help me some time, feel free! You'll always be very welcome.

Love,
Emily

D Exam practice

This exercise tests grammar from the rest of the book as well as the grammar in this unit.

Listening

🔊 **24b** You will hear four different extracts. For each, choose the answer (**A**, **B** or **C**) which fits best according to what you hear. There are two questions for each extract.

Extract One

You hear Mark Harris being interviewed about his new book on immunisation.

1 Why, according to Mark Harris, do most scientists support immunisation?
- **A** They are reluctant to disagree with the predominant view.
- **B** They believe it is the best way to protect public health.
- **C** They think it has worked effectively since it was developed.

2 In this interview, what is Mark Harris's main message?
- **A** Views on the effectiveness of immunisation have changed over time.
- **B** It is not desirable to immunise all children against disease.
- **C** All immunisation is unsafe to some extent.

Extract Two

You hear a woman talking about snowboarding.

3 According to the speaker, the public don't realise that
- **A** snowboarding is easier than skiing.
- **B** snowboarding is difficult for beginners.
- **C** snowboarders take their sport seriously.

4 According to the speaker, why don't skiers welcome snowboarders?
- **A** They resent the fact that snowboarders generally have more money than skiers.
- **B** They don't like the disruption that snowboarding causes.
- **C** They don't like snowboarding being dominated by one group.

Extract Three

You hear a woman talking about her job in a lost property office at a major railway station.

5 When she explains that their missing belongings aren't in the lost property office, most people
  A don't believe her.
  B are annoyed with her.
  C realise that they have probably been stolen.

6 She believes that most unusual items of lost property
  A are unwanted presents.
  B have been left deliberately.
  C have no value to their owners.

Extract Four

You hear a man on a radio travel programme talking about city audioguides for use on an MP3 player.

7 According to the speaker, the *City Sounds* audioguide
  A is no better than a guidebook.
  B explains architecture well.
  C includes irrelevant information.

8 The feature of *Walk and Talk* that the speaker particularly praises is
  A the style of presentation.
  B the accuracy of the information.
  C the selection of music.

Complete these sentences from Extract 3 by writing the object in brackets in one space and an appropriate particle in the other. In which can you reverse the position of the object and the particle?

1 It's always difficult when I tell people that no-one's handed .their property in / in their property . *(their property)*

2 I think most of them are secretly convinced that I'm hanging ....
.... *(lost property)* for myself or selling ....
.... *(it)*

3 People leave .... on trains that you really would not believe. *(some things)*

4 I really think that people 'accidentally' leave unusual things like this on the train because they don't know how else to get rid ....
(them)

5 You'd think people would be able to give .... or dispose of them in some other way rather than leaving them behind on trains, wouldn't you? *(them)*

Writing

The tourist authority is trying to increase the number of visitors from overseas that come to your region. It has asked for reviews of local tourist attractions which have some historical interest for publication in its magazine for visitors. Write your review of one tourist attraction. Describe it, outline its historical interest, give your personal view of the attraction, and say why it will appeal particularly to overseas visitors.

Write your **review** in **300–350** words.

This task gives you the chance to practise using complex prepositions:
in comparison with other tourist attractions; together with restaurants and clubs; away from the crowds; as well as other attractions.
(▷ See Appendix 17.)

Prepositions after nouns and adjectives

noun + preposition: related verbs and adjectives; noun + preposition + -*ing* or noun + preposition + noun; noun + *of* + -*ing* or noun + *to*-infinitive; noun + *in* or noun + *of*; adjective + preposition

A Context listening

1 Do you prefer reading the news online or in a newspaper? Why?

2 ⓟ25 Kate Pearce has set up an online newspaper called *Happening*. Recently she visited her old school to talk to students about how she set up the paper. Listen to the question and answer session and number these steps in the order Kate mentions them.

a contact advertisers ....

b learn how to design a website ....

c give more information about famous people ....

d gather feedback on the website ....

e respond to criticism ....

f borrow some money ....

g design a prototype website ....

h increase involvement of teenagers ....

i have the idea of a newspaper for teenagers ....1....

3 ⓟ25 Listen again and write the exact words you hear in the spaces.

1 I'd also had the opportunity to do a course on website design, and that ......*influenced*...... my decision.

2 I felt that there was a big .... an online newspaper.

3 But we did .... money to live on.

4 We had real .... persuading banks to lend us anything at all.

5 We took the .... work on it for six months.

6 It was .... generate business at first.

7 I think there'll always be a .... traditional newspapers.

8 And do many people .... *Happening*?

9 In the early days we used to get quite a lot of .... our news coverage.

10 Young people .... very high standards nowadays.

11 We've .... include a section on celebrities.

12 Young people may be able to have an .... government policies.

4 Underline the nouns you have written in Exercise 3, and find the related verb or adjective. Which nouns used the same preposition as the related verb or adjective?

B Grammar

START POINT

*I felt that there was a big **demand for** an online newspaper.*
*Every bank we approached was **sceptical about** whether the project would ever make money.*
Many nouns and adjectives are typically followed by particular prepositions.

1 Noun + preposition: related verbs and adjectives

Many nouns are followed by the same prepositions as their related verb or adjective:
(▷ See Appendix 20.1.)
*We used to get quite a lot of **complaints about** our news coverage.* or
*People used to **complain** a lot **about** our news coverage.*
*I wanted to increase young people's **awareness of** current affairs.* or
*I wanted to make young people more **aware of** current affairs.*

A few are followed by different prepositions from their related adjective:
(▷ See Appendix 20.1.)
*We take **pride in** the design of our website.* or *We are **proud of** the design of our website.*

Some take a preposition where their related verb does not:
(▷ See Appendix 20.1.)
*Young people may be able to have an **influence on** government policies.* or
*Young people may be able to **influence** government policies.*

2 Noun + preposition + *-ing* or noun + preposition + noun

Most noun + preposition combinations can be followed either by an *-ing* form or a noun:
*There have been **protests about locating** a new nuclear power station on the east coast.* or
*There have been **protests about the location** of a new nuclear power station on the east coast.*
(▷ See Appendix 20.2.)

⚠ Some noun + preposition combinations are more usually followed by a noun than an *-ing* form:
*I felt there was a **demand for the publication** of an online newspaper.* rather than
*I felt there was a **demand for publishing** an online newspaper.*
(▷ See Appendix 20.2.)

3 Noun + *of* + *ing* or noun + *to*-infinitive

Some nouns can be followed be either *of* + *-ing* or a *to*-infinitive with little difference in meaning:
*The **idea of setting up** some kind of newspaper for young people came from that time.* or
*The **idea to set up** ...*
*I had the **opportunity to do** a course on website design.* or
*I had the **opportunity of doing** a course on website design.*
(▷ See Appendix 20.3.)

Some nouns have more than one meaning and are followed by either *of* + *-ing* or *to*-infinitive depending on which meaning is used:
*Young people get the **chance to contribute** in various ways.* (chance = opportunity)
*The banks thought there was little **chance of making** it a commercial success.*
(chance = likelihood)
(▷ See Appendix 20.3.)

Some nouns can be followed by *of* + *-ing*, but not a *to*-infinitive:
*The **difficulty of persuading** the banks to lend us money meant that we had to borrow money from our parents.* (**not** ~~The difficulty to persuade the banks~~ ...)
(▷ See Appendix 20.3.)

Some nouns can be followed by a *to*-infinitive, but not *of* + *-ing*:
*We took the **decision to work** on it for six months.* (**not** ~~We took the decision of working on it for six months.~~)
(▷ See Appendix 20.3.)

4 Noun + *in* or noun + *of*

We use *increase / decrease / rise / fall* + *in* when we talk about what is increasing or decreasing, and *increase / decrease / rise / fall* + *of* to talk about the amount of an increase or decrease:
*The recent **increase in** hits on the website means that we can charge more for advertising space.* (**not** ~~The recent increase of hits~~ ...)
*We've had an **increase of** about 50% in the last three months alone.* (**not** ~~We've had an increase in about 50%~~ ...)
Other nouns like this include: *cut, decline, downturn, drop; gain, growth, jump, leap.*

5 Adjective + preposition: expressing feelings

Many adjectives which refer to feelings or opinions are followed by particular prepositions:
*Young people seem generally very **enthusiastic about** the site.*
*They were very **wary of** advertising on the site.*
(▷ See Appendix 20.4.)

6 Adjective + preposition: different meanings

Some adjectives are followed by different prepositions, depending on meaning:
*I knew they were **concerned about** what was going on in the world.* (*concerned about* = worried about)
*We have a reviews section, which is **concerned with** films, CDs, DVDs and books.* (*concerned with* = to do with)
(▷ See Appendix 20.5.)

C Grammar exercises

1 Complete each sentence with an appropriate preposition.

1 I've been afraid ......*of*...... the dark ever since I was young.

2 As the men came towards him, knives in hand, he felt afraid .... his life.

3 Get Brian to do the decorating. He's particularly good .... wallpapering.

4 We ought to get our website redesigned. I think it would be good .... business.

5 I was really furious .... Steve for turning up so late.

6 Local people are furious .... the decision to build a power station.

7 I think it's unfair .... you to blame me for missing the plane. It wasn't my fault the taxi was late.

8 The teacher kept the whole class in after school, which I thought was unfair .... those of us who hadn't been behaving badly.

9 I'm really sorry .... the coffee on the carpet. I didn't notice your cup there.

10 I feel really sorry .... Sarah. She lost all her work when her computer crashed.

2 Rewrite the sentences using a noun related to the underlined verb or adjective. Make as few other changes as possible.

1 At the meeting we discussed the pros and cons of private education.

At the meeting we had a discussion about / on the pros and cons of private education.

2 She admitted that the salary increase had influenced her decision to take the new job.

3 The children's spelling has improved noticeably since they were each given a dictionary.

4 Alex has done very well at university and we are very proud of his achievement.

5 Although I don't agree with his political beliefs, I greatly admire his writing.

6 The flooding seriously damaged many of the houses in the village.

7 When you come to collect the parcel, please bring documents to prove your identity.

8 Northern Rail has banned the use of mobile phones on its trains.

9 To solve the problem of severe traffic congestion, drivers are to be charged £10 a day for bringing their cars into the city centre.

10 The number of students dropping out of college has reduced substantially this year.

3 Choose the correct option. In some sentences both are correct.

1 Researchers have developed a treatment that they claim can significantly reduce the likelihood *of getting* / *to get* skin cancer.

2 After his heart attack, Tom had the sense *of cutting* / *to cut* down on the amount of fatty foods he ate.

3 The government has withdrawn its opposition to *using / the use of* private hospitals in the National Health Service.

4 Has there been an increase or decrease in *visiting / the number of visitors to* the National Park over the last ten years?

5 It was Gwen who had the idea *of organising / to organise* a fashion show to raise money.

6 Have you ever regretted your decision *of moving / to move* to Sweden?

7 It has been shown that people are more productive when they are given the option *of working / to work* flexible hours.

8 There seem to be two main factors behind *closing / the closure of* the car factory.

9 The focus of the conference is on *protecting / the protection of* endangered species in the rainforests of central Africa.

10 The party still shows no sign of *recovering / recovery* from its election defeat last year.

11 As she was writing, I noticed she had a very strange way *of holding / to hold* her pen.

12 A new advertising campaign is being launched today with the aim *of encouraging / to encourage* children to stay at school until they are 18.

4 **Add the missing prepositions to these texts.**

A A: I'm really fed up ˄ my job. I've been doing the
          ^{with}
    same thing at Trimstep for ten years, and I'm tired
    the same old routine.
 B: But I thought you were keen your job. You've
    always seemed so enthusiastic it.
 A: Well, I used to be very impressed the managers.
    But now they're only interested making money and
    they seem indifferent how the staff feel. There are
    rumours that business isn't going well, so a lot of
    people are worried their jobs. In fact, one of the
    senior managers left last week. He obviously wasn't
    satisfied the way the company's being run. Maybe it's
    time I started looking around for something new, too.

B (This is part of a speech made by a senior manager at Trimstep to employees.)
 I know that some of you have expressed anxiety Mr Madson's sudden departure the company last week. I was very disappointed his decision to resign. I must admit that the last few months have been difficult, and at times we've been very concerned ourselves the future of the company. However, we have now developed an association a firm of retailers in South-East Asia, and we're extremely pleased this development. We did at first have a disagreement safety standards, but this has been resolved and they have now indicated their satisfaction the design changes we've made. We hope to sign a major contract with them in the next few days. To all of you I want to express my gratitude your belief the company and your continuing support the management team.

D Exam practice

Use of English

For questions **1–12**, read the text below and then decide which answer (**A, B, C** or **D**) best fits each space. There is an example at the beginning (**0**).

Seasonal affective disorder

Seasonal affective disorder, or SAD, is a type of depression that follows the seasons, with most SAD sufferers **(0)** .... *C* .... symptoms during winter months. These symptoms include disturbed sleep and difficulty staying awake during the day. For many people, SAD is a **(1)** .... condition which causes **(2)** .... discomfort, but no severe suffering. This form of SAD is sometimes referred to as 'winter blues'. For others, however, it is a serious illness which might **(3)** .... them living a normal life.

SAD is clearly a response to the **(4)** .... of daylight hours and the lack of sunlight in winter. It is mainly found **(5)** .... people living in high latitudes. However, it is rare in those living within 30 degrees of the Equator, where daylight hours are long and constant. The relationship between **(6)** .... daylight and SAD is not clearly understood. It is thought that it affects the brain's production of the hormones serotonin and melatonin, but precisely **(7)** .... depression is triggered by a fall **(8)** .... the production of these hormones is an area for further research.

The most common treatment **(9)** .... SAD is light therapy in which sufferers are exposed to a very bright light, of at least ten times the intensity of ordinary domestic lighting, for up to four hours per day. This is **(10)** .... in around 85% of cases. Patients who do not respond to light therapy are usually prescribed antidepressant drugs, although there is a growing **(11)** .... in psychotherapy for SAD sufferers, enabling them to relax and **(12)** .... with the problems induced by the illness.

0	**A** feeling	**B** facing	**C** experiencing	**D** finding
1	**A** mild	**B** medium	**C** lenient	**D** slight
2	**A** the	**B** some	**C** a	**D** no
3	**A** limit	**B** prevent	**C** obstruct	**D** prohibit
4	**A** inadequacy	**B** shortage	**C** scarcity	**D** shortening
5	**A** by	**B** on	**C** among	**D** between
6	**A** weakened	**B** contracted	**C** reduced	**D** lowered
7	**A** if	**B** why	**C** whether	**D** that
8	**A** from	**B** to	**C** in	**D** of
9	**A** with	**B** for	**C** of	**D** by
10	**A** efficient	**B** active	**C** effective	**D** productive
11	**A** enthusiasm	**B** attention	**C** popularity	**D** interest
12	**A** cope	**B** manage	**C** face	**D** confront

Grammar focus task

Without looking back at the text, decide how many of these extracts have the preposition *of* after the noun in italics? What other prepositions are used after nouns in the extracts?

1 Seasonal affective disorder is a *type* ..... depression that follows the seasons.

2 This *form* ..... SAD is sometimes referred to as 'winter blues'.

3 SAD is clearly a *response* ..... the shortening of daylight hours ...

4 ... the *lack* ..... sunlight in winter.

5 The *relationship* ..... reduced daylight and SAD ...

6 ... it affects the brain's *production* ..... the hormones serotonin and melatonin.

7 ... triggered by a *fall* ..... the production of these hormones ...

8 ... at least ten times the *intensity* ..... ordinary domestic lighting ...

Writing

You are studying Business and English at your college. You want to spend two months during your vacation working in a company in an English-speaking country to get work experience and to practise your English. Write a letter to the Personnel Manager of Arcon, an international company with branches in many countries, explaining who you are, what you would like to do, and why the company should employ you temporarily. Offer to send further information about yourself if the company is interested in employing you.

Write your **letter** in **220–260** words. Do not write any postal address.

Writing hints

The task gives you the chance to practise using nouns followed by particular prepositions: *a possibility of (finding), the experience of (working), a good knowledge of (computers); the opportunity to (improve); an interest in (marketing), an expertise in (information technology); a demand for (temporary positions)*

Useful language
I am writing to enquire whether ...; I would like to be able to ...; to make a useful contribution; Thank you for your attention.

Key

Unit 1

A: Context listening

2 2 Dave 3 Karen 4 Dave 5 Keith 6 Karen 7 Beryl 8 Keith

3 2 'd (had) been waiting
3 've (have) been working 4 've (have) arrived
5 'm (am) now thinking 6 'm (am) working
7 'd (had) spoken 8 've (have) enjoyed
9 've (have) been trying 10 'd (had) finished

Six tenses are used in these extracts:
past simple (1), past perfect continuous (2), present perfect continuous (3 & 9), present perfect (4 & 8), present continuous (5 & 6), past perfect (7 & 10)

C: Grammar exercises

1 2 was driving 3 come / am usually coming (either is possible to describe something regularly done at a certain time)
4 went / was going (similar meaning) 5 saw 6 stopped
7 watched / was watching (similar meaning) 8 travelled / was travelling (similar meaning)
9 disappeared 10 believed / have never believed (similar meaning) 11 is forever trying 12 exist 13 think (suggests that her opinion has changed) / 'm thinking (suggests that her opinion is in the process of changing) 14 is / was 15 got / were getting (similar meaning) 16 was 17 received 18 saw / were seeing (this would suggest that the callers phoned while watching the light) 19 are now considering 20 offers / offered (similar meaning) 21 came / were coming (similar meaning) 22 suggest (implies that the likely explanation is that the lights were a meteor shower) / suggested (implies that this explanation is less certain) 23 was 24 is 25 seems 26 are getting 27 is currently researching 28 believe 29 observed / were observing (similar meaning) 30 says 31 take / are taking (similar meaning)

2 2 a expect b are ... expecting
3 a hated b was hating (focuses on the temporary effect of the waves) or hated (focuses on the more general activity of being in a boat)
4 a is attracting b attracts
5 a Do ... see b was seeing
6 a was measuring b measures
7 a 'm (am) looking or was looking (similar meaning, although the past continuous is more tentative, suggesting less chance of success) b looks
8 a appears or is appearing (suggests that this is unusual or temporary behaviour) b 's (is) appearing

3 1 b had played / played (similar meaning) c Did you play d had been playing / had played (similar meaning)
2 a made b had been making c had made / made (similar meaning) d have made
3 a had been eating b ate c had eaten d haven't eaten
4 a have run b had been running c had run d ran

4 2 has been dropping is more likely as a situation is being talked about which has changed over a period of time up to now and may well continue to change.
3 has belonged
4 has been serving is more likely because we are told how long it has continued.
5 have failed
6 Have you considered
7 Have you been swimming
8 've (have) tried
9 has burst

5 2 started 3 remember 4 had been working / had worked
5 was doing 6 I've been working 7 had just finished
8 was feeling / felt 9 have you been sleeping 10 hits
11 I've been having 12 I notice 13 Have you had
14 haven't had 15 I suggest 16 are working / work
17 doesn't solve

D Exam practice

Reading

1 C 2 D 3 A 4 D 5 B 6 C

Grammar focus task

2 wondered 3 had affected 4 did not care 5 had been
6 had fallen 7 took 8 added 9 was 10 had listened
11 had he heard 12 vanished 13 had learned

Writing *Sample answer:*

The most important invention of the last 100 years: television or the Internet?

Some people *consider* television to be the most important invention of the last 100 years. However, there *is* another invention, which *has had* an even greater impact on the world: the Internet. Developed in the 1990s, the Internet *provides* global communication, something no other invention *has achieved*. Never before has it been possible for people to communicate so easily, so rapidly and with so many others. An email, for example, can be sent from one side of the world and received on the other in a matter of seconds.

The Internet *has transformed* the way we *conduct* almost all aspects of our lives – social interaction, business, education, politics and leisure. Young people in particular *communicate* with friends and *exchange* information on social networking websites such as Facebook. The majority of businesses now *have* their own websites to inform their customers. On many of these sites it *is* also possible to order goods directly from the business. More and more educational courses *use* online resources to supplement face-to-face teaching and paper-based material. Political parties and individual politicians *have* websites to encourage people to vote for them, and oppressed minorities in many countries *call* for political reform in email and blogs. People *spend* their leisure time playing games on the Internet or downloading films to watch and music to listen to.

Until the Internet *came* along, it *was* hard to disagree that television *was* the major invention of the last hundred years. It *provided* entertainment, it *informed* us about events around the world, and it *allowed* advertising to reach into our homes. But the Internet can do all the things television can and many, many more. Above all, it *allows* us to interact directly with other people in a way that television never could. It *has already changed* the world and its potential to change it still further *is* enormous.

Unit 2

A: Context listening

2 The following activities are mentioned: visiting the Golden Gate Bridge in San Francisco, camping on a beach, sightseeing in New York, visiting the Grand Canyon.

3 2 arrive 3 'll (will) be looking 4 's (is) going to take 5 'm (am) going to fly 6 Will 7 'll (will) have been living 8 'll (will) be staying

4 Six ways of talking about the future are used in these extracts: present continuous (1), present simple (2), future continuous (3 & 8), *be going to* + infinitive (4 & 5), *will* (6), future perfect continuous (7)

C: Grammar exercises

1 2 departs 3 'm (am) having 4 is going to melt 5 will persuade 6 will rise (as weather is not something people can control, it would be unusual to use *be to* + infinitive here) 7 agrees 8 see (we usually use the present simple to refer to the future in a time clause with a conjunction such as *when*) 9 miss 10 is to be believed 11 will be enjoying

2 2 I'm going to do 3 I'll let (a promise; *I shall* is rather formal) 4 He'll cause / He's going to cause 5 I'll take (an offer or a decision made without planning) 6 are you doing / are you going to do (we don't use present simple for an informal arrangement); I'll 7 will commence (a formal arrangement) 8 is going to be / will be 9 is doing (an arranged event); Shall I (an offer) 10 will take 11 are starting / will start / start (*will* or present simple suggest a formal arrangement (perhaps these are public examinations); present continuous suggests a less formal arrangement (perhaps a teacher is announcing her intentions for a class test)) 12 is (present simple in time clause with *when*); is going to be / will be (we don't use *is to be* for something that people can't control, such as someone's age) 13 is probably going to burst / will probably burst

3 2 a 'm (am) going to buy b 's (is) going to have c 're (are) going to need
3 a will have been working b will have been watching c will have been negotiating
4 a won't be coming b will you be supporting c will be doing
5 a is to create b are to be left c is / are to launch
6 a will have moved b will have had c will have been analysed
7 a 's (is) making b 'm (am) not going c 're (are) having

4 2 was to have begun 3 will reduce 4 was to have carried / was to carry 5 will take place / is to take place / is going to take place 6 is to star / will star 7 was going to make 8 was to spend 9 was to be 10 will appear / is to appear / appears / is going to appear

D: Exam practice

Use of English

1 Because the decisions or actions (about ageing) taken now might damage society in the future.

2 We feel at the same time that old age is both a success and a failure.

3 inevitably

4 That the author sees disease in old age as very unpleasant. / That the author is shocked / frightened by disease in old age.

Grammar focus task

2 The decisions we take in the next few years *will have* far-reaching consequences for the state of future society.

3 Many are the news stories trumpeting that we *will* soon all *live* to 130, 200 or 400 years. ('... that we will soon all *get* to 130, 200 or 400 years' would also be possible, although *live* was used in the original text)

4 When we get these therapies, we *will* no longer all *get* frail and decrepit and dependent as we get older.

5 We *will* still *die*, of course.

6 So, *will* this *happen* in time for some people alive today?

Writing *Sample answer:*

Dear Delegate,

We look forward to welcoming you to the 15th annual conference of 'Sport for Youth', which *will be held* in the Town Hall in Congerton from 22nd to 25th September.

You already have a programme for the first day, but here are some further details. The registration desk *opens* at 8.30 and *stays* open all day. You can collect a Welcome Pack when you register, and this *will include* a Certificate of Attendance. In his opening speech, Peter Taylor *is talking* about the current state of sport in schools. Coffee and lunch *are served* in the Avon Room. The cost of these is included in the conference fee. If you need Internet access, then this *will be available* through computers in the basement at no charge.

No events have been arranged for the first evening, but there are lots of things to do in Congerton. The town has two cinemas, and a theatre which *is showing Romeo and Juliet* during the conference. There are many pubs and bars close to the conference venue, and some excellent restaurants offering a wide range of food and prices. The conference organising committee *will be* at the conference hotel to advise and guide you.

Please feel free to contact me before the conference *starts* if you need any additional information.

Regards,

Anna Reece

A: Context listening

3   2 must accept 3 were able to bring 4 will be 5 ought to be 6 have to play 7 should give 8 will be

4   2 extracts 2 and 6 3 extracts 5 and 7 4 extract 1
    5 extracts 4 and 8

C: Grammar exercises

1   2 We'll be able to 3 wasn't able to / couldn't 4 couldn't
    5 Could 6 could 7 might / could 8 could 9 mightn't

2   2 must 3 can't 4 mightn't 5 should / must / ought to
    6 did you have to 7 had to 8 have to 9 shouldn't 10 have to
    11 have to / 've got to / must

3   2 b 3 a and b 4 b 5 b 6 a 7 a and b 8 b

4   2 In just a few years from now everybody *will be able to* watch TV on their computers.
    3 I still remember how they *would* play together so well as children. (*used to* is also possible)
    4 Forecasters are warning that heavy snow *could* cause dangerous driving conditions. (*will* is also possible)
    5 Here's some really nice cheese that I don't think you *will* have tasted before.
    6 We live in an old house that *used to* belong to a politician.
    7 Writing my geography assignment *shouldn't* take me too long.

D: Exam practice
Listening

1 B 2 C 3 B 4 C 5 A 6 B

Grammar focus task

1   *may* (in recording); *could* also possible
2   *will* (in recording); *can* also possible
3   *'ve got to* (in recording); *should* also possible
4   *used to* (in recording); *would* also possible
5   *must* (in recording); *could* also possible
6   *could* (in recording); *would* also possible

Writing *Sample answer:*

Proposal to reduce car use by employees

The problem

Most employees drive to work, despite the provision of public transport in the city.

Benefits of reduced car use

Reducing car use by employees *would* have a number of significant benefits for the company as well as the wider world.

• It *would* ease parking problems for employees and this *ought to* decrease the number of people arriving late due to parking difficulties. Thus, the company's output *might* increase.
• It *would* reduce greenhouse gases emitted and thus lower the company's contribution to global warming.
• As we are an influential company in the city, it *may* encourage other companies to introduce their own schemes for reducing car use.

Possible ways of reducing car use

A number of possible ways of reducing car use are suggested:
• The introduction of a car-share scheme, organised by the company.
• Providing secure bicycle parking at the company to encourage people to cycle to work.
• Promoting the use of public transport by providing travel passes subsidised by the company.

Barriers to change

A number of problems *will* be faced when changes are implemented, including:
• Resistance to change. For example, some employees said that they take their children to school before coming to work, so *are not able to* share transport. Others said that they *would* be unwilling to cycle in wet weather.
• Limitations of the public transport system. Many employees said that the reliability of public transport *needs* to be improved substantially before they *would* consider giving up their cars.

Recommendations

None of the suggestions is supported by all employees. I therefore recommend that a mixed approach *should* be taken to the problem, with the company adopting all three of the proposals. To overcome barriers to change, the company *should* organise a publicity campaign highlighting the convenience and financial benefits of car-sharing and the health benefits of cycling. At the same time, the company *should* join with other major businesses to put pressure on local government to improve public transport.

Unit 4

A: Context listening

1   a, b, d and f

2   2 f 3 a 4 e 5 h 6 b 7 g 8 d

3   1 sentences 1 & 2 2 sentences 3 & 8 3 sentences 4 & 7
    4 sentences 5 & 6

C: Grammar exercises

1   1 must have got up / must have had to get up (*must have got up* is a conclusion that A got up early; *must have had to get up* is a conclusion that it was necessary for A to get up up early. Here, they have a similar meaning.)
    2 didn't dare admit / didn't dare to admit; would have been
    3 might be raining; we ought to / we'd better
    4 is supposed to start; couldn't
    5 must; might / could
    6 must have known; should have warned
    7 might; need never
    8 should / were supposed to (the meaning of *should* and *were supposed to* is similar, although *should* expresses the speaker's view more strongly); could / might

2   2 have been caused 3 have changed 4 have been working
    5 have found 6 be waiting 7 have been made 8 have been talking

3   2 have managed 3 there is a possibility of seeing
    4 I recommend you to / I recommend that you (should)

5 succeeded in taking 6 are to be taken 7 you are allowed to / we will allow you to 8 it is compulsory for everyone to

4 2 might have been working 3 must be getting easier
4 must have been going through 5 could be facing
6 must have to be 7 ought to have given 8 would not have been able to grow

D: Exam practice
Use of English

1 would sooner watch football than play 2 must have made
3 are required to fill 4 in order to be 5 have thought about
6 has succeeded in cutting 7 you'd (= had) better not miss
8 did they bring up

Grammar focus task

1 5 2 2 3 had better not (in 7)

Writing *Sample answer:*

Dear Martha,

It's great that you're thinking of a walking holiday. I enjoyed my week in Italy. But I'm not sure whether this is the holiday for you.

On the plus side, the scenery was incredible and the villages we walked through were lovely. Our guide knew all about the history of the area, so we learned a lot. Each night we stayed in a different hotel, and these were comfortable and served great food – as you'd expect in Italy! The others in the group were very friendly and interesting.

Unfortunately, the guide kept getting lost, even though he *was supposed to be* really experienced. Sometimes the hotel rooms weren't ready when we arrived, and I feel they *could have been* better prepared. Meals were included in the price except for lunch, but this was very expensive. I think they *should have warned* us about this. But the big problem was hill walking. It was exhausting, and I *couldn't* keep up. I think it *might have been* better for me to go on an easier walk.

And that's what I'd recommend to you. As (like me!) you're not very fit, maybe you *should* find a company that does easier walks. The company I went with only does tours in hilly areas. You'*ll* probably be able to find a company that's cheaper, too. The one I went with was overpriced.

Love,
Nathalie

Unit 5

A: Context listening

3 2 decision-making 3 rainforest 4 river levels 5 energy saving
6 lighting energy 7 recycling scheme 8 the arms trade
9 mountain environments

noun + noun: 1, 3, 4, 8, 9
noun + -*ing* form: 2, 5
-*ing* form + noun: 6, 7

4 For more details and examples, see Unit 5, Grammar, part 4
1 a the first time 'drought' is mentioned b it seems that 'drought' has been mentioned before, so the listener would know what drought is being talked about

2 a talking generally about something that is unique – there is only one future b a particular kind of future which is then specified
3 a talking about college (the institution) in general b talking about the particular college that Nazim hopes to study in

C: Grammar exercises

1 2 a colleague of hers 3 Adam's decision 4 a horror film; a documentary about apartheid (*an apartheid documentary* is not a commonly used combination – in the way that *a horror film* is – so we are more likely to use noun + preposition+ noun) 5 the brother of someone I worked with in Malaysia 6 the Earth's surface / the surface of the Earth 7 a moment's hesitation (we prefer noun + 's + noun to talk about time) 8 a children's playground 9 a cousin of John Lennon / a cousin of John Lennon's 10 The construction of the new library 11 letter box; a congratulations card 12 book reviews; crime reporter

2 2 is 3 is 4 live / lives 5 depend 6 has 7 is 8 has
9 has / have 10 is 11 is 12 means 13 are 14 are

3 2 fresh fruit / vegetables (both are possible) 3 advertisements
4 salt ('cups of coffee' might be used in informal contexts)
5 advice ('tips' might be used in informal contexts)
6 explosives / ammunition (both are possible)
7 work ('jobs' might be used in informal contexts)
8 rubbish ('empty bottles' might be used in informal contexts)

4 2 a a competition; b a competition 3 a paper; b a paper
4 a a shampoo; b shampoo 5 a iron; b an iron 6 a a time;
b time 7 a an importance (*importance* would also be possible here); b importance 8 a knowledge; b a knowledge

5 1 My brother wasn't very good at taking exams and he left school at 16. At first he went to work in the construction industry. But he didn't enjoy it, so he took an evening course in accounting. Eventually, he started a company offering financial advice. He's now the managing director, and it seems that the company's doing really well.
('He's now managing director' is also possible.)

2 A: Do you remember the summer we went to Sweden? 1995, I think it was.
B: It was a wonderful holiday, wasn't it? And so good to see Joakim again. I'll never forget the picnic we had with him. There were a huge number of mosquitoes.
A: Yes, I remember. And then when the sun was going down there was an amazing sky – bright orange.
B: And then his car broke down as we were going home, and we had to go back by bus.
B: No, we got a taxi, didn't we?
A: Oh yes, that's right.

3 Linda has a busy life as a lawyer, but in her free time she really enjoys hiking. Most weekends she drives out into the countryside and walks for a few hours. She says she likes to forget about work, and she doesn't even take a mobile phone with her. In the summer she's going hiking in the Philippines. She's never been there before, but the friend she's going with knows the country well.

D: Exam practice
Use of English

1 is 2 The 3 As / Along 4 the 5 each 6 being 7 from
8 come / stem / date 9 are / were 10 Although / While
11 across / through / throughout / around 12 By 13 most
14 the 15 is

Grammar focus task

1 b the
2 a The b –
3 a the b a
4 a a b the

Writing *Sample answer:*

Sports facilities: present and future

Introduction
Two hundred residents were questioned about their use of sports
facilities in the town and their views on these facilities. The
report outlines the most popular sports among those questioned,
assesses satisfaction with facilities, and makes suggestions for
future developments.

Popular sports
Only *20% of the people questioned have used* sports facilities in the
town within the last year, although over 70% said they did some
sport in their last year at school. The most popular sports among
men are football and squash. Women prefer swimming, dance or
the use of fitness centres. *The number of men using fitness centres
is* small, even though *the council has targeted* men in its recent
'Keeping fit' campaign.

Current facilities
The public are generally satisfied with existing facilities, although
a number of people consider the leisure centre in need of
refurbishment. *The council is / are to make a decision* on this soon.
It was pointed out that many of the facilities in the town are
becoming increasingly run-down; for example, the tennis courts
and the golf course. One person pointed out that *90% of funding
for sports facilities comes from* local taxes, and that taxes were
already very high.

Future developments
In my view, the council should invest in facilities for team
sports such as volleyball, hockey and rugby, to enable people to
continue playing sports they enjoyed in school after they leave.
A new campaign should be launched to attract men to fitness
centres. The council should also consider outside sponsorship
from local businesses to fund better facilities.

Unit 6

A: Context listening

2 The speakers mention the following benefits and problems:
benefits: enjoyment, (personal) satisfaction, fitness (good for
heart and lungs), sleep better, social contact / friendships
problems: time commitment, running injuries (aching muscles,
back pain), running in bad weather is unpleasant

3 1 b many
  2 a each b every
  3 a a few b the few
  4 a less b fewer

4 In sentences 2a and 2b: we can say *each / every day* and *every /
  each one of us.*

C: Grammar exercises

1 1 is / are (Both are possible in this informal context; however,
    is would be preferred in a formal context); have
    2 is; has; has / have (Both are possible, although *have* is more
    likely in this informal context.)
    3 has; seem; likes

2 2 each 3 all / the whole (Both are possible, with a similar
    meaning.) 4 little 5 We were all 6 not all of it was 7 Not all
    8 less 9 the few 10 will all be 11 less 12 every 13 few
    14 nearly every 15 the whole 16 your children all / all your
    children (Both are possible, with a similar meaning.) 17 a few
    18 fewer (*fewer* is grammatically correct, although *less* might
    be used in an informal context.)

3 2 a the many b many
    3 a a lot of (more natural than *much* in this informal context)
    b much (more natural than *a lot of* in this formal context)
    4 a many b a lot of (more natural than *many* in this informal
    context)
    5 a none of b not any of (*none of* would also be possible)
    6 a No b not any (probably written or said *wasn't any*; *no*
    would also be possible)

4 3 all (*many* would also possible be here)
    4 few of 5 None 6 Both of 7 much 8 many of 9 much of
    10 Both 11 None of 12 every 13 Many 14 All (of)
    15 little of 16 little 17 each of

D: Exam practice
Listening

1 commitments 2 impressed 3 patronising 4 irrigation
5 handouts 6 self-sufficient 7 surplus 8 prospects

Grammar focus task

2 Many 3 all 4 few 5 whole 6 less

Writing *Sample answer:*

Report on part-time employment

Types of employment
Forty-eight of the 50 students interviewed had a part-time job,
with 75% working in shops. Four students were involved in
education: three taught musical instruments and one helped in a
school for disabled children. The remaining eight did babysitting.

The students worked between 2 and 20 hours a week. Those in
shops worked longest, 15 hours on average, while those doing
babysitting had less regular hours. *Most weeks* they do very *little
work*, but occasionally work up to four nights per week.

Negative effects

Many of the students said their work made them stressed. They felt tired at college and unable to complete their work to the best of their ability. *A few* also mentioned that they had *less time* for relaxation.

Advantages

All of the students interviewed felt that a part-time job gave them independence and awareness of the value of money. *Some* noted that as their parents were not well-off it was the only way to get money for leisure activities. *Many of them* said that it would be advantageous when applying to university and to jobs in later life, and students working with children felt that their jobs were very rewarding.

Recommendations

The most negative comments came from students who worked longer, inflexible hours in shops. Those working *fewer hours* a week, on the other hand, said they felt *less stress* and that they gained more from their work. I therefore suggest that students should be advised to spend no more than 10 hours a week in part-time employment.

Unit 7

A: Context listening

1   From top to bottom: Sweden, Scotland, Norway

2   He used to live in Sweden. He was born in Scotland and he lives there now. He recently visited Norway.

3   2 I left teaching and I started writing professionally.
3 I go back on every possible occasion. (*every occasion possible* would also be possible.)
4 I always know how a book is going to end.
5 I'm generally up at about 7.00 in the morning. (*Generally I'm up* ... would also be possible.)
6 As a rule I prefer finding information from books. (... *finding information from books as a rule* would also be possible. *I prefer, as a rule, finding* ... would also be possible but less likely.)
7 I still speak Swedish quite well.
8 My mother was a rather gentle woman. (*was rather a gentle woman* would also be possible.)
9 I'm still sketching out the plot. (*I'm sketching out the plot still* would also be possible, but less likely.)

4   2 ✓ 3 ✓ 4 ✗ 5 ✗ 6 ✓ 7 ✗ 8 ✓

C: Grammar exercises

1   2 I sometimes take / sometimes I take (Both are possible.)
3 hardly ever visits
4 to shout angrily
5 I absolutely agree / I agree absolutely (Both are possible.)
6 left last week
7 We occasionally go / Occasionally we go (Both are possible.)
8 to Sweden before (*before to Sweden* is much less likely.)
9 seldom go out
10 started singing loudly

2   2 a technical b somewhat technical

3 a genuine b very genuine
4 a original b highly original
5 a thoroughly professional b professional
6 a rather odd b odd
7 a critical b severely critical
8 a wild b pretty wild

3   2 to live 3 to stay 4 to see / seeing 5 to fall 6 working
7 to leave 8 to turn down / turning down 9 not being able
10 to start / starting 11 asking 12 to blame 13 to get / getting 14 leaving

4   1   2 I haven't heard back from her yet. (*I haven't yet heard back from her* would also be grammatically correct, but less likely and rather formal in a conversation.)
3 a really bad cold
4 the only seats available / the only available seats
5 a quite ridiculous price

2   1 Have you seen anything unusual in the street
2 I only ever see him
3 He's the man living in
4 the house opposite
5 He's rather a tall man / He's a rather tall man. (Both are possible.)

3   1 the given instructions / the instructions given (Both are possible, but the second is more likely in this informal conversation.)
2 the suggested route / the route suggested
3 steepest imaginable road / steepest road imaginable
4 there are rather a lot
5 even I would be worried

D: Exam practice
Use of English

1 responsible 2 concerned 3 original 4 event 5 critical
6 perfectly

Grammar focus task

1   Question 3: a highly original mix (gradable); My original plan (non-gradable); the original painting (non-gradable)
Question 5: a critical moment (non-gradable); was critical of his performance (gradable); is critical to the prevention (non-gradable)

2   seemed perfectly well (no other positions possible for *perfectly*)
I perfectly understand your objections, *or* I understand perfectly your objections, *or* I understand your objections perfectly
to have perfectly combed hair (no other positions possible for *perfectly*)

Writing *Sample answer:*

I wish to nominate my teacher, Miss Petra Gunnarson, for the 'English Language Teacher of the Year' award. She is in her mid thirties and has taught English for ten years. She did a degree in English at Stockholm University, where she also trained to teach. She taught in Germany and Australia before coming to work at my college last year.

Miss Gunnarson is an *outstanding* teacher in many respects. Firstly, she has an *excellent* command of English. She not only studied it at university but she also lived in Australia, so she speaks *perfect* idiomatic English. She keeps her English up-to-date by reading and visiting friends in Britain. Secondly, she is *tremendously* enthusiastic about English. She is *fascinated* by the language and conveys her interest to her students. Thirdly, she clearly understands the best methods of language learning. Miss Gunnarson's lessons are *quite hard work*, but always *highly entertaining*. We play games and work in pairs so that we speak English as much as possible.

I was always *rather shy* about speaking English, but Miss Gunnarson has encouraged me to speak and not worry about making mistakes. She is never *critical* if I try but get something wrong, and full of praise when I get something right. She has also given me the *essential* skills to help me improve on my own by organising my time, and trying to learn a few words each day.

Without doubt Miss Gunnarson has had a huge impact on me and my fellow students. She is a *wonderful* teacher in so many ways.

Unit 8

A: Context listening

3 2 the best ... on 3 as little as 4 the most boring
   5 more peaceful than 6 as much as

4 1 *too* + adj + *to*-infinitive 2 *the best* 3 *as* + adj + *as*
   4 *the most* + adj 5 *more* + adj + *than* 6 *as much as*

C: Grammar exercises

1 1 most venomous (*most harmful* would also be possible)
   2 narrower / more narrow; deeper 3 more harmful / unhealthier / more unhealthy; most alert 4 closest; most magnificent / handsomest / most handsome 5 poorer; unhealthier / more unhealthy 6 handsomest / most handsome; more concerned 7 more thrilled; most respected; more sad

2 1 b the cheapest *or* cheapest
   2 a the oldest of b the most famous artist of his generation
   3 a the youngest in the team b fittest *or* the fittest
   4 a the most exclusive hotel on the island b most embarrassing

3 2 few 3 were the poll findings / the poll findings were 4 little
   5 as is 6 as much 7 serious a problem 8 normal a life
   9 not such a 10 as 11 so / as (Both are possible in informal speech, but *as* is more likely.)

4 2 Adam is so tall that he has to bend down to get through doorways. 3 The job offer was so good that I couldn't turn it down. 4 The comet is so bright that it can be seen with the naked eye. 5 The traffic outside the theatre was so loud that the actors couldn't make themselves heard. 6 The camera is so small that it can fit easily into your shirt pocket. 7 The results were so awful that our teacher made us take the test again. 8 The fire was so serious that the building had to be evacuated.

5 2 (3 from Ex 4) The job offer was too good (for me) to turn (it) down.

3 (6 from Ex 4) The camera is small enough to fit easily into your shirt pocket *or* The camera is small enough to fit into your shirt pocket easily.
4 (8 from Ex 4) The fire was serious enough for the building to be evacuated.

D Exam practice
Reading

1 C 2 A 3 D 4 D 5 B 6 C 7 A 8 B 9 B 10 D 11 A 12 C 13 C 14 C 15 A 16 B 17 D 18 D

Grammar focus task

1 as damaging ... as 2 the more ... better 3 so ... so ... that
4 as little as

Writing *Sample answer:*
Improving study skills

Do you find studying difficult? If so, this information sheet is for you. It provides tips to make studying *a more straightforward process*.

Time management

Managing time is one of *the biggest problems* faced by students: finding enough study time and making *the most effective* use of it. Try this:
- Identify periods you know you will be free to study in the coming week.
- Write a list of tasks you have to do – *longer tasks* like reading a chapter, and *shorter tasks* like organising notes.
- Match the tasks to the study periods.
- Keep to your timetable, and don't be distracted by *more interesting* activities like watching TV.

Reading

Reading a textbook is *more difficult than* reading a novel, so you need different strategies:
- Set reading targets, such as the number of pages to read each day.
- It's *better* to work on a difficult text for short periods, taking frequent breaks.
- If you get stuck, discuss it with a classmate or your tutor.

Remembering information

Everyone has their own methods of remembering information. Here are some of *the most popular*:
- Study a topic and then get a friend to test you – testing yourself is *not as effective as* having someone else do it.
- Record information onto a MP3 player and listen to it *as often as possible*.
- Use drawings in your notes – visual images are *easier to remember than* words.

Above all, be positive about studying. It's not *as difficult as* you might think!

Unit 9

A: Context listening

2 2 Early communication: parents and play
   3 Listening and learning: the interrelationships

4 Patterns of communication: learned behaviour?

5 Language learning problems: what and why?

3 2 giving a toy to their mother

3 offering her some food

4 Mend this for me

5 Reading stories for young children

6 describing this process to you

4 verb + person / people + thing(s)   1 and 3

verb + thing(s) + for + person / people 4 and 5

verb + thing(s) + to + person / people   2 and 6

5 2

✓ giving their mother a toy

✗ ~~giving a toy for their mother~~

✓ giving a toy to their mother (focuses attention on 'their mother')

3

✓ offering her some food

✗ ~~offering some food for her~~

✓ offering some food to her (focuses attention on 'her')

4

✗ ~~Mend me this~~

✓ Mend this for me

✗ ~~Mend this to me~~

5

✓ Reading young children stories

✓ Reading stories for young children (focuses attention on the young children and suggests that the children themselves aren't able to read)

✓ Reading stories to young children (focuses attention on the young children and highlights that something is being read out loud)

6

✗ ~~describing you this process~~

✓ describing this process for you

✓ describing this process to you (*describing ... for* and *describing ... to* have a similar meaning here)

C: Grammar exercises

1 Example answers:

  2 They agreed with each other.

  3 They always compete with each other.

  4 They respect each other.

  5 They trust each other.

  6 They miss each other.

  7 They have known each other for 20 years.

  8 They work with each other.

  9 They blamed each other.

  10 They disagreed with each other.

2 2 myself some chocolate 3 those letters for you / them for you
4 some apples for me / me some apples; you for them
5 you a favour (*a favour of you* would also be possible.); me how to print out a document 6 your car for you; you a lot
7 the mistake to the manager; me a £10 gift voucher / a £10 gift voucher to me 8 me your glass / your glass to me; some water for you / you some water

3 2 him guilty of the murder

3 themselves incapable of maintaining order

4 himself fit to play again 5 myself lucky to be alive
6 her responsible for its collapse 7 itself independent of the Soviet Union

4 2 himself on; (himself) to 3 herself (to make it clear that the chocolates were for Sarah); myself with 4 (myself) for; myself with 5 themselves; you 6 (himself); (no reflexive or personal pronoun needed)

D: Exam practice
Use of English

1 her responsible for

2 have made up

3 sooner had I got home than

4 get along with one

5 no difficulty (in) recognising

6 herself on her / an ability

7 clearly explained the procedure (to us) / explained the procedure clearly (to us) / explained the procedure (to us) clearly

8 with the exception of

Grammar focus task

1 impose herself <u>on</u>, organise themselves <u>into</u>, brace ourselves <u>for</u>, acclimatise himself <u>to</u>, distance myself <u>from</u>, console herself <u>with</u>, familiarise yourself <u>with</u>, establish ourselves <u>as</u>, tear myself away <u>from</u>, busy herself <u>with</u>

2 fetch ✗ collect ✗ owe ✓ offer ✓ build ✗ point out ✓ repair ✗ choose ✗ hand ✓ introduce ✓

Writing *Sample answer:*

To whom it may concern,

I am writing in support of Lucy Moseley's application for the post of newsletter editor.

I have known Lucy for five years since we met at university. We both worked on the university's weekly newspaper, and Lucy was editor for two years. In this role she demonstrated great enthusiasm and administrative skills. In addition to editing, she had to *write articles for the newspaper* and *set up interviews for the other student journalists* like myself. When we *asked her for advice*, she was always eager to help.

After university, Lucy and I both took jobs at our present company, and I have continued to work closely with her. During the time that I have known Lucy, I have *found her reliable* and honest in all aspects of her work. She has also *earned herself a great deal of respect* through her support for junior colleagues, always being happy *to explain procedures to them*.

Although she can at first appear to be rather a shy person, she is in fact very kind and friendly when you get to know her, and always willing to socialise with work colleagues.

I have no doubt that she will carry out every aspect of the position to the best of her ability and with great success. In addition, it will *give her the opportunity* to develop her editorial and communication skills still further. I am happy to *recommend her for the post*.

A: Context listening

1 passport left at home, missed flight, seasickness, stung by jellyfish

2 2 meant flying 3 made to wait 4 had encouraged me to go 5 hate swimming 6 felt it stinging 7 appreciated them looking after 8 stopped to admire 9 tried using 10 came to realise 11 considered staying

3 1 We can use either a *to*-infinitive or *-ing* form in sentences:
5 When I was younger I used to hate *to swim / swimming* in the sea.
8 As we stopped *to admire / admiring* the amazing sunset, it was almost possible to believe it.
9 I tried *to use / using* the camera in my mobile phone, but the quality was pretty poor.
2
Sentence 5 would have a similar meaning with either a *to*-infinitive or an *-ing* form.

C: Grammar exercises

1 2 advised him to give up 3 were asked not to use *or* were asked to not use (similar meaning but the first is more likely) 4 has suggested widening 5 showed him pointing 6 guarantee to reply 7 make it drink 8 appreciate you helping / appreciate your helping (*your* is more formal) 9 don't enjoy sitting 10 advertise for someone to share

2 A 2 him talking 3 him stealing 4 to have 5 to sack
B 1 to capture 2 for the bear / it to get 3 to eat / eating (both possible) 4 it / the bear escaping 5 to call / calling (both possible)
C 1 saying 2 having 3 to see 4 do 5 to collect 6 to get

3 2 to get more exercise
3 to have been killed in the earthquake
4 to go at the weekend
5 to be talking on my mobile
6 (to) argue with him
7 shouting / shout at anyone
8 to be a successful businesswoman
9 have been here an hour ago
10 paying for both of us
11 having her around
12 to have been caused by a virus

D: Exam practice
Reading
1 D 2 C 3 A 4 B 5 C 6 A 7 B

Grammar focus task
2 to narrow 3 travelling 4 enforcing 5 cutting 6 pushing 7 to reduce 8 to question
In 3 we could also use 'to travel' and in 6 'to push'.

Writing *Sample answer:*

Senior Citizens' Visit

In July, a group of local senior citizens *came to visit* the college.

The afternoon started with a welcome speech from the Principal, followed by a guided tour. We then provided entertainment – music, drama, and dance. It was described in feedback as 'superb' with the dancing singled out as 'very professional'. We *encouraged visitors to join* in songs from the 1950s, which they did enthusiastically. The rock band, though, was too loud for some!

Next came refreshments with cakes baked by students, praised as 'first class'. It was a great opportunity to talk, and we all *enjoyed sharing* our educational experiences. We were amazed to learn that some were taught in classes of 50 pupils!

Our visitors left at 4.30, and they all *seemed to enjoy* the afternoon. One wrote: 'We *appreciated the students looking* after us so well, and *we're looking forward to coming* back.' We enjoyed it, too, and *can't wait to see* them next year. Thanks to all who *helped make* it so successful.

Next year we will run a similar event, inviting local children with physical disabilities. But we need more helpers. If you play an instrument, be part of our entertainment. Or act as a guide – we need lots more. Come along and be part of a great day!

A: Context listening

1 The commentary is about the early development of radio.

2 The photographs and models are mentioned in the following order:
b, d, e, a, c

3 2 whose 3 when 4 of which 5 whereby 6 by which time

4 2 *whose* refers to *Guglielmo Marconi.*
3 *when* refers to *1901.*
4 *of which* refers to *wireless telegraphs.*
5 *whereby* refers to *a method.*
6 *by which time* refers to *1952.*

C: Grammar practice

1 2 b The photograph reminded him of the time **when** he used to live in New York.
3 a Any complaints should be sent to the Broadcasting Regulator, **whose** job it is to maintain standards in television programmes.
4 f The journalists have reached an agreement **whereby** they will be paid for a minimum 35-hour working week.
5 d I couldn't see any reason **why** Maude should be offended by my letter.
6 c The university has introduced an initiative in **which** talented students can complete their degree in only two years.

2 2 B / C (*committee* is a collective noun referring to a group of people, so we can use either *which* or *who*; *that* would also be possible)
3 A (some people might use *that* (B), but this is grammatically incorrect
4 A (formal) / B / D
5 A / C (more formal)
6 C

7 B / C / D (more formal)

8 A (formal) / D

3 2 in 3 at 4 from 5 of 6 for 7 by 8 of / about 9 in 10 by

4 2 A diving board is a narrow piece of wood at the edge of a swimming pool (**that / which**) people can dive from. (or **from which** people can dive)

3 Capri pants are women's narrow trousers **that / which** end just below the knee.

4 A shipper is a person or company **whose** job (it) is to organise the sending of goods from one place to another.

5 A *hakim* is a Muslim doctor **who** uses traditional methods to treat people.

6 A dumb waiter is a piece of equipment like a lift **in which / whereby** people can move food between the floors of a building. (or **which** people can move food **in** between the floors of a building)

7 The Stone Age is an early period in human history **when / in which / during which** people made tools and weapons only out of stone.

8 Proportional representation is a political system **in which / whereby** parties are represented in parliament according to the number of people who vote for them.

D: Exam practice
Use of English

1 which 2 whose 3 most / many / some 4 where 5 What 6 out 7 to 8 of 9 who 10 a 11 even 12 In 13 of / for 14 what 15 ever / yet

Grammar focus task

2 In general, these objects begin with a square sheet of paper, whose sides may be different colours. (Also possible is 'In general, these objects begin with a square sheet of paper, the sides of which may be different colours.')

3 Some believe that origami originated in China, from where it was taken to Japan in the seventh century.

4 Probably the most famous modern origami artist was Akira Yoshizawa, who died in 2005.

5 Akira Yoshizawa created more than 50,000 models, only a few hundred designs of /for which were shown in his books. (Also possible is 'Akira Yoshizawa created more than 50,000 models, of /for which only a few hundred designs were shown in his books.')

Writing *Sample answer:*

Fundraising for charity: a proposal

1 The cause

I propose that our college should raise money for the United Nations Children's Fund, UNICEF, *the aim of which* is to ensure children around the world have access to the support, healthcare and education necessary for a happy and healthy childhood. *The reason why* I have chosen this charity is that, as young people, we can empathise with *the people the charity aims to assist.* Supporting UNICEF should help us appreciate the opportunities we have, compared with young people *who are* less fortunate than ourselves.

2 Fundraising

I have various ideas for fundraising, *one of which* is to have a cake sale within the college. This could involve all senior students contributing some food, for example cakes or biscuits they have made themselves, and then selling these to the rest of the school. This way everyone could help make a contribution.

Another idea is to have a sponsored walk. For example, we could find out how far some children in developing countries have to walk to school, to water supplies or to hospitals, and then get sponsorship for walking this distance. This would allow students to experience the difficulties faced by many children in poorer societies, and also raise money at the same time.

3 My role

For the cake sale, I would arrange the time and place for the sale, and also organise people to bake enough cakes and biscuits.

For the walk, I would try to find a company *which* would agree to sponsor us. Then all participants could wear a T-shirt advertising the cause *that* they are supporting. I would also find out from UNICEF about the long distances walked by some children in a developing country, and would prepare maps for participants with walking routes of the same distance.

Before both events, I would organise a meeting for the whole college *where* a group of senior students could present the main aims of UNICEF, why we are supporting this specific charity, and how everyone can get involved.

Unit 12

A: Context listening

2 She uses:
   studio lights for lighting the shot
   glycerine to keep the food looking shiny and moist
   cotton wool balls soaked in water and heated in the microwave to create steam
   a blowtorch to brown or melt the food.

3 2 who wanted > wanting
   3 who encouraged > to encourage
   4 who won > to win
   5 that is produced > produced
   6 which are used > used
   7 that is not made > not made
   8 which contains > containing
   9 that have been soaked > soaked

4 1 Sentences 1, 2, 8
   2 Sentences 5, 6, 7, 9
   3 Sentences 3, 4

C: Grammar exercises

1 2 a The Internet is bringing about a degree of cultural change which /that has not been seen for centuries.
   The Internet is bringing about a degree of cultural change not seen for centuries.

   3 c All the passengers who / that were injured in the train crash have been released from hospital.
   All the passengers injured in the train crash have been released from hospital.

4 e People who want tickets for the cup final can expect to pay over 100 euros.

People wanting tickets for the cup final can expect to pay over 100 euros.

5 g Our teacher, who was carrying a huge pile of textbooks, came hurrying into the room.

Our teacher, carrying a huge pile of textbooks, came hurrying into the room.

6 f Is that woman who is playing the piano your sister?

Is that woman playing the piano your sister?

7 b Barton Green, which is situated five miles from the city centre, will be the location of the new sports stadium.

Barton Green, situated five miles from the city centre, will be the location of the new sports stadium.

2 1 The government has brought in new legislation affecting Britain's 5.4 million dog owners. From next year all dogs will have to be tagged with tiny electronic chips holding information about the dog's owner.

2 The inquiry into the wreck of the oil tanker *Patricia*, which sank off the south-west coast in 2007, has produced its final report. The report, (to be) published tomorrow / being published tomorrow, is thought to show that the captain was mainly responsible for the collision with a smaller vessel.

3 The road bridge being built across the River Neem at Walden will not now be completed until next January, nearly four years behind schedule, after yet another accident on the site. A section of the bridge being lowered into position fell from the cranes lifting it, causing major damage to parts already completed.

4 Demonstrators protesting against the play *Global Strife* at the Crest Theatre in London, claiming it to be 'anti-religious', have succeeded in preventing it being performed. The theatre management, advised by police that security could not be guaranteed, cancelled last night's performance. On Thursday, a number of demonstrators who broke through police lines caused damage to the theatre and terrified members of the audience.

5 Researchers in New Zealand are developing a new drug which might prevent memory loss in older people. A group of 20 elderly people suffering from dementia were given the drug over a two-year period, and results showed a significant slowing down in memory decline. The drug, derived from a plant found only in New Zealand, will now be tested on a larger group before being made more widely available.

3 2 to contact is the human resources manager
3 to look at the environmental effects of nuclear power
4 on the south side of the city
5 happy to help out
6 to take part / to have taken part in the London Marathon
7 very similar to Romanian
8 to pass / to have passed the French exam
9 to announce large-scale redundancies
10 to ring / to have rung today about the car

4 2 which have cut power use by up to 6.5% in Canada (no reduced relative clause possible)
3 who want them (*or* wanting them)
4 which are left on unnecessarily (*or* left on unnecessarily)

5 which use microchip technology and a digital display (*or* using microchip technology and a digital display)
6 that is being used in a house at any given moment (*or* being used in a house at any given moment)
7 that are provided free of charge (*or* provided free of charge)
8 that would give customers access to free monitors (*or* to give customers access to free monitors)
9 that should be considered (*or* to be considered)
10 which communicate electricity consumption both to the customer and the energy supplier (no reduced relative clause possible)
11 that are only able to do half the job (*or* only able to do half the job)

D: Exam practice
Reading
1 C 2 A 3 D 4 A 5 D 6 B 7 B

Grammar focus task
2 … there were clusters of dark freckles on his head, brown against the unconvincing wisps of his pale hair.
3 She put her hands into her pockets and pulled out a handful of small balls, multi-coloured and very bouncy.
4 I'm a Latvian sleeper. Waiting to be activated.

Writing *Sample answer:*

Salcombe – for a seaside holiday to remember

Salcombe is a delightful and charming town, *situated* in the south of Devon. The tranquil countryside *surrounding* Salcombe is ideal both for keen hikers and those who enjoy a more leisurely ramble, while the scenic coastline is breathtaking. It's a superb place *to spend* a relaxing week or weekend away, escaping from the fast pace of everyday life.

For those *wanting* a more active holiday, Salcombe is the place to come for sailing. It boasts some of the best sailing waters in England, as the sheltered estuary gives protection from Atlantic currents. There are many sailing schools within Salcombe *providing* first-class tuition for beginners as well as experienced sailors.

The town has all you need for the perfect holiday. There are cafes, restaurants, art galleries, museums, and great shopping. Find a shop *selling* Salcombe's famous dairy ice cream, and you'll be in for a real treat. Two glorious beaches can be found to the south of Salcombe, and across the estuary, a short boat ride away, lie the award-winning beaches of Mill Bay and Sunny Cove.

There are plenty of places to stay in and around Salcombe, *ranging* from old thatched cottages to four-star hotels. For those of you who love the outdoors, there are many camping and caravan sites *located* in quiet and pretty surroundings.

Come to the seaside at Salcombe for a more varied experience than a holiday in the countryside and a more peaceful holiday than a city break.

Unit 13

A: Context listening

1 1 processed food 2 a ready meal 3 a balanced diet
4 nutrition

2 2 + seeing that + **b** 3 + so that + **h** 4 + whereas + **a**
5 + because + **f** 6 + in order to + **e** 7 + although + **c**
8 + when + **g** 9 + while + **i** 10 + despite the fact that + **d**

3 *Seeing that* in sentence 2 has a similar meaning to *because*.
You could use *because* in sentences 8 and 9, but it would have
different meanings from *when* and *while*.

whereas and *Despite the fact that* in sentences 4 and 10 have
similar meanings to *although*.

C: Grammar exercises

1 2 as / when / while 3 as 4 when 5 While (= Although)
6 as / when 7 As 8 when (= every time; *whenever* would also
be possible) 9 As / When 10 When 11 While (= Although)
(In 2, 6 and 10, *as* and *when* (and *while* in 2) have a similar
meaning. However, *when* is more common than *as* or *while* in
informal contexts.)

2 2 c Although smoking is now banned in public spaces, sales of
cigarettes have actually increased.
Despite smoking now being banned in public spaces, sales of
cigarettes have actually increased.
3 g Although she fell heavily at the start of the race, she went
on to finish second.
Despite falling heavily at the start of the race, she went on to
finish second.
4 e Although we got lost on the way, we were eventually only
a few minutes late.
Despite getting lost on the way, we were eventually only a few
minutes late.
5 a Although the alarm went off when the house was broken
into, nobody bothered to call the police.
Despite the alarm going off when the house was broken into,
nobody bothered to call the police.
6 b Although we lived in the same village, we had never
spoken to each other.
Despite living in the same village, we had never spoken to
each other.
7 d Although she was badly hurt herself, she helped a number
of passengers out of the crashed coach.
Despite being badly hurt herself, she helped a number of
passengers out of the crashed coach.

3 2 People here don't put much effort into the job seeing that
it's so poorly paid.
3 My bike is unusual in that the front wheel is smaller than
the back.
4 You need to lift the plant carefully so as not to damage its
roots.
5 Pitcher plants are unique in that they are carnivorous.
6 The runway is going to be extended in order that larger
planes can land there.
7 She'll probably recover from the illness quickly seeing that
she's so fit.

8 She left work early in order that she could get to the concert
on time.
9 We spoke very quietly so as not to be overheard.

4 A
2 though 3 In spite of the fact that 4 before I go 5 seeing
that
B
1 Because 2 I'll have to 3 while (*whilst* would be very
formal in this context) 4 so that I can (Some people use *so
as + subject + verb* (e.g. *so as I can*) in very informal English.
However, this is grammatically incorrect and should be
avoided in examinations.) 5 you get
C
1 Inasmuch as 2 despite the fact that 3 in order not to
4 Although 5 as

D: Exam practice
Use of English

1 except / but 2 much 3 until / to / till 4 so 5 themselves
6 when 7 in 8 with 9 meet / turn 10 surprisingly 11 other
12 on 13 order 14 led 15 conflict

Grammar focus task

1 whenever 2 in that 3 although 4 in order to

Writing *Sample answer:*

I want to recommend two films with a romantic theme: *Chocolat*
and *Pride and Prejudice*. *Chocolat* follows the story of a woman,
Vianne, and her young daughter who travel constantly, never
settling down. They arrive in an old-fashioned village and open
an exotic chocolate shop. *Although* she is welcomed by some
villagers, the mayor becomes her enemy. How Vianne becomes
part of the community makes for an amusing and heart-warming
film. The film is shot in a beautiful setting and includes some
fine performances.

The second, *Pride and Prejudice*, follows the lives of the Bennet
family; five daughters and their father and mother. The mother's
aim in life is to help her daughters meet men, *so that* they
can get married. *When* Elizabeth, the second-oldest daughter,
meets Mr Darcy, she thinks he is incredibly proud. But *as* she
gets to know him, she discovers a gentleman beneath his proud
exterior. And, of course, they fall in love. The twists and turns
of the relationship keep the viewer gripped. *While* I don't always
enjoy Keira Knightley's acting, in this film she gives an excellent
performance.

The main difference between the films is their period and
location; *Chocolat* is set in twentieth century France and *Pride
and Prejudice* in eighteenth century England. But both films have
romance at their heart, and romance is a surefire winner with
cinema audiences whenever and wherever films are set.

Don't look for special effects in either of these films – they will
instead appeal to those who like their films clever, witty, well
acted and beautifully photographed.

Unit 14

A: Context listening

1 Picture a shows a zoo, picture b a game reserve and picture c a safari park.

2 2 M, W and D 3 D 4 M 5 D and W 6 M 7 D 8 D

3 2 unless 3 even if 4 provided that 5 even though
  6 so long as

C: Grammar exercises

1 Suggested answers:
  2 If you've got / If you have a student card you can get a discount at the bookshop.
  3 If you promise to bring it back tomorrow you can borrow my laptop for the evening.
  4 If we used /use more efficient light bulbs, there could be a 5% reduction in electricity consumption. *or* If people used / use…
  5 If I had been promoted, I would have had to move to our head office in Madrid.
  6 If you're going to catch the 8.30 train, you'll have to leave the house by 7.00. / If you leave the house by 7.00, you'll (be able to) catch the 8.30 train.
  7 If I'd known you were a vegetarian, I wouldn't have cooked lamb for dinner. *or* If I knew you were a vegetarian…
  8 If I had studied harder, I wouldn't have such a poorly paid job now.

2 2 if; didn't get / don't get
  3 if / even if (a similar meaning here); liked / likes
  4 even though; had been driving / had driven / drove
  5 if; was / were (*were* is more formal)
  6 even though; have been doing / have done / did
  7 If; enjoyed
  8 Even if; rains / rained
  9 unless; prefer / would prefer
  10 if; isn't
  11 Even if / Unless (*Even if* … means that the company is likely to close by the end of the week whether or not there is a buyer. *Unless* … means that the company is likely to close only if no buyer can be found.); can
  12 if /even if; was / were (*were* is more formal)
  13 if; was / were (*were* is more formal)
  14 even if / even though (*even if* = whether or not he has formal qualifications. *even though* = despite the fact that he doesn't have formal qualifications); doesn't have

3 2 f Aid must reach the refugees before the rainy season starts, *otherwise* many thousands will die.
  3 a The demonstrators arrested were allowed to go free *on condition that* they remained outside a 10-mile zone around the nuclear power station. ('providing' is also possible, although it would be rather informal in this sentence)
  4 c Car airbags were designed to prevent chest injuries to the driver *in the event of* a head-on collision.
  5 e He would have gone on working until he was 65 *but for* his poor health.
  6 b We should get to the airport by 5.00 *providing* the traffic isn't too heavy on the motorway.

4 1
  2 phone 3 will make / makes (similar meaning)
  2
  1 had bought 2 had 3 was 4 would stop
  3
  1 wasn't snowing 2 I'd have left 3 you'd got up
  4 could have got 5 will be / is (similar meaning)

D: Exam practice
Listening

Task One

Speaker 1 F   Speaker 2 G   Speaker 3 A
Speaker 4 C   Speaker 5 D

Task Two

Speaker 1 C   Speaker 2 H   Speaker 3 E
Speaker 4 B   Speaker 5 G

Grammar focus task

2 a *or* b 3 a *or* b 4 b 5 a

Writing *Sample answer:*

The growth of cities: present and future consequences

People have many different motivations for moving from the countryside to cities, but by far the most significant is the greater opportunity for earning higher wages in urban areas. Rates of unemployment in rural areas are generally higher than in cities and, *even if* people have a job in the countryside, they are likely to be earning less than they could in a city. Cities have other attractions, too, particularly for young people who want the kinds of educational and entertainment facilities – universities, cinemas, and clubs, for example – that they do not have access to *if* they live in the countryside. Older people, too, may be attracted to the healthcare facilities found in cities.

The growth of urban areas has consequences, mainly negative, for both cities and villages. Rural areas suffer from depopulation, which means that there may not be enough people to keep health centres and schools open. *If* a village loses a large proportion of its young people, the remaining older population may not grow sufficient agricultural produce for the village to survive. *Unless* urban growth is planned for carefully, there can be huge pressure on housing, with the resulting shanty towns seen in many cities in the developing world. The consequent overcrowding and poor sanitation can lead to the spread of disease.

It is vital that the trend towards urbanisation is slowed down; *otherwise*, the future is bleak. But *as long as* the world population continues to grow, this is unlikely to happen. The main priority, then, is education and access to birth control. In addition, life in rural areas must be made more attractive to young people, encouraging them to stay. *If* governments don't take steps to expand well-paid employment in the countryside, the flight to the cities will continue. The picture is not, however, all negative. In some countries, the problems of living in cities have encouraged older, richer people to move to the countryside, and with them have come educational, health and entertainment facilities. *If* this pattern continues, we may eventually see a slowdown in the expansion of cities.

(Note: *a shanty town* is an area in or on the edge of a city in which poor people live in small, badly built houses)

Unit 15

A: Context listening

1   1, 2 and 4

2   2 c 3 f 4 a 5 d 6 b

3   2 Exhausted 3 Before leaving 4 Having left 5 But opening up 6 Having been woken up

C: Grammar exercises

1   **2 b** Covered in oil, Colin got out from under the car. / Getting out from under the car, Colin was covered in oil.

3 h Not being able to speak Portuguese (*or* Not speaking Portuguese ...), I found travelling in Brazil difficult.

4 d Having already beaten Real Madrid twice this year, Manchester United are favourites to win again. / Having beaten Real Madrid twice this year already, ...

5 a Having been shown how to use the software, I found it easy to design my own website.

6 c Not having eaten or drunk anything for hours, I was starting to feel a bit faint.

7 e Putting on her glasses (*or* Having put on her glasses ...), she began to read her speech.

8 f Written in Latin, the two letters were sent in 1406 to the French king.

2   2 Seeing the pocket watches / On seeing the pocket watches (more formal)

3 some (of them) being / with some (of them) being

4 Living in Hong Kong / Having lived in Hong Kong

5 After looking at / After having looked at

6 I got there to find / on getting there I found (more formal)

7 Having spent

8 (in order) to get

9 (When) looked at

10 tired

11 before going out

3   2 S 3 D 4 S 5 S 6 D 7 D 8 S

Suggested improvements:

1 (Other possible answers) As the signs were painted bright yellow, I could see them clearly from a distance. / Painted (*or* Being painted ...) bright yellow, the signs could be seen from a distance. (The alternatives with *Painted* ... and *Being painted* ... are more formal than those with *Because* ... and *As* ... and would be more appropriate in writing.)

2 (No improvement necessary)

3 Because / When I laughed at her new hat, Kate looked really angry with me. / Because I was laughing at her new hat, ...

4 (No improvement necessary)

5 (No improvement necessary)

6 Because they were talking to each other in the library, I asked them to keep quiet.

7 Crayfish are caught in traps put on the riverbed at night, and many fishermen depend on them for their livelihood.

8 (No improvement necessary)

4   2 While researching 3 Although no longer involved 4 Before being made 5 Without asking 6 since leaving 7 once caught 8 With the wind reaching 9 until / before being woken 10 If found

D: Exam practice

Use of English

1 helping 2 instinctively 3 readily 4 ability 5 adaptable 6 starvation 7 learnt/learned 8 inadvisable/ill-advised 9 parental 10 independent

Grammar focus task

1   This kind of behaviour is vital for a young animal, *helping* it recognise danger and food.

Mammals often have an even greater degree of parental care, some *staying* with their mother even until her next offspring is born.

2   *Governed* by its genes, some parts of an animal's behaviour are innate.

Having *learnt* what she looks like, chicks are then able to avoid making inadvisable approaches to other potentially dangerous birds in the community.

3   *To survive*, an animal has to be able to do certain things as soon as it is born or it hatches.

Writing *Sample answer:*

Review of *Lucia, Lucia* by Adriana Trigiani

Lucia, Lucia is a riveting novel of passion and elegance. It is the story of a woman who believes that as a woman she could, and should, be able to have it all.

Set in dazzling and pulsating 1950s New York City, it is the enthralling story of how Lucia Sartori follows her heart, *changing her life forever*. She is the beautiful daughter of an affluent Italian grocer in Greenwich Village. *Although engaged* to her childhood sweetheart, Dante DeMartino, a chance meeting with a handsome stranger who promises her a life of uptown glamour causes her to become torn between the two. Their love affair takes a startling turn as secrets are revealed and she finds herself in the centre of a sizzling scandal. *With her reputation at risk*, the honour of the Sartori family is in jeopardy.

I found this a thoroughly enjoyable read, with an enchanting story and a set of lively and warm-hearted characters. An element of warm humour makes it pleasurable and light-hearted. I found the character of Lucia particularly entertaining, and her witty remarks to the men in her life often made me laugh out loud. *Having read it three times already*, I have found it to be a book that never loses its appeal, and I would strongly recommend it. It is a novel that should be read and passed on to a friend, as it is sure to bring a smile to anyone's day.

A: Context listening

1 **1** birdwatching **2** using the Internet **3** giving someone a lift
4 bricklaying / building a brick wall
5 having / organising a barbecue **6** building a fence

2 2, 3, 5 and 6

3 **2** F **3** F **4** T **5** T **6** T **7** F **8** F **9** T

4 **1** that you'll make a lot of new friends **2** whatever time
people can spare **3** when we usually meet **4** what to do
5 why the Marsh was given to the NWT

5 *wh-* words and *that*

C: Grammar exercises

1 **2** the fact that **3** The fact that **4** that **5** the fact that **6** that
7 the fact that **8** the fact that **9** that **10** the fact that **11** that

2 **2** whichever direction you approach it **3** whether to take a
guided tour **4** when the cathedral was built **5** where the
building materials came from **6** how they managed to do that
(*the way they managed ... is also possible*) **7** Who designed
the cathedral **8** what conditions were like for the builders
9 the way the light shines through them (*how the light shines
... is also possible*) **10** whoever wrote that **11** if I'd make it
(*whether I'd make it* is also possible)

3 **2 e** I must have that painting, and will pay *whatever* it costs.
3 d The police have said that to protect the public they will
take *whatever* action is necessary.
4 a I've bought this armchair that adjusts itself to the body
shape of *whoever* is sitting in it.
5 g We've got lots of cakes, so just choose *whichever / whatever*
one you want.
6 h At the first modern Olympic games in 1886, athletes could
wear *whatever* they wanted to.
7 b Houses next to the river are at risk of flooding, *whichever*
side they are on.
8 f Both the number 45 and 47 buses go into town, so get on
whichever comes first. (*whichever one you want* is also possible)

4 **2** told us what questions
3 do you know how to drive
4 to teach me / you what to do (*to teach me / you how to do it*
would also be possible)
5 showed me where to sit
6 about what would happen next
7 asked (her) when the doctor
8 the time when we were (*the time we were* would also be
possible)
9 the problem of how to get
10 The reason why I mention it (*The reason I mention it* would
also be possible)

D: Exam practice
Use of English
1 C **2** C **3** A **4** D **5** A **6** D **7** C **8** A **9** C **10** B **11** A **12** C

Grammar focus task

1 whether homework has a significant educational value
2 that it takes too much time away from other more useful
activities
3 What is often neglected in this debate
4 whether or not the child's home provides support for effective
homework
5 Whatever money they have
6 the idea that only middle-class parents support their
children's education

Writing *Sample answer:*

Dear Editor,

David Wallace is wrong to say that we need more nuclear power
stations. Until the issue of *what to do with nuclear waste* is
resolved, nuclear power can never be the answer to our energy
needs. He seems to forget *that as the number of power stations
increases, so does the chance of another huge nuclear disaster on the
scale of Chernobyl.*

He claims *that developing countries must have nuclear power
stations*, but few developing countries have access to the huge
amounts of money needed to build them. He also overlooks *the
fact that technological developments in coming years are likely to lead
to a rapid expansion in the use of renewable energy.* Although not
all countries have available to them the full range of renewable
energy sources – hydro, wind, solar, tidal and geothermal energy
– each country has the potential to develop at least one major
source.

Many countries in Africa and the Middle East have massive
potential for developing solar energy provided cheap technology
becomes available. Eventually, they may even be able to sell their
energy to other countries, enabling them to develop still further
economically.

Good examples of what might be done already exist around the
world. Iceland, for example, is aiming to become a carbon neutral
country, and already 99.9% of its energy comes from renewable
sources, mainly hydroelectric and geothermal power. Germany is
Europe's leading generator of wind energy, accounting for around
4% of all its energy use. Each country has to consider *how best to
exploit the renewable energy resources it has available.*

I do not believe, then, that it is necessary to drastically increase
the number of nuclear power stations. This would simply divert
funds from the research into new technologies that is needed for
the expansion of renewable energy. We have to face *the fact that
renewable energy sources are the only answer* and all our money and
effort should be directed towards their development.

Yours sincerely,

Laura Hernandez

Unit 17

A: Context listening

2   reversing around corners, overtaking and starting on a hill

3   Marie: the correct order is: c, b, a, d
Sam: the correct order is: h, f, g, e

4   2 however   3 even so   4 although   5 even though   6 as long as

C: Grammar exercises

1   **2 h** She always finds time to talk to students, no matter how busy she is. / No matter how busy she is, she always finds time to talk to students.
3 a The restaurant's closed next Monday because it's a public holiday. / Because it's a public holiday, the restaurant's closed next Monday.
4 e He's a seismologist. That is to say, he studies earthquakes. / He studies earthquakes. That is to say, he's a seismologist.
5 f Tuition fees have been increased. As a result, the number of applications has fallen.
6 c We travelled much faster once we got onto the motorway. / Once we got onto the motorway, we travelled much faster.
7 b The government is being urged to build more nuclear power stations. However, such a move would be controversial.
8 g He was wearing the same clothes as me, except that his shoes were black.

2   2 Firstly   3 hardly / scarcely (similar meaning)   4 until
5 Lastly   6 Even so   7 On the contrary   8 before / until
(similar meaning)   9 At last   10 At first   11 Even though
12 no sooner

3   1 Note that we can't use *while* here because it is a conjunction. A sentence connector is needed to link the two sentences.
2 in case there's a power cut
3 whereas I prefer Italian (*while* is also possible)
4 Consequently, it isn't very heavy
5 otherwise we'll have to walk miles to the bridge
6 while she's looking for a new flat
7 In contrast, in Marketing they get an hour
8 unless the weather's bad

4   A
2 while   3 because   4 At first   5 Even so
B
1 As well as   2 In spite of   3 until   4 hardly / no sooner
(similar meaning)   5 What's more

D: Exam practice
Use of English

1 on   2 something   3 if   4 Although / While   5 order   6 how
7 that / which   8 like   9 what   10 who   11 cope / deal   12 with
13 few   14 means   15 however

Grammar focus task

2 Although / While; Therefore; in order to   3 Nevertheless; however

Writing *Sample answer:*

Healthy eating – Learn to eat for a healthy life.

'Healthy eating' essentially involves following a balanced diet which includes all the different food groups in appropriate proportions. *Although* healthy eating is important for everyone, it is of particular significance for young people. In the early years of life people's bones and muscles grow rapidly, and a good diet is necessary during this period *in order to* avoid illness.

Deficiencies in important minerals can result in health problems, either immediately or in later life. Iron deficiency is common in young people, caused by rapid growth and a fast pace of life, and this can result in anaemia. *Consequently*, you should eat a diet rich in iron, including red meat and fresh vegetables such as broccoli. Calcium deficiency can lead to osteoporosis in old age, which causes bones to become very brittle and break easily. *Therefore*, a diet should be rich in calcium, from foods such as yoghurt, cheese and milk.

As well as preventing illness, there are other advantages of healthy eating. Healthy eating provides us with the energy needed for sport or simply going out with friends. *In addition*, it keeps your mind sharp and allows you to concentrate better on work. By eating well you can keep your skin, hair and nails looking good, *too*.

There are so many benefits of healthy eating and it doesn't have to be a chore. Eating well can be something enjoyable. Remember: invest in a balanced diet now and you will be rewarded with the health benefits throughout your life!

Unit 18

A: Context listening

1   1 STREET ART SPRAYED IN CAPITAL – **e** vandalism (here spraying graffiti)
2 MORE KIDS ATTACKED IN MOBILE THEFTS – **c** street crime (here stealing mobile phones from children)
3 GUN CONTROLS FAILING, SAYS POLICE CHIEF – **b** firearm offences
4 GANG LINKED TO 500 BREAK-INS – **a** burglary
5 VEHICLE THEFT COST £800M – **d** car crime (*car crime* can refer to stealing cars or stealing things from cars)

2   car crime, vandalism (damage to property, graffiti), street crime (stealing mobile phones), drug-related crime, burglary

3   2 F (Peter Miles was appointed head of the police service)   3 T
4 F (Other countries are thinking of copying the government's scheme.)   5 T (She agreed that there had been an increase in street crime.)   6 F (She said she didn't know)   7 F (She admitted that there might be mistakes in the figures.)
8 F (There is a campaign to reassure people it is falling)

4   1 was given (passive)   2 have been arrested (passive)
3 are seeing (active)   4 have become (active)   5 were caught (passive)   6 was broken into (passive)

C: Grammar exercises

1   A
2 is widely used   3 is viewed   4 are evaluated   5 is
6 is considered   7 collects   8 travels   9 believe   10 occur

11 is prevented 12 help

B

1 were constructed 2 be used 3 weighed 4 be carried
5 advanced 6 be held 7 became / had become 8 was banned
9 suggests / has suggested 10 has not discouraged
11 predict / are predicting 12 will be conducted

2 2 His name is Robin, but he is called Bobby by his friends.

3 (no passive) We might instead use *We had the procedure demonstrated to us ...*

4 The news will be announced to staff later today.

5 I have been offered a new job in Hungary.

6 He was seen to push the goalkeeper just before he scored. (*or* He was seen to have pushed ...)

7 The surgery has been declared a complete success (by the medical staff).

8 (no passive)

9 (no passive) We might instead use *I had the idea suggested to me ...*

10 This necklace was bought for me by my uncle when he was in Zimbabwe.

3 1 had / got her handbag stolen
2 was / got woken up; have been / have got thrown out
3 had / got his hair cut; had / got his jacket cleaned
4 's (is) owned; getting broken into
5 got it caught; be / get infected (*be* suggests that the speaker thinks it is infected now; *get* suggests that the speaker thinks it might become infected in the future)
(Note: The alternatives with *get* are more informal.)

4 2 we were made to run

3 she seemed to be supported by many of her colleagues

4 no passive (there is no passive form of 'want + object + *to-infinitive*')

5 remember being asked

6 not to have been picked / not having been picked / that she hadn't been picked / that she wasn't picked

7 he came to be liked by most of the children in the class

8 He was caught trying

9 likes being tickled / likes to be tickled

10 without having been asked / without being asked

11 She was heard to remark

12 no passive (there is no passive form of 'need + object + *to-infinitive*')

13 Over 100,000 demonstrators are expected to march

D: Exam practice
Reading

1 D 2 A 3 F 4 B 5 G 6 E
The extra paragraph is C.

Grammar focus task

1 decided (active) 2 is exposed (passive) 3 appointed (active)
4 assisted (active) 5 was greeted (passive) 6 attract (active)
7 sold out (active) (The passive form *was sold out* would also be correct.) 8 been played (passive) 9 has become (active)

Writing *Sample answer:*

Dear Editor,

I am writing in response to recent letters discussing the importance of university education. University is a very valuable experience for the overwhelming majority of students, and many skills *are learned* in addition to those gained in academic study.

The view *was expressed* that only those who go to universities should pay for them. But surely everyone in the country benefits when as many people as possible go to university. And access to university should not be confined to those whose parents can afford to pay. Students from poorer backgrounds also have talents to be developed in higher education. When those who do not attend complain about *being asked to fund* universities for young people, they should remember that graduates go on to support them directly. They become the doctors who care for them in their old age, the bankers who administer their pensions, and the engineers who build their roads and cities. And without university-educated people to fill these highly skilled jobs, we face *being left behind* by other countries.

In most countries, the percentage of the population having a university education is increasing, and this trend *is expected to continue*. However, this doesn't necessarily mean that high levels of graduate unemployment *will be seen*. In many parts of the world there is currently a shortage of students studying sciences, in particular physics and chemistry. It has to be acknowledged, however, that in some specialist areas too many graduates *are being produced*. For example, in the UK there are presently far more students graduating with a degree in forensic science than can be justified by the number of jobs available in forensic science. But as time goes by, such imbalances *will be put right* by the laws of supply and demand.

University-educated students contribute to our economic development, as they are the future workforce of this country, and without that workforce we cannot develop. Knowledge needs *to be passed on* to them and as they gain new skills they can become future leaders of our society, demonstrating that university benefits not only students but our nation as a whole.

Yours,

Carmen Alexander

Unit 19

A: Context listening

2 Advantages: it would create 2000 jobs at the airport; it might encourage tourism in the region; it would help local business
Problems: it would damage tourism; the noise; the danger of a plane crashing into the nuclear power station

3 2 said that 3 promised to keep 4 encouraged us to go
5 warned us that 6 advised us to write 7 've (have) volunteered to write

4

verb + *that*-clause	verb + *to*-infinitive	verb + object + *that*- clause	verb + object + *to*-infinitive
said	promised volunteered	told warned	encouraged advised

warned can also be followed by *that*- clause (e.g. *She warned that the airport authorities were not telling the truth*).

C: Grammar exercises

1 2 grumbled / were grumbling 3 claimed it 4 reassured me 5 reveal to 6 emphasised 7 whispered to 8 persuade him 9 commiserate with 10 explained to

2 2 me to apply / me that I should apply 3 me that my research 4 to complete / that I will complete 5 to publish / publishing / that I will publish 6 my qualifications and experience to be / that my qualifications and experience are / that my qualifications and experience will be 7 to hear / that I will hear 8 me to explain 9 told them (that) 10 (to them) that I had (had) problems / (to) having (had) problems 11 that I (should) look at / looking at 12 with me that my research 13 me to visit 14 me to write / that I (should) write / writing 15 to contact me / that they would contact me 16 to offer me / that they would/could offer me

3 2 He thinks (that) it's going to rain later today.

  3 She asked me why I don't / didn't walk to school any more. (We can use either a present or past tense verb if the situation (= not walking to school any more) still exists at the time of reporting.)

  4 She didn't think (that) it was her coat. (*She thought that it wasn't her coat* is also possible, although less likely.)

  5 He said (that) Diane can / is able to / could / was able to speak six languages.

  6 She asked (me) if / whether I'm /was going to college next year.

  7 She said (that) I had to / must set the alarm when I leave / left the house.

  8 She asked me who my favourite teacher was / who was my favourite teacher / my favourite teacher when I was at school.

  9 She couldn't remember where she left / had left her handbag.

  10 He said (that) he was playing football yesterday afternoon.

  11 He said (that) he won't / wouldn't be able to give me a lift after all, so I'll have to get a taxi.

  12 He wanted to know how much I earn / earned.

  13 She mentioned (that) they might go to France again in the summer.

  14 He wanted to know what he should do with the painting. / what to do with the painting.

4 2 She demanded that the debt of African nations be cancelled

  3 She argued that millions of people are / were being cheated of a proper living (a present subjunctive is not possible)

  4 She recommended that aid be focused / She recommended that we focus aid on basic health care and education

5 She said that the current trading rules are / were not fair (a present subjunctive is not possible)

6 She urged that poorer countries be allowed to trade as equals

7 She insisted that trade rules not be rewritten to favour richer countries

8 She advised that developing countries be helped to expand their own industries

9 She announced that *Stop Poverty!* is to launch a new public awareness campaign (a present subjunctive is not possible)

D: Exam practice
Listening
1 B 2 A 3 B 4 M 5 B 6 M

Grammar focus task

1 a no b yes
2 a no b no
3 a yes b no
4 a no b yes
5 a no b no

Writing *Sample answer:*

Report on English language course

Introduction

This report is based upon feedback from the five managers who attended the English language course in Britain this year.

Teaching and accommodation

The course lasted three weeks, with 75 hours of tuition. All participants *felt* that the teaching was excellent, and most *said* that with a longer course they would have made even more progress. Participants stayed with local families, and most *thought* this arrangement was successful. However, one manager *complained* that the food was poor.

Social activities

These included weekend trips arranged by the school, and informal evening activities organised by students. The participants *said* that all of these were enjoyable, although some *pointed out* that they were expensive.

Problems

In addition to those mentioned, some participants *grumbled* that the school was disorganised; for example, classrooms were often changed.

Recommendations

The overall cost was £2340 per person, and this seems reasonable value for money. However, this figure excluded social activities, books and midday meals, and some participants *reported* that these extra costs were a problem. My recommendation is that the exercise should be repeated with the same school for one more year for three weeks, but we should ask the school to include social activities and books in the figure of £2340. If they disagree, then we should try a different school.

Unit 20

A: Context listening

1 The pictures show:
   1 caving / potholing 2 camping 3 river rafting 4 paragliding
   5 (scuba) diving 6 surfing 7 sailing

2 Alison advises Ben to take a face mask, snorkel, sun hat,
   plastic trainers and insect repellent.

3 2 One of the local organisers did (met me at the airport).
   3 They should do provide all the equipment.
   4 But you don't have to be a very good swimmer.
   5 Preferably plastic ones trainers.
   6 By the end of the holiday I was exhausted, but I was very fit.
   7 You'll certainly need some insect repellent.
   8 I don't imagine so you'll need to take a tent and cooking
   things.

C: Grammar exercises

1 2 to ask you / to ask you
   3 has eaten anything today / has eaten anything today
   4 would have been shocked / would have been shocked /
   would have been shocked
   5 to leave work early / to leave work early
   6 might be a vegetarian would only be used informally;
   might be a vegetarian is more likely.
   7 to come on holiday with you / to come on holiday with
   you / to come on holiday with you
   8 had been opened / had been opened
   9 to get promoted
   10 did know I was getting married / did know I was getting
   married

2 2 No (ones is not used on its own to replace a noun phrase.
   We could say (some) new ones) 3 one 4 No (money is
   uncountable) 5 ones 6 (one) 7 (ones) 8 No (talking about
   specific items; we could replace the car keys with them)
   9 one 10 (one) 11 one 12 one 13 (ones) / (ones)

3 2 so did 3 So 4 do (do so would be unnaturally formal here)
   5 so 6 that 7 So 8 do 9 Yes, 10 (doing) that (doing so would
   be unnaturally formal here) 11 doing so 12 (that) she will
   (do) (do so would be unnaturally formal here, particularly
   after a modal verb. Note that do is optional here.) 13 so does
   14 Yes, (= this is my opinion, too)

4 Suggested changes in bold:

   Hi Chris,

   I tried phoning you earlier, but you must have been out. But I
   just have to tell somebody about the terrible day I've had …

   It started badly and got worse! When I got up the kitchen was
   flooded – I'd left the freezer door open! I've never **done that**
   before. By the time I'd finished mopping up all the water it
   was getting late. I was going to take my big handbag to work,
   but I was so rushed I picked up my small **one** by mistake,
   leaving my purse behind so I didn't have any money. Luckily,
   I bumped into Bob at the station and he was able to lend me
   some. My office key was also still at home, so when I got to
   work I had borrow **one**.

   Then I had to get to an important meeting. Our company is
   hoping to do some business with a Japanese firm. My boss

thinks we have a good chance of signing a deal soon, but I
don't think **so**. I thought the meeting was on the fourth floor
– in fact, I was certain **it was**. But it had been rearranged
and nobody had bothered to tell me. So I was 20 minutes
late. I wasn't very happy, and **neither was my boss / my boss
wasn't either**. To make matters worse, I'd been hoping to run
through my presentation over breakfast, but I'd had no **time
/ time to**. So my talk went really badly. Afterwards, my boss
said she was disappointed with the way the meeting went. But
so was I / I was, too.

After such a dreadful day, I was hoping I'd have a quiet
evening, but I **didn't**. When I got home I found that my cat
had knocked over some glasses – you remember the beautiful
old Swedish **ones** that my parents gave me? I wonder if I'll be
able to replace them? I **don't expect so / expect not**.

The only good thing is that it's the weekend. Come over
whenever you **want / want to**. In fact, are you able to come
over tomorrow? If you**'re not able to / can't**, how about
Sunday? Or are you still too busy decorating the house? I
hope not. But give me a call and let me know.

D: Exam practice
Listening

Grammar focus task

1 2 want 3 willing 4 able 5 advise
2 We can leave out to in:
   1 … she was determined to.
   3 … if they're willing to.

Writing *Sample answer:*

A PROPOSAL TO EXTEND THE LIBRARY

Introduction

Class 12Y proposes that the money put aside by the college for
the improvement of the building and facilities should be used
for an extension of the college library. We suggest that a wider
variety of books and new computers should be bought. *In doing
so*, the college can ensure that students have state-of-the-art
facilities for study.

The benefits

A number of benefits can be identified for both students and
teachers:
• The new library would provide a quiet working environment
  for students in their study periods.
• New reference books would be of value for students working
  on assignments and teachers preparing for their classes.
• The availability of a variety of novels of various genres would
  encourage students to read more widely outside school. A large
  collection of novels should be built up but, as paperback books
  are quite cheap, it would not cost a lot to *do so*.
• Computers with Internet access could be used by students and
  teachers for research purposes.
• Teachers could occasionally have the whole class using
  computers. *Doing so* will encourage new and innovative ways of
  teaching.

Recommendation

The college administration should consult with students and teachers on the design of the extension and on the new facilities. *By doing so*, it can be confident that they will meet the demands of the users.

Unit 21

A: Context listening

2 The speaker uses the following words in describing Maria Adams:
determined, persuasive, enthusiasm

3 2 F (the council lends them musical instruments)
3 T
4 F (the council backed down from their plan to make them pay)
5 F (People come from other countries to see the project)

4 The sentences you have written have a different emphasis from the ones given. The parts emphasised by the speakers are moved to (or closer to) the front of the sentence. These parts are underlined here:
2 Making music she sees as a fundamental part of a child's development,
3 What impressed us most was the way she calmly and clearly argued her case.
4 Rarely have I met anyone with such passion for their beliefs.
5 A number of times the council has tried to make changes to the *Music in Schools* project in order to save money.
6 Only after Maria threatened to withdraw her support from the project did the council back down.

C: Grammar exercises

1 2 It was at her eighteenth birthday party that she announced she was going to join the air force.
3 What we did was (to) ask a farmer to pull us out with his tractor.
4 What I really want is a cup of tea. / It's a cup of tea that I really want.
5 It could be the clutch cable that's broken.
6 What happened was that I wasn't looking where I was going and walked into a lamppost.
7 What I don't know is who sent them.
8 It must have been my parents who / that gave Colin my telephone number.
9 What the research shows is a link between salt intake and rates of heart disease.
10 It was his nervous laugh that made me think he was lying. / What made me think he was lying was his nervous laugh.

2 2 f Should today's match have to be postponed, it will be replayed next week. *or* Were today's match to be postponed, it will be replayed next week.
3 g Had anyone been looking at Martha when the police arrived, they would have noticed the expression of panic on her face.
4 d Were taxes to be increased further, there would be a huge public outcry. *or* Should taxes be increased further, there would be a huge public outcry.

5 a Had the doctors operated sooner, she might have made a full recovery.
6 h Were I president, I would introduce three-day weekends.
7 b Should your flight be cancelled, the insurance covers a full refund. *or* Were your flight to be cancelled, the insurance covers a full refund.
8 e Had heavy snow been forecast, we would not have begun the climb.

3 *Suggested answers:*
2 have I heard 3 did he discover / find / realise
4 did I know/realise 5 have there been 6 did she answer
7 had he got 8 did she say 9 should/must you turn/switch

4 2 It was the hotel that was the real problem. / What was the real problem was the hotel.
3 Along came the hotel porter
4 Away he went
5 in walked a man
6 There they told her
7 that she really got furious about
8 First came an electrician
9 Three days it took them
10 what annoyed me most was the attitude of the staff / it was the attitude of the staff that annoyed me most
11 Never have I seen
12 Not once did anyone apologise

D: Exam practice
Use of English

1 do the islanders / they take pride in
2 appreciated them / their putting me / appreciated the fact that they put me
3 was her hatred / dislike
4 explanation was given of / for his sudden departure from / reason was given for his sudden departure from
5 was no alternative (for her) but / was no alternative but for her
6 had the President / he been voted in than / had people voted for the President than
7 were she ever to become / if she were ever to become / if she ever were to become
8 distinct possibility of my / me getting

Grammar focus task

Sentences 1, 3 and 6. Sentence 7 would also be an example of inversion if your answer was *were she ever to become.*

Writing *Sample answer:*

Global warming: it's our planet

Never before has the world faced a threat like global warming: a potential catastrophe for the Earth, brought about by human activity. And it will have the biggest impact on young people, with climate set to change dramatically in our lifetime. *What's worrying, though, is that we are the group that does least about it*, leaving the hard choices to others. So what more can we do?

It's in our daily lives that we can make the biggest difference.
Turning off one light might not seem important, but turning it
off every day for a year saves a significant amount of energy. The
same goes for TVs and computers. *What we have to do is change
our habits* – if it's not being used, turn it off! Try walking to
college or getting the bus, rather than getting a lift from parents.
Not only is this better for our health, but it also saves energy.

Naturally, *it is governments who take the big decisions*, but here
we can play a part, too. Write to your council encouraging
them to invest in cycle paths and recycling. Email your MP
asking for more renewable energy. We need to put pressure on
governments. *Only then will they make the changes to our economy
and society that are needed.*

Of course, we could just do nothing. But *it is our generation
who will suffer the future flooding, storms and high energy prices
resulting from indifference now.* So whatever you can do to help,
do it. It's our planet, after all!

Unit 22

A: Context listening

2 The correct order is: g, c, e, a, d, f, b.

3 2 increase in 3 closure of 4 rise in 5 discovery of
   6 evacuation of

4 *Suggested answers:*
   2 The number of people living close to the lake has increased.
   3 Thousands of homes and businesses would be left without
   electricity if the power stations closed.
   4 The level of radon gas in the soil rose dramatically.
   5 Scientists discovered thousands of dead fish, which
   increased their concerns.
   6 30,000 people began to be evacuated two days ago. /
   The army began to evacuate 30,000 people two days ago.

C: Grammar exercises

1 2 made a start
   3 do some / the gardening.
   4 Give (me) a shout
2 1 made / taken a decision
   2 I have a feeling
   3 made an arrangement
   4 take a deep breath
   5 give him an explanation of
3 1 have a talk with
   2 gave her a call
   3 had a chat
   4 gave a sigh
4 1 take / have a shower
   2 have a rest
   3 do the cooking
   4 have / take a look

2 *Suggested answers:*
   2 The organisation of the conference was very professional.
   3 The turnout for the match was huge. / There was a huge
   turnout for the match.

4 The withdrawal of the troops was immediate. / There was
an immediate withdrawal of troops.
5 A shake-up in /of top management is needed for the
company to be successful again.
6 The increase in interest rates was the third in two months. /
There was an increase in interest rates for the third time in
two months.
7 An agreement was reached on extra funding for the
project. / There was an agreement reached on extra
funding for the project.
8 The breakout from the jail took place / happened /
occurred during a power cut. / There was a breakout from
the jail during a power cut.
9 The announcement of the merger came / was made / took
place last week.
10 The decision to postpone the race was taken / was made /
was reached at the last moment.

3 *Suggested answers:*
   2 John's obsession with cars started when he was quite young.
   3 The expansion of the nuclear power programme has been
   criticised by opposition politicians.
   4 The reduction in the price of petrol is good news for drivers.
   5 The abolition of parking charges in the city centre has led to
   / has resulted in increased business for shops.
   6 The demand for healthier food in school is the result of / is
   due to growing concerns about childhood obesity.
   7 The departure of the train will be delayed for half an hour
   because of engine problems.
   8 The appointment of a new college principal may lead to /
   result in staff leaving.

4 2 the complexity of the English spelling system
   3 the response to its recruitment drive
   4 the threat to animal and plant species
   5 the strong resistance to increased taxation *or* the strength of
   the resistance to increased taxation
   6 the extent of the damage to property

D: Exam practice
Reading

1 E 2 E 3 B 4 C 5 A 6 A 7 B 8 D 9 A 10 C 11 A 12 D
13 E 14 B 15 D

Grammar focus task

in is used in 3 and 7.

Writing *Sample answer:*

**'The Meadows' out-of-town shopping centre: a report on its
impact on Fairfield**

Introduction

The aims of this report are to identify *the impact of the new out-of-
town shopping centre*, The Meadows on:
• transport
• the environment
• people's shopping habits
• shops and recreational facilities in the centre of Fairfield.

Transport

Overall, there has been a positive impact on transport facilities. This is mainly due to *the expansion of bus and tram services*, providing easy access to The Meadows for customers. These services are regular, punctual and popular with users.

Environment

There have been some negative environmental impacts:
- *The construction of The Meadows* has destroyed a huge area of land, previously occupied by fields, trees and grasslands. *The damage to the ecosystem* is considerable, although difficult to measure. Furthermore, *the physical attractiveness of the area* has been substantially reduced.
- *The increase in traffic* has not only led to more exhaust pollution, damaging the nearby natural environment further, but also noise pollution, which disturbs local people and wildlife.

However, there are have also been positive effects:
- *The implementation of modern, clean public transport systems* along with the limit placed on the number of cars that can access The Meadows, have encouraged more people to use public transport.

Shopping habits

When asked where they prefer to shop since *the building of the new centre*, an overwhelming majority of people chose The Meadows. The main reasons given were:
- Good accessibility
- A wide variety of shops available
- *The proximity of shops* to recreational facilities such as cinemas and restaurants
- A more pleasant shopping environment than in the town centre
- Longer opening hours.

Impact on Fairfield town centre

The presence of the new shopping centre has caused *a slight reduction in the amount of business* conducted by shops and recreational facilities in Fairfield town itself. However, as far as it is possible to tell at this stage, the new facilities have not had a significant negative impact on the economy of the town centre.

Unit 23

A: Context listening

3 2 T 3 T 4 C 5 C 6 T 7 C 8 C 9 T 10 C
4 2 It's obvious why they've been having problems selling **it** (= the town apartment).
3 It really shocked me to see how bad **it** (= the decoration in the town apartment) was.
4 It's about 15 kilometres from **there** (= Canley) into the centre.
5 **There's** bound to be a regular bus service from **there** (= Canley).
6 **There's** no special parking area for the apartments.
7 **There's** that lovely little river that runs nearby.
8 You couldn't even fit a chest of drawers in **there** (= one of the bedrooms in the Canley apartment).
9 The rooms in **it** (= the town apartment) are quite dark and that made **it** (= the town apartment) feel cramped.
10 **There** is expected to be a lot of interest in the property.

C: Grammar exercises

1 2 there was nobody in the room 3 X 4 X 5 there is one opposite the railway station 6 X 7 There are only ten places available 8 there was no milk left 9 X 10 Is there anyone who would 11 X 12 There was something on the radio

2 2 Fraser has said he will retire from football if **there** is thought to be no chance of his ankle injury healing in the foreseeable future.
3 Is **there** a swimming pool at the hotel we're staying at?
4 It worried me to see Heather looking so thin.
5 In December 1944 **there** took place a secret meeting between the countries' leaders.
6 Although it took hours of practice, I eventually managed to play a simple tune on the saxophone.
7 Most people had left the party and I decided that it was time I went home, too.
8 The scientists said that **there** is very little evidence that mobile phone use has any adverse effect on health.
9 How far is it from Paris to Berlin?
10 They travelled by bus, **there** being no railway line in that part of the country.

3 2 It's no good 3 It's no secret 4 there's no harm in 5 there's no chance of 6 There's no doubt / It's no doubt true / It's no doubt the case 7 There's no need 8 it's no longer 9 There's no (need to) hurry

4 2 it doesn't hurt to 3 there is (there's) nobody by 4 it turned out that 5 noticed that she was 6 don't expect there to be 7 see it as my role 8 thought it best not to tell 9 had ('d) mentioned (it) to me (*it* can be included in informal contexts) 10 think there is Internet 11 there might be some left 12 remember you saying that 13 I prefer it if 14 there are thought to be

D: Exam practice
Use of English
1 question 2 content 3 anxious 4 thought 5 coincidence

Grammar focus task
1 **New information:**
All the tickets have been sold so *there's* no question ...
There are thought to be fewer than ...
Mr Turner claimed that *it* was mere coincidence
Perhaps *it* is no coincidence that poets ...
2 **Place:**
I left *there* early ...
... he thought nothing of walking *there* ...
Previously mentioned:
If the salt content of food is high, I try to avoid *it*. (*it* = food with high salt content)
It's an interesting idea, but I wouldn't have thought *it* was very practical. (*it* = both times is the idea)
... he sold his share of the company the day before *it* was declared ... (*it* = the company)

Writing *Sample answer:*

Introduction

I undertook a survey to identify staff views on the time, duration and location of the annual sales conference.

Time

The conference is traditionally held in the spring and this seems to suit the majority of staff members. The survey indicated that *there is an overwhelming preference for the conference to take place in February or March*, with only a small minority favouring April.

Duration

In the past, the conference has lasted three days. However, *it appears that most staff members consider this to be too long*. The general view is that the information could easily be covered in two days. *It is possible that the conference could be held over a weekend*, although this may inconvenience staff members with families.

Location

This year's conference should be held somewhere different. *There was considerable negative feedback* on last year's venue. People felt confined to the countryside centre for the whole three days. If the conference were held in town, *there would be many more facilities available*.

Recommendations

I propose that we hold our conference for two days during the working week in early spring. *I think it essential that it takes place in town*. This would appeal to most staff members, with the likely result of increased motivation and participation.

Unit 24

A: Context listening

2 Instruction 3

3 2 you up 3 out the train times 4 on the train 5 into the hotel
   6 out the bill 7 around town

4 The order can be reversed in sentences 1, 3 and 6:
   1 I'm afraid I've messed **our plans up** for tomorrow.
   3 I've found **the train times out** from the SNCF website ...
   6 I'll sort **the bill out** when I pick you up on Thursday afternoon.

C: Grammar exercises

1 2 throw away some of my old exercise books from school
     (more natural than 'throw some of my old exercise books
     from school away' because the object is long)
   3 gathered her papers up / gathered up her papers
   4 bumped into Cherie
   5 (have) left Dave's name out / (have) left out Dave's name
   6 tell the twins apart
   7 talk you out of leaving college
   8 get some food down / get down some food
   9 woke me and my husband up / woke up me and my
     husband
   10 try them out
   11 (has) made the whole story up / (has) made up the whole
     story (or is/was making)

2 2 as against the 10,000 predicted
   3 in place of cream
   4 irrespective of their ability to pay
   5 in the event of a terrorist attack
   6 thanks to a strict protein-only diet
   7 in accordance with his wishes
   8 for the sake of their health
   9 along with an excellent art gallery
   10 by way of an apology
   11 with effect from 30th September
   12 on the part of the train driver

3 1 advised against using
   2 dismissed the reports as; prevent her (from) doing
   3 congratulated them on achieving; had benefited from taking
     part in
   4 has quarrelled / has been quarrelling with her European
     counterparts over; ended in / with her walking
   5 protect the country from / against; rush into investing

4

Dear Jodi,

Sorry I haven't been **in** touch **with** you for such a long time, but it's been a busy few months.

Earlier this year I heard that my great-aunt had died. Apart **from** seeing her a couple of times at my parents' house, I didn't really know her. So you can imagine my surprise when I found **(out)** *(optional)* she'd left me a cottage along **with** some money in her will!

When I saw the cottage, I just fell in love with it. It's close **to** a beautiful little village, and looks out **over / on** the sea. My great-aunt used it as a holiday home, and I've decided to do the same. Unfortunately, it's been badly looked **after**, so I've had to spend most weekends this year sorting **(out)** the place **(out)** *(Either position is possible. Very informally, 'out' could be omitted.)*

I knew it was **in** need **of** some work, and at first I thought I could get away **with** giving it a quick coat of paint. But I soon realised it was a much bigger job. There were holes in the roof, and the window frames were so rotten some of the panes of glass were **in** danger **of** falling out.

I was walking around the village one Saturday, wondering what best to do, when who should I run **into** but Barney Adams. Do you remember him from school? As luck would have it, he now works in the village as a builder and decorator. We got talking, and he said he'd come **(over/round)** *(optional)* and look **(a)round / at / over** the house. Naturally, I took him up **on** his offer! He got really enthusiastic about it. He talked me **into** *('talked to me about' is also possible)* replacing all the windows, and he's put in a new central heating system **in** place **of** the old coal fires. I've had to prevent him **(from)** *(optional)* extending the kitchen, which he was keen to do! He's checked **(over)** the roof **(over)** *(Either position is possible; 'over' could also be omitted)*, and fortunately that doesn't need replacing. Thanks **to** Barney, the house is now looking brilliant, and **in** comparison **with** other builders, he doesn't charge very much.

The next project for me is to clean **(up)** the mess **(up)** *(Either position is possible.)* in the garden, as it's completely overgrown. If you want to come **(over/round)** *(optional)* and help me **(out)** *(optional)* some time, feel free! You'll always be very welcome.

D: Exam practice
Listening
1 A 2 B 3 C 4 B 5 A 6 B 7 C 8 A

Grammar focus task
2 onto lost property; it off 3 some things behind *or* behind some things 4 of them 5 them away

Writing *Sample answer:*

Birmingham's canals: an undiscovered attraction

The city of Birmingham in the English Midlands may not be glamorous *in comparison with* Venice, but it has more canals – over a hundred miles of them! In 1800, Birmingham was at the heart of the Industrial Revolution, and the meeting place of five major canals. Throughout the nineteenth century, the city's canals were alive with activity, as cargoes were loaded, unloaded and transported *as far as* Liverpool and London. But in the twentieth century the canals went into decline *as a result of* competition from railways and then road transport, and the network was *in danger of* being filled in.

Today, however, Birmingham's canals are once again buzzing with life. Where they cut through the city centre, they are surrounded by restaurants and clubs, *together with* concert venues and shopping malls. The canal boats are busy once again, but *in place of* the cargoes of coal and iron, they carry residents and tourists enjoying the leisurely pace of life along the waterways.

It is equally enjoyable to walk the miles of towpaths *next to* the canals. These were the paths originally walked along by horses, pulling barges in the early days before motorised boats. *Away from* the crowds, it is possible to explore the industrial heritage of the city, *as well as* make use of the new facilities that have developed around the canals. Recently, I had an excellent dinner on board a restaurant canal boat as it made its peaceful way around the city. The following morning, I was back, drinking coffee on a boat moored in an oasis of calm in the city, watching the world go by.

It is a pity that visitors from overseas usually bypass Birmingham, heading instead for nearby Oxford and Stratford. The canals are a gem in one of the country's most underrated cities, and they offer a view of life in Britain that overseas visitors rarely see. And visitors can be certain that they will be given a warm welcome by those living and working on and around the canals.

Unit 25

A: Context listening
2 2 b 3 g 4 f 5 a 6 d 7 e 8 h 9 c
3 2 demand for 3 need 4 difficulty in 5 decision to
6 difficult to 7 need for 8 complain about 9 complaints about 10 demand 11 decided to 12 influence on

4 2 <u>demand</u> + for; 10 demand (verb) + no preposition
4 <u>difficulty</u> + in; 6 difficult (adjective) + to
5 <u>decision</u> + to; 11 decided (verb) + to
7 <u>need</u> + for; 3 need (verb) + no preposition
9 <u>complaints</u> + about; 8 complain (verb) + about
12 <u>influence</u> + on; 1 influenced (verb) + no preposition

C: Grammar exercises
1 2 for 3 at 4 for 5 with 6 about 7 of 8 on 9 about 10 for
2 *Suggested answers:*
  2 She admitted that the salary increase *(had) had an influence on* her decision to take the new job.
  3 *There has been a noticeable improvement in* the children's spelling since they were each given a dictionary. or *The improvement in the children's spelling has been noticeable* since they were each given a dictionary.
  4 Alex has done very well at university and *we take (great / considerable) pride in* his achievement.
  5 Although I don't agree with his political beliefs, I *have great admiration for* his writing.
  6 The flooding *caused serious damage to* many of the houses in the village.
  7 When you come to collect the parcel, please bring documents *as proof of (your) identity.*
  8 Northern Rail *has imposed / placed / put / introduced a ban on* the use of mobile phones on its trains.
  9 *As a solution to* the problem of severe traffic congestion, drivers are to be charged £10 a day for bringing their cars into the city centre.
  10 *There has been a substantial reduction in* the number of students dropping out of college this year.

3 2 to cut
  3 using / the use of
  4 the number of visitors to
  5 of organising / to organise
  6 to move
  7 of working / to work
  8 the closure of
  9 protecting / the protection of
  10 recovering / recovery
  11 of holding
  12 of encouraging / to encourage

4 1 A: I'm really fed up **with** my job. I've been doing the same thing at Trimstep for ten years, and I'm tired **of** the same old routine.
    B: But I thought you were keen **on** your job. You've always seemed so enthusiastic **about** it.
    A: Well, I used to be very impressed **by / with** the managers. But now they're only interested **in** making money and they seem indifferent **to** how the staff feel. There are rumours that business isn't going well, so a lot of people are worried **about** their jobs. In fact, one of the senior managers left last week. He obviously wasn't satisfied **with** the way the company's being run. Maybe it's time I started looking around for something new, too.

2 I know that some of you have expressed anxiety **about** Mr Madson's sudden departure **from** the company last week. I was very disappointed **with** his decision to resign. I must admit that the last few months have been difficult, and at times we've been very concerned ourselves **about** the future of the company. However, we have now developed an association **with** a firm of retailers in southeast Asia, and we're extremely pleased **with / about** this development. We did at first have a disagreement **over** safety standards, but this has been resolved and they have indicated their satisfaction **with** the design changes we've made. We hope to sign a major contract with them in the next few days. To all of you I want to express my gratitude **for** your belief **in** the company and your continuing support **for** the management team.

D: Exam practice
Use of English
1 A 2 B 3 B 4 D 5 C 6 C 7 B 8 C 9 B 10 C 11 D 12 A

Grammar focus task
of is used after the noun in 5 extracts (1, 2, 4, 6, 8)
to is used in 3, *between* in 5, and *in* in 7

Writing *Sample answer:*

Dear Mrs Adams,

I am writing to enquire whether there is any *possibility of finding* temporary work at Arcon in one of your branches in an English-speaking country this summer.

I am a student of business and English, near the end of the third year of a four-year course at City College in Athens. I would like to spend some time during the college vacation gaining *experience of working* in a multinational company. Although I have *a very good knowledge of spoken and written English*, I would welcome *the opportunity to improve* my language skills further by working in an English-speaking environment.

I have a particular *interest in marketing*. If there is a post in the marketing department, I am sure I could make a useful contribution as well as develop my own *understanding of the area*. I also have *an expertise in information technology*, and have designed websites for organisations at college. My skills in this area might be useful to you.

I am happy in principle to work for no salary, and will be able to pay for my own accommodation and living expenses. However, if Arcon could pay a salary this would be gratefully received.

I realise there must be *a great demand for temporary positions* of this kind. However, if you feel there is *a chance of arranging* work for me, I would be pleased to provide further details about myself. In the meantime, I enclose a copy of my CV.

Thank you for your attention, and I look forward to hearing from you.

Yours sincerely,

Nikolaos Kovaios

Recording scripts

Recording 1

Presenter: And our next caller is Karen. Karen, what's your experience of public transport?

Karen: Yes, hello, Gary. Well, I commuted to London for over ten years. I caught the train every morning at 7.15 to get to work for nine o'clock, and I wouldn't get home until about seven o'clock in the evening. And frankly it was a terrible period of my life, really stressful, mainly because of the unreliability of the train service. I was forever arriving late for work. One day I was travelling home when the train broke down and I eventually got back at midnight. Of course, I had to go to work the next day, so off I went for my 7.15 train. I'd been waiting over an hour when they announced that the train was cancelled. That really was the end for me. I arranged with my employer to work at home and I've been working at home happily for the last five years. Of course it meant a big salary cut, but I haven't regretted it for a moment.

Presenter: Thanks for that, Karen. Can you just stay on the line? I'm hoping we've got Dave on the line. Dave, are you there?

Dave: Yes, I'm here, Gary.

Presenter: Great. And what point do you want to make?

Dave: Well, I just wanted to say that my experience is similar to your last caller, although I'm a newcomer to commuting by public transport. I've just sold my car and now I go to work by bus. I'd owned a car ever since I left college, but I wanted to do my bit to cut down on pollution. But I have to confess that I'm regretting it already. I've arrived late for work twice this week because the bus hasn't turned up on time. It's got so bad that I'm now thinking of buying a motorbike. It'll cause less pollution than a car, and be more reliable than public transport.

Presenter: Well, it sounds like you're another dissatisfied customer, Dave. But we've also got Beryl on the line, and I think she's more positive. Beryl, are you there?

Beryl: I am, Gary, good afternoon.

Presenter: Hello, Beryl, what do you want to tell us?

Beryl: Well, I'd like to put in a good word for train travel. I'm working at home while our office block is being renovated, and while I'm appreciating being able to get up later than usual, I really miss my daily commute. You get to know the people you travel with every day. I remember one day I dropped my purse while I was getting off the train. Another passenger picked it up, found my address in it, and brought it round to my house later that evening. Another time, I'd been working really hard and went to sleep and missed my station. One of the other passengers was getting off at the next station and she had her car parked there. She woke me up and offered me a lift back to my home. I'd spoken to her only a couple of times before then, but now she's a really good friend. You meet a lot of nice people, and become a part of the travelling community.

Presenter: Thanks, Beryl. That's a side of commuting we don't often hear about. Now somebody else who sees the good side of train journeys – Keith. Are you there, Keith?

Keith: Yes, indeed. Actually, I'm phoning from the train on my way home from work.

Presenter: And are you having a good journey?

Keith: Yes, it's been fine. But then I love trains. I've enjoyed travelling by train ever since I was young. I admit that it can be frustrating at times. There are delays and cancellations, and there are minor irritations like poor mobile phone reception – I've been trying to phone in to your programme for the last half hour, in fact – but I catch the 7.05 at the station near my home every morning, and still find there's something quite magical about stepping on to the train. And there are clear advantages over driving, apart from the lack of stress. I reckon that over the years I've saved a huge amount of money by using public transport. I've never really considered buying a car. You can also get a lot of work done. On the train yesterday morning, for example, I'd read a couple of reports and prepared for an important meeting before I even got to work. Admittedly, I'm quite lucky. The train company I travel with have invested a lot of money recently. They've bought new trains and have really improved the service.

Karen: Gary ...

Presenter: Karen, were you wanting to say something?

Karen: Yes, I just wanted to pick up Keith's point that travelling by train is less stressful than driving. Public transport can be stressful, too, when trains don't turn up or are delayed. What's less stressful is working at home. At eight o'clock I'm usually having a leisurely breakfast when most people are in their cars or on the train. Yesterday, I'd finished all my work by 2.30, so I drove to the local pool for a swim. And today I've been working hard all day, so now I've got time to relax by listening to the radio for a while. Much better than the stress of commuting.

Presenter: You're very lucky, Karen. We've got another caller on the line ...

Recording 2

Kelly: You must be really looking forward to going to America. When are you actually leaving?

Jessica: I'm flying on 15th July. I'm spending a few days sightseeing in New York, and then I arrive in Los Angeles on the 20th. Lectures start on 27th July.

Kelly: Sounds great. And what about accommodation?

Jessica: Well, first I'm going to stay with Don and Suzanne, some friends of my parents.

Kelly: You're not staying with them the whole time you're there, are you?

Jessica: No, I'll be looking for my own place. But I'm really pleased they'll be around. It'll be good to know I can contact them in case I have any problems. They're meeting me at the airport, too. Mind you, I haven't seen them for years. They'll have forgotten what I look like.

Kelly: And what about the course?

Jessica: It looks really interesting. They sent me a reading list but of course I haven't got round to opening any of the books yet. So it's going to take a long time to catch up. I'll be studying really hard during the semesters so that I don't have to do much work in the vacations.

Kelly: And when does the first semester end?

Jessica: 7th December. Then I'm going to San Francisco for a week. I've always wanted to see the Golden Gate Bridge. I'm going to fly up there if it's not too expensive.

Kelly: Do you know when you'll be back in Los Angeles?

Jessica: Probably mid-December. So you can come any time after that.

Kelly: I'm so looking forward to it. I've always wanted to go to the States. I was going to see my aunt in Seattle a couple of years ago, but I cancelled the trip because she got ill.

Jessica: Will you stop over anywhere on the way out? Maybe New York or Chicago?

Kelly: I haven't really thought about it. But I've only got three weeks, so I think I'll fly directly to Los Angeles.

Jessica: Fine. And I'll meet you at the airport, of course. By the time you come I'm sure I'll have got to know LA really well, so I'll be able to show you all the sights.

Kelly: Yes, I suppose you will. When I come to see you, you'll have been living in California for nearly six months.

Jessica: Hard to imagine, isn't it? After Los Angeles, I thought we could go down to a place called Huntington Beach. If you bring your tent, we'll camp there for a few days. The weather will still be quite warm even in the winter.

Kelly: Isn't it your birthday around then?

Jessica: That's right. I'll be 21 on 2nd January.

Kelly: Well, that'll be a really good way to celebrate.

Jessica: The best! I'll need to get back to Los Angeles for when the second semester starts. But you'll be staying longer, won't you?

Kelly: That's right. I don't have to be back in England until later.

Jessica: Well, why don't you go to the Grand Canyon? It's supposed to be spectacular.

Kelly: Yeah, I might think about that. Anyway, as soon as I book my tickets, I'll let you know.

Jessica: Okay. We can sort out the details closer to the time.

Kelly: Fine. Look, it's nearly two o'clock. If I don't go now, I'm going to be late for my next lecture. I'll text you.

Jessica: Yeah, see you.

Recording 3a

Presenter: And now on Radio Nation it's 8.30 and here's a summary of the latest news.

Air passengers could be hit badly today as cabin crews stay at home in the latest in a series of one-day strikes. The major airlines are warning that up to 100,000 people may experience delays. The managing director of Travel Air, David Wade, had this warning to the unions:

David: I'm sure I don't need to spell out the chaos being caused in the airline industry as a result of these strikes, and I would like to apologise to all our customers. However, the cabin staff must accept the new working conditions if the airline is to compete, and the management has no choice but to stand firm on this issue.

Presenter: But he didn't have to wait long for a response. A union spokesperson said: 'I can't believe Mr Wade is being so confrontational. We will not be bullied by management. Eventually the airlines will have to return to the negotiating table.'

Up to 200 teachers and pupils had to be evacuated from Northfield Primary School in South Wales today after a fire broke out in an adjacent building. Although firefighters were able to bring the fire under control fairly quickly, they couldn't prevent the fire damaging the school's sports centre. The headteacher said it might be a number of months before the sports centre is back in operation, although the school itself should be able to reopen early next week.

The new Borland Bridge, connecting the island to the mainland, was officially opened today by the Transport Minister. However, it's been in operation for a few weeks already and has received a mixed reception from islanders. From Borland, here's our reporter, Anna Curtis.

Anna: Yes, the new bridge has stirred up a lot of strong emotion on Borland, and I'm here to gather the views of some of the island's residents. Excuse me, what do you think of the new bridge?

Resident 1: I think it will be of great benefit to the island. We used to be terribly isolated here because the ferry service was so bad. It's only a short distance, but the crossing would take over an hour at least. It could be a very rough journey, too. Many passengers would get seasick during the crossing.

Anna: Excuse me. I'm asking people about the effects of the new bridge. They reckon that tourism on the island is set to expand …

Resident 2: Is that such a good thing? There are already far too many cars and people. We'll also get wealthy people from the mainland who can afford second homes. That will push up house prices and islanders won't be able to buy properties. That can't be right, surely? There ought to be restrictions on the number of people moving here.

Anna: It's certainly true that the bridge is going to have a major impact on the way of life of the people here over the next few years. But whether that will be a positive or negative effect, only time will tell.

Presenter: Following her report on the high levels of obesity among children, the government's chief health adviser, Professor Carmen Brady, has said that schools have to play a more active role in encouraging children to take up sports. She has also criticised parents.

Carmen: Parents needn't be very interested in sport themselves – but they should give their children whatever encouragement they can. While we were gathering information for our report, we found that some parents will actually discourage their children from taking up a sport on the basis that they might get distracted from their academic studies. This negative attitude to sport mustn't be allowed to continue – not if we are to get on top of the obesity crisis facing the country.

Presenter: And finally the weather. Well, if you're in the south of the country you shouldn't be troubled by any rain today. It will be warm, sunny and dry, with temperatures up to 22 degrees Celsius. However, in the north you're likely to see an occasional shower, with maximum temperatures of around 15 degrees. Radio Nation news …

Extract 1

Man: Research shows that the optimum time to start music education is between the ages of three and four. As well as improving manual dexterity and concentration, it seems that it may help emotional development, too. The piano is the instrument that many parents want their children to start learning, and I think three years old is the right time to start.

Woman: Personally, I don't think the piano is the best instrument to start with so early. Children have to show the mental, physical and emotional readiness to learn an instrument like the piano, which obviously takes a lot of effort and commitment. In my experience very few children under six are able to take on that kind of challenge. Starting early is vital, yes, but less demanding instruments would be my choice, things like the recorder or a half-size guitar.

Man: No, I think children of that age can learn to play simple tunes on the piano and they soon progress to more complicated pieces. And starting young on understanding musical notation lays down an excellent foundation for later on.

Woman: But a rather academic approach like that will turn children off for life if they're not ready for it. Enjoyment has got to be the priority.

Man: Well, enjoyment is certainly important, but …

Extract 2

Interviewer: So, Ben, you're well known in the climbing world as a bit of a loner; you prefer climbing without other people. Is that true?

Ben: Well, to some extent. I've always talked to other climbers about the technical side of things – training, equipment, and things like that. But at the end of the day you've got to learn independently, through trial and error. If you're climbing in a group you'll always compare yourself to others, and that doesn't always help you to improve. It's good to admire other climbers, but different things work best for different people.

Interviewer: So you never climb with other people?

Ben: As far as possible, I climb alone, but occasionally I look to others for support. When I was younger I used to do most of my climbing during the summer holidays, and I haven't done much winter climbing. So I still feel out of my depth climbing alone on icy rock faces. In those conditions you need people who've been brought up with it. It's good to have people around to advise you on what's a safe manoeuvre to make in the conditions.

Extract 3

Interviewer: You're such a household name, it must be terrifying for staff when you go into a restaurant. How do they react?

Amanda: It's true that a lot of people know me, at least in the restaurant world, so I always eat with a friend and they'll make the booking. Often, though, I get recognised and when that happens it's inevitable, I suppose, that they take a bit more care over serving the food. I've never been offered complimentary wine, though, or anything like that. That would be just too obvious, and of course it could be considered unethical to accept a gift like that.

Interviewer: And what makes a good restaurant?

Amanda: A good restaurant is one where the management and waiting staff have given some thought to why their customers are there. Most restaurant owners believe that the main reason people go to restaurants is for the food, but that's completely wrong. The main reason people go to restaurants is to have a good time, not because they're hungry. So there might be a big difference between the priorities of a restaurant and the priorities of diners. For example, one thing that a restaurant gets judged on is the quality of service. What restaurant owners think is good is service that is efficient, but what customers have as their priority is friendly service.

Police Officer 1: So how on earth did they manage to get in? There's no sign of a forced entry.

Police Officer 2: Well, I suppose they could have got in through a window up on the fourth floor.

Police Officer 1: But no one would have dared climb up the outside of the building. Anybody trying to do that would have been seen from the street below. You don't think they would have been able to jump from the block across the road, do you?

Police Officer 2: No, it's much too far. Of course, there's always the fire escape around the back of the building. They could have climbed up there reasonably easily, and after that they might have been lowered by rope from the roof. If that was the case, people living in the block of flats behind the museum might have seen something, so we need to talk to them.

Police Officer 1: Right, but we needn't interview everyone in the block, just the people who have windows facing the museum. I'll arrange that.

Police Officer 2: If it wasn't a window, the only other possibility is that they went in through the front door. Perhaps they forced the lock, but the door didn't appear to be damaged at all.

Police Officer 1: And the entry code is supposed to be known only by the security guard.

Police Officer 2: So someone else must have opened the door from the inside.

Police Officer 1: Only the security guard was allowed to stay in the museum after it closed. Do you think they somehow persuaded him to let them in? Maybe they just knocked on the front door and he opened it.

Police Officer 2: He surely wouldn't have done something as stupid as that. Do you think he might have been expecting them and that he was part of the gang?

Police Officer 1: But then why would they have attacked him?

Police Officer 2: I don't know, but we'd better find out all we can about that guard as soon as possible. Now, who was it that raised the alarm?

Police Officer 1: It was the head cleaner who went into the building early this morning. He must have to know the entry code, too.

Police Officer 2: Yes, maybe. He says the front door was unlocked when he got here. But he claims he didn't see anything else unusual until he got to the fourth floor. But of course, he might be lying.

Police Officer 1: Yes, he must know that he ought to have called the police as soon as he found the door open. I wonder why he didn't. I think we should talk to him again. I suppose he could be hiding some information from us, and he might be prepared to tell us more if we put a bit of pressure on him.

Police Officer 2: The other puzzling thing is how they took the paintings away. Apparently, they're very big, so the robbers must have had to bring a van around to the front of the building.

Police Officer 1: The driver must have been waiting nearby and drove up when they'd got the paintings. They could have loaded the paintings up very quickly, and might have driven straight to a port or airport. Anyway, the forensic team should have finished examining the building by now. Once they've done that, I think we should go and look around ourselves ...

Recording 5

Interviewer: Right, perhaps you could tell me something about how you got interested in environmental science, and what experience you have in the subject.

Nazim: Well, I've always been fascinated by plants and animals, and then last year a friend of mine, Mike Proctor, invited me to Brazil. He's the head of a project there run by a European charity. The charity's aim is to help groups of villagers set up their own schools and medical centres. They also encourage sustainable agriculture and the setting up of businesses to sell local handicrafts. Anyway, it was during my stay that I really began to understand the impact of climate change. I want to learn more about this and more generally how decision-making on environmental issues in one part of the world can affect the lives of individuals elsewhere.

Interviewer: You say you 'began to understand the impact of climate change'. Could you give me an example of what you saw in Brazil that influenced you?

Nazim:	Yes, of course. We've all heard about the destruction of the rainforest, and I was able to see examples of that. But also people don't realise that the climate in the region is changing, and that the speed of change is frightening. There's been a drought there for a number of months, and river levels are low. I had direct experience of this when I travelled with Mike. Having responsibility for the whole project in the area means that his job involves travelling to some pretty remote areas. Sometimes we had to go by boat to get to some of the villages, and we had to carry the boat because there wasn't enough water in the river.
Interviewer:	And is this change affecting the lives of local people?
Nazim:	A huge amount. The main problem has been the effect of the drought on food supplies. The majority of people there are farmers, and all of them have lost animals and crops. The charity's project has been a success so far in that levels of income from the sale of handicrafts have increased. But, of course, financial success isn't everything. It's hard to imagine a future without farming in an area like that.
Interviewer:	Your trip to Brazil sounds like an amazing experience. And since you've been back, have you done anything to develop your interest in the area?
Nazim:	Yes, I've read a book about energy conservation and how this might slow down climate change. And I was particularly interested in how the Netherlands has begun to tackle the problem. The government has introduced some really interesting projects on energy saving in cities – the use of low-energy light bulbs to reduce the consumption of lighting energy, better insulation for homes, and things like that. There's also a massive recycling scheme, which is saving a huge amount of our natural resources. What's needed now, though, is to expand work like this across the world.
Interviewer:	And what are your plans for the future, after you've left college?
Nazim:	Actually, I'd like to go into politics. We've got somehow to persuade governments

	in developed countries to change their priorities. For example, even if just a small percentage of the money spent on the arms trade could go into tackling climate change, I'm sure we could make a difference.
Interviewer:	And you think that as a politician, you'd be able to do this?
Nazim:	I'd certainly like to try.
Interviewer:	Before we finish, have you got any questions about the course here at the college?
Nazim:	I've noticed that statistics is included in the course. I'm a bit concerned about that.
Interviewer:	I wouldn't worry about it. You'd be able to get by with a reasonable knowledge of maths.
Nazim:	That's very reassuring. I also wanted to ask about the field trip for second year students.
Interviewer:	Okay. Second year students go to Nepal in June, looking at the ecology of mountain environments.
Nazim:	That sounds like a fantastic opportunity.

Recording 6a

1 I took up running a couple of years ago. Until then I did a bit of sport at school, but I didn't do much outside school at all. In fact, I suppose I didn't have many interests – except playing computer games. Then I went to watch my uncle in a 5k fun run – it was to raise money for charity. I thought the whole event was brilliant and every runner there seemed to be enjoying it. There was another fun run later in the year and I signed up for a laugh. I didn't do any proper training for it, just a bit of jogging around the park after school, so I was really surprised when I managed to run all the way. Now I run nearly every day and I get a lot of satisfaction out of it. My friends all think I'm crazy. None of them like the thought of running long distances. I think about all kinds of stuff when I'm running, and I know it's really good for my heart and lungs. Sure, some people get running injuries, but I've been lucky – I've had none so far.

2 I'd never really thought about exercise and keeping fit until a couple of years ago. My boyfriend and I were in town late and we had to run to catch the last bus home – just a couple of hundred metres. By the time we got to the bus stop both of us were completely exhausted! On the way home we started talking. Neither of us did

any exercise and I didn't do much with my free time – just reading magazines and eating biscuits! By the time we got home we'd each decided to take up a different activity for six months and see who could lose the most weight. My boyfriend joined a gym, and I started running in the local park – just a few hundred metres at first, and gradually building up. Now I run a few kilometres each day. Of course, that takes up quite a lot of time and my boyfriend moans about that sometimes. But after I've been sitting at my computer all day I can't wait to go out for a run. We certainly both got a lot fitter and I've lost a lot of weight. Not all the effects are positive, of course; I've had a few problems with sore knees and sprained ankles. I suppose all exercise carries some risks, but there isn't much evidence that running causes major problems if you warm up carefully and have good footwear. It's one of the few sports where no special equipment's needed – just a pair of running shoes.

3 I had three older brothers and I think they could all have been Olympic athletes if they'd had the opportunity. So it was quite natural that I would go out running with them. I think I started at about the age of 10, and I've been running regularly all my life. Now that I'm getting older I go out running every couple of days, but if the weather's bad I might go all week without a run. I certainly go out a lot less during the winter. Well, who would want to go running on a horrible rainy day? Inevitably you get a few injuries, too – everyone gets aching muscles after a long run, and I used to get back pain occasionally. But surprisingly I seem to have fewer injuries now than when I was younger. Maybe it's because I run more slowly! Actually, I feel a lot healthier, and I even sleep a little better after I've been out running. But I think the best thing for me is the social contact. We've got a running club in our village – I moved here when I retired – and before I joined the club I had very few friends who lived nearby. Now, many of my closest friends are the runners in the club. Next spring we're all going to Madrid to run in a marathon for over 60s only. Of course, we know that not all of us will finish, but you can be sure that every one of us will have a really good time. My aim is to complete the course and do it in less than six hours. But I know it won't be easy!

Earlier this year I fulfilled a lifelong ambition of mine by working for three months as a volunteer in an African country. I'm in my late 50s now and I don't have the commitments that have previously held me back. I've worked in marketing for much of my life, and I wanted to use the skills I have to help out in a small way.

I applied to do voluntary work a couple of years ago, but it wasn't until about a year later that a suitable scheme came up and I was asked to go. The reaction of my friends to the news was interesting. Many were impressed, I think, and a lot said that given the opportunity they'd like to do something similar – although I must say that not all of them were so keen when I told them later about how basic the conditions were. But a few clearly disapproved of what I was doing. They argued that I was patronising Africans by intervening and telling them how to run their lives. But I saw it rather differently. Ideally, development schemes should be set up by the communities themselves. But sometimes local people don't yet have the necessary skills to make them effective, and need some kind of outside, expert support. And that's where I came in.

The scheme I worked on was based in a village of about 200 people in Tanzania. It involved building concrete tanks to capture water during the wet season with the aim of reducing the problem of drought during the rest of the year. With better irrigation would come more reliable crops, so that eventually the villagers would become self-sufficient. There had been a severe drought in the area for the previous three or four years. The whole region was on the brink of starvation and handouts from charities were the only thing that kept people alive. The scheme had been underway for less than a year when I arrived, and my brief was to suggest ways in which the villagers could market any agricultural production that was surplus to their own requirements – any food that they didn't need themselves. I've heard now that the village is making money from its crops and it's built a primary school and a small health centre. It's very gratifying to know that the scheme has completely transformed its prospects, and the village is now well on its way to becoming a thriving community.

Interviewer:	In the studio today we have the novelist David Bardreth, whose most recent book, *A Woman Alone*, was published last week. Welcome to the programme, David.

David: Thanks for inviting me.

Interviewer: Now, David, you came relatively late to writing, didn't you?

David: Well, I suppose I'd always been a writer – poems, short stories, and so on – but only my close family had read anything I'd written until I had my first novel published in my early forties.

Interviewer: And how did you feel about that?

David: Oh, it felt fantastic having my first book published.

Interviewer: At that time you were a primary school teacher in your native Scotland. At what stage did you leave teaching?

David: Until my third novel was published I was happy to teach during the day and write in the evening and at weekends. But I found that there wasn't enough time to do both as well as I wanted to, so I left teaching and I started writing professionally. Some of my close friends thought I was mad to give up my job, and I was greatly relieved that my subsequent books sold quite well.

Interviewer: So no regrets about leaving teaching?

David: Oh, it was the most difficult decision imaginable! I'd worked at the same school for about fifteen years, and I felt bad leaving the children and also some very close colleagues and friends. But I still live near the school and I go back on every possible occasion.

Interviewer: Tell us something about the process of your writing. How carefully do you outline the story at the very beginning?

David: Before I start writing I always know how a book is going to end, although I rarely have a clear idea at the beginning of how the characters will develop. As I write, gradually they grow into real people in my own mind. But sometimes even I'm surprised at how they turn out!

Interviewer: And what about your daily work routine?

David: I suppose I'm fairly disciplined in my writing. I'm generally up at about 7.00 in the morning, and I usually start work by about eight o'clock. I work upstairs – we've converted our attic into a study. In the early stages of a new book I'll often go to the city library in the afternoon to do some research.

Interviewer: You don't use the Internet?

David: As a rule I prefer finding information from books, and I only turn to the Internet as a last resort.

Interviewer: Let's go on now to your latest novel, *A Woman Alone*. I was surprised to find it set in Norway.

David: Yes, I finished my previous book last January. I'd been feeling really tired, and I was aware that I needed rest and a source of fresh ideas. I taught English in Sweden after I left university – and I still speak Swedish quite well – but I hadn't been to Norway before. There are a lot of historical links between Norway and the north of Scotland, so I decided to spend some weeks there. Some of the geographical settings used in *A Woman Alone* are based on places I visited while I was travelling around.

Interviewer: And *A Woman Alone* seems to be more personal than many of your other works.

David: I'd already decided that I wanted to write about a single-parent family. As you may know, my sister and I were brought up by my mother on her own. The mother in the story, Elsa, is very protective of her children, as was my own mother. But although they have certain common characteristics, Elsa is not really modelled on my mother. Elsa is quite a dominant figure and a woman susceptible to periods of depression, whereas my mother was a rather gentle woman and always even-tempered.

Interviewer: And when you're researching and writing books, do you have time to read other people's novels?

David: I do, yes. One novelist I greatly admire is William Boyd. He writes simply, but with great control of language. I've just finished his excellent novel, *Restless*. It's a quite remarkable story.

Interviewer: I'll certainly add that to my list of books to read. And what about your present writing project? What are you working on now?

David: Well, I don't know if I can tell you yet! I'm still sketching out the plot, so it's very much in the early stages.

Interviewer:	I know there'll be a lot of people waiting eagerly to get hold of it... David Bardreth, thank you for talking to us.
David:	My pleasure.

Alice:	Hi everyone!
Ryan, Luke, Kathy:	Hi / How are you doing?/ Hi, Alice.
Alice:	Listen, we need to make a decision about our holiday. If we don't decide soon, it'll be too late to get anywhere to stay. It's got to be Corfu, hasn't it?
Ryan:	I'm not sure how we'd get there.
Luke:	Well, my brother went there last year. He flew to Rome, then took a train to Brindisi, and then had to get a boat.
Kathy:	No, it's not as difficult as that. We could fly from London to Athens and then take a flight from there to Corfu. It takes about six hours. I've had a look on the Internet and it looks like there's a flight that leaves London at about ten in the morning. But we need to book soon. The longer we leave it, the more expensive it's going to be.
Ryan:	But obviously it would be much easier getting to Athens – there's lots of flights and we wouldn't have to change.
Luke:	Then what about somewhere to stay? Aren't hotels supposed to be pretty expensive in Corfu?
Alice:	Well, I've found three that seem possible. I've printed off the details here. They all look pretty good, and they're right next to the best beach on the island.
Luke:	Which one's cheapest?
Alice:	Er ... this one here. Sixty euros a night for a double room.
Luke:	Well, accommodation would be cheaper in Athens, I think. It says in my guidebook that there are reasonable hotel rooms for as little as 40 euros a night. There's one here recommended. It's a bit far from the city centre, but it's on the metro, so it's easy enough to get into the centre from there.
Kathy:	It wouldn't be as nice as being able to look out over a beach ... What worries me is what we'd do in Athens for a couple of weeks.

Ryan:	Look, Athens is one of the oldest cities in the world. There's lots of museums, and then there's the Acropolis with the Parthenon.
Kathy:	I remember going to Rome with my parents once. We spent the whole time looking at museums and art galleries, and it was the most boring holiday I've ever had.
Alice:	Yeah, I think it'd be more fun to go to Corfu. I much prefer lying on a beach to walking around art galleries all day. And it would be more peaceful than being in a city. I want to come home more relaxed and healthier ... not unhealthier than when I went away!
Kathy:	Yes, I'd prefer to go to an island, too, although I don't want to lie on the beach all day. Maybe we could hire a car and explore the island a bit.
Alice:	Yeah, we want to see as much as possible, and a car would be the easiest way of getting around. It's probably not as unspoilt as some of the other Greek islands, but it's still supposed to be a really beautiful place, so we'll want to see as much as we can. What about the weather in August? I know we all want to see some sunshine, but isn't Athens supposed to be incredibly hot in August? I've heard that it gets so hot that a lot of people leave the city to find somewhere cooler.
Ryan:	No, my friend Mark used to work there as an English teacher, and he reckons the heat is nowhere near as bad as people say. Anyway, isn't Corfu likely to be as hot as Athens at that time of the year?
Alice:	I think you get the breezes off the sea ...

First, let me introduce myself. I'm Dr Lynn Jones, and I'll be taking you for the first five lectures in this course on first language learning. I'd like to begin today's session by highlighting some of the main areas that I'll be covering with you.

From the moment they wake up, infants are keen to interact and communicate with others. This interaction may not, of course, be with people. Early morning sounds from a child's bedroom may be them babbling to themselves or speech as a child speaks to their toys. I recently bought my two-year-old daughter a cuddly elephant, and it has become the 'person' she talks to each morning lying in bed. And as my three-year-old dresses herself, she likes to talk to each item of clothing: 'Red jumper, your turn ...'. So the first lecture will be about what I call 'private' conversations.

Of course, a child's parents are usually their most important focus of interaction, and in the second session we'll be exploring the part that parents play in very early communication. The first stage of interactive play might be a child giving a toy to their mother or offering her some food. And even before they can use words, infants employ their faces, bodies and sounds to communicate what they want. A hand outstretched to a toy could mean 'Give it to me', or a broken toy handed to a parent with an 'Aaa' might mean 'Mend this for me'. Parents encourage this kind of interaction by, for example, hiding an object behind them and asking 'Where's it gone?' At first infants point, and then later verbalise a response.

The importance of infants listening to adults speaking for the development of their own language cannot be overestimated. Many parents play 'follow the instructions' games with their children when they first become mobile, saying things like 'Go to the toybox and find the car for me' or 'Fetch me your hat', although as the parents of older children will know, the novelty for children of following instructions soon wears off! Reading stories for young children is a similarly important part of this process of listening and understanding. But even when children are not being actively encouraged to listen, they will be seeking to make sense of the language they hear. When children appear to be busying themselves with their toys, or applying themselves to painting a picture, they will be absorbing the speech they hear around them and often copying what they hear in their own speech. So the third area we'll be looking at is the relationship between listening and the development of speech.

Interactions between infants will often copy parental speech and behaviour. Two small children at a nursery school might hug each other when they meet each morning, because that's what parents do to the children when they are collected from school. Most parents at some time hear their child say something and ask themselves the question: 'Did they copy that from us?' Of course, it is very difficult to assess exactly the extent of parental influence. Take, for example, the area of conflict. It is not uncommon to see in a nursery school two small children playing with each other peacefully one moment, but they might be hitting each other the next. If their language is more developed, they might each blame the other for a broken toy or a spilt drink. While these would be uncharacteristic of normal adult interaction, perhaps the conflicts between parents witnessed by small children somehow are mimicked in these arguments. A fourth area, then, will be the extent to which patterns of communication are copied.

A final subject I will examine during the course is that of problems in language acquisition. We might consider first language learning natural, a normal process that everyone goes through, and Dr Jackman will be describing this process to you in detail in later talks. However, a significant number of children either acquire language more slowly than the usual rate, or never reach an average level of language proficiency. This topic will obviously be of particular importance to those of you who are going on to work with children with learning difficulties, or as speech therapists.

So, first of all then, let's look at the private conversations that infants engage in ...

Presenter: Hello. All you regular listeners to *Traveller's World* will know that our intrepid reporters are sent around the globe, coming back with stories of marvellous times spent in exotic locations. In today's programme, however, we begin with a trip that had a nightmare start – just to reassure you that even professional travellers can get it wrong. So, Simon Richer, tell us your sorry tale.

Simon: Hello, Jackie. Yes, my assignment was to visit the beautiful island of Lombok in Indonesia. I was supposed to have been flying from London to Singapore and then from Singapore to Mataram in Lombok. I arranged for a taxi to collect me from home in good time, but it eventually turned up an hour late.

Presenter: So you were late to the airport.

Simon: Got there just as they were closing the check-in desk. I handed over my suitcase but then, to my horror, I found I didn't have my passport! I'd been so anxious to get into the taxi that I'd forgotten to pick it up.

Presenter: How very unprofessional of you!

Simon: I know. In 25 years of air travel, that's the first time it's ever happened to me. So back home I went to get it, and then off to plead with the airline. Eventually they found me an alternative flight a day later. It meant flying to Bali and then taking a ferry to Lombok, but I decided to go ahead. The journey went very smoothly until we got to Lombok. Apparently, there'd been a fire and we were made to wait outside the harbour for hours, and the sea was very rough ...

Presenter: ... and you were seasick.

Simon: Very! And, of course, because I'd changed my flight, I also had to stay in a different hotel. I'd really been looking forward to staying at the Hotel Sanar in Mataram, but I had to make do with a less luxurious place – no pool, and no TV in my room.

Presenter: And what about Lombok itself?

Simon: Oh, it was beautiful. A number of people had encouraged me to go to the coral reefs off the northwest coast of the island. I managed to find a friendly taxi driver called Arun to take me and wait for me there. Now, when I was younger I used to hate swimming in the sea. But I went snorkelling for the first time just last year and loved it, so I couldn't wait to have another go. The coral was just a few metres off the beach, so it was quite safe ...

Presenter: Until ... ? What happened?

Simon: Well ... I'd been swimming for a few minutes. The coral was fantastic – some of the best I've seen. And then all of a sudden there was this huge jellyfish in front of me, and I couldn't get out of the way. As it swam past I felt it stinging me across the stomach. I started screaming – it was incredibly painful – and headed back to the beach. Fortunately, there was a small settlement nearby and some of the villagers helped carry me back to my taxi. Arun was fantastic. He took me to the local clinic and the doctors were excellent. I really appreciated them looking after me so well. It was sore for a few days, though, and I was told to take things easy.

Presenter: So how did you spend the rest of your time there?

Simon: Well, Arun really took care of me. The next day we went on to drive towards Mt Rinjani, the highest mountain in Lombok. The mountain's thought by some to have been created by the god Batara. According to tradition he created light and the Earth and still lives in Rinjani. And as we stopped to admire the amazing sunset, it was almost possible to believe it. I really regret not having taken my camera with me.

Presenter: No camera?

Simon: Ah, no. That was another of my disasters. I'd picked up my passport, but then I'd left my camera. I tried using the camera in my mobile phone, but the quality was pretty poor.

Presenter: And what about the people in Lombok?

Simon: Arun's family lived close to the mountain. I was really interested in seeing what it was like in a traditional Lombok family and he invited me to stay with them. Very soon I came to realise that the Lombok people are very kind and hospitable. It wasn't long before I was beginning to feel quite at home there. Arun's family are Sasak, who make up about 80% of the population. The Sasaks are thought to have originally come to Lombok from India or Burma.

Presenter: So the trip actually ended quite positively?

Simon: Absolutely! I considered staying for a few more days, but I didn't have time. But I really hope to go back in the next few years. The island obviously wants to encourage tourism to boost the economy, but I'd love to think that it could avoid a huge expansion in visitors.

Presenter: Thank you, Simon.

The story of radio probably begins with Heinrich Hertz, who was the first to produce radio waves in a laboratory. He devised an experiment in which a spark jumped across a gap in a metal ring when a sparking coil was held a few metres away. The model that you can see in Case 1 shows how this works.

For most people, however, it is the Italian Guglielmo Marconi whose name is mainly associated with the development of radio. Before Marconi's breakthrough, it was possible only to send electrical messages, or 'telegraphs', along fixed wires. This obviously greatly restricted the places to which telegraphs could be sent. Marconi's goal was to find a system where telegraphic messages could be transmitted without the need for the connecting wires that were used in the electric telegraph. For some time he was only able to transmit signals over a few hundred metres, and there were many people who doubted Marconi would ever succeed. The first public demonstration of the power of radio came in 1901, when Marconi announced that he had received a transmission from across the Atlantic. The old photograph that you can see ahead of you shows Marconi at Signal Hill in St. John's, Newfoundland, where this first transmission was received. Soon after, Marconi opened a 'wireless telegraph' factory in England, which employed around 50 people. There are just a few of the 'wireless telegraphs' the factory produced left in the world, an example of which you can see in Case 2. These early radio systems could only be used for Morse code, in which each letter of the alphabet is represented by a combination of dots and dashes. Radio waves could not carry speech until a method had been developed whereby the low-frequency waves produced in a microphone could be combined with high-frequency radio waves. The invention that made this possible was the vacuum tube or thermionic valve. You can see examples of these in Case 3.

In several countries, radios became the main means of communication during the 1930s and 1940s. The next photograph shows friends gathered around the radio in the mid-1930s. Radio entertainers, many of whom became household names, were highly paid. In Britain, the popularity of radio increased until 1952, by which time four out of five households owned one. You can probably guess the reason why radio began to lose some of its popularity in the early 1950s – competition from television.

Move now to Room 36, where you can find information and displays about the early days of television ...

Interviewer: Photographs of food are all around us, in advertisements, magazines and cookbooks. Today's guest is Helena Palmer, who has made a highly successful career out of food photography. Welcome, Helena.

Helena: Thank you.

Interviewer: So how did you become involved in food photography – was your first interest the food or the photography?

Helena: Oh, definitely photography first. When I was quite young – 10 or 11 – I started using an old camera belonging to my father. I became fascinated with taking shots of people – my friends and my family in particular.

Interviewer: And were you also interested in the way food was presented – in restaurants, for example?

Helena: My parents – not having much money – rarely took us to restaurants. But my mother was an excellent cook. I used to take shots of her in the kitchen, and also some of the special things that she'd prepare – birthday cakes, and things like that.

Interviewer: And you left school quite young.

Helena: Yes, I wasn't very gifted academically, so at 16 I left school and went to help out at a local photographic studio. It was easy to find a photographer wanting to take on an assistant for no pay! For a couple of years I lived at home with my parents, who supported me financially. And I was very lucky that the photographer who took me on taught me a lot. She was really the first person to encourage me to take up food photography. She always let me help out with 'food shoots' – wedding cakes, publicity photos for local restaurants, and so on. Then, when I was 18, there was a major photography competition being held in London and one of the categories was 'Celebrations'. So I entered a portfolio of photographs – just for the experience, I thought. By that time I was getting quite into it.

Interviewer: And you won.

Helena: That's right. At that time, I was the youngest person in the competition to win any of the major categories.

Interviewer: Now, it's sometimes said that photographing food is the most difficult job for a professional photographer. Is that really true?

Helena: It can certainly be very difficult to make it look appetising. Food photography is all done in studios, and the biggest problem is the heat produced by the lights. It can take a very long time to get everything exactly right for a shot, and by that time a chef's carefully prepared salad might look limp or a cream cake becomes a mound of wet sponge.

Interviewer: So how do you get round that?

Helena: Well, firstly, the food in photographs used to illustrate cookbooks and magazine articles isn't always entirely authentic.

Interviewer: You mean it's made of plastic?

Helena: Well, some of it, perhaps, but not all of it! If great food could be copied in plastic,

I'd be out of a job! We have a number of techniques to help us out. First, a lot of the items in the photograph can be set up early – glasses, cutlery, flowers, perhaps. And then we put in some material to substitute for the food – something with the same size, shape and colour. Often we just make this quickly in the studio from cardboard or any other material available, and paint it.

Interviewer: Personally, I prefer food not made of cardboard!

Helena: Don't we all! In the meantime, a food stylist prepares the food to be photographed.

Interviewer: A food stylist!

Helena: Oh, yes, most professional food photographers employ a food stylist nowadays. As soon as I'm satisfied with the setting, lighting, and so on, we take out the artificial food and put in the real thing. But the food starts to dry out very quickly. So I generally have with me a spray bottle containing glycerine mixed with water. Glycerine's a liquid, completely colourless, that's often used to sweeten food. It's great for keeping food looking shiny and moist. Another difficulty is that food is sometimes meant to be hot and steaming, but of course by the time we photograph it, it's completely cold. The only thing to do in that case is to create steam from elsewhere. We use cotton wool balls soaked in water and then put in a microwave. These steam nicely for a couple of minutes, and we position them so that it looks like it's the food steaming. Something else I wouldn't be without is a small blowtorch.

Interviewer: What do you use that for?

Helena: Hundreds of things – quickly melting butter over vegetables, browning toast ... A technique that might be used in photographing meat is to take a piece of, say, chicken, use the blowtorch for a while so that it's nicely golden brown, and then spray some glycerine on the outside to make it look moist. It looks great in the photo, but it might be raw on the inside.

Interviewer: Helena, it's been fascinating talking to you. Thank you so much for coming into the studio.

Helena: My pleasure.

Recording 13

Researcher: Thanks to both of you for filling in the questionnaire about your diet, and for agreeing to discuss the issues that it raised. First of all, Sarah, could you describe your eating habits on a typical day?

Sarah: Well, on a typical working day I usually start with a piece of toast and a glass of orange juice. For lunch I generally have a sandwich and a packet of crisps as I'm sitting at my desk. When I get home late I take a ready meal out of the freezer and put it in the microwave. Curries are really good, or something with noodles.

Researcher: And what about you, Don?

Don: I'm pretty much the same, actually, although at the weekend I like to make something myself so as not to eat processed food all the time. I'll perhaps roast a chicken, or do a salad.

Sarah: At the weekend, I'm often with friends and we'll usually go out to eat seeing that none of us likes cooking.

Researcher: Okay. Can you tell me how your diet now is different from when you were younger – say, when you were a teenager?

Sarah: Well, when I was younger, my mother used to keep an eye on what I ate. She tried very hard to encourage me to eat healthily. I think she made a particular effort as I was often ill as a child. She also talked to me about the food she made so that I'd learn about diet and nutrition.

Researcher: Right. Don?

Don: Yes, I suppose because it's so easy to buy ready meals from the supermarket, it makes me quite lazy about cooking, and in that way my diet isn't so good. But in some ways, it's better now, though. If I get hungry, I'll eat some fruit, whereas at school I'd buy a bar of chocolate. I remember once I was eating some sweets in my bedroom when my mother walked in. I got a long lecture on the dangers of too much sugar.

Researcher: But overall you feel your diet is less healthy than it was, say, ten years ago?

Don: Yes, I think that's true, in that I ate more regularly then and had a more balanced diet.

Researcher: Okay, so what are the main problems you see in your present diet, and what would you most like to change?

Sarah: Well, for me, I think the biggest problem is breakfast. I don't eat much for breakfast because I'm always in a rush. I know that's not good for me, and I'd like to have something more substantial before I leave home in the morning. But I have to get out by 7.30 in order to catch my bus, so I really don't have time.

Don: My biggest problem is that I tend to snack a lot. When I've had one of those ready meals, I feel hungry by the time I go to bed. So sometimes I get up in the night and have a snack, although I know it's bad for me. I must be eating too much because I've been getting a bit overweight recently. And as I put on weight, it gets more and more difficult to exercise. I was absolutely exhausted when I had to run for the bus yesterday.

Researcher: Thanks. And what's preventing you from making the changes that you'd like to make in your diet?

Sarah: I suppose time is the big problem. Although I'd like to eat more fresh food, I don't have time to prepare meals in the evenings. And I don't have the opportunity to go shopping while I'm working.

Don: Well, my problem is that I'm not a very good cook! I actually read a lot about food and health, and what I should be eating. But it's very hard to put a healthy diet into practice despite the fact that I know all about the theory. And most recipes in magazines are no use to me because of the time they take. It would be really helpful to ...

Recording 14a

Presenter: Plans to open a new zoo at Twyford have caused a major outcry among animal rights campaigners. With me in the studio to discuss the issue are Debbie Hall, from the organisation Save the Animals which campaigns against zoos, Mark Archer, who plans to open Twyford Zoo, and Wendy Khan, who runs a safari park in the south of England, where visitors can drive their own cars through large enclosures where wild animals run free. Mark Archer, if I could come to you first, why is another zoo needed? Aren't there enough already?

Mark: Well, zoos have a number of very important roles. First of all, they're of enormous educational value. If we didn't have zoos, most people would never see wild animals in real life. The fact that there is no large zoo in this part of the country means that there's a real need for a zoo at Twyford. We want to make it as easy as possible for young people to come along so that they can learn about wild animals. Second, rare and endangered species can be preserved, and, hopefully, bred in captivity, making sure that the species survives. If we'd introduced captive breeding earlier, we would have prevented the extinction of a number of animals. I'm thinking of animals like the Tasmanian tiger or the Chinese river dolphin. Unless we expand captive breeding, many more animals will die out.

Presenter: Debbie Hall. Your view on this?

Debbie: Well, certainly we should have captive breeding programmes if it will help save species. But this doesn't have to be in a zoo, where animals are often kept in small enclosures and cages. If they were in the wild, they would have more space to roam free. And so many other aspects of zoos are unnatural for wild animals. It's not natural for different species to live separately from each other, or for them to be given food at regular times rather than hunt for it. And then there's the cruelty involved in capturing and transporting wild animals to zoos.

Mark: But what you've got to remember is that many animals in zoos nowadays were actually born in captivity.

Debbie: That's no excuse. Even if wild animals are born in a zoo, it's still cruel to keep them in a small enclosure where they often become unhappy and prone to illness.

Mark: But if there's a health problem, vets deal with it quickly. In the wild, an animal that becomes ill is much more likely to die or be eaten.

Debbie: That's true, of course. In the wild, animals do die through illness or are attacked by other animals. But this is perfectly normal and how they lived for centuries before we started hunting them.

Presenter: Wendy Khan. Can I bring you in here? You were disappointed that Twyford was to be a zoo and not a safari park.

Wendy: Yes, I certainly was. First of all, I agree with Debbie that it's inhumane to keep animals in the conditions you find in most zoos. Safari parks offer all the educational experience of zoos – the close contact with animals – but they also allow animals to roam free in large enclosures. Safari parks are also very active in captive breeding programmes, of course. The decision to make Twyford a zoo rather than a safari park is a lost opportunity.

Mark: I'm all in favour of safari parks provided that the animals are well looked after. Unfortunately, that hasn't always been the case in the past. But they can never replace zoos. They're places where large animals, mainly from Africa – giraffes, elephants, lions, and so on – roam free. But you can't have small animals roaming around – if they're not eaten by the larger animals first, they'll be killed by visitors' cars.

Debbie: If I could just get a word in here ... Save the Animals believes that safari parks are **not** an acceptable substitute for zoos. Even though they say they are concerned about the welfare of animals, just like zoos, they are still businesses mainly out to make a profit. Entertaining visitors is the priority, not the welfare of animals. Our view is that wild animals should be protected in their natural habitat. There are many successful reserves in Africa, for example, where wild animals roam peacefully.

Wendy: But all that costs huge amounts of money that can only be provided by rich tourists who come to see the animals. Most families can't afford to make trips like that to see them. Safari parks allow city-dwelling children from all levels of society access to ....

Debbie: But animal welfare is more important! In reserves, animals can be monitored and treated for illness and they can be protected from poachers. And they have as much space as they need to live their lives freely. So long as developed countries put money into these reserves, species will be preserved.

Mark: I'm sorry, but that's unrealistic.

Presenter: Well, I'm afraid that's all we have time for tonight. Wendy Khan, Debbie Hall, Mark Archer, thank you.

Recording 14b

Speaker 1

By the time I get home after a hard day, and with the prospect of an evening of preparation and marking ahead of me, the last thing I want to do is spend a lot of time in the kitchen. I live on my own, so dinner isn't a time to talk and relax, unless I've got friends round. I just tend to grab a sandwich and eat it while I'm watching the news or working. If I want good food, there are some pretty good restaurants around here.

Speaker 2

Even when I'm abroad, I'd rather go somewhere that serves the kind of food I'm used to – steak and chips, and things like that. Sometimes this gets to be a bit of a problem if I'm transporting stuff to somewhere off the beaten track. If I don't know the place I'm going to, I'll generally take food from home to keep me going for a few days, and eat in the cab rather than eat out.

Speaker 3

When I was training, I lived at home and my mum did all the cooking unless she was away from home. She really enjoys it, so she didn't mind. Now I realise I should have paid more attention to what she was doing, but she's offered to lend me some recipe books and give me some tips, so that will really help. But just now I'm rushed off my feet. I'm working in the accident and emergency department and we have to do long hours and night shifts every other week. If I wasn't so busy, I'd certainly like to cook more. Hopefully, things'll be less frantic when I get moved to the children's ward at the end of the year.

Speaker 4

I went off to France for a year after school and really got hooked on good food and cooking during that time. Unless I've got lectures first thing, I generally go down to the market to get the best-quality stuff. None of us has got a lot of money to spare, but you can get real bargains at some of the stalls. Then in the evening I cook for my flatmates. They're pretty appreciative, and if they enjoy what I've cooked – well, that's what it's all about.

Speaker 5

I'm at home most of the time and I don't have a set pattern of work. If the writing's going well, I might work through from eight in the morning to three in the afternoon without a break – unless the sun's shining and then I might go out for a walk. This means that I tend not to eat regularly or I forget to buy anything in the shops. I'll often go out and get a take-away or something late in the day. Not very nutritious, I realise, but it's difficult if you've got deadlines to meet.

Recording 15

Linda: Have you seen Sam's article for this week?

Bob: No, not yet. He'd got as far as Naples last week, hadn't he? Go on, read it out.

Linda: Right. He's called it 'Rest and rats: from Naples to Amalfi'.

'When I last wrote I was just north of Naples. I was tired, had big blisters on my feet, and, having fallen over a number of times, I was feeling thoroughly miserable. Now, a week later, I'm sitting in a restaurant looking out over the Mediterranean watching the sun go down – and life has improved greatly.'

Bob: That's a bit better! To hear him grumbling last week, you'd think he was about to get on the next flight home!

Linda: He sounds in good form now. Listen to this. 'I had no idea where I was heading when I walked into Naples. Exhausted by a difficult few days, I was only interested in finding a bed for the night. Not wanting to carry my backpack any further than I needed to, I went to the first hotel I came across. But I struck lucky! I'd found a small, friendly hotel. In fact, the welcome I got at the hotel made me decide to stay for a couple of days. While in Naples, I did what all visitors do – I took a tour to Vesuvius and Pompeii. Fascinating places, and it was so good to sit on a coach and give my feet a rest.'

You've been there, haven't you?

Bob: Yes, I went a couple of years ago. Pompeii is amazing. I don't imagine he rested his feet that much, though – it's such a big place to walk around. What else does he say?

Linda: Let's see … 'But after a couple of days of rest and relaxation, I was ready to get back on the trail. Before leaving Naples, I bought yet more walking socks and a new pair of boots. These are not just any old boots, though. Made from the softest leather imaginable, they are as comfortable as a pair of slippers.'

He must be really pleased. He was getting so many blisters with the old pair.

'Having left the sprawl of the city behind me, I walked up into the hills to avoid the long trek around the coast. There's spectacular scenery up there and beautiful views to the sea. On the downside, though, the hills are covered in thorny bushes, and the whole area is very rocky. At times it was difficult to follow the paths as they're not well marked, and I often had to retrace my steps. I also had a few unpleasant encounters with the local wildlife. Walking into one village I was met by a pack of unfriendly dogs. Snarling aggressively, the dogs were pretty terrifying at first. But I found that if I ignored them, they soon lost interest in me. I met some smaller wildlife, too. The first night on the hills, I pitched my tent, and was ready to sleep. But opening up my sleeping bag, I discovered a scorpion.'

Bob: You're kidding! Aren't they dangerous?

Linda: Well, Sam obviously wasn't sure.

'I'm no expert on scorpions, and I didn't know if this one was poisonous. I shook it out of my sleeping bag well away from the tent, and made sure it was heading off in the opposite direction before I settled down for the night! But then, around two in the morning, having been woken up by a scratching sound, I found a large rat trying to get into my backpack. Fortunately, it ran off when I threw my boots at it. What with sleeping so badly, and a long and difficult walk along some treacherous paths down from the hills, it was quite a relief to get to Amalfi this afternoon. I'm now ready for dinner – I've been recommended the local speciality of lasagne with ricotta cheese – and a few more miles of walking tomorrow towards Ravello. This time, though, it will be along the coast and (I hope) scorpion and rat free! Another report next week.'

Bob: Well, it sounds like he's enjoying Amalfi, anyway. He hasn't got much further to go, has he?

Linda: No, probably another two or three weeks and he'll be back with us.

Recording 16

Joe: First of all, thank you for giving me the opportunity to come and talk to you this evening. I'm sure you all know the area a couple of miles out of the village known as the Norton Marsh. You've probably also heard that the Marsh has been given to the NWT to look after. Unfortunately, the Marsh has been neglected for many years. It's overgrown, paths have disappeared, and the stream running through the area is blocked by rubbish. Our plan is to return the Marsh to its natural state as far as possible. We'd like to follow the example of what they've done at Broadstone Park, which many of you will have been to. A few years ago it was a wilderness. Now it's a thriving nature reserve full of animal, bird and plant life, with a popular nature trail for visitors.

Broadstone Park is part of the Montague family estate and, as such, was largely funded by private means. As a charitable trust, we have to rely on contributions from the public, and we have to face up to the fact that we don't have the resources at the moment to achieve our aims. Don't worry, I'm not asking you for your money this evening, but I **am** asking for your help. We're looking for volunteers to help us work on the Marsh over the next few years. For example, we need people to clear the vegetation, maintain paths, clear the stream and build fences. Clearing the vegetation is something that is urgently needed.

But why should you volunteer? Well, the reason for most people is that they want exercise and fresh air – and it's also good to know they're helping the environment. There's a great social side to the NWT, too. I can guarantee that you'll make a lot of new friends, and we organise barbecues and other social events. If you don't fancy the physical work that's involved at the Marsh, you can still help. We also need people to address envelopes, deliver promotional material, and publicise the NWT on the Net. Whether you help with the outdoor or indoor work depends on you. It's entirely up to you to decide how much time you can give to work at the NWT. We will be very grateful for whatever time people can spare. Nine o'clock is when we usually meet, on Saturday and Sunday mornings. Just come along to the Marsh and we'll show you what to do.

You don't have to make a decision tonight – you can get in touch with me at any time. If you've got any questions about what I've said so far I'd be very happy to answer them.

Man 1: What you've told us is very interesting and I'd like to be involved, but I'm not a member of the NWT. And I've heard it's quite expensive to join.

Joe: The fact that you're not a member of the trust makes no difference. We're just looking for people with enthusiasm, commitment and some spare time.

Woman 1: Can I ask why the Marsh was given to the NWT?

Joe: Well, Mr Reynolds, the man who gave us the land, has been a supporter of the NWT for many years and wanted us to take over the area a long time ago. Unfortunately, he'd been in a dispute over property with his brother and there was some debate as to whether he could legally give us the land. That dispute has now been resolved, so he got his wish, and the land is now ours.

Woman 2: I'd like to be involved, but I don't know whether or not I'd be able to come on a regular basis. Would that be a problem?

Joe: Not at all. Come when you can. You'll be made very welcome.

Man 2: I don't have a car. Does the NWT organise lifts to the Marsh as I don't know if I can get there by public transport?

Joe: There is a bus – the number 45 – that goes from town past the Marsh, although I can't remember whether it runs on Sundays.

Woman 2: No, the Sunday service was cancelled a while ago.

Joe: Anyway, we organise lifts for people who don't have their own cars and each weekend one person is responsible. You can phone whoever is in charge of arranging lifts on the weekend you want to come and we'll make sure someone will collect you from your home – and take you back, of course!

Recording 17

Marie: I learnt to drive with a driving instructor, and I think there are lots of advantages to this. Firstly, cars like the one I learnt in have dual controls so the instructor can take over accelerating, braking and stuff. Also, my instructor never got annoyed, however badly I was driving. Even if I did something incredibly stupid like stalling in the middle of a busy road, he'd stay completely cool. He was really encouraging as well as being incredibly patient. We used to stop driving at some point during the lesson, and he would ask me how I felt I'd improved, so he'd always be focusing on what I was doing right. Another thing is that being so experienced, he'd got lots of really useful tips to pass on. Like, for example, reversing around corners. At first, I couldn't get the hang of this at all. However I had the mirror positioned, I just couldn't judge where the back of the car was. But he told me exactly what to do – how to sit, what I should be able to see out of the mirror and windows, and so on. After that it was dead easy.

There were disadvantages, of course. Occasionally, my usual driving instructor was ill, so the driving school sent along a replacement. That was a bit disappointing because he was great and I didn't want to be taught by anyone else. Even so, I always found the replacements very patient and helpful.

Another advantage is that experienced instructors know when you're good enough to pass, which I think is kind of difficult for non-professionals to judge. I just carried on having lessons until my instructor said I was ready to take the driving test. And he was right – I passed first time. Although it's expensive having driving lessons, I'd really recommend it.

Sam: My mum taught me to drive 'cause I couldn't afford to pay for driving lessons. I think there's a lot of other good things about having your parents teach you, besides saving money. You've got to book driving lessons in advance, but you can go out with your parents whenever it suits you. And you can spend a lot more time practising, as well. For example, my mum used to come and collect me from college in the car and I'd drive home. What's more, she'd let me drive when we went shopping.

My mum was a great teacher. Even though she doesn't have a professional qualification or anything, she's got lots of experience to pass on. I was lucky, though, because she knew a deserted airfield near to where we live, and for the first few lessons Mum took me there to practise. She wouldn't let me drive on busy roads before I could control the car reasonably well. And as long as I didn't do anything stupid, she stayed pretty calm. The only time I remember her getting stressed was when I was overtaking. I used to find it really hard.

It was very different with my dad, though. He took me out once when Mum was away. We'd hardly driven out of our road before we were shouting at each other. Then he made me practise hill starts for an hour – that's something I still have problems with – and we just snapped at each other all the time.

Of course, one disadvantage of learning with your parents is that you have to pay a lot to insure the car. But apart from that, I think it's much better.

Recording 18

Interviewer: A government report published today has shown a dramatic fall in recorded crime over the last ten years. With me to discuss the report is the Home Affairs Minister, Kate Pullman. Minister, you must be very pleased with the findings.

Minister: Yes, indeed, I was delighted when I was given the figures. When we got elected ten years ago, one of our priorities was a reduction in the disturbingly high crime figures. Obviously, the policies that we've put into place have had a significant impact, so that during our period in office there's been a 40% fall in the risk of being a victim of crime.

Interviewer: So can you pinpoint what measures have had the most significant effect?

Minister: Well, I think I'd highlight three things. First, attitudes to committing crime have changed significantly since Peter Miles was appointed head of the police service. He's been successful in getting more police officers on the streets, and this has meant that a much higher proportion of offenders have been arrested during the last ten years than ever before. Second, a huge amount has been invested in surveillance, particularly closed-circuit television. CCTV has been introduced into most city centres, and it's used widely now in helping to prevent car crime in particular. And third, I'd pick out our

Make Amends scheme. Most people found guilty of vandalism are now made to repair the damage they've caused, and this has discouraged young people in particular from causing damage to property. The effect of this is becoming obvious. People are seeing less graffiti in city centres, for example. It's been so successful that a number of other countries are considering adopting a similar policy.

Interviewer: But it's not all good news, is it? While overall crime levels have fallen, some categories of crime have risen quite sharply, haven't they? Street crime is up over 25%!

Minister: It's true that there has been a surge in street crime. The reason for this can be found in the huge increase in the number of mobile phones. These have become a particular target for street robbers. But this figure is expected to fall rapidly as new technology starts being introduced to trace stolen mobiles. If they can be traced, they'll be a much less attractive target.

Interviewer: And drug-related crime is on the increase.

Minister: Well, it's certainly true that more people were caught selling drugs. It's not clear, though, whether there are more people out there selling drugs or whether there has been better policing and so more arrests.

Interviewer: There have been some questions raised about the accuracy of the figures in the report.

Minister: Well, it may be that some minor mistakes were made in collecting the figures, but I don't think anyone would deny the general trends that are reported.

Interviewer: Finally, can I turn to the issue of the public perception of crime, which the report also investigates. It must concern you that despite the number of crimes falling in recent years, a majority of people believe that the crime rate has actually gone up. Everyone you speak to seems to have been a victim or know a victim of crime. If I can give a personal example, my house was broken into only last week and I had my TV and stereo taken. Virtually every person in my road has had a burglar alarm fitted recently.

Minister: I'm very sorry to hear that. Yes, there is a problem of public perception, but we're taking steps to improve this. For example,

our latest poster campaign is intended to reassure people that violent crime is falling nationally. But it'll take a long time for perceptions to change, I think.

Interviewer: You don't believe then, as many people do, that crime is actually on the increase but that fewer crimes are reported to the police?

Minister: I do accept that some of the fall might have been caused by lower rates of reporting, but I'm sure this has had a very small impact on the figures.

Interviewer: Kate Pullman, thank you very much.

Minister: Thank you.

Recording 19a

James: Oh, there you are, Kath. I've been looking for you. So how did the meeting go?

Kath: Well, it was really interesting. There were a couple of representatives from the airport, and one of those, a Mr Kelly, spoke first. Then there was a short presentation by Sue Ray.

James: Who's Sue Ray?

Kath: The head of the No to Airport Expansion group. After that there were questions from the audience. Some of the people there got pretty angry.

James: I'm not surprised! Everyone I've spoken to thinks it's awful.

Kath: Yeah, I thought so, too, before the meeting, but I'm not so sure now. I agree with the anti-expansion group that the plans will change the area, but maybe change isn't such a bad thing.

James: So the airport authorities have convinced you, then?

Kath: Not entirely. They told us that the expansion would create around 2000 jobs directly – people employed at the airport. They also said that it might increase tourism in the region. I wasn't so sure about this. I asked how it would boost tourism, and they admitted that they're not sure exactly how many more people it will attract, although they said it would certainly make it easier for people to get here. Actually, Sue reckoned the expansion would **damage** tourism because people won't want to go on holiday anywhere near an airport. They said that a growing number of people in the local area supported the expansion, particularly local business.

James:	But what about the noise?
Kath:	Mr Kelly said the airport had carried out trial flights last month and no complaints had been received from people in the village. He convinced me that noise wouldn't be a problem for us.
James:	And what were the airport people like?
Kath:	Well, I expected them to be confrontational, but in fact they seemed quite understanding of the complaints. They promised to keep us informed about future developments. They say they'll be putting copies of the plans in the village hall. They encouraged us to go there and look at the plans in detail. They also announced that there would be a public enquiry before any final decision is taken.
James:	I'm worried about the nuclear power station on the coast. Won't planes fly directly over it? And if ever a plane crashed into it, it would be a disaster.
Kath:	They said that the flight paths they're proposing would keep planes away from the power station. Mind you, when Sue gave her presentation she warned us that the airport authorities were not telling the truth. She obviously doesn't trust them, and demanded that we be shown the details of the flight paths. She wanted to know why we should believe them when they had denied for years that they wanted to expand. They avoided replying to that.
James:	And what does the No to Airport Expansion group want to happen next?
Kath:	Well, we had a talk about that after the meeting. Someone asked Sue what we should do to protest about the proposal and she advised us to write to our local politicians with our objections and she also suggested inviting the Minister for Transport to hear our complaints. I've volunteered to write to her. And I'm going to go and have a look at the plans. Do you want to come with me?
James:	Yes, it'd be interesting to see …

Recording 19b

Alan:	So how did you get into landscape photography?
Maggie:	It started at school, really. There was an exhibition of landscape photography on in town, and my art teacher suggested that I go along. I was just bowled over by it and decided then and there that's what I wanted to do.

Alan:	In my line of work, portrait photography, I rarely venture far from the studio. I like the degree of control you have there. I mean, outside you're dependent on the weather and being able to get access to just the right place to shoot from.
Maggie:	But that's part of the attraction of it for me. I love searching for the best vantage point, the quietness of waiting for the perfect moment for the shot – which may never come – and seeing the way a scene changes over time.
Alan:	So you've never been tempted by studio work?
Maggie:	Well, early on I didn't have access to a studio, and later, when I was commissioned to do portraits, I found it quite restricting. It took me hours to set up the lighting and the position of the subject. I felt that creativity was lost, and this was reflected in my photographs.
Alan:	That's certainly a risk. The temptation is to set things up so meticulously that by the time of the shoot the subject has lost interest and can't help looking rather false, as if they'd rather be somewhere else.
Maggie:	And there's so much more involved in photography than just the techniques of using the camera and lighting.
Alan:	Yes, it's not just a question of imagining what you want a portrait to look like, you've also got to be able to convey this to the subject: how you want them to sit, what kind of emotion you want expressed. These aren't the kinds of things you can demonstrate, but you've got to get that message across.
Maggie:	It's similar in landscape photography to some extent. Most of the work is for clients – tourist authorities and the like. You've got to listen to your clients and match their needs with your own preferences, and negotiate an agreement on what the end product should look like. If clients want something that I know isn't going to work, I encourage them to look at the location in a different way.
Alan:	Yes, negotiating with clients is something that all photography courses include these days.
Maggie:	Of course, we're both of a generation where it was rare to have formal training. Personally, I learnt from looking at the photographs of other professionals, making my own judgements about their quality.

Alan: I suppose that's where I wanted a teacher of some kind. I remember the hours I would spend poring over an image, trying to discover how they got some lighting effect.

Maggie: It's true it can take a huge amount of time, but you end up with skills that you'd never be able to learn from someone else. You've got to work these things out by yourself, without other people influencing you. Cartier-Bresson claimed that photography is a way of life, and he was right.

Alan: But I think the way you develop is through comments from people on your own work. Negative feedback can be quite hard to take, but it's a great help in shaping what I do.

Maggie: Yes, it's an important influence on any artist's work. I quite like getting negative feedback because it can point the direction I should be taking in a way that praise never can. In some ways it's great when people consider that an exhibition of mine is a success, but what do I learn from that?

Alan: And of course our lives have been changed radically by the advent of digital photography. A colleague of mine persuaded me to switch to a digital camera shortly after they first appeared in the 1990s, and I've never looked back. Being able to see an image that you've captured pretty well instantaneously is amazing. And the biggest impact of all is on what happens after the image is captured – I mean, being able to adjust images on the computer.

Maggie: But we get into difficulties here with the purpose of photography. For me, a drawing or painting can show something that never actually existed: something that can come entirely from the artist's imagination. A photograph, though, should show something that was in front of the camera when the photograph was taken. Digital technology allows you to interfere with a photograph to show as real what the photographer prefers.

Alan: But don't you think that ...

Recording 20a

Alison: Are you still using the computer?

Ben: I won't be long. I was just looking at some of these adventure holidays in Australia. You've been to Australia, haven't you? Who did you go with?

Alison: A company called TransWorld Adventures.

Ben: Oh, that's who I was thinking of going with! They do diving holidays in quite a few places – Perth, Brisbane, Sydney ...

Alison: I went for the one based in Brisbane. It was a fantastic experience.

Ben: The website's a bit short on detail, though. What happened when you got there? Who met you at the airport?

Alison: One of the local organisers did. And then he drove me to a diving school just outside the city, where I met the others in the group. We had a week there learning to dive, and then we went to the Gold Coast where we had a week of sailing.

Ben: Do they provide all the equipment? It doesn't say much about that on the website.

Alison: They should do. They certainly did for us – all the air tanks, weights and things that you need – although it's useful to have your own face mask and snorkel.

Ben: I'm a bit concerned about the diving. I'm not really a very good swimmer.

Alison: No, neither am I. But you don't have to be. That's the great thing about diving – you don't actually have to be a strong swimmer. What else were you thinking of doing?

Ben: Well, sailing would be great, but I've never sailed a boat before.

Alison: That doesn't matter. Nor had I, but it's really not that difficult, and the instructors are brilliant. And anyway, it doesn't matter if you fall in. The water's warm, and they give you life jackets to wear.

Ben: You think I'd enjoy it, then?

Alison: Oh, I'm sure you would.

Ben: So have you got any good tips?

Alison: Well, make sure you take a sun hat. It's easy to get burned. And take a couple of pairs of old trainers – preferably plastic ones because they get really wet on the boats. I took leather trainers that fell apart, and I had to buy new ones while I was out there. I suppose the other thing is that I didn't realise what hard work sailing is. By the end of the holiday I was exhausted, but very fit!

Ben: Yes, I need to get into better shape. I was also thinking about spending an extra week in Tasmania going river rafting. That's probably hard work, too.

Alison: Sounds great, but I don't think TransWorld Adventures do that, do they?

Ben: Yeah, it mentions it here on their website.

Alison: Let's see ... So it does. That's new!

Ben: It looks amazing. You travel down the Franklin River in a rubber dinghy and then camp by the river at night.

Alison: Wow! Well, if you're going camping, don't forget to take a really good insect repellent. You'll certainly need some. Tea tree oil works very well.

Ben: What about other camping equipment – a tent and cooking things – do you think I'll need to take those?

Alison: I don't imagine so. Usually they provide that sort of stuff. But why not contact them and ask them for more information?

Ben: Yeah, maybe I'll email them now.

Recording 20b

Interviewer: Today I'm talking to David Evans, who's a school chef at Academy School in Wales. Now, David, this is a new school, isn't it, and it takes a rather unusual approach to school meals?

David: That's right. When the school opened about this time last year the new Principal proposed that school dinners should be compulsory. Some people thought she'd be crazy to go ahead with the plan, but she was determined to. Obviously, this was quite a risky experiment. Students aren't allowed to bring in sandwiches or fizzy drinks. And each day there are only two options available, one vegetarian. We try to introduce a wide range of styles of cooking. Naturally, at first, students were a little dubious about the food. Most had only eaten what you might call 'traditional' British food, so I think it was quite adventurous for them to try what they saw as unusual, the kinds of foods they normally wouldn't have the opportunity to eat at home, or wouldn't want to.

Interviewer: And rather than having a typical school canteen with individual students lining up to collect food from the kitchen, you have a different arrangement.

David: Yes, we have our restaurant system. We get everybody seated at about 12.30 on tables of six and then one student from each table collects the food from the kitchen and serves it to the others. It's slow, but we deliberately encourage students to sit and talk around the table, including about the food they're eating. There's still some resistance to this, particularly as a lot of our students come from homes where fast food and ready meals are what's normally eaten, and family members eat at different times. They don't have the habits of conversation over a meal or discussions of food. But we see this as part of our mission, to give them basic social skills so they can operate in an adult world.

Interviewer: And what about staff here? What's their part in this?

David: Staff are expected to eat in the restaurant and sit with students, but they're not there to control things. They're there to talk to students about the food they're eating and in this way they learn about nutrition and how important it is to get the right amounts, and that having too much carbohydrate or fat isn't a good thing. Of course, it's not all food talk. An unexpected benefit is that the teachers learn more about students outside the classroom. At first there were grumbles from teachers about being forced to eat with students rather than sitting with other members of staff, but now I think they prefer to.

Interviewer: And you always try to cook with fresh ingredients.

David: Yes, that's right. Although we offer international dishes, both for nutritional reasons and because of environmental concerns, pretty much all of the produce we use is locally sourced. We've also got a small herb garden behind the science block. Students can help with this if they're willing to. So as well as having fresh food, we're reducing the environmental problems associated with transporting food over long distances. We put up a map in the restaurant to show where food has come from. It's not always possible to get local produce, of course, but we do what we can.

Interviewer: Now what about you personally, David? How did you come to take on the post of school chef here?

David: Well, I've had a varied career. I've been a waiter and a chef in a London restaurant, I've run two small companies, and I went on to train as a teacher. I taught domestic science in a secondary school for ten years before taking on this job. I've found that probably the most important part of the job is to listen to what the students say about the food. I spend a lot of time in the restaurant. I go and talk to the students. They'll always give me an honest opinion on whether or not they've enjoyed something. The time I spent in management has helped me most with this. You need to listen to what people are saying to get the best out of them and make the right decisions.

Interviewer: And do you think the approach to food you've taken here could be adopted in any school?

David: No, I don't think all schools would be able to. We're lucky in that we're a new school and we set it up with the ethos that learning about healthy eating is an important life skill, and students and their parents accept that, although sometimes rather unwillingly. It could be difficult to introduce this into an established school where, for example, chips and burgers are a regular feature of school dinners. Introducing a radical change when students are used to doing things in a certain way can be difficult. But any school could take some steps to make students aware of the importance of healthy eating. I'd certainly advise them to. Over time I think we'll see most schools moving in this direction.

Recording 21

The final presentation to be made tonight is an award for Lifetime Service to Music Education, and I'm delighted to say that this goes to ... Maria Adams.

Before I ask Maria to come up and accept the award, I'd just like to say a few words about her. All of you will know of her achievements, first as a highly successful violinist, and then as conductor of the York City Orchestra, but fewer of you will know about her contribution to music education in this country and beyond.

It was in the mid-1990s that we first met. She had been conductor of the YCO for about a year, and I was head of education on York city council. For some time Maria had been writing to me, saying that the council should do more to help children's musical development in the city, particularly for those who came from poorer backgrounds. What she was suggesting was that members of the YCO would volunteer their services, either individually or in groups, to go into schools and play for children and run music workshops. In exchange, she wanted the city council to lend instruments to children and provide free music lessons for children whose parents weren't able to afford them. This was at a time when the government had cut funding for music lessons.

Eventually, I invited her to talk to the committee, so along she came to present her proposal. What she did first was convince us of the value of a musical education. Making music she sees as a fundamental part of a child's development, as essential as an ability to read or write. What impressed us most was the way she calmly and clearly argued her case. By the end of the meeting, all of us had been won over by Maria's arguments and the Music in Schools project was born. Somehow we found the money to support it!

Rarely have I met anyone with such passion for their beliefs. And thanks to Maria's enthusiasm the project has been a tremendous success. Not only has she persuaded YCO members to give up their time willingly, but she has also encouraged visiting musicians to give free concerts in schools when they come to play in the city. Well, 'encourage' perhaps isn't the right word – she's a very persuasive person!

A number of times the council has tried to make changes to the Music in Schools project in order to save money. When this has happened, Maria has demonstrated that she is a determined and persuasive character. Five years ago, for example, there were plans to start charging all children for music lessons, but this she resisted. Only after Maria threatened to withdraw her support from the project did the council back down.

Maria's dream was always to extend her work beyond this city, and with typical energy she set about persuading the government to adopt the project throughout the country. What's happened as a consequence is that music has become established as an important part of the national curriculum. I think it's fair to say that, had Maria not been around, music education in most schools in this country would have practically disappeared. Instead, so successful has it been, that those involved in music education around the world have visited the city to see the project in action.

And then came an invitation to be a special adviser to the government on music education. In this role, she has worked closely with the Minister for the Arts. Were he here tonight, I know that he would want to express his thanks personally to Maria.

And as a further acknowledgement of her enormous service to music education we'd like to present her with this lifetime achievement award. Maria Adams, if you'd like to come up onto the stage.

Recording 22

Newsreader: People living close to Lake Taal on the island of Luzon in the Philippines continue to be evacuated from the area as the Taal volcano threatens to erupt. Over to our reporter, Katie Hill.

Reporter: Lake Taal lies in the huge crater of the Taal volcano. In the middle of the lake is a smaller volcano which has been showing signs of increased activity over the last few weeks. Taal is one of the most active volcanoes in the world. In 1911 an eruption claimed over a thousand lives and in 1965 villages on the lakeshore were devastated by falling rocks and huge waves on the lake. Although scientists predicted the 1965 eruption, the authorities failed to warn villagers and the breakdown in communication cost at least a hundred lives.

After the disaster of 1965, the government introduced the Taal Emergency Strategy. This involved monitoring the volcano for early signs of an eruption and the drawing up of an evacuation plan. Since that time, however, there has been an increase in the number of people living close to the lake, and the government has also encouraged the industrial development of the area. The building of two power stations just a few kilometres away was strongly criticised by environmentalists. In the event of an eruption, these would have to be shut down, possibly for a long period if damage occurs. The closure of the power stations would leave thousands of homes and businesses without electricity.

Last month, scientists noticed a sudden rise in the temperature of the lake. There was also a dramatic rise in the level of radon gas in the soil. Their concerns increased with the discovery of thousands of dead fish, apparently killed by acidic volcanic gases rising from the bed of the lake. As a result they gave a warning that Taal could erupt again at any moment. The authorities took immediate action. The President put government authorities on a state of high alert, saying that the danger of the situation made it necessary to bring in the army to oversee operations. The decision was made to evacuate an area of five kilometres around the entire lake, and two days ago the evacuation of around 30,000 people began.

The provision of temporary shelter in a safe location for those displaced is the army's top priority, and it is now estimated that about 25,000 evacuees have arrived at makeshift camps. Conditions in the camps are reasonably comfortable, and there are adequate supplies of food and water. But no one knows here how long they will be away from their homes – or, indeed, if Taal erupts again, whether they will have homes to go back to. All they can do is watch and wait for nature to take its course …

Katie Hill in the Philippines.

Newsreader: The government has announced that …

Recording 23

Father: So, what do you think? It's going to be hard to choose between them, isn't it?

Liz: Yes, there's so many things to think about. But overall I prefer the out-of-town apartment – the one in Canley.

Mother: Well, look, don't rush into a decision. It might help just to run though the pros and cons of each of them again.

Liz: Okay. Well, one obvious factor is price. The town apartment's about a third more expensive than the one in Canley.

Father: True, although maybe you could get them to lower the price a bit. It's been on the market for a long time, so they're probably keen to sell it.

Liz: Yes, and it's obvious why they've been having problems selling it – it hasn't been decorated for years. I couldn't believe it when the agent said the decoration was 'in good condition' – it clearly wasn't! It really shocked me to see how bad it was.

Father:	I'm sure you could get it decorated quite cheaply.
Mother:	And what about location? One of the things that worries me about the Canley apartment is that it's about 15 kilometres from there into the centre. Living in town would make it so much easier to get to work.
Father:	It's certainly an advantage being able to walk to work rather than having a long commute. It would save you a lot of money.
Liz:	Yes, but lots of people work in town and live in Canley, so there's bound to be a regular bus service from there. Didn't the agent say there's a bus stop just outside the apartment block?
Mother:	Well, you'd need to look at the bus timetable to check how long it takes to get into town. Personally, I wouldn't like it if I had to get up at six o'clock in the morning to get to work for nine.
Liz:	Another thing is that if I ever bought a car, there's the problem of parking at the town apartment. There's no special parking area for the apartments, is there? On the other hand, there's a car park behind the Canley apartment block.
Mother:	But you're not likely to be able to afford a car for ages ... It struck me that the Canley apartment might be quite noisy with that busy road nearby.
Liz:	But it's in such a great location. There's a lot of open space at the back of the block. It'll be great in summer. And there's that lovely little river that runs nearby.
Father:	Yes, but I wonder whether it floods in heavy rain? I've heard there have been problems in the past ...
Mother:	It's a pity that the Canley apartment is so small. There wasn't much space in the bathroom, was there? Nowhere to store towels and things. And did you notice that in one of the bedrooms there was just a bed, a small wardrobe and some bookshelves? You couldn't even fit a chest of drawers in there.
Father:	The kitchen was quite small, too.
Liz:	I must admit the town apartment is a bit bigger, but the rooms in it are quite dark and that made it feel cramped. I really like the light in the Canley apartment.
Father:	Another thing to consider is whether the apartment is going to be a good investment.

Mother:	Yes, they say that the cost of property in the town centre is going to go up with more people wanting to move in. Apparently, there are plans to build new apartments not far from the one we looked at.
Liz:	Maybe, although the agent's advertisement for the Canley apartment says 'There is expected to be a lot of interest in the property'.
Mother:	Oh, I'm sure it's just a way of encouraging people to buy quickly. But take your time to think about it, there's no hurry to decide.
Liz:	You really want me to take the town apartment, don't you?
Father:	Well, it's obviously your decision, but there are so many advantages of living in town ...
Mother:	Yes, and it would be so much easier for us to come and visit you there ...

Recording 24a

Dan:	Dan Seville.
Jess:	Oh, hi, Dan, it's Jess. Look, I'm really sorry, but I've messed up our plans for tomorrow.
Dan:	Oh, no. What's happened?
Jess:	Something's come up at work. Well, to be honest, it's a really important meeting. I'm so silly! I arranged it weeks ago and I forgot to put it in my diary. It means I've got to spend a couple of days in Marseille and I'll be heading off there early tomorrow morning.
Dan:	Right.
Jess:	So I won't be able to pick you up at the airport after all. I tried to reschedule the meeting for next week, but it's just impossible. I'm really, really sorry about this.
Dan:	No, don't worry. I'm sure I'll be able to get to your place somehow.
Jess:	Well, it means that you'll have to get to Perpignan from Montpellier airport on your own, and I'm afraid it's a bit complicated. You've got to get to Montpellier railway station and then catch a train to Perpignan. If you've got a pen handy, you might want to take down some of the information I'm going to give to you.
Dan:	Okay, just a second ... Right, go ahead.
Jess:	Okay, now, I know that you get to Montpellier airport at eight in the evening.
Dan:	Ten past eight, that's right.

Jess: I've found out the train times from the SNCF website and it appears that the last one from Montpellier to Perpignan is at ten minutes to ten. You really need to catch that train or an earlier one, so the first step is to get from the airport to the railway station in the centre of Montpellier. I know you're on a tight budget, so you could get the bus instead of a taxi but to be honest I'd advise you against catching the bus. It can be quite unreliable and it will only take you as far as the main square, and then it's a bit of a walk to the railway station from there. For the sake of a few euros, it's worth taking a taxi right to the station.

Dan: Right. Okay, I'll do that.

Jess: You'll need to buy a ticket before you get on the train. I think it costs about 25 euros. The last train's due to get in at about 11.30. Because I won't be in Perpignan, I've booked you into a hotel not far from the station.

Dan: That's great! Thanks!

Jess: It's called Le Metropole. I haven't stayed there myself, but one of my friends recommended it to me.

Dan: Le Metropole. Right ... That sounds good. Thanks.

Jess: Now, depending on the weather you could either take a taxi there or walk from the station. Actually, it's probably best to walk, as it's really not far. Don't worry about getting lost – everyone knows Le Metropole and will be able to give you directions, and there'll still be plenty of people around at that time of night.

Dan: Okay, that's fine.

Jess: It'll be quite late when you arrive, so when you've checked into the hotel, I suggest you get a meal there. The hotel restaurant is very good and they'll still be serving food at that time. And have whatever you like – I'm paying for your room and the meal.

Dan: No! You don't need to do that.

Jess: Yes, I want to. It's the least I can do. I'll sort out the bill when I pick you up on Thursday afternoon.

Dan: Well, I'll buy you a meal later in the holiday.

Jess: All right, then. I'll take you up on that.

Dan: Fine.

Jess: Relax on Thursday morning and walk around town. Perpignan's a lovely place. While you're strolling around, look out for Café Mathis. You might want to try their hot chocolate. It's the best in town. I should be with you at about two and I'll meet you in the foyer at Le Metropole.

Dan: Sounds wonderful. Thanks for organising that. I'm looking forward to seeing you.

Jess: Okay, Dan. And I'm really sorry again. Hope the journey goes well, and I'll see you on Thursday.

Dan: Great. See you then. Bye, Jess.

Extract 1

Interviewer: Now, Mark Harris, your new book includes some opinions on immunisation that are likely to arouse a strong reaction.

Mark: I hope they will! There's an overwhelming picture presented to the public, and that is that immunisation is a safe, scientific procedure which safeguards our health. But this message that is put out by governments, the medical establishment and the media is not supported by fact. Historically, supporters of immunisation have made grandiose claims about its effectiveness, while scientists have distorted the objective evidence to the contrary for fear of going against the mainstream. Very few are prepared to speak out and highlight the findings that much immunisation is not safe in the short term and that the long-term effects of certain forms of immunisation may constitute a major health hazard.

Interviewer: So in your view we should stop immunising all children against disease.

Mark: No, no, not at all. The need for immunisation is closely linked to a child's level of well-being. For a child living in hygienic conditions and receiving proper nutrition, immunisation has a minimal effect on the body's ability to fight off disease. But of course, this doesn't apply to a malnourished child living in insanitary conditions, who will be less able to fight off disease. And also there are all shades of variation between these two extremes in both rich and poor countries.

Extract 2

I first got keen on snowboarding during a skiing holiday in Switzerland when I was about 15. The first couple of hours I spent most of my time on my back. My legs just kept buckling. But it didn't take me long to get fairly good at it, which is the experience most people have. It's no surprise that, apparently, around 80% of people going to ski slopes for the first time take up snowboarding now rather than skiing. I've got to admit, though, that snowboarding has an image problem among the general public. Snowboarders are very committed to their sport, but people have the impression that we spend most of our time sitting around chatting and having a laugh rather than being on the slopes.

There's a great deal of rivalry between skiers and snowboarders, and skiers are typically not very welcoming to snowboarders. I guess it's to do with who snowboards – it's still very much a young person's sport, whereas skiing is for all the family. So snowboarders are viewed as pretty wild and crazy people, who upset the rather sedate feel of the slopes that skiers have always been used to. But they're just going to have to accept it. Without the money that snowboarders bring in, a number of ski resorts will go out of business.

Extract 3

It's always difficult when I tell people that no one's handed their property in. I think most of them are secretly convinced I'm hanging onto lost property for myself or selling it off. I do nothing of the sort, of course! Usually they'll ask me if I'm really sure or say 'Can you have another look for me, please?' It doesn't seem to occur to them that **anyone** could run off with a coat or a laptop left unattended on a train.

People leave some things behind on trains that you really would not believe. You get a load of clothes and umbrellas, of course, the kinds of things you'd expect. But also carpets, vases, lampshades, ironing boards ... It's not even as if they're things that are cheap and easy to replace. We've even had animals, as well. We had a huge spider once in a shoebox. I really think that people 'accidentally' leave unusual things like this on the train because they don't know how else to get rid of them. You'd think people would be able to give them away or dispose of them in some other way rather than leaving them behind on trains, wouldn't you?

Extract 4

More and more audioguides are becoming available, which you simply download onto your MP3 player and listen to as you walk around a city. I tested four of these out in my favourite city – Florence.

The first was from *City Sounds*. I'm afraid I didn't like this. The delivery is terribly deliberate, and an occasional change of pace would have been welcome. The effect was closer to someone reading out a guidebook, in a rather flat style, rather than a friend showing you around.

Frustratingly, it frequently fails to guide you round the interiors of the buildings it takes you to, but wastes time talking about sights that aren't even on the walk. It's professionally produced, though, and considerably cheaper than the others.

The second, *Walk and Talk*, was much better, in my view. The polished speaker sounded like an enthusiastic old friend, and the information never felt like a lecture. There's just the right level of detail on the art and architecture you're looking at, and a clever use of a second voice to break in and recount tales about various artists – very entertaining, although some of those stories sound rather far-fetched. The directions are clear, although the music used to accompany you as you walk wasn't to my taste. Perfect for anyone wanting to get to grips with the history and architecture of Florence.

The third guide is ....

Recording 25

Teacher:	Thanks, Kate, for showing us *Happening*. I'm sure there'll be lots of questions about it from students. Sarah, yes, you first.
Sarah:	Where did your idea of a newspaper for teenagers come from?
Kate:	Well, I used to spend a lot of time reading newspapers when I was at school. But my friends didn't read them much, even though I knew they were concerned about what was going on in the world. So, I suppose the idea of setting up some kind of newspaper for young people came from that time.
Teacher:	Hannah?
Hannah:	Why did you go for an online newspaper?
Kate:	Well, I did a journalism course at university. I'd also had the opportunity to do a course on website design, and that influenced my decision. It just seemed natural to combine the two, so I designed a prototype of an online newspaper for teens. My main motivation was that I wanted to increase young people's awareness of current affairs, but I also realised that there might be a chance of making it a commercial success. I felt that there was a big demand for an online newspaper aimed specifically at teenagers.
Teacher:	Sarah, your question.
Sarah:	Didn't you need a lot of money to get it started?

Kate:	Not really, no. I talked to a couple of university friends, and when the course finished we just went ahead. That's one of the great things about most online business – you don't need huge amounts of money at the outset. But we did need money to live on, of course. We had real difficulty in persuading banks to lend us anything at all. Every bank we approached was sceptical about whether the project would ever make money. But eventually, we managed to borrow some money from parents and we took the decision to work on it for six months. If we weren't making money after that, we'd give the idea up.
Teacher:	Can I ask a question here? How do you actually make money when people don't have to pay to access the site?
Kate:	All the money comes from advertising. Organisations pay us to put their adverts on the site. When we started we immediately contacted companies, but it was difficult to generate business at first. They were very wary of advertising with us, but as the number of hits we got started to increase – that's the number of people accessing the site – the number of companies wanting advertising space went up as well.
Teacher:	I see, thanks. Er ... Hannah, you've got another question?
Hannah:	Do you think online newspapers will ever take the place of traditional newspapers?
Kate:	I doubt it. Being able to access news online is right for some people, but not others. A lot of people want to be able to read a newspaper on the bus or train, or at home away from their computer. So, no, I think there'll always be a need for traditional newspapers.
Teacher:	Any more ... Tom?
Tom:	What's been the reaction of teenagers to *Happening*?
Kate:	We average about 20,000 hits a day and the number's steadily growing. We've had an increase of about 50% in the last three months alone. When I talk to young people, they seem generally very enthusiastic about the site. And hundreds of comments get posted on our message board each day.
Tom:	And do many people complain about *Happening*?
Kate:	Yes, we get both complaints and praise. In the early days we used to get quite a lot of complaints about our news coverage because it didn't feature young people's perspectives enough. We've tried to take that on board. So, for example, as you know, a recent big news story has been the protests about the location of a new nuclear power station on the east coast. As part of this, we covered what school students had been doing to protest. We also occasionally get complaints about how well the website works. Young people demand very high standards nowadays.
Teacher:	Hannah.
Hannah:	Are any young people directly involved in producing *Happening*?
Kate:	Yes, young people get the chance to contribute in various ways. For example, we have a reviews section, which is concerned with films, CDs, DVDs and books. All of the reviews are written by young people.
Teacher:	And what future do you see for *Happening*?
Kate:	That's a good question. First, I'd like to see it expanding. We've decided to include a section on celebrities, and also do more on science and technology. For that, though, we need more staff, and that means more money. But the recent increase in hits on the website means that we can charge more for advertising space. So we're quite optimistic about that. More generally, though, politicians seem to be getting interested in *Happening* as a place where young people express their views. If I'm right about this, then young people may be able to have an influence on government policies through *Happening*.
Teacher:	Interesting. Gerry, you've got a question ...

Appendices

Appendix 1: State verbs

➤ See Unit 1.

1 State verbs

- referring to emotions, attitudes and preferences:
  *agree, appreciate, attract, *desire, *doubt, expect, hate, hope, like, love, *prefer, regret*
- referring to mental states: *anticipate, assume, *believe, consider, expect, feel, find, imagine, *know, realise, think, understand*
- referring to senses and perceptions: *ache, hear, *notice, see, *smell, sound, *taste*
- others: *appear *belong to, *consist of, *constitute, *contain, cost, *differ from, fit, have, look, *mean, measure, *own, *possess, *resemble, *seem, weigh*

(The verbs marked * are rarely used with continuous tenses, but may be if they refer to actions rather than states.)

2 Verbs with both 'state' and 'action' meanings:
anticipate, appear, cost, expect, feel, fit, have, imagine, measure, see, think, weigh

3 Verbs that describe what we are doing as we speak:
acknowledge, admit, concede, contend, deny, guarantee, predict, promise, suggest, swear

Appendix 2: Future in the past

➤ See Unit 2.

The future seen from the past:

*As it was such a lovely morning, Emma thought she **would walk** to work.*
*I had no idea what **was going to happen** next.*
*I couldn't go to the meeting because I **was leaving** for Paris later that day.*
*Greg rang to tell me when he **would be arriving**.*
*Seeing there **was to be** no more entertainment, the crowd began to disperse.*
*It was announced that two new nuclear power stations **were to be built** by the end of the decade.*
*I **was about to start** my lecture when the fire alarm went off.*

Appendix 3: Subject noun–verb agreement

➤ See Unit 5.

1 Nouns with a singular form that can be used with either a singular or plural verb (collective nouns):
army, association, audience, club, college, committee, community, company, crowd, electorate, enemy, family, generation, government, group, jury, opposition, orchestra, population, press, public, school, university

In addition, the names of specific organisations:
Apple, the Bank of England, the BBC, Greenpeace, IBM, Sony, the United Nations

2 Nouns that usually have a plural form (and take a plural verb):
belongings, earnings, goods, outskirts, particulars (= information), premises (= building), riches, savings, stairs, surroundings, thanks; jeans, pyjamas, shoes

⚠ The nouns *police* and *people* always take a plural verb, and the noun *staff* usually does.

Appendix 4: Countable and uncountable nouns

➤ See Unit 5.

1 Nouns that are usually uncountable:
advice, applause, assistance, camping, cash, chaos, clothing, conduct, employment, equipment, evidence, furniture, health, homework, information, leisure, luggage, machinery, money, music, parking, pollution, research, scenery, shopping, sightseeing, transport

2 Nouns used uncountably when talking about the whole substance or idea, but countably when talking about units or different kinds:
beer, coffee, tea; fruit, shampoo, toothpaste, washing powder; business, cake, land, paint, stone; abuse, conversation, (dis)agreement, difficulty, improvement, language, pain, pleasure, protest, sound, space, thought, war

The following nouns are only used countably in the singular:
education, importance, knowledge, resistance

3 Nouns with different meaning when used countably and uncountably:
accommodation, competition, glass, grammar, jam, lace, paper, property, room, sight, speech, time, tin, traffic, work

> See Unit 6.

1 We use a singular verb with:
   - *any of, none of, the majority of, a lot of, plenty of, all (of), some (of)* + an uncountable noun:
     None of the information is very helpful.
     All the money has now been spent.
   - *everyone, everybody, everything* (and similar words beginning *any-, some-* and *no-*):
     Everyone agrees with me.
     If anybody phones, tell them I'll be back later.
   - *every* or *each* + a singular noun:
     Every attempt to rescue them has failed.
     Each chapter consists of three sections.
     However, when **each** follows the noun or pronoun it refers to, the noun / pronoun and verb are plural:
     We each pay a small fee.
   - *one of* + a plural noun / pronoun:
     One of my brothers lives in Alaska.
     There are three main characters in the book. One of them comes from Thailand.

2 We use a plural verb with *a / the majority of, a number of, a lot of, plenty of, all (of)*, or *some (of)* + a plural noun / pronoun:
   A majority of the people questioned think that the government is doing a good job. A lot of changes are planned for this part of the city.

3 We can use a singular or plural verb with *any of, each of, either of, neither of, none of* + a plural noun / pronoun:
   Do you think any of his colleagues support / supports his decision? Neither of my parents is / are particularly musical.
   (However, a singular verb is preferred in formal contexts.)

> See Unit 7.

1 Adjectives that can be used before or after a noun with a different meaning:
   The medicine was supposed to help me sleep, but it had the opposite effect. (= completely different)
   Who owns the house opposite? (= facing; on the other side of the road)

He plans to spend a year travelling around Australia doing temporary work, before coming back to Scotland to get a proper job. (= real)
Before the meeting proper, I'd like to get your views on the appointment of a new personnel manager. (= the main part of)
And also: *concerned, involved, responsible*

2 Adjectives which have both gradable (G) and non-gradable (NG) uses with different meanings:
   My music teacher was critical of my piano playing.
   (G = not pleased with it)
   Investing in sources of renewable energy is absolutely critical to the survival of our planet. (NG = very important.)
   It seemed an extremely odd thing to say in an interview. (G = strange)
   I noticed he was wearing odd socks. (NG = not matching)
   I like their music, even though it's not very original. (G = different)
   Our house is 100 years old and has still got some original features. (NG = from the beginning)
   And also: *civil, clean, false, old, particular*

3 Adjectives which have both gradable and non-gradable uses with only small differences in meaning between them:
   She didn't go to university – she's never been very academic. (G = good at learning things by studying)
   We were all impressed with his academic achievements. (NG = achievements in studying at college or university)
   The house has a very private garden at the back. (G = it can't be seen by many people)
   We had to hire a private plane to get to the island. (NG = used only by a particular group of people)
   And also: *adult, average, diplomatic, foreign, genuine, guilty, human, individual, innocent, mobile, professional, public, scientific, technical, true, wild*

> See Unit 7.

When an adjective comes after a linking verb, we can use a number of patterns after the adjective:

1 + *to*-infinitive:
   Are you ready to go now?
   I was keen to hear more about his trip.
   And also: *(un)able, careful, easy, free, inclined, interested, (un)likely, (im)possible, prepared, quick, slow, welcome, (un)willing*

2 + -ing:

He was busy cooking when I called him.
I felt awful making her walk all the way.
And also: (usually after the verb *feel*) *awkward, bad, comfortable, fantastic, stupid, terrible*

3 + to-infinitive or -ing:

It was really good to see her again. or *... good seeing her again.*
And also: *crazy, difficult, foolish, (un)happy, mad, nice, safe* and (usually after verbs other than *feel*) *awful, awkward, fantastic, stupid, terrible*

4 + that- clause:

I was aware that I needed new ideas.
They were angry that I was late.
And also: *afraid, alarmed, amazed, annoyed, ashamed, astonished, certain, concerned, confident, disappointed, glad, (un)happy, pleased, positive, shocked, sorry, sure, thankful, upset, worried*

5 + to-infinitive or that- clause:

I was greatly relieved that my subsequent book sold well. or *... relieved to find that my subsequent book sold well.*
And also: the adjectives in 4, except *aware, confident, positive*

6 + -ing or that- clause:

I felt bad leaving the children. or *... that I was leaving the children.*
And also: (usually after the verb *feel*) *awful, awkward, bad, good, guilty, terrible*

Appendix 8: (In)transitive verbs, verb + two objects, verb + each other / one another

➤ See Unit 9.

Common transitive verbs, intransitive verbs and verbs with two objects:

1 Verbs usually transitive (verb + object):

arrest, avoid, copy, describe, do, enjoy, find, force, get, grab, hit, like, pull, report, see, shock, take, tell, touch, want, warn

2 Verbs usually intransitive (verb + no object):

appear, arrive, come, cough, faint, fall, go, happen, hesitate, interact, matter, occur, remain, sleep, sneeze, swim, wait

3 Verb + indirect object + direct object:

allow, ask, bet, cost, deny, envy, fetch, fine, forgive, give, guarantee, permit, refuse

4 Verb + direct object + for + indirect object:

(i) *book, collect, fix, mend, repair*
(ii) *build, buy, catch, choose, cook, cut, fetch, find, get, make, order, pour, save* (can also be used in verb + indirect object + direct object)

5 Verb + direct object + to + indirect object:

(i) *admit, announce, confess, demonstrate, describe, explain, introduce, mention, point out, prove, report, say, suggest*
(ii) *award, give, hand, lend, offer, owe, pass, show, teach, tell, throw* (can also be used in verb + indirect object + direct object)

6 Verb + direct object + for / to + indirect object:

bring, leave, pay, play, post, read, send, sing, take, write (can also be used in verb + indirect object + direct object)

7 Verb + object + adjective:

assume, believe, consider, declare, find, hold, judge, pronounce, prove, report, think

8 Verb + reflexive pronoun / personal pronoun:

She took some deep breaths to compose herself, and then walked onto the stage. (= to calm)
Mozart was only 13 when he composed it. (= produced)
He joined the navy at the age of 18, and distinguished himself in the Seven Years' War. (= did so well that he was admired)
The pills were in different coloured bottles to distinguish them. (= show the difference between)
I don't need to explain myself to you. (= give reasons for my behaviour)
The procedure was complicated, but she explained it very clearly. (= made it clear)

9 Verb + reflexive pronoun + preposition

acclimatise ... to, avail ... of, brace ... for, busy ... with, console ... with, content ... with, distance ... from, establish ... as, familiarise ... with, impose ... on, occupy ... with, organise ... into, pride ... on, tear ... away from

Verbs commonly used in the following patterns with *each other* and *one another*:

10 Verb + each other / one another:

attract, avoid, blame, call, complement, face, fight, help, hit, hold, hug, know, (dis)like, love, meet, miss, resemble, respect, see, trust, understand

11 Verb + with + each other / one another:

(dis)agree, argue, coincide, compete, cooperate, get along / on, live, play, work

Appendix 9: Verb + *to*-infinitive / *-ing* / bare infinitive

➤ See Unit 10.

1 **Verb + *to*-infinitive:**
   agree, aim, ask, consent, decide, decline, demand, fail, guarantee, hesitate, hope, hurry, offer, plan, prepare, pretend, refuse, threaten, volunteer, wait, wish

2 **Verb + *-ing*:**
   avoid, delay, deny, detest, envisage, feel like, imagine, miss, recall, resent, risk

3 **Verb + bare infinitive:**
   modal verbs (e.g. *will, could, may*); *dare, help, need*

4 **Verb + object + *to*-infinitive:**
   advise, allow, believe, cause, command, enable, encourage, entitle, force, invite, order, persuade, remind, teach, tell, urge, warn

5 **Verb + object + *-ing*:**
   catch, feel, find, hear, notice, observe, photograph, prevent, show, watch

Appendix 11: Noun clauses

➤ See Unit 16.

1 **Verb + *the fact that*:**
   change, discuss, disguise, face, hide, highlight, ignore, overlook, reflect, welcome

2 **Noun + *of* + *wh-* noun clause:**
   account, description, discussion, example, idea, issue, knowledge, problem, question, reminder, understanding

3 **Verb + object + *wh-* noun clause:**
   advise, ask, assure, convince, inform, instruct, persuade, remind, show, teach, tell, warn.
   (*ask* and *show* don't always have an object before a *wh-* clause
   *It **shows (us) how** little we know about wildlife in the area. Can I **ask (you) why** the Marsh was left to the NWT?*)

4 **Verb + *how-* noun clause:**
   ask, consider, decide, describe, discover, explain, know, remember, reveal, show, tell, understand, wonder

Appendix 10: Verbs with different meanings followed by *to*-infinitive or *-ing*

➤ See Unit 10.

	+ *to*-infinitive	+ *-ing*
forget / remember	*I'd forgotten to bring my passport.* *I remembered to apply for a visa.* (= to talk about actions that are necessary and whether actions are done or not)	*I don't remember putting my camera on the table.* *I'll never forget visiting Lombok.* (= to mean that the action comes before the remembering or forgetting)
go on	*We went on to drive towards Mt Rinjani.* (= to mean that something is done after something else is finished)	*I went on watching the sunset until it started to feel cold.* (= to continue)
mean	*I meant to take my camera with me.* (= to say that we intend(ed) to do something)	*But it meant flying to Bali.* (= to say what a particular attitude or action involves or implies)
regret	*We regret to announce that flight XZ345 to Bali has been cancelled.* (= to say that we are about to do something we are not happy about)	*I regretted not speaking Bahasa Indonesian.* (= to say we are sorry that we did or did not do something)
stop	*We stopped there to admire the amazing sunset behind the mountain.* (= to say why we stop doing something)	*We stopped talking immediately.* (= to say what it is that we stop doing)
try	*I tried to get on a later flight.* (= to say that we attempt to do something)	*I tried using the camera in my mobile phone.* (= to say we test something to see if it improves a situation)

Appendix 12: Common conjunctions and sentence connectors

➤ See Unit 17.

1 Conjunctions

- TIME *after, as, as long as, before, hardly, no sooner, once, since, when, while* (more formally *whilst*), *until* (less formally *till*), *whenever*
- CONDITION *assuming (that), considering (that), even if, given that, if, provided that, providing, unless*
- CONCESSION / CONTRAST *although / though, even though, no matter (what /who / which / how), while* (more formally, *whilst*), *whereas, whatever, whichever, wherever, whenever, whoever, however, yet*
- EXCEPTION *except (that), only*
- PURPOSE *in order (not) to, in order that, so as (not) to, so (that), to*
- REASON *as, because, for, in case, in that, insofar as, seeing that, since*
- RESULT *so that, such that, in such a way that*

2 Sentence connectors

- TIME *after, afterward(s), before, earlier, later, meanwhile, in the meantime, previously, simultaneously, subsequently*
- CONDITION *if not, if so, otherwise*
- CONCESSION / CONTRAST *all the same, alternatively, anyway* (less commonly *anyhow*; both used mainly in informal speech), *by / in contrast, conversely, even so, however, in any case, instead, nevertheless, nonetheless, on the contrary, on the other hand, still, though*
- RESULT *as a result, because of this, consequently / in consequence, hence, therefore, thus*
- ADDING *above all, in addition, after all, also, as well, besides, further, furthermore, indeed, likewise, moreover, similarly, too, what is more*
- GIVING EXAMPLES *for example, for instance*
- REWORDING *in other words, namely, that is, that is to say*
- LISTING *first(ly), first of all, to start / begin with, last(ly), finally, next, then*
- ENDING *(all) in all, in conclusion, to conclude, to sum up*

A few words can be either a conjunction or sentence connector. Compare:

- *I usually go for a run **after** I've finished work.*
  *Let's try to finish the meeting by 12.00. **After / Afterwards**, we can go out and have some lunch.* (**after** as a sentence connector is mainly used in spoken English.)
- *I'll write the number down **before** I forget it.*
  *She's become much more confident since she went to university. **Before**, she was really shy.*

- *I don't often see Margaret, **though** she only lives in the next road.*
  *I've got your mobile number. I don't know your email address, **though**.*
- *Take a warm coat, **otherwise** you'll get cold.*
  *I knew you were busy. **Otherwise** I'd have come earlier.*

3 *Except (for)* is usually used as a preposition, but *except (that)* can be used as a conjunction meaning 'not including'. Compare: *Everyone was wearing fancy dress **except (for)** Nickie.*
*Hugh didn't say much in his letter **except (that)** he's going on holiday to Spain next month.*

4 *Hence* can be used as a sentence connector, but more often is followed by a phrase giving the result of an action in the previous clause or sentence. Compare:
*The south of the country is much more industrialised. **Hence**, income levels are higher.*
*You've broken a small bone in your foot − **hence** the pain.*

Appendix 13: Passive verb forms

➤ See Unit 18.

1 The most common passive verb forms are:
Present simple *All this land is **owned** by Mr Harris.*
Past simple *The cakes **were made** by Janet.*
Present perfect *The conference **has been arranged** by the university.*
Past perfect *The exam time **had been changed** by our teacher.*
Present continuous *I am always **being asked** for money by James.*
Past continuous *The lecture **was being given** by Dr Goodman.*
Future simple *You **will be met** at the airport by Miss Turner.*
Future perfect *The work **will have been finished** by the builders before the weekend.*

2 **State verbs not usually made passive:** *be, become, belong, exist, have* (= own), *lack, resemble, seem*

3 **State verbs that can be made passive:** *believe, intend, know, like, love, need, own, understand, want*

4 **Verb + *to*-infinitive + object** (active) / **verb + *to be* + past participle** (passive): *appear, begin, come, continue, seem, start, tend* (with these verbs, active and passive have corresponding meanings: *He began to annoy me* corresponds to *I began to be annoyed*); *agree, aim, arrange, attempt, hope, refuse, want* (with these verbs, active and passive do not have corresponding meanings: *I refused to help him* does not correspond to *He refused to be helped*).

5 **Verb + *-ing* + object** (active) / **verb + *being* + past participle** (passive): *avoid, deny, describe, dislike, enjoy, face, hate, (not) imagine, like, love, remember, report, resent, start*

6 **Verb + object + bare infinitive** (active) / ***be* + past participle + *to*-infinitive** (passive): *feel, hear, help, make, observe, see*

   (*help* can also be followed by object + *to*-infinitive in the active; *let* can be followed by object + bare infinitive in the active, but is never passive.)

7 **Verb + object + *-ing*** (active) / ***be* + past participle + *-ing*** (passive): *bring, catch, hear, find, keep, notice, observe, see, send, show*

8 **Verb + object + *to*-infinitive** (active) / ***be* + past participle + *to*-infinitive** (passive): *advise, allow, ask, believe, consider, expect, feel, instruct, invite, mean, order, require, sing, tell, understand*

9 **Verb + object + *to*-infinitive** (active) / **no passive:** *(can't) bear, hate, like, love, need, prefer, want, wish*

10 **Verb + object + complement** (active) / ***be* + past participle + complement** (passive):
   • (verbs to do with giving someone a particular position) *appoint, declare, make, nominate, vote*
   • (verbs to do with 'naming') *call, name, title*

Appendix 14: Reporting verbs

➤ See Unit 19.

Reporting verbs followed by the pattern shown. Some verbs can be followed by more than one pattern.

1 **Verb + *that*- clause** (usually reporting statements *She agreed that the rule was unfair.*): *add, agree, announce, answer, argue, comment, confirm, deny, emphasise, grumble, guarantee, insist, note, object, observe, point out, predict, protest, remark, repeat, reply, state, swear, think*

2 **Verb + object + *that*- clause** (*He reminded me that it's Hannah's birthday next week.*): *assure, convince, inform, notify, persuade, reassure, remind, tell*

3 **Verb + (object) + *that*- clause** (with these verbs an object is usual, but not always necessary *They warned (us) that swimming there was dangerous.*): *advise, promise, show, teach, warn*

4 **Verb + *that*- clause or verb + object + *to*-infinitive** (the *to*-infinitive is often *to be*; *They expected that the concert would be cancelled.* or *They expected the concert to be cancelled.*): *acknowledge, assume, believe, claim, consider,*

declare, expect, feel, find, presume, suppose, think, understand

5 **Verb + *that*- clause or verb + *to* + object + *that*-clause** (*They complained that my lectures were boring.* or *They complained to me that my lectures were boring.*): *admit, announce, complain, confess, explain, indicate, mention, propose, recommend, report, reveal, say, suggest, whisper*

   Verb + *that*- clause or verb + *with* + object + *that*-clause (*She joked that she had lost their presents.* or *She joked with the children that she had lost their presents.*): *agree, argue, check, commiserate, confirm, disagree, joke*

6 **Verb + *to*-infinitive** (*He offered to give us a lift to the airport.*): *apply, offer, refuse, swear, volunteer*

7 **Verb + object + *to*-infinitive** (*She told me to phone her at any time.*): *advise, allow, ask, call on, command, encourage, forbid, force, instruct, invite, order, persuade, recommend, remind, request, teach, tell, urge, warn*

8 **Verb + *to*-infinitive or verb + object + *to*-infinitive** (*I asked to wait* (= I asked if I could wait) or *I asked her to wait.*): *ask, beg, expect*

9 **Verb + *to*-infinitive or verb + *that*- clause** (*He decided to go to Greece.* or *He decided that he would go to Greece.*): *agree, claim, decide, demand, expect, guarantee, hope, promise, propose, request, swear, threaten, vow*

10 **Verb + object + *to*-infinitive or verb + object + *that*-clause** (*He advised me to travel by train because it would be cheaper.* or *He advised me that it would be cheaper to travel by train.*): *advise, order*

11 **Verb + *-ing* or verb + *that*- clause** (*She regretted starting the course.* or *She regretted that she had started the course.*): *admit, advise, deny, mention, propose, recommend, regret, report, suggest*

12 **Verb + *that*- clause with *should* or the present subjunctive** (*They proposed that Sociology (should) be taught as an undergraduate subject at the university.*): *advise, ask, beg, command, demand, direct, insist, instruct, intend, order, prefer, propose, recommend, request, require, stipulate, suggest, urge, warn*

   We can also use a *that*- clause with *should* or the present subjunctive after nouns related to these verbs, such as *advice, command, demand, direction, insistence, instruction, proposal*:
   They put forward the proposal that Sociology (should) be taught as an undergraduate subject at the university.

Appendix 15: Substitution

➤ See Unit 20.

1 **Verbs commonly followed by *so*** (substituting for a clause):

be afraid (= expressing regret), *appear / seem* (after *it*), *assume, believe, expect, guess, hope, imagine, presume, say, suppose, suspect, tell* (with an indirect object), *think*

Verbs not followed by *so* (substituting for a clause):

accept, admit, agree, be certain, doubt, hear, know, promise, suggest, be sure ·

2 **Verbs, nouns and adjectives after which we can leave out *to*** (*Do you think Paul will come? He promised (to).*):

Verbs: *agree, ask, begin, forget, promise, refuse, start, try*

Nouns: *chance, idea, opportunity, promise, suggestion*

Adjectives: *afraid, delighted, determined, frightened, willing*

3 **Verbs after which we can't leave out *to*** (*Would you like to be a fire officer? I'd hate to.* not ~~I'd hate.~~): *advise, afford, be able, choose, deserve, expect, hate, hope, intend, love, mean, need, prefer*

These verbs must have a complement; that is, a word or phrase that completes their meaning *I can't afford a car* (*a car* is the complement) not ~~I can't afford.~~)

4 **Common omissions and changes to verbs in order to avoid repeating words in a previous clause or sentence:**

- auxiliary + main verb > auxiliary

  *He says he **has** finished, but I don't think he **has** ~~finished~~.*

- auxiliary + auxiliary + main verb > auxiliary (+ auxiliary)

  *I **hadn't been** invited, but my sister **had been** ~~invited~~* or *my sister **had** ~~been invited~~.*

- auxiliary + auxiliary + auxiliary + main verb > auxiliary (+ auxiliary) + (auxiliary)

  *A: We **could have been** arrested.*
  *B: Yes, we **could have been** ~~arrested~~* or *we **could have** ~~been arrested~~* or *we **could** ~~have been arrested~~.*

- (*do*) + main verb > *do*

  *David goes running every morning, and I **do**, too.*
  *A: I **didn't take** her bike. B: Nobody said you **did**.*

- *be* (= auxiliary / main verb) > *be* or modal + *be*

  *A: The cat's asleep in the kitchen. B: It usually **is**.*
  A: Ann's late again.
  *B: She said she **might be**.* (or informally *she **might**.*)
  A: Are Tom and Mel staying overnight?
  *B: Yes, I think they **are / will be**.* (or informally *they will.*)

Appendix 16: *It* and *there*

➤ See Unit 23.

1 **Verbs used in the following patterns with introductory *it* as subject:**

- *it* + verb + *to*-infinitive clause: *not do, help, hurt, pay*
- *it* + verb + object + *to*-infinitive clause: *amaze, annoy, frighten, hurt, scare, shock, surprise, upset, worry*

We can use *it* + *take* + object + *to*-infinitive clause when we say what is or was needed in a particular activity: (*It took (them) a week to mend our roof.*)

- *it* + verb + *that*- clause: *appear, come about, emerge, follow, seem, transpire, turn out*

Alternatives with the *that*- clause in initial position are not possible:

It turned out that I was wrong. not ~~That I was wrong turned out.~~

- *it* + verb + object + *that*-clause: *dawn on, hit, strike* (all meaning 'occur to'); and also the verbs listed above for the pattern *it* + verb + object + *to*-infinitive clause.

2 **Verbs used in the following reporting patterns with introductory *it* as subject:**

- *it* + passive verb + *that*- clause:

  agree, allege, announce, assume, believe, calculate, claim, consider, decide, demonstrate, discover, establish, estimate, expect, feel, find, hope, intend, know, mention, plan, propose, recommend, reveal, say, show, suggest, suppose, think, understand (**but not:** *encourage, inform, persuade, reassure, remind, tell, warn*)

- *it* + passive verb + *wh*- clause: *discover, establish, explain, find, know, reveal, show, understand*

These verbs can also be used in the pattern *it* + passive verb + *that*- clause.

3 **Verbs used in the following patterns with introductory *it* as object:**

- verb + *it* + *that*- / *if*- or *wh*- clause:
  can't bear, hate, like, love, resent, can't stand
- verb + *it* + *if*- or *wh*- clause:
  dislike, enjoy, prefer, understand
- verb + (*it*) + *that*- clause:
  accept, admit, deny, guarantee, mention
- verb + *it* + adjective + *that*-, *wh*- or *to*-infinitive clause:
  believe, consider, feel, find (= discover from experience), *make, think*
- verb + *it* + *as* + adjective + *that*-, *if*- or *when*- clause:
  accept, regard, see, take (= interpret something in a particular way), *view*

Many other verbs that can be followed by a *that-, wh-, if-,* or *to-*infinitive clause are not used with introductory *it* as object: *argue, discover, emphasise, notice, predict, recall, remember.*

4 **Common expressions with *it's no* and *there's no*:**
it's no secret that, it's no surprise that, it's no use / good +-ing, it's no coincidence / accident that, it's no longer necessary to, it's no bad thing to, it's no doubt true that, it's no doubt the case that, it's no exaggeration to say that, there's no doubt that, there's no chance / denying that, there's no choice / alternative but to, there's no chance / hope of +-ing, there's no need to, there's no point in +-ing, there's no question of +-ing, there's no reason to, there's no harm in +-ing

Appendix 17: Complex prepositions

> See Unit 24.

1 **Two-word prepositions:**
- ending *for: as for, but for, except for, save for*
- ending *from: apart from, as from, away from*
- ending *of: ahead of, as of, because of, devoid of, instead of, irrespective of, out of, outside of, regardless of, upwards of*
- ending *to: according to, as to, close to, contrary to, due to, near to, next to, owing to, prior to, relative to, subsequent to, thanks to, up to*
- ending *with: along with, together with*
- others: *such as, as against, as regards, depending on, all over, rather than, in between*

2 **Three- and four-word prepositions:**
- ending *as: as far as, as well as*
- ending *for: in exchange for, in return for*
- ending *from: as distinct from, with effect from*
- ending *of: by means of, by virtue of, by way of, for lack of, for want of, in aid of, in case of, in charge of, in danger of, in favour of, in front of, in lieu of, in light of, in need of, in place of, in respect of, at risk of, in search of, in spite of, in terms of, in view of, on account of, on behalf of, on grounds of, on top of; as a result of, for the sake of, in the case of, in the event of, on the part of, with the exception of, on the strength of*
- ending *to: as opposed to, by reference to, in addition to, in contrast to, in reference to, in regard to, in relation to, with regard to, with reference to, with respect to*
- ending *with: at variance with, in accordance with, in comparison with, in compliance with, in conformity with, in contact with, in line with, in touch with*

Appendix 18: Verb + preposition – common patterns

> See Unit 24.

Some verbs can be used in more than one pattern.

1 **Verb + object + prepositional phrase** (*I grabbed the boy by the hand.*):
protect / insure ... against, dismiss / condemn ... as, (re)schedule / exchange ... for, isolate / protect ... from, implicate / interest ... in, translate ... into, rob / deprive ... of, force / feed ... on, explain ... to, associate / confuse / discuss ... with

With a few verbs we change preposition if we change the word order: *Our tutor issued us **with** a reading list.* or *Our tutor issued a reading list **to** us.*
Other verbs like this: *present ... with / to, entrust ... with / to, supply ... with / to (or for), trust ... with / to, blame ... for / on*

2 **Verb + preposition + object + preposition + object** (*They **collaborated with** Russian scientists **on** the research.*): *(dis)agree / argue / quarrel with ... about / over, count / depend / rely on ... for, complain / boast to ... about, refer to ... as, apologise/appeal/apply to ... for, react / respond to ... with, compete / contend with ... for*

3 **Verb + preposition + -ing** (*When he failed his driving test he **reacted by kicking** the car.*): *inquire / worry about, end / start by, apologise / vote for, benefit / refrain from, persist / succeed in, rush into, disapprove / dream of, concentrate / insist on, admit / confess to, go ahead / help with*

4 **Verb + object + preposition + -ing** (*She **accused me of copying** her work.*):
advise ... against, blame / prosecute / thank / praise ... for, discourage / prevent ... from, talk / trick ... into, suspect ... of, congratulate ... on

5 **Verb + preposition + subject + -ing** (*My place at university **depends on me getting** high grades in my exams.* or *... **depends on my getting** high grades*): *worry / think / know about, protest / laugh at / about, arise / come / follow from, result / end in, speak / (dis)approve of, depend / count / insist / rely on, lead to, end / start / finish with*

Appendix 19: Phrasal verbs – position of objects

➤ See Unit 24.

1 Phrasal verbs that can be used transitively or intransitively with the *same* meaning: *answer back, call back, clear away, cover up, help out, take over, tidy away, wash up*

2 Phrasal verbs that can be used transitively or intransitively with a *different* meaning: *break in, cut out, hold out, look out, look up, pick up, split up, turn in, wind up*

3 Phrasal verbs whose object can go *before or after* the particle: *bring about, check over, clean up, drink up, gather up, get down, leave out, make up, mess up, shoot down, sort out, throw away, try out, use up, wake up*

4 Phrasal verbs whose object must go *after* the particle(s): *account for, act on, approve of, bump into, call on, check into, flick through, look after, look around, provide for, result from, run into, stick at, take after, take against; do away with, get away with, grow out of, look out over, make up for, send away for*

5 Phrasal verbs whose object must go *before* the particle (i.e. between the verb and the particle): *hear out, order about, pull to, push to, shut up, stand up, tell apart*

6 Three-word phrasal verbs with two objects, one after the verb and the other after the particles: *help on/off with, set off against, talk out of, take out of / on, take up on*

Appendix 20: Prepositions after nouns and adjectives

➤ See Unit 25.

1 Examples of nouns in the following groups:
- nouns usually followed by the same prepositions as their related verb or adjective (after *to be*): *to accuse – accusation of, to (dis)agree – (dis)agreement with / about / on, to amaze – amazement at, to annoy – annoyance about / at / with, to be anxious – anxiety about, to apologise – apology for, to associate – association with, to be aware – awareness of, to believe – belief in, to be bored – boredom with, to complain – complaint about, to contribute – contribution to, to depart – departure from, to be grateful – gratitude for, to insist – insistence on, to insure – insurance against, to object – objection to, to be satisfied – satisfaction with, to succeed – success in, to worry – worry about*
- nouns usually followed by different prepositions from their related adjective (after *to be*): *to be fond of – fondness for, to be proud of – pride in, to be ashamed of – shame about / at*

- nouns which take a preposition where their related verb does not: *to admire – admiration for, to answer – answer to, to attack – attack on, to ban – ban on, to damage – damage to, to decrease – decrease of / in / by, to delay – delay in, to demand – demand for, to discuss – discussion about, to fear – a fear of, to ignore – ignorance of, to improve – improvement in / on, to influence – influence on, to interview – interview with, to lack – lack of, to prove – proof of, to question – question about / of, to reduce – reduction in, to solve – solution to, to support – support for*

2 Examples of nouns in the patterns shown:
- noun + preposition + noun or noun + preposition + *-ing*: *approval for, change from, focus on, interest in, opposition to, protest about, sign of*
- noun + preposition + noun: *damage to, decrease in, demand for, factor behind, increase in*

3 Examples of nouns in the patterns shown:
- noun + *of* + *-ing* or noun + *to*-infinitive with a similar meaning (usually after *the*): *aim, idea, opportunity, option, plan*
- noun + *of* + *-ing* or noun + *to*-infinitive with a different meaning: *chance, sense, way*
- noun + *of* + *-ing*: *cost, difficulty, effect, fear, likelihood, possibility, probability, problem, prospect, risk, sign*
- noun + *to*-infinitive: *ability, attempt, concern, decision, desire, determination, failure, inability, permission, proposal, reason, refusal, reluctance, (un)willingness, wish*

Many of these nouns can be used with other prepositions + *-ing* (*attempt at -ing, reason for -ing*)

4 Adjective + preposition: expressing feelings and opinions: *amazed at / by, ashamed of, bored with, confident of, content with, crazy about, critical of, enthusiastic about, envious of, fed up with, impressed by / with, indifferent to, interested in, intolerant of, jealous of, keen on, nervous about / of, proud of, satisfied with, scared of, shocked at / by, surprised at / by, tired of, upset about, wary of, worried about*

5 Adjective + preposition: different meanings: *afraid of / for; angry / annoyed / furious about / with; answerable for / to; anxious about / for; bad / good at / for; concerned about / with / for; disappointed with / at / about / in; frightened of / for; good about / to / with; glad for / of; pleased about / at / with; right about / for; sorry about / for; unfair of / on; wrong about / of*

CD Tracklist

CD1

Recording	CD track	Accents
1	2	Southern English
2	3	Southwest English
3a	4	Borland residents speak with a slight southwest English accent.
3b	5	Southern English
4	6	Liverpool
5	7	The interviewer has a Central English accent, while Nazim's accent is UK Asian.
6a	8	Speaker 1 has a Central English accent.
6b	9	Southern English
7	10	David has a Scottish accent.
8	11	Southern English
9	12	Lynn has a Canadian accent.
10	13	Simon has a Northern Irish accent.
11	14	Southern English
12	15	Southern English
13	16	Liverpool
14a	17	Mark has a slight South African accent.
14b	18	Southern English

CD2

Recording	CD track	Accents
15	2	Both speakers have Irish accents.
16	3	All speakers have Welsh accents.
17	4	The first speaker has an Australian accent, while the second voice is from New Zealand.
18	5	Northern English
19a	6	Southwest English
19b	7	Southern English
20a	8	Alison's accent is from Newcastle-upon-Tyne, while Ben speaks with a northern English accent.
20b	9	Southern English
21	10	Northern English
22	11	US accents
23	12	Australian
24a	13	Scottish
24b	14	Southern English
25	15	Northern English